Foundations of Ministry
An Introduction to Christian
Education for a New Generation

BridgePoint,
the academic
imprint of
Victor Books:
Your connection
for the best in
serious reading
that integrates
the passion of
the heart with
the scholarship
of the mind.

FOUNDATIONS OF MINISTRY

EDITED BY

MICHAEL J. ANTHONY

A
BRIDGEPOINT
BOOK

Scripture quotations are from the following translations. Chapters 1, 5, 8, 9, 13, 14, 15, 24, 25
are from the *New American Standard Bible* (NASB),
© the Lockman Foundation 1960, 1962, 1963, 1968, 1971, 1972, 1973, 1975, 1977.

Chapters 3, 4, 12, 22, are from
the *Holy Bible, New International Version* (NIV),
© 1973, 1978, 1984, International Bible Society.
Used by permission of Zondervan Bible Publishers.

Chapter 18 is from the *New King James Version* (NKJV).
© 1979, 1980, 1982, Thomas Nelson, Inc. Publishers.

Chapter 23 is from J.B. Phillips: *The New Testament in Modern English* (PH), Revised Edition. ©
J.B. Phillips, 1958, 1960, 1972, permission of Macmillan Publishing Co. and Collins Publishers.

Copyediting: Robert N. Hosack

Cover Design: Scott Rattray

Cover Photography: Karl Knize

Library of Congress Cataloging-in-Publication Data

Foundations of ministry / by Michael J. Anthony, editor.
p.   cm.
Includes bibliographical references.
ISBN 0-89693-955-3
1. Christian education. I. Anthony, Michael J.
BV1473.F69   1992
268–dc20   91-42034
                                                                          CIP

BridgePoint is the academic imprint of Victor Books.
© 1992 by SP Publications, Inc.
All rights reserved. Printed in the United States of America.

1   2   3   4   5   6   7   8   9   10   Printing/Year   96   95   94   93   92

Contents

Dedication

Each generation has had its leaders and trailblazers. In the field of Christian Education we have had those who have shaped our thinking and provided us with godly role models both in and outside the classroom. Our history is rich with professors and practitioners who have led the way for those of us currently in the field.

This book is dedicated to Dr. E. Stanley Leonard, teacher and mentor who served as a master in the field of Christian Education to the generation represented by the authors of this book. Most of us had Dr. Leonard as a teacher and can attest to his close walk with God. Many of his class sessions continued in his home with his wife Donna. Together they served Biola University and the local churches in Southern California for over twenty years of faithful service.

It is our hope that this text will serve a new generation of Christian educators by standing on the shoulders of those who have gone before us in the field.

Introduction

Anytime an editor attempts to compile a comprehensive "Introduction" text in a given field, he does so knowing his job can never be complete. There is simply too much in the field of Christian Education to include within one manuscript. Decisions must be made on the basis of priority, readability, and cost effectiveness which will ultimately limit the size and scope of the book. In addition, each contributor has a personal theology and philosophy which has shaped his or her own perspective of ministry. To be honest to the authors, these views must also be interwoven into each chapter without disrupting the flow of the overall text.

It is my desire to present an overview of the discipline to the student who is new to the field of Christian Education. This book is not intended to be the final word. An introductory text should provide the reader with a concise look at the subject and then point him or her to additional sources for further reading and investigation.

The most significant challenge in compiling a book of this nature is finding a balance between theoretical foundations and current practice in the field of ministry. If the gap between these two entities is too large, then the value of the book is diminished. Each of the authors who contributed to this book currently serves as a practitioner in the C.E. field. In addition to our appointments at Talbot School of Theology at Biola University we are also pastors, Christian educators, consultants to mission boards, and conference speakers. The benefit to the student is that the content of our curriculum is more "user friendly." The student should not have to search the pages of a text to find the applicability of the content—especially in ministry.

Each chapter begins with an overview of both the biblical and theoretical foundations of the subject. Building upon this base is a set of practical guidelines and principles for ministry application. This text is designed to meet the needs of both the undergraduate and the graduate student. We also want it to be a valuable ministry resource for those serving in the local church who need to see Christian Education ministry from a broader perspective. It is more than just Sunday School! Because of this diverse audience, we wanted to keep each chapter brief and to the point. Documentation is not intended to impress the reader with our breadth of reading, but rather to honestly reflect the contributions which others have made to our thinking. Students are encouraged to explore the "for further reading" section at the end of each chapter to expand upon the issues presented therein. The student who majors in Christian Education will no doubt have the opportunity to take entire classes in many of the areas covered in these chapters (e.g., C.E. of Children, History & Philosophy of C.E., Ministry to Single Adults). The sources at the end of each chapter will serve students in years to come as a guide for further bibliographical investigation.

Christian Education ministry is one of the most exciting forms of service in the kingdom of God. Whether it be serving in a local church, a parachurch organization, at home, or on the mission field abroad, people need to hear the message of salvation in Christ and, for those who respond to God's calling, be built up and strengthened in their faith. Discipleship is at the heart of Christian Education, and the process of becoming a discipler of men and women is deeply entrenched in the contents of this book. It is my hope that the message contained in these pages will strengthen the reader to be a worker who does not need to be ashamed and who correctly handles the word of truth.

Michael J. Anthony, Ed.D., Ph.D.

PART ONE.
Foundations of
Christian Education Ministry

One
Putting Ministry in Perspective

Ministry: How would *you* define it? It means different things to different people and thus there are as many definitions as there are varied ministries. If you became a Christian at an early age and began attending a small rural church your concept of ministry will be strongly shaped by that experience. But perhaps you came to Christ in your adolescent years as a result of a parachurch organization's outreach effort. Your first ministry experience probably took place in the context of a home Bible study taught by a parachurch leader. These two examples illustrate some of the many differences that exist in ministry. It isn't that one is right and the other is wrong. They simply represent different elements of a very broad spectrum of ministry experience that believers share.

Many people come to faith through the efforts of the local church and for this reason have a church perspective on how ministry is conducted. However, even in this there are vast differences in ministry due to the differences that exist in church size, denominational affiliation, church traditions, and pastoral leadership styles. Each of these elements will influence how things are done in the name of ministry. Traditions, old and new, greatly influence ministry perspectives.

There are other believers who came to Christ through the efforts of a missionary sharing Christ on the foreign field. These believers view the way ministry is done in their homeland as an indication of how ministry should be done around the world as well. When these believers travel to others parts of the world and see the differences in ministry perspectives they ask the simple question: What is ministry? The answer, however, is not as simple for there are many common misconceptions about ministry evident in our churches today.

Misconceptions of Ministry

Before attempting to answer the above question we would do well to first identify what ministry is not. Knowing this will help us dispel some of these common misconceptions of ministry and allow us to determine just what it truly is.

1) *Ministry is not a social agency.* Many churches are involved in activities which contribute to our society's needy, (such as ministries for the homeless, unwed mothers, and various recovery groups). Their involvement in such programs fulfill the biblical mandate of clothing the needy, feeding the hungry, and visiting prisoners, widows, and orphans (James 1:27; Matt. 25:35-36). The difficulty comes when these programs take on such a significant role that the church ceases to fulfill its primary role of evangelism of the lost and edification of the body. There are a number of distinctive biblical functions, which will be covered in subsequent chapters, which only the church can accomplish. The issue here is balance. When the church ceases to function as a church, then the social programs have blurred its vision to be far more than just a social agency.

2) *The church is not an educational institution.* This is a common misconception among many new Christian college students. They come to campus and enjoy Bible classes taught by knowledgeable professors; they experience dynamic speakers in their daily chapel hour. The temptation to allow their school experience to double for their church involvement is obvious. However, the church, as Christ intended, is to be far more than a Bible college experience. There are many components of the New Testament church which the Christian college is not able to replicate. We should therefore not see it as a substitute for church ministry.

3) *The church is not a program.* Many churches have numerous programs designed to minister to the needs of their community (AWANA, VBS, youth groups). Some pastors today measure the effectiveness of their ministry based on how many people they can involve in their church's programs. If not careful, the pastor will fall prey to the temptation of promoting programs instead of Christ and thus lead the congregation into the false assumption that ministry is simply a matter of implementing a new program every few months. But real ministry is more than a program.

4) *Ministry is not a building.* It is easy for young believers to equate the church ministry with a building. They say to their friends, "I'll meet you at the church after school." Such a statement promotes a common misconception among many Christians that limits their church ministry to a building. The church, as it is described in the New Testament, is not limited to a geographical location or building. The New Testament church is comprised of believers in Christ who choose to associate together. They remain the church

whether they meet in a building, a park, or at the side of a lake. A building is not a necessary requirement for a church ministry to fulfill the Great Commission. Buildings can contribute a great deal toward the effectiveness of ministry in a local community. The danger comes when one equates the building with the ministry of the church.

5) *The church is not an organization.* This last misconception of ministry is also common among believers. This is a popular misconception among Christians who attend large churches. The extent to which many of these large churches are organized is very impressive. Christ has called us to be good stewards of our resources, and there is nothing wrong with sound principles of church administration. The danger comes when believers view church ministry as being the same in scope and content as an organization. They see that both have board members, budgets, staff members, employment policies, job descriptions, organizational charts, goals and objectives, etc. If not careful, the business procedures of the church can so overwhelm believers that they view the church as nothing more than an organization with a Christian emphasis. But the church is not an organization. According to Scripture, the church is an organism. It is the body of Christ incarnate in the world today.

The Early History of Ministry

Theologically speaking, the church began in the mind of God. The Bible teaches that before sin entered the world, God had already planned the course of redemption for mankind (Eph. 3:9-11; 1 Peter 1:20). God had planned that Christ would have to be born a man, incarnate for the purpose of redemption. He was to be the Lamb chosen by God to remove the sin of the world (John. 1:29) and make fellowship with an eternal Father possible. God had ordained that Christ would be offered up as an atonement for humankind through His death on the cross (Rom. 3:35; Heb. 2:17).

Historically speaking, the church began at Pentecost. The feast of Pentecost was a Jewish harvest festival which took place fifty days after Passover. The people came to Jerusalem after they had brought in their crops and were in a mood to celebrate their bountiful harvest. It was also a time for them to reflect upon their religious origins and thank God for giving them the Law on Mt. Sinai. It was in this context that the book of Acts records the birth of the church: "And when the day of Pentecost had come, they were all together in one place. And suddenly there came from heaven a noise like a violent, rushing wind, and it filled the whole house where they were sitting. And there appeared to them tongues as of fire distributing themselves, and they rested on each of them. And they were all filled with the Holy Spirit and began to speak with other tongues, as the Spirit was giving them utterance" (Acts 2:1-4).

Merchants, from around the world, who were in Jerusalem for the festival began to stare in amazement as they observed this phenomenon taking place. Peter stood up in the midst of this assembly and began to preach a sermon which resulted in the salvation of approximately 3,000 people. The church was born. It's first membership consisted of more than 3,120 people (cf. Acts 1:15, 2:41).

Characteristics of the Jerusalem Church
Most of these new believers were from Jerusalem and had grown up as devout members of the Jewish faith. They had a strong affinity for the Old Testament, and it was only natural that their new Christian form of worship reflected elements of their Jewish upbringing. The first church, located in Jerusalem, maintained its Jewish cultural and religious heritage. They continued to honor the Sabbath Day as holy (Acts 17:2), went to the temple for regular periods of prayer and worship (Acts 3:1ff.), kept the Jewish dietary laws (Acts 10:14), read from the Jewish sacred Scriptures (Acts 2:42-43), and continued the practice of circumcision (Acts 15:1).

In addition to these practices, which were heavily influenced by their Jewish ancestry, they also began to meet on the first day of the week to commemorate the resurrection of Jesus Christ. They met regularly together in homes to enjoy fellowship meals (Acts 2:42-43) and ended each of these meetings with the celebration of the Lord's Supper, in remembrance of His death and eventual return (1 Cor. 11:17-34).

Characteristics of the Church in Antioch
Shortly after the birth of the church in Jerusalem the Jewish city leaders began efforts to extinguish this new cult from their city. They prohibited Christians from buying and selling in the city. In addition, they appointed leaders from among themselves to seek out these Jewish defectors and persecute them. This persecution was successful to some degree for the Bible tells us that many believers left Jerusalem for other parts of the world, taking the Gospel with them.

One of these new places was Antioch, a northern city in the middle of a strategic location for commerce and trade. Over several years believers settled in Antioch and established pockets of home fellowships where the Gospel was preached and where the Word of God was taught on a regular basis (Acts 11:19-20). The church in Antioch developed a reputation for rapid growth and became known to the Jerusalem church (Acts 11:21-22). In an effort to guarantee that the Gospel in Antioch was being preached according to the truth, the church leaders in Jerusalem wanted to send some of their members to ascertain the legitimacy of this northern church.

A church leader by the name of Barnabas was selected for this important assignment (Acts 11:22). During the period of time that this northern church was being established, Saul, a member of the ruling council of the Sanhedrin in Jerusalem, had come to faith in Christ. Unsure of his motive for becoming a Christian, the Jerusalem church was wary of accepting him so they sent him to Antioch with Barnabas. It was in this location, for at least a year, that Barnabas discipled Saul into a strong Christian believer (Acts 11:25-26). This man, now with his name changed to Paul, would become one of the leading authors of the New Testament.

The church in Antioch was significantly different from the church in Jerusalem. Their ministry reflected its cultural and geographical context. Made up of Grecian Jews, this church had a cosmopolitan composition. Christians in this church had a diverse background. A few were Greeks who had subsequently become Jews. Having heard the message of the coming of the Jewish Messiah, they converted to Christianity. Many members of this church came to Christ directly from a Greek or Roman background. The cultural and religious heritage of these Greeks and Romans would give this church a significantly different appearance from the church in Jerusalem.

These Antioch believers had a different concept of ministry due to their diverse heritage. They did not see the need to keep the Jewish Sabbath since many of them had never kept it before. They saw no need to maintain the Jewish dietary lifestyle, visit the Temple in Jerusalem, or become circumcised. To them, these were remnants of a Jewish faith which had never been their own. Their ministry reflected their social, geographical, and cultural backgrounds. They were distinct from their Jerusalem brothers and sisters in Christ in many respects. It was in Antioch that believers were first called Christians (Acts 11:26), where a relief effort was first organized to help another church (Acts 11:29-30), and from where the first missionaries were sent out (Acts 13:2-3).

Principles of New Testament Ministry

Scripture provides us with a number of important ministry *principles* which can be drawn by watching these two churches in action. Observing the differences between them helps us understand the nature of how ministry should be structured in our churches today.

1) There are no prescribed patterns of worship for the church. The early church chose to conduct its worship services in different ways. We are never told that the pattern of worship in the Jerusalem church was duplicated in the church in Antioch, Ephesus, Corinth, or any other group of that day. Each church was allowed the freedom to structure their worship service according to the various social, cultural, and geographical influences in their fellowship.

2) Some program elements in the early church are noticeably absent from church ministry today. The early church did not have Sunday Schools. They did not have youth groups or church choirs. Parachurch ministries were non-existent as well. Each of these program elements, and countless more, have come as a result of differing church contexts. Ministry should not be duplicated in the same way in all churches. Each congregation should take into consideration what their local needs are and not feel compelled to replicate the ministry practices of another church.

3) Ministry should always be based upon the needs of the people. Perhaps one of the most important skills a pastor will ever learn in seminary is the ability to determine the needs of his or her congregation. The churches in the Book of Acts selected their church ministry programs based upon evident needs. A partial survey of the church in the Book of Acts, as depicted in the following chart, will illustrate this point. Read the passages of Scripture presented and you will notice that once a need became evident the church responded by developing a program to meet that need.

Need-Based Ministry in the Early Church

Acts	Evident Need in the Church	Action Taken
2:37-42	Due to their phenomenal growth, they needed a place where they could gather together for fellowship.	A small group ministry was established so they could meet together for fellowship.
6:1-6	The Hellenistic Jewish converts had widows who were not being taken care of by the church.	The church responded by establishing the first deacon board.
12:1-17	The church needed to get their leader out of jail. Peter was about to be killed by Herod.	They established the first prayer meeting to ask God to deliver Peter.
Chap. 13	The early church recognized the need to take the Gospel to other cultures in the surrounding region.	The church established their first missions program to send out two missionaries.
Chap. 15	The church was about to split over a controversy regarding the new Gentile converts.	The church leaders convened a special conference to come to a peaceful resolution.

Figure 1.1

There are many other examples of this ministry principle which could be highlighted from Scripture. Unfortunately, many churches today select a new program from their local Christian bookstore or denominational publishing company on the basis of slick marketing or advertising materials, without taking the time to see if the program relates to their church's needs. Once the program is implemented and it begins to fail, the pastoral leadership, fearing embarrassment over the failure of a church program, may put inappropriate pressure on the congregation to support the new program. This tension can be avoided if the principle of need-based ministry is observed.

4) Ministry should seek to gain total member involvement. This principle comes from the biblical teaching on spiritual gifts. The basis of New Testament ministry is the identification and development of one's spiritual gift(s). The Bible clearly teaches that every believer has at least one spiritual gift (1 Cor. 12:7; 1 Peter 4:10) and that these gifts provide the church with its foundation for ministry. This principle, known as Pedagogical Ecclesiology, comes from Ephesians 4:11-16 and is illustrated in figure 1.2.

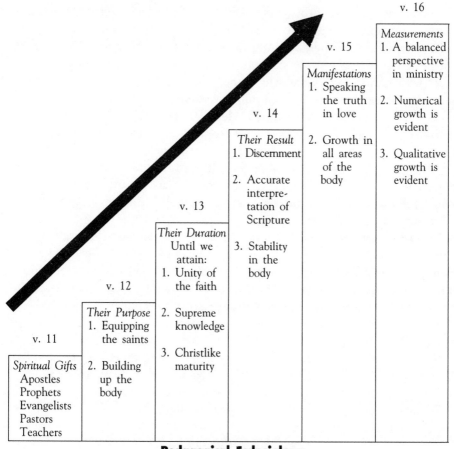

Pedagogical Ecclesiology
Figure 1.2

As each member determines his or her spiritual gift and employs it in the life of the church the local body is built up and strengthened. In turn, the member that expresses the gift experiences a degree of spiritual maturity as well. The goal of ministry is for members of the church to determine their gifts and then find areas where those gifts can be employed. Spiritual growth will take place in the body of Christ and in the life of the individual believer only as each member is involved in some aspect of ministry.

5) *Each church should determine what areas of ministry involvement they feel called to accomplish.* No individual church can meet all the needs of a given community. Some churches may feel called to a particular ministry program but not feel called to others. For example, not every church has to have a ministry to unwed mothers. Neither does every church have to have a choir to be spiritually mature. The program elements a particular church offers should be determined through the guidance of the Holy Spirit. In addition, human and physical resources must also be taken into consideration.

Some smaller churches, realizing their limitations, are joining their efforts with other churches in their community to provide their combined memberships with ministry programs which they could not afford to offer by themselves. For example, an AWANA ministry requires many trained leaders to be done right. If there are not enough adult leaders available, churches should consider combining their leaders to sponsor an AWANA ministry together. One church may have a gymnasium as part of their facilities, but not enough adult leaders. Another church may have limited facilities but a lot of willing adults. Whatever the situation, where needs demand, efforts should be combined for the benefit of the kingdom of God. For further information on Christian Education in the small church see chapter 16.

6) *The church must find a balance between evangelism and edification in its ministry programs.* Not all activities in the church have to be evangelistic. Some may emphasize growth. However, the church that does not have a strong emphasis in evangelism is spiritually incomplete. Both are essential! Without evangelism the church will have no one to edify. Without edification the body of Christ will not be trained to proclaim Christ in the marketplace.

Some churches have a tendency to emphasize one aspect over the other. Pastoral and lay leadership must examine each program activity carefully to see that the totality of their ministry programming includes elements of both. A balanced physical diet makes for a healthy physical body. The same applies for the spiritual body as well.

Christian Education: An Integrative Discipline

During the early period of historical development, Christian Education placed its focus on the agency of the Sunday School as the main avenue of ministry.

The primary professional who provided the oversight of this educational ministry was the Christian Education Director (D.C.E.). However, during recent years there has been a shift toward a more holistic and comprehensive approach to Christian Education ministry in the local church. This has resulted in a diverse number of specialized ministry positions such as Children's Ministry Director, Youth Pastor, Minister to Single Adults, and Minister to Families.

Part of the reason for this shift in ministry direction has been the emergence of more open-minded professional ministers. Directors of C.E. are now more willing to investigate, and in some cases integrate, principles and methods which can be learned from other related disciplines. The academic disciplines of education, psychology, sociology, intercultural studies, and business have much to contribute to the ministry of the local church. Indeed, one must examine these disciplines with a degree of godly wisdom so as to avoid their excesses and shortcomings (e.g., humanism, determinism, behaviorism), but an educated student should be able to sort through these disciplines and select those elements with merit and value. Obviously, such disciplines must be viewed through the lens of authoritative biblical absolutes.

One need not read far through the pages of Scripture before finding insights regarding human nature, leadership and administration, cross-cultural communication, group dynamics, and the teaching/learning process. The Bible has much to say regarding these important elements. There is a great deal of biblical truth which can be seen in the principles of the behavioral sciences. Figure 1.3 demonstrates a model which may be helpful for the new student of Christian Education. It depicts the systems approach to understanding the contributions of other disciplines to Christian Education.

This model demonstrates our dependence on the Word of God as our absolute authority and guide for ministry application. Biblical imperatives must be seen as guidelines which the church is called to fulfill. Beyond these truths comes the manner in which we have come to understand and organize them. This organization of themes is called Bible doctrines (e.g., Christology, Eschatology, Pneumatology). Knowing how the church has historically interpreted these themes and applied them to ministry is important for it serves as a backdrop for present and future ministry programming.

Once having passed through these elements ministry then considers and integrates the contributions of other related disciplines (e.g., intercultural studies, sociology, business, psychology, and education). Flowing out of these disciplines come the functional purposes of ministry (e.g., worship, evangelism, discipleship, fellowship, service). The end result of this process is spiritual fruit, that is, changed lives. The only fruit which will last for eternity is that of people whose lives have been brought into relationship with God in Christ and whose lives reflect the risen Lord.

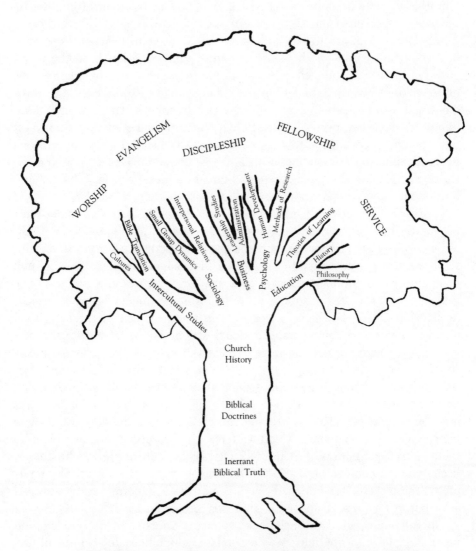

An Integrated Systems Approach to Understanding Christian Education
Figure 1.3

Summary

The Christian Education ministry of the local church must be comprehensive and balanced. It should take into consideration the outreach needs of its community as well as the growth needs of its local congregation. The various church programs of music, missions, evangelism, discipleship, Bible study, prayer cells, support groups, men's/women's fellowships, children's ministry, youth ministry, and various forms of adult ministry must all be taken into consideration. No one church should try to be all things to all people. The members should feel the freedom to determine the needs of their community and congregation and then plan their programs accordingly. Since, as we noted, church ministry varied from one church to another in the New Testament, then it should offer a similar diversity today as well.

The church must be both culturally relevant and socially sensitive. It should base its ministries on evident needs and find a balance between both evangelism and edification. Those who would want to model our ministries today after the Jerusalem church do not understand that social, geographical, and cultural issues must be taken into consideration if contemporary ministry is going to be relevant and meaningful.

As the church takes the message of hope and salvation to a lost and needy world and seeks to apply the Word of God to the complex social needs evident today, it will be fulfilling the Great Commission of Christ to make disciples of all nations.

Two
The Theology of Christian Education

When most of us think about theology, we think of orderly explanations of doctrine gleaned from the Bible. These collections of Scripture-based teachings are sometimes arranged according to biblical designations such as Old Testament theology or Pauline theology. In other instances they are compiled in relation to "systematic" themes such as pneumatology and ecclesiology. Many times they are mixed, covering topics like the pneumatology of the Old Testament or the ecclesiology of the epistles of Paul. Such is the language of theology.

On the other hand, contemporary thought in Christian Education, like its secular education counterpart, is normally expressed in behavioral science terms with reference to the cognitive, affective, and psychomotor domains. Often, philosophical categories like epistemology, metaphysics, and axiology are the basis for presentations of educational theory. Such is the language of education.

Because of differences in terminology, theological concepts are not easy to fit into educational discussions. There doesn't seem to be much of a relationship between the loci of theology and age-graded curriculum or behavioral objectives. As a result, in Christian Education, theology is usually related only to the content of instruction. It is infrequently employed as a guide for Christian Education theory and practice. This is unfortunate, for theology is vitally related to what Christian Education has been, is, and should be.

Theology and Attitudes in Christian Education
In 1948, after pastoring two small churches in Pennsylvania, a young man named Francis A. Schaeffer became a missionary involved in children's ministry in post-war Europe. During his third year in Switzerland, Schaeffer experi-

enced a personal spiritual crisis, after which he carefully reconsidered the divisive attitude that characterized his organization's approach to ministry—a disposition that was so intensely concerned about personal and ecclesiastical purity that joy had been removed from ministry. In a 1951 article in *The Sunday School Times*, Schaeffer declared that there were significant theological reasons for a more biblical spirit in those who minister in the name of Jesus Christ. He explained that consistent power and enjoyment of the Lord in ministry do not rest upon a single foundation of ecclesiastical purity. Rather, they are supported by a dual foundation of both purity and love (see figure 2.1).[1]

It was not sterile dogma that Schaeffer forcefully applied to the practice of Christian ministry: "If we have come to the frame of mind where we are so occupied with the struggle against fleshly sin, or unbelief, that we act as though any means is permissable, then the love has gone, and the power has gone. Combat, to be for God's greatest glory, must be fought according to

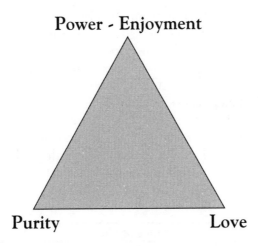

Power - Enjoyment

Purity   Love

Figure 2.1

God's rules. It is possible to struggle for personal purity and the purity of the church without having the struggle based upon love and leading to a deeper love of God and man. When this is done it leads inevitably to dead orthodoxy, and dead orthodoxy is always the threshold to new heresy."[2]

This simple doctrinal distinction may seem innocuous today, but Schaeffer's theological thesis caused great consternation amongst the hierarchy of "the movement."[3] Even some close colleagues concluded that Schaeffer was becoming "soft" in regard to orthodox doctrine, rather than recognizing that he was heralding a ministry attitude that reflects the character of Jesus Christ, who was "full of grace and truth" (John 1:14). In any event, this important theological perspective had revolutionary implications for Francis Schaeffer's educational mission. It fostered a balanced attitude that matured into a genuinely Christian ministry characterized by both gentleness and precise theology for the remainder of his life.

Theology and the Practice of Christian Education

Like Schaeffer, every Christian educator has a theology. At some point one's theology must be demonstrated in relationship between oneself and God, and between oneself and other people. It is in relationship when we are able to examine the values, beliefs, and behaviors which flow from our theological convictions. Since there is room for disagreement in theological issues, there must be a corresponding degree of tolerance in the church for the way that one's theological convictions are displayed in the church. An example of this is seen in the way a church is led.

Theology Applied to Church Leadership Models

A similar effect of theology upon ministry is found in the initial pages of *A Theology of Church Leadership* by Larry Richards and Clyde Hoeldtke. The following chart represents three major types of relationship between church leaders and members that these authors discuss in some detail.[4]

Richards and Hoeldtke believe column A represents a "Command" model in which leaders "lord it over" (Luke 22:25) members. Their rejection of this style of ministry leadership prevents the recommendation of an authoritarian approach to church leadership. The authors believe that column B represents a "Sharing" model that is related to the biblical ideal, but falls short of the

A	B	C
Command Model	Sharing Model	Servant Model

H = Headship

Figure 2.2

example of Jesus. Moderate approval of this model causes Richards and Hoeldtke to value the roles of both leaders and members in the work of the ministry. Richards and Hoeldtke believe that the biblical ideal for New Testament church leadership is represented by column C. Consequently, their text is a manual for "Servant" leadership in ministry. The authors' theological position determines the approach to ministry leadership that they recommend. In fact, they declare that "If we are to serve as leaders in the body of Christ, whatever that leadership may involve, it cannot be biblical if it is constructed on a distorted idea of what headship means."[5]

With that injunction in mind, we might take a closer look at the above model to see if there is an alternative theological perspective. While the columns do appear to represent distinct approaches to ministry, they also display three crucial and correct aspects of biblical leadership that are clearly defined in Scripture. Column A represents the *position*[6] of a leader *over* the members—as an overseer to be honored (1 Tim. 3:1 and 5:17). Column B represents the *identity* of a leader *as* one of many valuable members (1 Cor. 12:12-31). Column C represents the *function* of a leader, serving *under* the members of the body, building them up for the work of the ministry (Eph. 4:11-13).

Because the text by Richards and Hoeldtke is primarily concerned with the *function* of ministry leadership, the skewed theological foundation has a minimal effect. The recommendation of a servant model in church leadership is right on target. However, a member who believes that column C represents the *position* or *identity* of a church leader is not likely to respond well to servant leadership. In a similar fashion, a leader who accepts column C as a representation of his *position* or *identity* may not respond confidently in circumstances that call for church discipline or in congregational discussions of controversial issues. However, a leader or member who clearly understands the theology of position, identity, and function is apt to promote order, unity, and service in the church. Theological precision can have a dramatic effect upon the practice of Christian Education and the effectiveness of ministry programs and organizations.

Theology and Authority in Christian Education

The Theological Encyclopedia

The determinative effect of theology in regard to ministry has often been displayed in a hierarchical device called a "theological encyclopedia"—a visual representation of the continuum from biblical exegesis to application of truth. Though encyclopedic presentations of the progression from text to life can be complex, the general scheme usually can be reduced to three basic components. Figure 2.3 demonstrates an example of a theological encyclopedia model.[7]

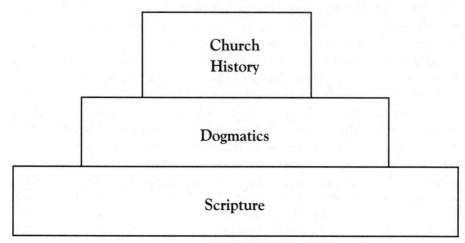

Figure 2.3

The encyclopedia starts with Scripture at its foundation. This demonstrates that accurate interpretation of the Bible should be the basis for all Christian thought and practice. The foundation of the theological encyclopedia is biblical exegesis. Dogmatics, including both biblical and systematic theology, rests upon the foundation of Scripture. This placement indicates the fact that though personal beliefs influence interpretation of the Bible (it is humanly unavoidable), theology should not control exegesis. Finally, in a theological encyclopedia, church history, the practice of God's people through the ages, is customarily pictured as emerging from the theological level. In turn, theology is to inform the practice of the Christian life.

The strength of the encyclopedia is that it displays that the practice of the Christian life (church history) can be guided by precise thought (dogmatics) based upon the authority of the Word of God (Scripture). However, the progression displayed in the encyclopedia also reflects a weakness in much C. E. theory. The encyclopedia removes the Christian life from the direct influence of the Word of God by a secondary, theological discipline. Theological explanations based upon careful study of the text of Scripture are extremely helpful. Further, correct theology is essential for the practice of the Christian life. However, theology is meant to be neither a barrier nor a necessary mediator between the Scriptures and Christian Education.

In a direct historical manner, the encyclopedic approach has led to the potential for the separation of components of Christian thought that must remain united. It has inspired the creation of "divisions" and "departments" within theological education that, all too often, compete with one another for prominence. It has depicted Christian Education as a tertiary appendage to the true sciences of biblical and theological studies.

Theological Integration

An unfortunate effect of encyclopedic thought is described by Kirk E. Farnsworth in relation to the integration of theology and the behavioral sciences. He correctly explains that because scientific research findings are the result of inductive procedures (which yield probabilities rather than certain results), conclusions based upon empirical research are subject to various levels of error. Farnsworth takes this one step further by demonstrating that theology has the same potential weakness. He argues that because theology is derived from Scripture by a process that is subject to misinterpretation, it may be in error as well. Speaking of the Scriptures, Farnsworth explains his understanding of the nature of theology:

> The logical conclusion is that the data base is privileged, but the interpretations are not. For example, the Bible itself has priority over theological facts derived from the Bible. Assuming this to be the case, we can further conclude that theological facts are not necessarily superior to any other kind of facts (e.g., psychological facts). What we must not conclude, however, is that all data bases are on a par. The inerrant Bible stands alone. It occupies a special position in God's revelation of truth through His creation. In other words, biblical data are privileged . . . in comparison with all other kinds of data—such as data generated by human subjects in a psychological experiment."[8]

Following similar lines of reasoning, Christian philosophers, psychologists, sociologists, and educators have attempted to defuse controversy concerning discrepancies between theology and science by claiming that "all truth is God's truth" whether it is discovered through study of the Scriptures (special revelation) or the study of creation (general revelation). They claim that because both theology and empirical research are subject to errors of observation and interpretation, they are epistemological equals and must be "integrated."

Some integrationists, however, have become so disillusioned by disagreements between evangelical systematic theologies and by disparate formulations of God's will for Christian living that they have almost given up on knowing truth itself. One writer has expressed his frustration in this way: "The existence of numerous, conflicting, and constantly changing theories about truth, as it is revealed through both general and special revelation, suggests that efforts to observe and interpret revealed truth are plagued by error and inaccuracy. Therefore, it appears that we are unable to fully know the truth since our knowledge is partial, at best."[9]

There is a widespread desperation concerning the possibility of divine guidance in the Christian life, Christian psychology, and Christian Education that is rooted in the misconception that fallible theology is the ultimate source of truth. Many Christian educators and scientists mistakenly believe that the text of the Word of God is unable to guide human conduct with authority, that the errors of individual interpreters equalize the authority of the Scriptures and empirical research, and that church history (the practice of believers through the centuries and today) is subject to only general biblical principles.

It would be an error to believe that this confusion and lack of authoritative guidance is a modern phenomenon. In fact, the history of Christian Education is intricately interwoven with the history of philosophy. Often, this relationship has led Christian educators away from the text of God's Word and the development of a strong biblical foundation for education.

Theology and Philosophy in Christian Education

As Christians have struggled with the questions of knowing (epistemology), being (metaphysics), and acting (axiology), they have adopted a variety of theoretical constructs. The urge to discover ultimate organizing principles in regard to these cognitive, affective and overt behavioral aspects of life has led them along many different philosophical roads. Some have been useful. Others have been almost totally devoid of significance for truly Christian Education.

An Eclectic History

Gangel and Benson have scrutinized this sometimes godly but somewhat worldly heritage. They state that the Christian philosopher "has generally found himself in a 'Paul-in-the-marketplace' situation as a *spermalogos* — one picking up the seeds of truth from various systems and forming a 'system' that displeases proponents of any worldly pattern because of its primary concern to be biblical."[10]

This interactive development of Christian Education has resulted in some benefit. The claims of Christ and the educational implications of biblical revelation have confronted challenges of human reason and have fended off attacks of those who view a bibliocentric world view as unscholarly at best. However, a negative aspect of this adaptive growth pattern has been a tendency for C.E. to sink its roots too deeply into ground that has been cultivated by philosophers and educators with distinctly non-Christian presuppositions. The foundation of Christian Education has frequently been an eclectic mixture of biblical content and non-biblical theory.

A Structuralist Conformity

In the last half of the twentieth century, a body of literature has evolved within evangelical Christian Education that is dependent upon the theories of Jean Piaget, Lawrence Kohlberg, and, more recently, James Fowler. At the forefront of this trend, Norman Wakefield[11] and Lawrence Richards[12] produced excellent presentations of how Piaget's developmental constructs involving cognitive growth in children relates to Christian Education. Ted Ward[13] and Donald Joy[14] have produced sharp analyses of Kohlberg and have explored the educational implications of a stepwise, unvarying, universal pattern of moral development from a Christian perspective. Fowler's faith development theory has also generated an evangelical response.

The almost total acceptance of the structural development viewpoint and the extensive conceptual accommodation to this approach within Christian Education has provided a convenient bridge by which to move quickly from a general Christian "world and life view" to educational planning and curriculum design. The natural maturation of cognitive and moral ability that is a prime tenet of developmentalism has been widely accepted as a sufficient basis for methodology in Christian Education. By adding a "supernatural/revelational" component,[15] Christian educators have adopted the structuralist approach as a foundation for the practice of Christian moral development and spiritual nurture.

Unfortunately, the creation of a theologically corrected developmental perspective has not yielded a more biblical approach to Christian Education. In the presence of theory and research that explain the "natural" appearance of mature thinking and moral reasoning, many Christian educators have ceased depending upon precise biblical exegesis in the process of determining guidelines for ministry.

Theology and Hermeneutics in Christian Education

Paul has provided a construct (faith, hope, and love) for the application of truth to life that may be used with confidence as a biblical foundation for Christian Education in every age. However, if the concepts of faith, hope, and love are to be more authoritative than mere principles or participial functions, their content must exceed a few favorite Bible verses or selected tenets of systematic theology. To be authoritative guides for educational ministry, faith, hope, and love must be related to specific behavioral directives found in relevant portions of the Word of God.

An Interpretive Foundation

Contemporary educational thought and practice must be guided by directives from the Bible. However, the text of Scripture was addressed to individuals in a wide range of circumstances over more than 2,000 years. It is actually somebody else's mail! It is this indirect applicability that has frustrated Christian educators. How do historical directives found in archaic documents addressed to ancient people apply to ministry programs of the contemporary church?

The customary approach is to seek definitive guidance from the general principles offered by theology. However, as noted earlier, the terminology of theology does not easily translate into the categories that form the structure of educational thought.

In order to receive authoritative directives from the Scriptures, Bible interpretation must be accomplished through a natural approach to the reading of Scripture. A historical-grammatical method of Bible interpretation is used to determine the meaning of biblical passages by analysis of word usage in specific contexts. Both the historical circumstance and the grammatical structure of any passage must be analyzed thoroughly. The uniting of the context and the content of a passage yields interpretation. In passages that are difficult to interpret, more thorough contextual research and content analysis are necessary. Even in these cases, the historical-grammatical method remains the proper vehicle for accurate interpretation.

Thus, it is not surprising to discover that in evangelical theological education, where the historical-grammatical method is fully accepted there is an emphasis on historical background research as a necessary component of interpretation.

A survey of hermeneutics textbooks reveals many fine presentations of the process of textual observation. However, it also reveals a neglect of the process of historical background research.[16] This neglect has resulted in an imbalanced emphasis upon precise grammatical analysis almost to the exclusion of thorough analysis of the historical background of the Scriptures. Inadequate attention to historical context has produced weak interpretation of specific behavioral directives that were given to individuals in specific biblical contexts, and has led to a lack of authority in the application of those directives to contemporary life.

The crucial nature of historical background research is based upon the realization that God's Word was God's will for those to whom the message was delivered. The Scriptures are statements of specific truth in the form of specific direction for specific circumstances. Consequently, the historical-grammatical method produces an understanding of God's will in the form of definite "historical directives" that were given to real people in real life circumstances. Thorough historical-grammatical interpretation makes it possible to know God's will for specific situations in history. This is the body of inspired knowledge from which all understanding of God's will for life today must be derived.

Educational Orientation
As the words of an author are interpreted on the basis of usage in a well-researched historical context, the intent of his or her communication can be identified. That intent is actually educational content involving the cognitive, affective, and/or overt behavioral activity of the recipients. The original recipients received facts to believe, perspectives to adopt, and actions to perform in their specific circumstances. They were also expected to apply the author's faith, hope, and love directives appropriately in similar circumstances in life and ministry as they occurred. The recipients were given definitive guidance that not only directed current behavior, but enhanced knowledge of God's will for thought, perspective, and behavior for related experiences in life.

Today, Christians reading Scripture can understand what God's will was in the historical setting. They can discern how to think, view circumstances, or act in specific *kinds* of circumstances. Further, they can learn to apply authoritative historical faith, hope, and love directives from analogous biblical circumstances to contemporary life and ministry with a high degree of precision.

Application by Analogy
In the same way that a judge in a court of law applies historical legal precedent to analogous cases before him, students of God's Word can apply revealed directives to current life circumstances. In this manner, cognitive content, affective perspective, and overt behavior can be identified and instituted as the biblical foundation for the theory and practice of Christian Education. The "historical directives" regarding facts to be believed, perspectives to adopt, and actions to perform that were given by inspiration of the Holy Spirit can be applied with confidence to similar circumstances today.

Summary
Rather than remaining constantly at the mercy of every behavioral science theory that appears on the scene, we need to develop a theology of Christian Education that is built upon extensive knowledge of the truth of God's Word.

Theology based upon accurate interpretation of the Scriptures is a valuable aid to Christian thought and is the content of much instruction in C.E. However, theology is not ultimate. Similarly, interaction with behavioral science research and theory is necessary. It provides valuable insight and encourages creative thinking. However, it must not be the sole pattern for Christian Education.

Epistemology, metaphysics, and axiology govern educational theory and practice. In Christian Education, these significant knowledge, perspective and overt behavior constructs must be guided by an active allegiance to a historical-grammatical interpretation of the Scriptures. Our commitment must be to the truth that produces faith, hope, and love in the development of a biblical foundation for Christian Education.

Notes

1. Francis A. Schaeffer, "The Secret of Power and the Enjoyment of the Lord," *The Sunday School Times*, 16 and 23 June 1951, 539-40, 555-56.

2. Ibid., 555.

3. In Lane T. Dennis, ed., *Letters of Francis A. Schaeffer* (Westchester, IL: Crossway Books, 1985), 46. Schaeffer described the reaction to a related article as ". . . being pursued into my work here, and that a determined and successful effort was made . . . to turn some from these spiritual matters, and to make them fasten their eyes on loyalty to the external machinery and human leadership."

4. Lawrence O. Richards and Clyde Hoeldtke, *Church Leadership: Following the Example of Jesus Christ* (Grand Rapids: Zondervan Publishing House, 1988), 22-26.

5. Ibid., 25.

6. In an October 1990 discussion with Larry Richards concerning this reinterpretation of his diagram, he stated that he prefers the term *office* to *position* in reference to column A in this revised perspective.

7. The threefold conceptualization used here reflects the approach of Friedrich Schleiermacher. A discussion of the history of the theological encyclopedia may be found in Edward Farley, *Theologia: The Fragmentation and Unity of Theological Education* (Philadelphia: Fortress Press, 1983).

8. Kirk E. Farnsworth, *Wholehearted Integration* (Grand Rapids: Baker Book House, 1985), 14.

9. James D. Guy, Jr., "The Search for Truth in the Task of Integration," *Journal of Psychology and Theology* 8 (1980): 30.

10. Kenneth O. Gangel and Warren S. Benson, *Christian Education: Its History and Philosophy* (Chicago: Moody Press, 1983), 339.

11. Norman Wakefield, "Children and their Developmental Concepts," in

Roy B. Zuck and Robert E. Clark, eds., *Childhood Education and the Church* (Chicago: Moody Press, 1975), 119-33.

12. Lawrence O. Richards, *A Theology of Christian Education* (Grand Rapids: Zondervan Publishing House, 1975), 170-87.

13. Ted Ward, *Values Begin at Home* (Wheaton, Ill.: Victor Books, 1989).

14. Donald Joy, "Human Development and Christian Holiness," *Asbury Seminarian*, (April 1976), 5-27.

15. Richards, *Theology of Christian Education*, 74-76.

16. I'm not aware of any hermeneutics or exegesis text that provides an adequate explanation of how to conduct historical background research as one of the two crucial components of the historical grammatical method of biblical interpretation.

For Further Reading

Boys, M.C. *Biblical Interpretation of Religious Education.* Birmingham, Ala.: Religious Education Press, 1980.

Byrne, H.W. *A Christian Approach to Education.* Milford, Mich.: Mott Media, 1978.

Daniel, E., J. Wade, and C. Gresham. *Introduction to Christian Education.* Cincinnati: Standard Publishing, 1980.

Farnsworth, E. *Wholehearted Integration.* Grand Rapids: Baker Book House, 1985.

Ferré, N.F. *A Theology for Christian Education.* Philadelphia: Westminster Press, 1967.

Gangel, K.O., and W.S. Benson. *Christian Education: Its History and Philosophy.* Chicago: Moody Press, 1983.

Getz, G. *Sharpening the Focus of the Church.* Chicago: Moody Press, 1974.

Graendorf, W.C., ed. *Introduction to Biblical Christian Education.* Chicago: Moody Press, 1981.

Guy, Jr., J.D. "The Search for Truth in the Task of Integration." *Journal of Psychology and Theology* 8 (1980).

Person, P.P. *An Introduction to Christian Education.* Grand Rapids: Baker Book House, 1979.

LeBar, L. *Education That is Christian.* rev. ed. Edited by J.E. Plueddemann, Wheaton, Ill.: Victor Books 1989.

Powers, B.P. ed. *Christian Education Handbook.* Nashville: Broadman Press, 1981.

Richards, L.O., and C. Hoeldtke. *A Theology of Church Leadership.* Grand Rapids: Zondervan Publishing House, 1981.

Richards, L.O. *A Theology of Christian Education.* Grand Rapids: Zondervan Publishing House, 1975.

Sanner, A.E. and A.F. Harper, eds. *Exploring Christian Education.* Kansas City: Beacon Hill Press, 1978.

Taylor, M.J. *Foundations for Christian Education in an Era of Change.* Nashville: Abingdon Press, 1976.

Thompson, N.H. ed. *Religious Education and Theology.* Birmingham, Ala.: Religious Education Press, 1982.

Tidwell, C.A. *Educational Ministry of a Church.* Nashville: Broadman Press, 1982.

Three
The History of Christian Education

The history of Christian Education is the history of humankind. In the beginning God created the heavens and the earth (Gen. 1:1). A significant part of that act was the creation of man and woman—the beginning of the human race. And the first direct interaction between God and man, recorded in the second chapter of Genesis, was an educational event. The Lord had placed the man in the Garden of Eden for a purpose. The man was to work his environment and take care of it (2:15). In order for the man to do this properly, within bounds that God had established, he needed instructions. Thus, "the Lord God commanded the man, 'You are free to eat from any tree in the garden; but you must not eat from the tree of the knowledge of good and evil, for when you eat of it you will surely die' " (2:16-17).

From the very beginning, the existence of the race depended upon a philosophy of education that required man and woman to listen, to learn, and to act upon knowledge acquired by revelation from God. It was very clear that allegiance to knowledge derived from other sources could lead to condemnation and death. This was confirmed when the woman that God created as a suitable helper for man (Gen. 2:20-23) listened to the serpent, learned of an alternative, and acted upon an interpretation of righteous behavior in direct opposition to the Word of God (Gen. 3:5-7). The man also chose to act upon "gained" rather than revealed wisdom, and a form of "enlightenment" occurred in which the eyes of the man and the woman were opened to all the created world has to offer, but were closed to the intimate communion that had existed between themselves and the only source of wisdom (Gen. 3:8-24).

In a very real sense, this was the beginning of Christian Education, for it was immediately revealed that Christ would be the solution to a conflict between the will of God and the deceptions of Satan that has characterized all of history. He is the only offspring of the woman who can crush the head of the great deceiver (Gen. 3:15). That humankind would be plagued for centuries by the deceptions of the serpent was revealed in the statement that Satan would strike the heel of the Son of God.

The educational conflict continued as Cain, the first individual born through childbirth, ignored God's direct instruction concerning righteousness and murdered his own brother (Gen. 4:6-8). Eventually, this pattern of response to God's revelation became characteristic of the entire human race. In fact, the great flood, from which only Noah and his family were delivered, was a result of the wickedness of man and the fact that "every inclination of the thoughts of his heart was only evil all the time" (Gen. 6:5).

After the flood, as humankind proliferated, individuals conspired to build cities, to make a name for themselves, and to disobey God's command to scatter over the face of the earth (Gen. 9:1; 11:4). By direct intervention, God created various language groups, making it impossible for people to understand one another without great difficulty. This produced an involuntary adherence to His command — the nations scattered over the face of the entire earth (Gen. 11:8-9).

The significance of this event in the history of Christian Education is found in the name of the location that this event occurred. The place was Babel, a word meaning "confusion." The fact that Babel is identified with Babylon, one of the great empires of the ancient world, should not pass without notice. The confusion of language at Babel was provoked by a human culture that repeated the arrogant rejection of God's will that characterized the generations from Adam to Noah. The pagan culture that developed at Babylon is representative of the confusion of knowledge that has characterized the history of humankind.

Every age has its Babylons. There has been no apparent limit to the alternative interpretations of reality and wisdom with which godly educators have had to contend through the ages. In many periods of history, the confusion of a culture has spread like an infection through the body of Christ. Occasionally, however, the church has been a source of light in ages darkened by the deception of the devil. This is the uneven story of God's people through the centuries. This is the history of Christian Education.

Education in Ancient Civilizations

Five major cultural systems of the ancient world made significant contributions in education. As far back as 3,500 B.C., in connection with the development of written language, formal schools were established in *Sumer* (present day Iraq). Artifacts from the area reveal that reading, writing, arithmetic, vocational skills, and allegiance to the king were primary foci of this education. Instruction was conducted mainly by priests who emphasized worship of the false gods of the Sumerians in their teaching. The *Persians* adopted the educational heritage of the Sumerians, whom they conquered. Basic academic subjects and vocational education were continued, but more emphasis was placed upon the character of male students and preparation for military and political service. In Persian education, however, the tenets of Zoroastrian religion were central and preparation for the hereditary priesthood was a major factor in schooling.

Further East, in *China*, formal schools were established as early as 3,000 B.C. A broader cultural enrichment was present, with character education, music, and poetry predominating. Philosophy took a central place in the curriculum, culminating, centuries later, in almost total alignment with the elitist philosophy of Lao-tzu (ca. 600-500 B.C.) and the writings of Confucius (551-479 B.C.) which included moral character traits and man-centered philosophical perspectives.

At about the same time (ca. 500 B.C.), schools were emerging in *Egypt*. Here, a dual educational system emerged. Schools sponsored by the government emphasized vocational and military training. Temple schools focused upon scholarly pursuits such as reading and writing as well as leadership in religious thought and observance.

In view of the pagan character of all ancient education, it is understandable that the *Hebrew* nation was founded by the call of God to Abram (later Abraham) to "Leave your country, your people, and your father's household and go to the land I will show you" (Gen. 12:1). From that time forward in the history of Israel, the Promised Land was the place of blessing. The place of unfaithfulness was outside the borders of the land — among the nations, the confused offspring of Babel, who bowed to idols and served man, rejecting the wisdom of the Most High God.

Hebrew education was focused upon monotheistic beliefs that shaped the culture of the community. The nation was God's treasured possession. Though the whole earth belongs to God, He said that Israel was "a kingdom of priests and a holy nation" (Ex. 19:6). The standard for righteous behavior in the nation was not a set of arbitrary character traits, it was the character of God. He required no less than perfection of His people, saying unto them, "I am the Lord your God; consecrate yourselves and be holy, because I am holy. . . . I am the Lord who brought you up out of Egypt to be your God; therefore be holy, because I am holy" (Lev. 11:44-45).

The Law (including the Ten Commandments and the entire regulatory system of Israel) was actually a revelation of the character of God in terms of human behavior. The Law was God *telling* man how He would act if He were to become a man. Later, in the incarnation of God in the person of Jesus

Christ, this Law was not abolished. Rather, it was fulfilled (Matt. 5:17) as "The Word became flesh and made His dwelling among us" (John 1:14). In the incarnation, God was *showing* man how He would act if He were to become a man (which He did). Consequently, the history of God's people in the Old Testament Scriptures is an integral part of the history of Christian Education.

The life-related educational philosophy of the Hebrews did not, at first, foster a schooling approach to learning. The ritual observances of the community and the home life of children were the primary vehicles for transmission of the God-centered culture. Just before entering the Promised Land (a return to the place of blessing after 400 years of exile in Egypt), God's people were commanded through Moses to not only *know* the commands, decrees, and laws of God, but to *obey* them in every aspect of life (Deut. 6:1-5). Obeying the commandments was to be a sincere commitment of every parent (Deut. 6:6). Children were to learn the ways of God through deliberate instruction as well as through informal discussion in the teachable moments of life that occurred all the time and everywhere (Deut. 6:7). Parents were to demonstrate how the Word of God affects behavior and assigns significance to every thought (Deut. 6:8). The commandments of God were also to be evident in the way that relationships were maintained in the home and in the community (Deut. 6:9).

In contrast to the school-based education available only to the elite in the pagan cultures of the Ancient Near East, Hebrew education pervaded the lives of all the people. The nation was to be separate from the influence of the nations (Gen. 12:1; Deut. 4; Ezra 10:11). There was to be a clear rejection of all "wisdom" that was not in accord with the will of the Lord as revealed in the Word of God.

Education in the Greek and Roman Periods

Education in Western civilization is largely a product of *Greek* philosophy and its corresponding educational system. The triumph of the more democratic society of Athens over the militaristic Spartans led to the development of a relatively free and flexible society often referred to as the Age of Pericles (459-430 B.C.), or the Athenian Golden Age.

Much of the educational progress that was accomplished at Athens was due to the affluence of the city. Athens emerged from the Persian Wars (5th century B.C.) with a prosperity that was able to subsidize a significant scholarly community and an elite class of citizens with the leisure time necessary for advanced learning. It is estimated that for every Athenian freeman there were seven slaves to do the productive work of the society. Further, neither voting nor education were available to women or slaves. Men, on the other hand, possessed the opportunity and the privilege for much contemplative thought. Predictably, Athenian education was theoretical, elitist, and ethereal. God was only an idea. Truth, like justice and happiness, was always beyond the reach of man.

The Greeks produced a culture that was rich in philosophy, literature, and art. The thought of Socrates (469-399 B.C.), Plato (420-348 B.C.), and Aristotle (384-322 B.C.) shaped human critical reasoning in such a focused manner that many educational historians believe the Athenian period provided the foundation for the Renaissance as well as the modern scientific age. But Greek thought had little practical benefit. Matters of everyday life were not the concern of the philosopher-educators. Common men were only capable of *doxa* (unproven opinion). It was believed that *doxa* must be elevated, by critical thinking, to the level of *orthe doxa* (correct opinion) and then *episteme*, the true knowledge that is attained by contemplation—which was the privilege of only a few.

The *Romans* conquered Greece in 146 B.C., but they did not obliterate Greek civilization. Instead, they recruited (enslaved) Greek educators to develop the Roman educational system. In this manner, Athenian educational influence spread gradually until it pervaded the entire Roman empire, which endured for over 1,000 years. The Romans carried the Greek educational impact to the farthest reaches of the known world. However, the practical Romans did not perpetuate the aloof Greek philosophical perspective. They did subsidize, organize, and administrate a commendable network of elementary and secondary schools as well as institutions for higher education. The goal of this formal school system was to produce citizens with strong character and allegiance to the state.

The Roman influence upon education is typified in the writings of Quintilian (A.D. 35-95). In a twelve-volume work, *The Institutes of Oratory*, this educational visionary presented the following principles (a few of many significant concepts):

- The maturity level of individual children is a significant determinant of learning.
- Individual mental and physical differences between children affect their rate of learning.
- Excessive corporal punishment hinders schooling.
- Encouragement and rewards are significant learning motivators.
- School subjects should be practical—learning should be life-related.

Formal education among the *Hebrews* developed slowly during the Greek and Roman periods. After the exile, Hebrew culture developed to a point beyond which the home or even the synagogue were considered sufficient educational vehicles. Schools were created for formal instruction in the theological and cultural values that were considered important by the temple leadership. Eventually, the elitism of Greek education was reflected in the Hebrew system. Only a few individuals were privileged to participate in all levels of the educational system. To a large extent, Hebrew education became as man-centered and aristocratic as the surrounding Greek culture. The temple leadership led the nation into a condition characterized by ritual and self-defined righteousness. Truth became as abstract as Athenian philosophy and the Law was viewed as impractical and irrelevant.

In its more advanced stages, Hebrew education was organized on a four-level continuum:

Birth to age 6	Home-based education.
Ages 6 to 12	Synagogue schools in which literary and mathematical training accompanied religious instruction.
Ages 12 to 16	Comprehensive study of the Law in small groups "at the feet" of a rabbi.
16 through adulthood	Individualized higher education in the Law and advanced theology under the supervision of respected authorities.

At the time of Christ, the fully subsidized Roman educational system was expanding. However, Roman culture was losing the vitality and creativity infused by the Greek conquest. Hebrew education, with its separatist stance and religious orientation, was not to be a source of progressive ideas in the Roman world. Reform would come from an unlikely source. There was a new movement afoot that would transform both culture and education in the West for centuries to come.

At the outset, *Christianity* did not appear to offer much in the way of educational innovation. Its leader, Jesus of Nazareth, claimed to be the Messiah of the Hebrews, but was rejected by the leaders of the nation. He was executed by the Romans and was represented by a small band of followers who had little formal education. His disciples were common men, ill-equipped to launch a system of moral thought with philosophical implications that would be a landmark in Western history. However, two significant differences between Christianity and the Hebrew religion define the essence of its potential impact.

The first was the reversal of the separatistic character of Jewish society. In what has been called The Great Commission, Jesus gathered His disciples about Him at the end of His earthly ministry and declared, "All authority in heaven and on earth has been given to Me. Therefore go and make disciples of all nations, baptizing them in the name of the Father and of the Son and of the Holy Spirit, and teaching them to obey everything I have commanded you. And surely I am with you always, to the very end of the age" (Matt. 28:18-20).

The second, implied in the first, was revealed when, just before ascending to the right hand of the Father, Jesus declared, "you will receive power when the Holy Spirit comes upon you; and you will be My witnesses in Jerusalem, and in all Judea and Samaria, and to the ends of the earth" (Acts 1:8).

As Christianity spread, the contrast between the teachings of Jesus of Nazareth and the philosophy of the Age of Pericles became apparent: "Gone is the unambiguous superiority of contemplation over active life; gone is the notion that all necessary activities are beneath the freedom and dignity of perfect life; gone, finally, is the notion that all human doing is either an activity thoroughly meaningful in itself or else only a 'purification.' For Christian deeds of charity serve a world which is not the Christian's homestead, and yet, they have to be carried out almost as if they were the only thing which really mattered."[1]

Pinar and Grumet expand upon the revolutionary impact of Christianity and relate it to the theory and practice of education: "For the Greeks, contemplation was reserved for the prosperous male. For Christians, even the poor can be saved. . . . Nor did one need to be brilliant, a philosopher, in order to achieve wisdom. Acceptance and belief require no sophisticated mental operations; even the illiterate and the enslaved can achieve the Christian equivalent of wisdom: Salvation."[2]

Writing to the church at Corinth in the first century, Paul confronted the Corinthians' inclination to adopt the wisdom of the world and the morality of the age. He sought to dispel any embarrassment at believing the truth of the Gospel and being devoted to the quality of life that is found in the example of Jesus Christ:

We do, however, speak a message of wisdom among the mature, but not the wisdom of this age or of the rulers of this age, who are coming to nothing. No, we speak of God's secret wisdom, a wisdom that has been hidden and that God destined for our glory before time began. None of the rulers of this age understood it, for if they had, they would not have crucified the Lord of Glory. . . . This is what we speak, not in words taught to us by human wisdom but in words taught by the Spirit, expressing spiritual truths in spiritual words. The man without the Spirit does not accept the things that come from the Spirit of God, for they are foolishness to him, and he cannot understand them, because they are spiritually discerned. The spiritual man makes judgments about all things, but he himself is not subject to any man's judgment: "For who has known the mind of the Lord that he may instruct Him?" But we have the mind of Christ (1 Cor. 2:6-8, 13-16).

Unfortunately, the history of Christian Education is littered with educational theory and practice based upon the wisdom of the rulers of the age rather than the Lord of the ages. Too frequently, the Word of God has been viewed as inferior to human wisdom. Whether through imperial edict, church ordinance, or academic intimidation, human judgment has been preferred to divine revelation.

Early Christian Education (To A.D. 476)

In the early years of the church, the aim of Christian Education was to provide doctrinal instruction and to provide training in godly behavior after the model of Jesus Christ. In many locations, Christians were persecuted, leading to close-knit, separated communities that utilized informal approaches to education. As in Hebrew education, teaching began in the home. It continued in the gathered assemblies of the believers. There is some evidence, however, that early Christians, when not persecuted, participated in the Roman society around them—including government subsidized schools. However, home education and the instruction that took place in the Christian community stipulated a body of truth and a view of life that was in direct opposition to the philosophy that permeated the state education.

Soon, however, a blending of pagan thought and Christian Education began to take place. First, "catechumenal" instruction was instituted for adults wherever Christianity reached, providing foundational doctrinal orientation and moral education as well as instruction in reading and writing. In the year 179, the first "catechtical" school was opened by Pantaenus in the large Christian community at Alexandria, Egypt. Other schools were developed at Caesarea, Antioch, Edessa, and Nisibis. The establishment of these schools accompanied a formalization of conversion and the rite of baptism within the Christian churches.

The first 500 years of Christian Education were characterized by a gradual institutionalization of instruction. Various forms of Greek and Roman educational methodology were employed as the emphasis shifted from faithful Christian living to scholarly reflection. Origen (185-254), who developed the catechtical school at Alexandria, sought to fully integrate Greek philosophy and Christian doctrine. He employed standard Greek educational methodology and utilized an allegorical approach to Bible interpretation that facilitated his attempt to unify philosophy and theology. By the fourth century, training of the professional clergy was conducted in cathedral and monastic schools that, in addition to teaching Christian doctrine, provided instruction in the seven liberal arts and training for formal worship in the church.

There are differences of opinion concerning the vitality and relevance of Christian Education near the end of this period. For example, many Christian educators laud Augustine (354-430) as a great force for moral reform in the church and the world. Others feel that his systematization of Christian doctrine delayed the Renaissance, impeding scientific progress for over six centuries.

Christian Education during the Medieval Period (476-1500)

Prior to the fall of Rome in 476, Christians had begun to withdraw from the moral decadence of Roman culture. Ignoring the Great Commission of Jesus Christ, they formed monastic communities, many of which provided formal education. The first Cenobite institutions were founded in Egypt as early as 350. Monastic education was introduced to Greece by Basil (331-374) and to Rome by Jerome (331-420). This genre of Christian Education carried with it many of the otherworldly and impractical traits from which true Christianity sought to deliver the people of God.

The Germanic conquest of Rome resulted in a fragmented feudalistic society that was not able to sustain the coordinated empire-wide educational system that had characterized the West. In this environment, the church assumed almost all educational activity as well as a powerful political function. However, the predominance of ascetic contemplation and suffusive heresy within various branches of the church silenced the reforming potential of the Good News of Jesus Christ. The impractical orientation of institutional Christianity combined with the lack of central governmental authority to produce "the Dark Ages."

Christianity became the nominal religion of the Western world. But the life was gone. The Holy Spirit, though active in scattered remnants of the true church, was largely ignored in the ritualism and decadence of the church. Education prospered, but it was Christian Education only in a vague sectarian sense. The scholastic developments of the later Middle Ages, such as libraries and universities, were significant. However, to include these as a part of the history of Christian Education is not entirely useful.

Christian Education and the Renaissance (1300-1500)

In secular educational history, the Renaissance is viewed as an intellectual awakening that ushered in the modern era. For Christian Education, the Great Awakening is a sober monument for a lost opportunity to claim the course of history for the kingdom of God in this present age. The Renaissance was a time of unparalleled human progress. Increase in wealth and international commerce accompanied the growth of large cities. A revival of Greek and Latin literature coincided with an explosion of creativity in music and art. But the progress was almost entirely in pursuit of a good life in this world. It was a secular Renaissance, and the stress was upon development of the individual in human society.

The establishment of public and private schools that were liberated from the control of the church set the stage for education that was free from the influence of the Gospel. The human mind was elevated to a place of sole authority. Even the great Christian scholars of the Renaissance were so critical of the "gloomy ignorance," as well as abuses and evils within the church, that they participated in the development of secular scholarship rather than biblical correctives to the humanistic speculation that characterized the era.

Near the end of the period, Vittorino De Feltre (1378-1446), operating from a distinctly Christian value system, blended fine educational innovations with advanced insight into human development. However, his superb educational methodology focused upon the enrichment of human character and allegiance to learning—with little, if any, emphasis upon the necessity of a commitment to the truth of the Gospel. This was excellence in education produced by an individual whose personal morality was undergirded by the truth of God's Word, but no ground was claimed for the Lord of the earth whose commandments are life.

In like manner, Desiderius Erasmus (1467-1536), who had received his early education under the Brethren of the Common Life in the Netherlands, became "The Prince of the Humanists." His attacks on ignorance, immorality, and superstition led the way to much educational progress and innovation. His criticism of the institutionalized church was a primary impetus for the Protestant Reformation. However, his life's work was more in support of a general biblical morality than a distinctive Christian testimony.

Christian Education and the Protestant Reformation (1500-1600)

Although the Protestant Reformation was developed and sustained through the efforts of many individuals (including Philip Melancthon [1497-1460], Huldreich Zwingli [1484-1531], and John Knox [1505-1572]), the Reformation impact upon Christian Education can be traced to the thought and vision of two primary individuals.

Martin Luther (1483-1546) was an Augustinian friar and a professor at the University of Wittenberg (Germany). He revolted against the oppressive and unbiblical practices of the Roman Catholic Church. His posting of Ninety-five Theses in opposition to Catholic doctrines and excesses sparked the Reformation in 1517. But it was Luther's approach to the interpretation of the Bible and his concern for the education of the common man that established his significance in the history of Christian Education. At stake in his revolt was the authority by which men would judge the truth or falsity of all knowledge in the church as well as in academics.

Luther's translation of the Bible into the language of the people and his commitment to the singular authority of the Scriptures are not merely symbols of the Reformation. Rather, they are central tenets of evangelicalism that distinguish Christian Education from all other systems of instruction—secular or religious. Luther's return to the priority of the home in the educational cycle (as in Hebrew and early Christian Education) was not an accident. It was a renewal of the purpose and practicality of the Great Commission versus Greek philosophy and Renaissance humanism. Luther's commitment to *sola Scriptura* (only Scripture) was not just a rallying cry. It was a world and life view that elevated the Word of God to its rightful place in life and in learning. All human thought, perspective, and behavior was to be normed by the Word and will of the living God as revealed in the Holy Scriptures.

John Calvin (1509-1564), the Genevan reformer, was responsible for exegeting and applying scriptural and theological teachings concerning the nature of national, church, and personal life. The Calvinist perspective of the complementary responsibilities of the state, the church, and the home (all under the authority of God) shaped many aspects of European and American government and education. However, though accepting a separation between home, church, and state, Calvin never envisioned a separation between the sovereignty of God and any sphere of authority on earth.

Calvinist, as well as Lutheran, approaches to education did not reject contemporary educational theory and methodology. In fact, the religious zeal of the reformers often led to educational innovation and instructional creativity. However, the objectives of education had to be in accord with ultimate aims and behavioral guidelines of the Scriptures in terms of godly character and the disciplines of the Christian life. Not all reformation education fulfilled this ideal. Much did.

Christian Education in the Post-Reformation Period (1600-1800)

Since the sixteenth century, education in general and Christian Education in particular has been an extension of the Renaissance in theory and the Reformation in practice. It is, therefore, not so remarkable that educational historians in the twentieth-century often identify Johann Amos Comenius (1592-1626) as the father of modern education. Comenius received a Lutheran theological education at the University of Heidelberg. He returned to his native Moravia where he was too young to be a pastor among the Hussite congregations. Consequently, he was given an appointment as a schoolmaster.

This set the course for a lifelong blending of pastoral and educational ministry during a period of scientific progress in methods of instruction. Comenius was not really ahead of his time. Rather, he excelled at all that he did in an enlightened and reformed period of history. The educational theory of Comenius, as well as that of John Locke (1632-1704), was given motivation and perspective by a definitive Christian heritage during an age that prized human reason and where many exciting educational ideas were being generated.

Unfortunately, the two centuries after the Reformation were also characterized by the creation of a significant amount of educational theory by individuals who, in whole or in part, rejected biblical authority and theological integrity. The Renaissance roots of modern secular education sprouted into philosophical thought and instructional intent that elevated human reason above Christian heritage. Cutting a fine edge between Christian Education and secular developmentalism was the work of Jean Jacques Rousseau (1712-1778). Born into a French Calvinist family that had fled to Switzerland, Rousseau experienced a troubled childhood and an indiscriminate young adulthood. As an author, however, he excelled, producing the great educational novel, *Emile*. This depiction of ideal education from infancy through early adulthood is considered to be one of the most significant influences upon twentieth-century educational philosophy and psychology.

Christian Education in the Nineteenth Century

Johann Pestalozzi (1746-1827) ushered in the modern psychologically-oriented approach to learning theory at the dawn of the nineteenth century by utilizing Rousseau's philosophy. Pestalozzi's educational methodologies were carried throughout Europe and the United States by educators who came to examine his schools in Switzerland. He marks the point at which the world of education shifted to dependence upon man rather than God for the answers to life's great questions.

"Pestalozzi had a great faith in the power of education to combat poverty, ignorance, disease, fear, and vice among the poor. He was a pioneer educational social worker and believed that:

1. to improve society reform must begin with the individual;
2. the individual must be taught to help himself;
3. education can develop the innate powers of the individual to improve himself and society."[3]

Perhaps innocently, Pestalozzi, as well as Johann Herbart (1776-1841) and Friedrich Wilhelm August Froebel (1782-1852), represented the race as they gazed upon the forbidden fruit of man's reason and chose to act upon "gained" rather than "revealed" wisdom. And, as in the Garden of Eden, a form of "enlightenment" occurred in which their eyes were opened to all that the created world has to offer, but were closed to the communion that had existed between themselves and the only true source of wisdom (Gen. 3:8-24). These men elevated instruction to an art form as they psychologized education apart from the Word of God.

However, a beacon of light pierced the descending darkness of Western educational history. Beginning in England with the work of either Hannah Ball or Robert Raikes, an institution now known as the Sunday School was created for the specific purpose of providing moral instruction for destitute children. The Sunday School was brought into existence to fill a void left by the secularization of education. From humble beginnings, the Sunday School became an organized lay movement in direct opposition to the humanistic sophistication of secular education.

The significance of the Sunday School movement can hardly be overestimated in the history of Christian Education. "For over 100 years the Sunday School was the dominant and, exclusive of the home, almost sole agency of Christian Education of Protestant children and youth."[4] For a while, it appeared that other parachurch organizations such as the Young Men's Christian Association (YMCA), and the Young Women's Christian Association (YWCA) would enjoy the same success as the Sunday School. However, their impact for the Gospel of Jesus Christ was only occasionally noteworthy.

But the Sunday School movement could not stem the tide of incipient naturalism. During the middle and late years of the nineteenth century, as if on a true course set by a master deceiver, secular educational theory emerged with ethical aims and attendant educational excellences (behavioral objectives) incompatible with revealed truth.

Basing his thinking upon the relativistic philosophical psychology of William James (1842-1910), John Dewey (1859-1952) intentionally deserted theistic presuppositions—first in favor of idealism, and then mere pragmatism. It was as if Greek philosophy, awakened from slumber in the Renaissance, had come of full age in the modern era. The starting point for education was now the raw experience of created man rather than the sovereign will of the Creator. Truth was to be found in science rather than the Word of God.

Christian Education in the Twentieth Century

Gangel and Benson recount a brief anecdote that captures the essence of Christian Education in the twentieth century:

> Wayne Rood tells the story of a meeting that took place in Chicago the year before Dewey left for Teacher's College, Columbia University. The

purpose of the gathering was the formation of a new professional association, presumably to enrich secular education. At least that is what one
segment of the group hoped, and their leader was the popular professor
of education at the University of Chicago, John Dewey.

Members of another wing, however, were concerned about the development of religious education, particularly an attempt to link theology
and science within the strongly emerging liberal patterns at the turn of
the century. Said Rood, "Their spokesman was a youngish professor of
the philosophy of religion at Northwestern University named George
Coe. His address, 'Salvation by Education,' stated the position that won
the conference. It became the Religious Education Association, and
John Dewey dropped out."[5]

From that point in the twentieth century there existed three entities that are
of primary interest to biblical Christian Education:

• Purely secular education, espousing speculative philosophical aims and
relying upon scientific and/or pragmatic methodology.
• Religious education, espousing theologically liberal social aims and relying upon scientific and/or pragmatic methodology.
• Evangelical Christian Education, espousing educational aims based upon
biblical authority while struggling with the extent to which scientific
and/or pragmatic methodology can be utilized.

Secular education in the twentieth century has been dominated by the
impact of the psychology of learning and human development. Though based
upon evolutionary presuppositions in the service of humanistic (though often
humanitarian) aims, much educational research and theoretical study related
to the practice of teaching has resulted in a body of knowledge that is of
value to evangelical Christian Education. Scientific study of humans and their
behavior (individually and in groups) has yielded general revelation concerning how growth and learning take place. The findings of this research, properly evaluated, can enhance precision and efficiency in the practice of evangelical Christian Education.

Research and theory that has had a noteworthy impact upon evangelical
Christian Education has been contributed by Albert Bandura (learning theory), Benjamin Bloom (learning theory), Jerome Bruner (learning theory),
Edgar Dale (instructional methodology), Robert Havighurst (lifespan human
development), Lawrence Kohlberg (moral development), Robert Mager (behavioral objectives), Erik Erikson (psychosocial development), and Jean Piaget (cognitive development).

The research and theory generated by the *religious education* movement has been of moderate value to evangelical C.E. From its founding, the Religious Education Association (REA), generally to the left of most evangelicals, has been characterized by educators whose beliefs are aligned with theological liberalism and neo-orthodoxy. A hallmark of liberalism is the persistent redefinition of traditional doctrinal terms and the reinterpretation of both the Scriptures and Christian experience. As a result, though religious education has confronted church education issues with commendable zeal and precision, the contributions of this movement are of questionable merit. Advanced students and experienced practitioners within evangelical Christian Education have profited from participation in the REA, as well as the Association of Professors and Researchers in Religious Education (APRRE). However, this association has had a limited effect upon the practice of evangelical Christian Education.

There are several individuals identified with religious education whose writings have been particularly informative. These include George Albert Coe, Iris V. Cully, James Michael Lee, Thomas Groome, Sara Little, Randolph C. Miller, Mary C. Boys, C. Ellis Nelson, James Smart, and John Westerhoff. D. Campbell Wyckoff is noteworthy for his significant contributions, particularly in curriculum theory, to both religious education and evangelical C.E.

Evangelical Christian Education has only recently come of age. For most of the twentieth century, the Sunday School, characterized by content-oriented curriculum and inadequate teaching methodology, was the only regularly scheduled instrument of Christian Education in churches. Individual churches organized Vacation Bible Schools for children, youth meetings and, in some cases, Bible training hours for adults. But the Sunday School was the only consistent educational agency—supported mainly by independent curriculum publishers such as David C. Cook, Gospel Light, Baptist Publications, Scripture Press, and Standard.

Of particular note has been the growth of Bible colleges, seminaries, Christian colleges and universities, and then Christian day schools in this century. Both public and private elementary, secondary, and higher education was distinctively Christian during most of the Puritan era in American history. However, the doctrinal integrity and Christian character of these institutions was eroded—first by secularism, and then by modernism. By the late 1800s, evangelical involvement in school education at any level was minimal. A few Bible colleges (such as Nyack Missionary College, Moody Bible Institute, and Gordon College) were founded near the turn of the century, but their influence grew slowly. This circumstance persisted through the period of fundamentalist-modernist controversy (ca. 1910–1930).

The last half of the twentieth century, however, has witnessed a virtual explosion of evangelical Christian involvement in school education. Small Bible colleges have grown into Christian colleges and universities enrolling thousands of students. Seminaries have expanded their curriculum offerings and degree programs to include many forms of graduate education and vocational training. Parachurch organizations and publishing houses have established C.E. training programs that deliver a wide range of skill development opportunities.

Individuals who have made significant contributions to evangelical Christian Education include Clarence Benson, Kenneth Gangel, Henrietta Mears, Howard Hendricks, Lois LeBar, Larry Richards, Finley Edge, Ted Ward, and Donald Joy.

The expansion of two Christian Education organizations in recent years is an indication of the maturity of evangelical Christian Education. The National Association of Directors of Christian Education recently became PACE (The Professional Association of Christian Educators) in order to more adequately reflect the multi-national membership of this association of hundreds of Christian educators around the world. Further, the North American Professors of Christian Education recently attracted more than 200 professors to its annual meeting representing thousands of C.E. students in evangelical institutions of higher education.

The challenge of the twenty-first century is for a mature evangelical Christian Education to remain true to the authority of the Scriptures. The temptation to be psychologically correct and methodologically sophisticated must be balanced with a commitment to the values of the Word of God. There is much to be learned from secular as well as religious educators that will be of benefit to evangelical Christian educators. But care must be taken to maintain allegiance to the will of the only source of wisdom.

Educational implications of scientific church growth research must be evaluated to guarantee that methods are consistent with biblical learning objectives. Moral development theory must not be permitted to dictate educational techniques without careful scrutiny of presuppositions and the meaning of developmental distinctions. Interest in research concerning faith development must be moderated until it is determined that it is, in fact, biblical faith that is the focus of investigation.

In the final analysis, evangelical Christian Education will continue to grow and thrive as it remains faithful to its heritage. Evangelical Christian Education will remain *evangelical* only if it maintains its place in the center of.the Great Commission of Jesus Christ (Matt. 28:18-20). Evangelical Christian education will remain *effective* only if it is sustained by the source of life in educational ministry—the promised Holy Spirit (Acts 1:8).

Notes

1. Nicholas Lobkowicz, *Theory and Practice* (Notre Dame: University of Notre Dame Press, 1967), 74.
2. William F. Pinar and Madeleine R. Grumet, "Socratic *Caesura* and the Theory-Practice Relationship," *Theory into Practice* 21 (Winter 1982): 32.

3. Oliver S. Ikenberry, *American Education Foundations* (Columbus, Ohio: Charles E. Merrill Publishing Company, 1974), 104.

4. Kenneth O. Gangel and Warren S. Benson, *Christian Education: Its History and Philosophy* (Chicago: Moody Press, 1983), 287.

5. Ibid., 304-5.

For Further Reading

Barclay, W. *Educational Ideals in the Ancient World.* Grand Rapids: Baker Book House, 1974.

Butts, R.F. *The Education of the West.* New York: McGraw-Hill, 1974.

Gangel, K.O. and W.S. Benson. *Christian Education: Its History and Philosophy.* Chicago: Moody Press, 1983.

Lynn, R.W. and E. Wright. *The Big Little School: 200 Years of the Sunday School.* Rev. ed. Birmingham, Ala.: Religious Education Press, 1980.

Towns, E.L., ed. *A History of Religious Educators.* Grand Rapids: Baker Book House, 1975.

Ulrich, R. *A History of Religious Education.* New York: New York University Press, 1968.

Four
Philosophical Foundations of Ministry

Students of ministry generally approach the subject of philosophy with a degree of skepticism. They are unsure of the purpose for such a discussion in the context of the kingdom of God. However, any meaningful ministry must be based upon a reason for doing it. Simply stated, a philosophy of ministry explains why you are doing what you are doing. This philosophy also generates answers to other important questions such as, "What is our vision for this ministry?" "What methods are appropriate to use?" and "By what criteria will we determine our ministry's effectiveness?"

This chapter will not promote or describe the ideal philosophy of ministry. Rather, we will see why it is important to think through foundational philosophical questions. Then we will suggest some relationships as a framework for building personal philosophical foundations for ministry. We will then conclude our discussion by examining how different philosophical foundations are being applied in a variety of church settings.

Articulated Versus Operant Philosophy
One of Webster's definitions describes philosophy as, "an analysis of the grounds of and concepts expressing fundamental beliefs." As applied to ministry it asks, "What are the grounds for your beliefs about ministry?" If you can succinctly state the grounds and concepts upon which you base ministry, you have an *articulated* philosophy and can develop a cohesive, holistic purposeful ministry. When you're unable to articulate your philosophical foundations you have an *operant* philosophy. The latter is a set of assumptions about people and ministry that give your actions purpose. But in this case, you may not have stopped to identify them.

When you minister, you play out a philosophy of ministry. You may not have articulated it yet. You may not even understand it. If asked, "Why are you ministering the way you do?" your answer will reveal part of your operant philosophy of ministry. Maybe you minister the way others ministered to you. It worked for you, so you have a sense that what you do will work for others. In fact, a person's sense of purpose is often stronger in an operant philosophy that has not been systematized than in a thoughtfully chosen, articulated philosophy.

Churches have philosophical foundations for ministry just as individuals do. They may be articulated or operant foundations. For example, you may move to a new city and visit six churches within the same denomination and have six different experiences. Why? Because they have six different philosophies of ministry. If a church or pastor can articulate their philosophical foundations, they have at least eight *advantages* over a church or pastor that cannot.

1) A church that can articulate its philosophical foundations can determine the scope of its ministry. The church without an articulated philosophy of ministry is defined by the experiences of the people who come into it and become its leadership. Their vision for ministry comes with them. For instance, if in previous churches they experienced an annual revival, then they will insist on an annual revival in their new church. If they came from a highly liturgical background, they want a similar worship experience in their new church. It is difficult, without an articulated philosophy of ministry, to lead people from diverse church backgrounds since they come with differing expectations. The articulated church philosophy allows people from diverse backgrounds to understand the church's vision for ministry. This allows them to set aside their personal expectations for the benefit of the body. Likewise, a minister who can articulate a personal philosophy of ministry will not simply be performing a job or running a program to the specifications of a job description. He or she will develop the job description by doing the ministry.

2) A church that can articulate its philosophical foundation can continuously reevaluate it's corporate experience in the light of its message. The old adage "what you do speaks so loudly I can't hear what you're saying" is valid for how both the unsaved and the layperson view the local church. We believe our message is summarized in John 3:16, but from the perspective of the unsaved we build buildings with steeples, go into them on Sundays, do religious things, and avoid certain vices.

However, an articulated philosophy of ministry keeps a church evaluating its corporate experience to ensure that it is consistent with its message. A minister with an articulated philosophy of ministry can keep evaluating what he or she is doing to be sure that activities are consistent with the Gospel message of love, forgiveness, and salvation. Anything less is hypocrisy.

3) A church that can articulate it's philosophical foundations can evaluate its ministry in the light of thoughtful criteria rather than on the basis of a program's popularity. Many pastors and laypeople evaluate church ministries on the basis of attendance alone. They believe that if attendance is growing, the ministry must be good. Such a standard, however, is not altogether biblical. Attendance may be a helpful guide, but it cannot be the sole indicator of success. Maybe the program is growing just because it is popular. Many faithful attenders come out of loyalty or for reasons that are not intrinsic to the ministry itself. On the other hand, some churches continue business as usual even though no one attends or responds. Figure 4.1 illustrates a philosophical schema that can be used to evaluate ministry.

The Pragmatist makes decisions about ministry based on what works and is endorsed by the most people. It is the philosophical equivalent of a market economy brought into the church. In many churches pragmatic responsiveness goes beyond program decisions to muting those parts of Scripture deemed unpopular.

The Realist makes decisions about ministry based on a balance between scriptural commands and the responsiveness of people. This approach is not so scriptural that it is legalistic and neither is it so responsive that it ignores Scripture. In attempting to keep both the message of Scripture and the needs of people in balance, this kind of ministry maintains a delicate tension.

The Idealist makes decisions about ministry that are so oriented to biblical purity and righteousness that he or she loses sight of the needs of people and often of his or her own sinfulness. Idealists interpret scriptural mandates such as "Be perfect" (Matt. 5:48) as the only acceptable standard. There are no ethical social dilemmas, only biblical absolutes to be applied according to their prescriptions.

To the Traditionalist the church exists to carry on "the faith of our Fathers." When faced with a ministry program decision they ask themselves, "Which option will be consistent with the programming of our past?" In many ways this church is a museum—usually close to empty, but a center for cultural traditions on certain holidays.

Ministry is too important to be done without purpose and intent. Both the church and the pastor need objective criteria by which they can evaluate their ministry effectiveness. Judging purely on the basis of popularity alone is simply not a biblical standard.

4) A church that can articulate its philosophical foundations is more likely to keep its ministry balanced and focused on essentials. It is easy in ministry to focus so much on our area of strength that we neglect other areas of equal importance. For example, some pastors feel their primary calling is to the pulpit ministry of preaching. If they are not careful, other, equally important areas such as worship, education, and administration, can go unattended. Some pastors feel their

Philosophical Schema for Evaluating Ministry

Philosophy:	Pragmatist	Realist	Idealist	Traditional
Ministry Question:	Is It Responsive?	Is It In Balance?	Is It Right?	Does It Keep Tradition?
Criteria for starting a ministry	Will people come?	Does it fit our goals?	Is it biblically mandated?	Is it a lost treasure?
Goals for ministry	Are more and more people coming?	People who are growing	Righteous people	Faithful people
Criteria for evaluating a ministry	Is it growing numerically?	Is it producing spiritual fruit?	Is it truthful?	Is it ritual?
Criteria for ending a ministry	Is there a more attractive way?	Has it lost its charter?	Are no leaders available?	Ministries never end

Figure 4.1

only calling is evangelism. The result is that they can become so engrossed in evangelism that they neglect the counterpart of edification.

When a church or pastor articulates its philosophical foundations and regularly communicates them, the congregation and the pastor can keep each other accountable for the implementation of a well balanced overall church ministry. Most churches have far more opportunities than resources when it comes to ministry planning. If a church is not careful it will fall into the temptation of trying to do a little bit of everything, with the result being that they end up doing nothing well. Keeping the church's (and the individual minister's) philosophical foundation in sight reduces sidetracking and imbalance.

5) *A church that can articulate its philosophical foundations can mobilize a greater proportion of its congregation as ministers.* For many ministers, the most difficult aspect of Christian Education is recruiting people for ministries. This is more difficult now than ever before in our North American culture, as time becomes our most precious commodity.[1] Some churches, however, have discovered that Christians will generously commit time and resources when they can clearly see and value the intended outcomes. The commitment is there, it's just the loyalty that has declined. People don't have time for programs they don't see contributing to a worthwhile cause. They want a deep sense of purpose in a ministry before they will divert time from other very purposeful activities in their lives. A church's program may be extremely worthwhile, but if its foundations are not articulated well, people will not value and respond to even the best of appeals and programs.

6) *A church that can articulate its philosophical foundations can determine the relative merits of a prospective ministry.* Today's minister is bombarded with a multitude of ministry options. He or she hears about ministries in other churches that are succeeding in great ways. New members who are transferring from other churches suggest ministries that made a great impact on them. Parachurch organizations offer ministry programs that are very attractive. Consultants also add to the list of possibilities. In a church with poorly articulated and understood philosophical foundations, new ministries are added on the basis of the persuasiveness of those presenting the ministries, not on the basis of their integration into the total church program. A church can end up with a patchwork quilt of ministries all struggling for resources and support.

7) *A church that can articulate its philosophical foundations can be a clear, attractive alternative community to people seeking relief from systemic failure.* If a church's philosophical foundations are apparent not only to its community of believers, but also to the larger community in which it ministers, it changes from being just another service organization into being a lighthouse for lost souls. Lost

people are trying desperately to find answers to their hurts, pains, and disappointments. In their quest for answers they explore a multitude of resources: drugs, alcohol, sex, social agencies, or civic clubs. Ultimately, they fail to find the answers for which they are looking. A church that articulates its philosophy of ministry and lives it out will appear as a beacon on a dark and stormy night. A church that fails to articulate its philosophical foundations will not appear to be a viable alternative.

8) *A church that can articulate its philosophical foundations can choose to cooperate or not cooperate with other churches and parachurch ministries.* One of the great tragedies of the early 1990s is the inability of evangelical churches to cooperate with one another. Where there is cooperation, it is usually done within a denomination. Periodically there may be city-wide cooperation in a crusade, but most of the time churches are competing rather than cooperating. If more churches clearly articulated their philosophical foundations they might find handles for cooperation and mutual benefit. Conversely, cooperation just for the sake of cooperation may divert a church from its primary goals. If a church has clearly articulated foundations, it is able to continue progressing toward its goals in spite of attractive, sidetracking alternatives.

Inoculating in Ministry

If a church can clearly articulate its philosophical foundations of ministry, it can develop goals which are appropriate to those foundations. It can then evaluate the strategies chosen to reach its goals. Strategies will be based on the church's goals which, in turn, are based on its philosophical foundations. Figure 4.2 illustrates this flow of ideas. When a church fails to articulate its philosophical foundations, goals, or strategies it can lose sight of its foundations and even its goals and become program oriented. The result is that programs become ends in themselves rather than means to accomplishing purposeful ends.

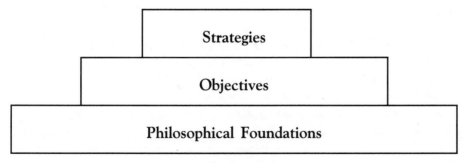

Figure 4.2

For example, a philosophical foundation for a church might be that Bible study is important. A goal based on this foundation might be that "Each member of the church will become an active student of Scripture." Flowing out of that goal is the strategy that, "Scripture will be preached from the pulpit, taught in Sunday School, and promoted in all weekly Bible study/home fellowship sessions." But if you question the members of most churches you would find that very few members actually study Scripture on their own. Few are able to explain central biblical principles to others who inquire about them. What has happened? Is the problem philosophical, directional, or strategic? We may have problems at all three levels, but in this chapter we are focused on the philosophical level.

If Christians are studying the Bible in church, Sunday School, and in home Bible studies, why aren't they valuing it enough to integrate it into their lives? The answer is that pastors and leaders are doing the Bible study, not the average Christian. The average Christian is passively receiving someone else's Bible study. Since the Christian is sitting and listening, what he or she is investing in is sitting and listening!

In the world of medicine, doctors prevent many diseases by inoculating people against them. They do this by giving a person a small dose of dead virus—the very virus being defended against. The body forms antibodies against the dead virus. An immunity is built up against the virus. Later when a live virus of the same kind invades the body, it is neutralized before it can cause illness. In ministry, we may inoculate Christians against the very things we think they should develop.

Philosophically speaking, we inoculate Christians against Bible study in several ways: First, by associating Bible study with sitting and listening. Second, by assuming that understanding the truth is the same as obeying the truth. We don't acknowledge this assumption, but we imply it in the way we teach—understanding is usually the end of the session. Third, by aimless teaching (teaching without a clear sense of what the learner can do with the truths taught), even though our teaching follows a passage of Scripture. It lacks application. Further, we inoculate by teaching in self-contained units that do not illustrate dependence on other passages of Scripture. Fifth, by teaching unguided by a curriculum, leaving laypeople to believe a seminary degree is essential for organizing scriptural truth. Sixth, by withholding support of learners who are appropriating the truth. And finally, by building a heavy dependency on the teacher for learning.

It is all too easy to imagine the additional ways we unknowingly inoculate Christians against prayer, worship, fellowship, evangelism, stewardship, and redemptive living. Such a philosophical approach to ministry must end if the church is going to be equipped for ministry in the twenty-first century.

Four Paradigms of Ministry Philosophy

Having described the need for an articulated philosophy of ministry, and a framework for building an individual or church philosophy of ministry, it might be useful to see how several philosophical foundations are expressed in ministry.

Most evangelical churches fit into one of four paradigms of ministry. In each case, the paradigm is the participant's, but this paradigm is maintained by the ways church leaders minister. The result is that churches can come to be characterized by these paradigms. Not every church member is characterized by the kind of church he or she is in, but people do tend to conform to the predominant trend in their churches. A church can be in transition from one paradigm to another, and segments of a congregation might be responding to two different paradigms. Each paradigm has a different foundational philosophy, so eventually people and churches tend to center around one paradigm.

The Spiritual Day Care

The philosophical foundation of the Spiritual Day Care church is that the church exists to serve its people. It's existence as a local body of Christ is for the purpose of determining its congregation's needs and then meeting them.

Focus: The focus of the average person in the Spiritual Day Care church is on the self and problem solving. People attend this church to meet their needs and solve their problems. They look for problem-solving hints in the pastor's messages and for elective class titles that will meet felt needs. As a result, the church is viewed as another form of service industry. Giving one's tithe is much like tipping at restaurants. If the service is good, the tip is larger. If the church doesn't meet their needs, people will find another one that does. The resulting low level of commitment takes its toll on the pastoral staff. The level of ministry satisfaction of the pastoral staff is in direct proportion to the attendance of the last worship service. They cannot afford to slow down their drive for popular-oriented programs since competition with other neighboring churches is always at the forefront of the mind.

Attitudes: The attitudes in the Spiritual Day Care church are basically consumer attitudes and are reflected in one of three ways: the Service Station, the School of Doctrine, or the Christian Manufacturing Company.

The Service Station attitude is reflected in people who need a weekly spiritual shot in the arm to face the cold, cruel world. Just as the HMO is responsible for their physical health the church is responsible for their spiritual health. The pastor's job is to reinforce their theological point of view, making them feel more warm, stable, and secure.

The School of Doctrine attitude is reflected in people who need the reassurance of knowing the right answers. To them, learning the Bible means being able to respond correctly to life's questions. The assumption is that if a person knows what to believe, those beliefs will eventually work into correct values and behaviors. Exegesis is the paramount church function for those in the School of Doctrine. It takes place not only in the pulpit, but often in classrooms as well. Although the message of the ministry is highly injunctive, the application of that message is left to the individual to discover at a later date.

The Christian Manufacturing Company attitude is reflected in those that assume God has left us in the world for the sole purpose of spiritual reproduction. Therefore, their sense of mission is defined in terms of evangelism, missions, and other measures of quantitative growth. There is an urgent call to salvation in every church service. Every church agency's primary goal is evangelism. Doctrine and discipline are usually secondary.

The result of each of these attitudes is the same — performance by professionals. In the Spiritual Day Care church, the people see the pastor as a professional caregiver. In the School of Doctrine the people see the pastor as the professional educator. In the Christian Manufacturing Company the people see the pastor as the professional evangelist. Either way, members of the congregation are unable to provide for their own spiritual development and must rely upon the food provided by professional clergy.

Motivation: The motivation for involvement in the Spiritual Day Care church is belonging and reassurance. Church membership is important, and in teaching, questions are only rhetorical, not challenging. The results of this motivation are conformity and intolerance. People find others like themselves with whom to associate. In this way churches become very homogeneous. Conversely, people who visit a homogeneous church and don't fit in culturally, socio-economically, or even politically, find it hard to feel at home.

Values: Individuals in the Spiritual Day Care church value being correct, solving problems, and achieving success. There is a low tolerance for ambiguity; things need to be black or white. The results of these values are 1) that it is difficult for a church to change. There is a vested interest in the statusquo. 2) Individuals grow if they apply biblical solutions to their problems. 3) Churches develop what some have called an "edifice complex." The success that people value is mirrored in the church's buildings.

The Fitness Center
The second philosophical paradigm of ministry is characterized by the Fitness Center with its emphasis on healthy growth and development. The Fitness Center views the church as existing as the incarnate body of Christ in the world. To gain a glimpse of Christ, one need only examine the lifestyle of one of its members.

Focus: The focus of the Fitness Center church is on one another, body life, and growth. The focus is less on the quantitative growth of the church and more on personal, spiritual development and the growth of others in the body. As a result the church slowly takes on the characteristics of an organism, rather than just being another organization. This church is alive, growing, and dynamic in nature. There is a genuine desire for development and an excitement about what the future holds.

Attitude: The attitudes of people in the Fitness Center are seen in their responsibility for personal and corporate growth. People here come to church with a different purpose than in the Spiritual Day Care church. It is not that the people in the Fitness Center have no needs, but there is an expectation of giving as well as receiving. There is an ongoing interest in the growth of others in the Fitness Center. As a result, a sense of mutual concern, trust, and accountability develops among people. This is usually evident in small group ministries such as fellowship groups and Bible studies. These small groups tend to stay together far longer in Fitness Center churches than in any other paradigm.

Motivation: The motivation for involvement in the body develops quickly from belonging to participation, and then eventually to leadership. Upon perceiving a need for ministry, people are more likely to move ahead to meet the need than waiting for church staff people to develop programs. As a result, ministries spring up, some within the church structure, some outside of it. As they do, because of the concern for one another, there are opportunities for discipleship. The danger for church leaders in the body is the impulse to organize and control these ministries.

Values: The values of people with a Fitness Center orientation are other Christians, whole persons, interpersonal giving, and relationships. As a result, relationships in the Fitness Center tend to be deeper, but fewer. One cannot be deeply committed to everybody, so levels of relationship develop where individuals operate mutually with a few people, then function in more of a discipling-parenting way with others. People in the Fitness Center also tend to exercise their spiritual gifts more readily. They may not have been taught about spiritual gifts, they just gravitate toward exercising them as they function with other members. The spontaneous exercise of spiritual gifts in the Fitness Center is an interesting contrast to the passive teaching on spiritual gifts that might occur in Spiritual Day Care churches where congregants sit and listen, but rarely put into practice.

The Cathedral

The third philosophical paradigm of ministry, the Cathedral, is characterized by its emphasis on worship. The philosophical foundation is that the church exists primarily as a place for God's people to gather and worship.

Focus: The focus of people in the Cathedral paradigm is on God Himself. They perceive the church as a place set aside to worship God. Other aspects of church life are incidental. The sermon is secondary. The church is primarily God's house. As a result, less emphasis is placed on the individual being the temple of the Holy Spirit. In other words, it is not that we are God's house as much as we enter into God's house for worship. For this reason services of worship are critical. Liturgy and the symbols of God's presence become very important.

Attitudes: The attitudes of people in the Cathedral are those of respect and reverence for a holy God. As a result there is sometimes a division between the sacred and the secular in the lives of people in the Cathedral paradigm. It becomes easy to lose sight of the presence of God when away from His house. Consequently, the individual comes into God's presence in His Cathedral, confesses his or her sins, gets back into His grace and worships Him. The individual then leaves the Cathedral, going forth from God's presence to live as a light in a dark world. The flame soon needs rekindling.

Motivation: The motivation for involvement in the Cathedral is appropriate response to God, the Creator and Sustainer. It is acknowledgment of the attributes of God and a sense of dependence upon Him. If one is not careful involvement can become a duty bound, even legalistic formal worship where the symbols and liturgy lose their meaning and relationship. In this context intimacy with God is conceptually impossible.

Values: The values of the individual in the Cathedral are God's holiness, the individual's inclusion in the community of faith, confession, and thankfulness. Inclusion in the community of faith insures eventual salvation; confession insures ongoing relationship; and thankfulness is the appropriate attitude basis for other aspects of life. As a result, the symbols of worship can take on their own reality, and people sometimes worship the symbols themselves. Other results can be humility and privatism. An awareness of God's awesome holiness and man's sinfulness is the source of humility. Privatism evolves from valuing one's individual relationship with God, while neglecting the lostness of people who have no relationship with Him. In essence, other's relationship with God is their business; my relationship with God is my business.

The M*A*S*H Unit
The fourth philosophical paradigm is the M*A*S*H unit approach to church ministry. The philosophical foundation is that the church exists to reach out to a lost world and reconcile people to God. Ministers who serve with this philosophical mind-set conduct business with a high level of intensity and a sense of spiritual urgency.

Focus: The focus of the M*A*S*H unit church is on ministry to the lost. The individual in this paradigm is not content to stay in the comfort of the church. He or she is burdened by the lostness of those who have not heard or responded to the claims of Christ. Some in this paradigm have grown beyond their own spiritual and emotional disabilities. Others are able to identify with lost people because even though they are found in Christ, they are still struggling emotionally or relationally. As a result of focus on the lost and time spent in ministry outside the church, M*A*S*H unit people tend to be misunderstood by other Christians. M*A*S*H unit churches develop as people with ministry burdens begin ministering together. These units sometimes become parachurch ministries. If they become churches, they tend to stay small and concentrate on reaching out to rescue others rather than focusing on the needs of those already reached.

Attitudes: The attitudes of people in M*A*S*H unit churches are those of responsibility for proclamation and redemption. They take seriously the condition of people on their way to hell. They realize that no one else will reach out to the people they are focusing on, and these target people will not respond to invitations. They go to lost people rather than inviting them to come away from their turf. They minister to the lost "on location." As a result, M*A*S*H unit ministers can be impatient with Christians who do not share their sense of urgency and mission to the lost.

Motivation: The motivation for people in the M*A*S*H unit church is love for God and identification with people. It's not that they don't have needs of their own; the needs of the lost are just more important to them. As a result, they make sacrifices other people would not make. Their investments in people are in "the bank of eternity." Ironically, this devotion can sometimes be so extreme that their family members and friends feel abandoned or neglected.

Values: The values of people in the M*A*S*H unit church are justice, mercy, salvation, faith, stewardship, reconciliation, and redemption. These are qualities that most Christians believe in, but Christians in the M*A*S*H unit church go beyond belief to valuing. As a result, they reorder their lifestyles and tend to identify with and invest in the downtrodden and the neglected.

Each of these philosophical paradigms can be seen by observing a church's ministry programming. A knowledgeable observer should be able to visit a church (or observe a minister) and determine which philosophical paradigm the church incorporates into its ministry. Some churches are able to articulate their philosophical foundations and others are not. But either way, knowing what to look for allows you the ability to see if there is a consistency between what they preach and what they live out. A graphic overview of each of these philosophical paradigms is represented in figure 4.3 on page 66.

Four Paradigms of Ministry Philosophy

	Spiritual Day Care	Fitness Center	Cathedral	M*A*S*H
Focus:	Self-absorbed Problem solving Meet felt needs	One another Spiritual growth Desires development	Corporate worship Worship setting Formal liturgy	Reach out to the lost Evangelism/missions Teamwork
Attitudes:	Service Station School of Doctrine Manufacturing Company	Responsibility for another Expect to give Mutual trust & love	Reverence for God High respect for God Self-reflection	Proclaim redemption Seek the lost Bring the lost in
Motivation:	Need for belonging Needs reassurance Homogeneous groups	Stage 1–Belonging Stage 2–Participation Stage 3–Leadership	Responsible to God God's attributes Emphasis on symbols	Love of God Love for people Bank of Eternity
Values:	Always being right Success-oriented Solutions to problems	Other Christians Deep relationships Use of one's gifts	God's holiness Personal humility Privatism	Justice, mercy, faith, salvation, stewardship, and reconciliation

Figure 4.3

My Personal Philosophical Foundations

	Scriptural Teaching:	Personal Beliefs and Convictions:
Focus: Who or what will be the purpose of my ministry?		
Attitude: How do I feel about the people to whom I am sent to minister?		
Motivation: Why do I seek to minister?		
Values: What are those things which I hold to be most important?		

Figure 4.4

Developing Your Own Philosophical Foundations

If you've not yet articulated your own philosophical foundations, take some time to do so before you read other chapters in this book. On the other hand, don't wait until you have a well-developed philosophy of ministry to read the rest of this book. What you learn in other chapters will help you develop your philosophical foundations. If you already have developed your philosophical foundations, this chapter may have challenged you to rethink them.

Take a moment and think through the essential components of building a philosophical foundation of ministry that have been presented in this chapter:

1) Focus: who/what which is at the center of your worldview.
2) Attitudes: how you feel about those to whom you minister.
3) Motivation: that which gives you your drive and desire.
4) Values: that which you feel is important and essential.

To help develop your own personal philosophy of ministry (or that of your church), fill in the chart (Figure 4.4) with your own focus, attitudes, motivation, and values.

Summary

Everyone has a philosophy of ministry. Those who have spent the time to formulate it and put it in writing will have a number of advantages over those who have not. Tradition is a powerful force in many churches across the country. However, experience tells us that tradition alone does not contribute toward the growing of a dynamic ministry. At the end of the twentieth century the church cannot afford to spend its limited resources on programs just because they have worked well in the past. It has been estimated that a culture undergoes significant change every three to seven years. If this is true, the church that stays on the cutting edge will be the one that understands why and how change is needed. As noted in chapter 1, programs are not biblical absolutes; they are only chosen strategies for reaching chosen goals. Our church and para-church programs must be built upon a clearly developed philosophy of ministry. This philosophy, with Scripture as its guide, can strengthen and encourage the church through the many years of contextual and cultural change.

Notes

1. George Barna, *The Frog in the Kettle.* (Ventura, Calif.: Regal Books, 1990), 39.

For Further Reading

Allen, R. & Borror, G. *Worship: Rediscovering the Missing Jewel.* Portland: Multnomah Press, 1982.

Ford, L. *Design for Teaching and Training.* Nashville: Broadman Press, 1978.

Griffin, E. *Getting Together.* Downers Grove, Ill.: InterVarsity Press, 1982.

Groome, T.H. *Christian Religious Education.* New York: Harper and Row, 1980.

Innovations in Learning (1981-1986) *Equipping Christians for Helping Ministries.* 7018 El Paseo, Long Beach, Calif. 90815 (213) 594-4823.

Moreland, J.P. & Nielsen, K. *Does God Exist?* Nashville: Thomas Nelson Publishers, 1990.

Ott, E.S. *The Vibrant Church.* Ventura, Calif.: Regal Books, 1989.

Steinbron, M.J. *Can The Pastor Do it Alone?* Ventura, Calif.: Regal Books, 1987.

Tillapaugh, F. *Unleashing the Church.* Ventura, Calif.: Regal Books, 1982.

Willard, D. *The Spirit of the Disciplines.* San Francisco: Harper and Row, 1988.

Five
Foundations of Human Development

Bible in one hand and visual in the other, the leader holds the class in rapt attention. The hour goes by quickly. With solid content broken occasionally by interest-arousing illustrations and humor, few moments are lost. Application is made and the lesson is closed in prayer.

Another effective lesson? Perhaps. The leader seemingly was prepared; otherwise the class would not have lasted the hour. Interest levels were kept high. God's Word was the core of the lesson. Yet, with all the skills this leader had to offer, the study still may have been ineffective. If little or no thought was given to understanding the nature of the students, the relevance of Scripture to issues of life may have been missed.

Life-changing effectiveness depends in large measure on a leader's knowledge of the individuals who are being taught or led. The effective teacher identifies the developmental issues of the group, and adjusts the content and methods accordingly. Significant damage has resulted from well-intentioned instruction that failed to consider developmental characteristics of students. Understanding the person is essential, nearly as important as the message itself.

The need to understand people is rooted in the theological concept of anthropology, or the nature of persons. Scripture provides what is necessary to understand their spiritual condition and needs. God's Word also gives us the *goal* of instruction. As the Apostle Paul stated it, "And we proclaim Him, admonishing every man and teaching every man with all wisdom, that we may present every man complete in Christ" (Col. 1:28). The word "complete" has the idea of maturity or wholeness. To address spiritual needs, instruction should aim at spiritual completeness or maturity.

While Scripture describes the nature of people and a maturity goal for teaching them, research in human development, on the other hand, provides an understanding of the *process* of becoming whole or complete. Insights of developmental theories can be applied to spiritual growth to give a more complete picture of the process of maturing. Both a biblical understanding of people and an understanding of human growth are essential for an effective ministry of Christian Education.

There is another advantage which developmental research provides. It identifies crucial issues at each stage of development throughout life that must be addressed from a biblical perspective. They must be addressed, that is, if the person is to avoid unbalanced spiritual growth, or little growth at all. These issues are signposts to assist the leader in knowing where to show the relevance of biblical truth. Developmental issues are at the same time potential prompters of spiritual development. Though seemingly unrelated to the faith, they have the potential of signaling the need for considering God's truth in light of the concerns of developmental periods of life.

Spiritual development is not something mysterious. It does not occur without direction. There is a path and pattern. It occurs in a human life context, following an agenda structured by God. It involves the whole person. God has ordained an unfolding life pattern, some of it unique, some of it similar, in each of His children. The psalmist describes it like this, "And in Thy book they were all written, the days that were ordained for me, when as yet there was not one of them" (Ps. 139:16). Developmental research helps us understand the way in which God has designed the life patterns of His created beings.

Major Theories of Development: An Overview

A theory is more than an educated guess. It is not even something hypothetical. Rather, it is a means of classifying what is observed and studied. Theories are ways of describing, and human development theories are descriptions of growth toward maturity. For most purposes, they may be divided into three major categories, each with its own distinctive approach: cognitive-structural, psychoanalytic, and behavioral theories. Each theory depicts development from a different perspective. Though differing, theories of development should not be thought to be in competition with each other. They are a bit like the multiple cameras and screens used in 360 degree motion pictures at Disneyland. Each projector portrays on the screen a different portion of the landscape. Neither is necessarily more accurate than the other. One projector isn't "right" while the others are "wrong". Rather, each shows a portion of the whole.

Cognitive-structural theories: Cognitive-structuralists focus on innate potential for growth in perception of, thinking about, and understanding one's world. They have discovered patterns in development, rather than random-ness. In part, it is the orderliness of growth and the cognitive-structuralists' affirmation that the individual carries a large portion of the responsibility for development that makes Christian educators feel comfortable with the cogni-tive theories. They are compatible with much of the perspective of Scripture. Jean Piaget, the foremost researcher in cognitive development, along with Jerome Bruner, identified stages of intellectual growth. Lawrence Kohlberg, drawing on Piaget's theory, identified stages of development in moral reasoning.

Psychoanalytic theories: Most psychoanalytic theories trace their roots to Sigmund Freud and his identification of the id, ego, and superego as the primary components of personality. It was Freud's contention that growth occurs as inner conflicting forces are recognized and controlled. Perhaps the most lasting contributions to Christian educators have come from Eric Erikson who built upon the work of Freud when he identified the eight ages of psychosocial development. In each stage, Erikson described a primary issue or conflict which must be resolved if the individual is to develop and mature. Daniel Levinson enlarged educators' understanding of adult development by identifying the primary issues with which most adults are concerned, from adolescence through late adulthood.

Behavioral theories: Developmental theories that are considered to be behav-ioral generally are based on the concepts of conditioning, reinforcement, stimu-lus, and response. B.F. Skinner is considered by many to be the primary contribu-tor of behaviorism in this century. His views, however, have been controversial when applied in the classroom. His concepts seem mechanistic, denying the dignity of individuals made in the image of God. Other behaviorists such as Albert Bandura, Justin Aronfreed, and Robert Sears, considered to be social learning theorists, emphasize means by which growth occurs through experiences of modeling, identification, and imitation. Christian leaders have been quick to note the value of each of these elements of learning and their close affinity to certain biblical concepts of spiritual growth.

Cognitive-Structural Development

Life constantly changes. Little remains the same. Yet, despite change, there is some predictability in growth. Clearly, physical growth follows a pattern. The same is true for cognitive development. Patterns of cognitive growth and change have been identified. Such predictable characteristics of development are compatible with the biblical description of an orderly God who established a process of growth in those He created.

While patterns of growth are innate, cognitive growth occurs only when there is interaction with others, with knowledge, and with the experiences of life. Development, for the most part, does not occur in a vacuum or in isolation. A multitude of influences such as family, teachers, friends, and culture affect development. This is one reason New Testament writers were so eager to promote fellowship and community among believers. As Christians interact with each other in the expression of faith, the potential for growth is immeasurably enhanced. Growth that is long-lasting and that involves the whole person requires active involvement.

There are differences between learning information, whether biblical or otherwise, and internal cognitive-structural changes. Generally, learning is more narrowly-focused and more specific than development. In part, it involves increases in the amount of knowledge. Cognitive development, on the other hand, involves fundamental, sweeping changes in the way a person thinks and responds, making it possible to handle more advanced concepts. Development is not merely adding more knowledge, or learning more facts.

The Apostle Paul referred, in part, to developmental changes when he commented, "When I was a child, I used to speak as a child, think as a child, reason as a child; when I became a man, I did away with childish things" (1 Cor. 13:11). Paul was not making a commentary on the foolishness of children. He was not saying that the thinking of children is wrong and adultlike thinking is right. Paul is pointing to the fact that there are differences. And it is appropriate that differences take place and that growth in thinking occurs.

Most researchers concur that cognitive development takes place in stages. Characteristics of thought are different from one stage to the next, with each stage representing qualitative changes in thinking. Although each stage builds on preceding stages, there is little similarity in the thought process of one stage and another. The writer of Hebrews pictures similar qualitative differences when he contrasts babes in Christ, who need milk, with the mature in Christ, who require solid food (Heb. 5:13-14). The young Christian thinks differently about spiritual things than the more mature Christian.

Although Paul makes reference in a general way to two primary periods of growth (childhood and adulthood), research has shown that there are more than two stages of development. There are multiple stages that occur in sequence; that is, there is no skipping around between stages. Instead, there is orderly progression. It has also been discovered that stages are found in all human beings in all cultures of the world. God's plan for growth to maturity has been imprinted in all.

One temptation of Christian leaders is to attempt to speed the rate of spiritual development. New converts are sometimes expected to think and act as mature believers. Frequently, they are given positions of responsibility and exposure and are pressured to handle the faith as mature believers. Children are often treated the same way. They are expected to understand abstract spiritual concepts or go through the motions of adult worship, but without the benefit of understanding.

Studies in human development have demonstrated the damage of pushing children and adults to develop too quickly. The result is what Elkind described as "the hurried child."[1] When believers, children or new adult converts, are pushed too far too fast, the stage is set for arrested spiritual development and even for later dumping of the faith. The young believer pushed too rapidly finds little in the faith to which he or she can relate. Sooner or later, the stress created by differences between a limited ability to understand, and the expectations of others for rapid understanding and growth, takes its toll.

It is possible to significantly increase a child's level of performance by concentrated encouragement toward high achievement. Bloom, in his study of highly talented individuals, noted that elevated achievement can be a result of such nurturing.[2] However, it generally exacts a toll on the child and on the family which pours its energies into the one child at the expense of the others.

Cognitive Development

We are indebted to Jean Piaget, a Swiss researcher, for describing the characteristics of intellectual, or cognitive, development.[3] Piaget found that the human mind has a drive to make sense of experiences, thoughts, and feelings. This is accomplished through the process of *organizing*, a procedure by which concepts are formed. For example, a young child receives the affectionate care of loving parents and hears their words of love. These experiences are slowly organized into a concept of love. In similar manner, all biblical truth is organized by the mind. Knowledge of Scripture and experiences with other Christians are systematized into spiritual concepts which become more complex and complete as the believer develops.

The mind also tends to adapt to knowledge and experience. This process of *adaptation* is of two kinds. In the first type, *assimilation*, the person deals with new knowledge by changing that knowledge to fit what is already understood. As adults, we know, for example, that the word "church" represents the biblical concept of the body of Christ. However, the young child is unable to comprehend such an abstract concept. Instead, the child understands church to be a building. It may be a building associated with pleasant memories of kind people, interesting activities, and where stories about Jesus are heard. But it is a building, nonetheless. The biblical concept of church is in this way modified to fit what the child is capable of understanding. It is important to realize that what we teach is always modified by the learner to fit what the learner can already perceive.

A second type of adaptation, *accommodation*, involves a different kind of change. Rather than modify the concept to fit present understanding, internal thought structures are changed to fit incoming knowledge or experience. Let's assume, for example, that a child's early experiences at church were unpleasant. Perhaps there was little that captured the child's interest. Maybe the teacher expected absolute quiet. Church, then, became distasteful. But let's assume that a new teacher provides interesting learning activities and is pleasantly involved with the children. The child then accommodates or changes his or her concept of church to one where there is joy and meaningful interaction.

Through adaptation and organization, individuals develop thought *structures*. These structures are ways of viewing life that are constantly being formed. As the person grows, structures develop in an orderly sequence known as stages. Each stage represents increasingly more complex structures. As an example, the childhood hand game, "Here is the church and here is the steeple; open the doors and see all the people," begins with the child perceiving nothing more than the physical characteristics of church. People are present, as represented by the fingers. Gradually, there comes a time when the child's idea of church as a building yields to more complex understandings of church. In later childhood or adolescence, church is seen as an organization. Still later, as thought structures change, this develops to understanding the church primarily as people.

All of us tend to resist change. There is a built-in drive toward stability known as *equilibrium*. This God-created characteristic is necessary to avoid becoming overwhelmed with ideas. Without it, there would quickly be chaos. In fact, mental dysfunction occurs when someone is unable to regulate the amount of change taking place within. Yet it is this same resistance to change, in addition to our sin nature, that sometimes makes it difficult for us to grow in Christ. Part of the process of developing to spiritual maturity is overcoming the inertia that prevents us from becoming increasingly "conformed to the image of His Son" (Rom. 8:29). Experiences of pain and suffering serve this purpose.

Piaget identified four primary stages of intellectual development. The first stage, the *sensorimotor* period, occurs during infancy up to approximately 4 years of age. The young child at this stage begins life centered on self, relying a great deal on reflexes. Gradually, the infant decenters from self to an awareness of objects around. Reflexes become action patterns. Soon the child is able to remember and to imitate. Interaction with people and objects, which for the child is play, is essential during this period if further development of complex thought and language is to occur. It is in this crucible of early life that the child's intellectual abilities to comprehend God and His Word are formed. For this reason, careful and creative attention must be given to designing, equipping and staffing church nurseries and infant care facilities. Here, the child's experiences provide a foundation for lifelong spiritual growth.

Preoperational thought, the second stage, occurs during the years 4-7. The thought of the child at this stage is *animistic.* The child tends to think that natural events are alive, just as people are alive. To the young child, the crashing waves of the ocean are living. There is belief, known as *artificialism,* that either people or some great power cause natural events. For example, to the child, thunder may be caused by an angry parent. The child has the idea that the actions of people and natural processes are interrelated, a characteristic known as *participation.* Thought at this stage tends to be *syncretistic.* Unrelated thoughts or events are grouped together. The child, for example, may bring parts of two different Bible stories together in a confused tale. Or, cartoon stories and biblical events may be combined. Because of the characteristic of *juxtaposition,* the child fails to see relationships between things or events. Even the relation of parts to the whole escape the child's understanding.

Egocentrism is a characteristic of the young child's thought which involves an inability to see things through the eyes of someone else. It should be noted that this is not in itself willful selfishness, although it may seem so at times. Rather, it is a limitation of the child's thought process. It leads the child to think solely of his or her own point of view. It also results in frequently breaking rules. The fact that rule-breaking is a natural consequence of developmental limitations is not to say that rules should not be enforced. Holding the child accountable to rules in a loving, understanding manner, is essential for development to the next stage of thinking. It is, however, helpful to understand why rules for a child at this age are so difficult to maintain.

There is a tendency for children to focus on parts rather than the whole, a phenomenon called *centration.* This characteristic leads, for example, to concentrating on the slingshot in the story of David and Goliath, rather than on the power of God through David. Thought lacks *reversibility.* The child is unable to think backward to make certain of accuracy. This often leads the young child to erroneous conclusions, such as thinking that Jesus and Superman are not very different.

Concrete operations, the third stage of development in a child's thinking, takes place during the years of approximately 7 through 11. Thought which was rather rigid and simple in preoperations becomes more flexible and complex. The child's thinking becomes *decentered.* That is, the child is able to handle several aspects of an issue at the same time. Thus, the biblical idea of sharing can begin to be perceived as an aspect of loving. No longer is one aspect of thought isolated from others. *Reversibility,* a second characteristic of concrete operations, means that the child is able to arrive at a conclusion and then reverse the process to return to the starting point. It allows the child to check on the accuracy of a conclusion by assuring its logical consistency. Children at this stage can think about what will happen if something is or is not done.

The fourth stage of cognitive development, *formal operations,* occurs primarily during the period of adolescence. While the concrete operations child is generally limited to what can be observed, the adolescent in formal operations is open to a vast array of possibilities. In fact, noting possibilities becomes the first way in which a new situation is approached. Thought at this stage is flexible and alert to multiple combinations of ideas. The adolescent becomes capable of dealing with the more complex, abstract issues of biblical faith and their expression. For example, now the teen becomes alert to many ways in which servanthood can be shown.

Piaget's Four Stages of Cognitive Development

Age	Stage	Characteristics
Birth–2 years	Sensorimotor	Reality is determined based upon the child's senses (e.g. taste, touch, see, smell, hear). Objects of thought are limited to these senses alone.
2–7 years	Preoperational	Incomplete thinking
a) 2–4 years	— Preconceptual	The child's ability to understand is incomplete, since the child cannot differentiate identical items from the same class.
b) 4–7 years	— Intuitive	Thinking in this substage is more logical, although governed more by perception than by logic.
7–11 years	Concrete Operations	Logical thought can now be applied to specific (concrete) situations which involve real objects.
12–15 years	Formal Operations	Logical thought can be applied using abstract concepts and examples with symbols substituting for real objects.

Figure 5.1

Jerome Bruner, who aligned himself rather closely with the cognitive development approach of Piaget, identified three primary characteristics of knowledge acquisition as people develop.[4] First, to know is to do. This does not mean that there is necessarily consistency between knowledge and behavior. Rather, it refers to the fact that learners constantly shape and reshape knowledge. Facts are explored, tested, and revised. Knowledge is never given nor received in a shape that is already formed. This is related to the second characteristic of acquiring knowledge: the learner must do something with knowledge for that knowledge to become meaningful. Third, knowledge acquisition requires interaction with someone else. It necessitates a social or community context.

Implications for guiding spiritual growth. Characteristics of thought at each stage of cognitive development provide helpful insights to the Christian leader for developing appropriate experiences for learning God's truths. Biblical teaching must take into account the intellectual abilities of the learner. To do otherwise runs the risk that learners will begin to feel that Scripture and biblical faith have little to say to them personally. Learners who are capable of doing so should be helped to develop to formal operations in relation to their faith. Neither a full understanding nor an adequate practice of faith are possible when spiritual things have been conceptualized only on a concrete level. At the same time, it should be recognized that not all learners are capable of formal operational thought.

Cognitive research has demonstrated the importance of actively engaging the learner in the learning process. The "tried-and-true" methods of telling and lecturing have minimal impact on learner development. But student participation in learning experiences influences not only cognitive development. It is also a means by which biblical truth is processed for life action.

Teaching to nurture learner thinking is an essential goal that is often missed in Christian Education. It involves leading students to reflect on biblical truth, its implications, and its application for life. Likewise, teaching for thought includes reflection on life experiences in light of Scripture. We want to equip believers to avoid what T. S. Eliot described as having an experience but missing the meaning. One effective method is to ask questions that "haunt" the learner, that continue to pester the mind long after the teaching hour has concluded.

Intellectual-Ethical Development

William Perry, who built on Piaget's understanding of formal operations, studied the intellectual-ethical development of college students.[5] He identified three basic levels. The first, *dualism*, views life through black and white lenses. The world is reduced to simple right and wrong. Diverse viewpoints are seen as aberrations, incorrect and unnecessarily confusing. Those who hold differing views are suspect. Biblical concepts at this level are seen simplistically. There is inability to perceive either the complexity of an issue or the way in which faith applies. Beliefs in large part are limited to those passed down by parents, pastors, and other teachers.

Gradually, there is growing awareness of a multiplicity of views, developing to a level Perry described as *pluralism*. Here, the student develops from conviction that there is one correct answer among all competing answers, to a belief that knowledge and solutions to issues are determined by context. "It all depends" is a common phrase. There is openness to the many ways in which God's Word relates to situations. Faith applied to life is not nearly so simple as previously believed. Honest doubts about the faith may even be experienced.

In the final level, *commitment*, the individual recognizes the need to press through pluralism to the point of making personal commitments. Such commitments are not simply accepted with little question, as in former dualistic thought. Rather, they are reflected upon and become far more secure and fixed. A high level of personal ownership develops. There is active engagement in working through the multiplicity of views in light of the student's commitments.

A number of alternatives to intellectual-ethical growth and development have been identified. The individual may draw back to or fail to develop beyond dualism, a condition known as *retreat*. The comforts of not having to face the multiple aspects of faith and its relationship with life are too enticing. There is safety in a world of black and white. But there is also the tendency to label as enemies viewpoints that are different from one's own. A second alternative is to *escape* at level two by avoiding commitments and responsibility. Often there is detachment and cynicism regarding the faith. There may even be passive or exploitative challenging of faith concepts. A final alternative to development is *temporizing*. Generally, this involves a delay of up to one year at the same sub-level within one of the three major levels of intellectual-ethical development. Temporizing may reveal a hesitancy to explore implications of the faith. Or it may simply be a time of consolidation of the previous level of development, a time of "equilibrium", to use Piaget's terminology.

Implications for guiding spiritual growth: Simple dualism is hardly faith that is reflective and mature. There is little at this level that could be called "thinking Christianly." The need to help Christians develop beyond dualism is obvious. Exposure of students to a variety of applications and interpretations of God's Word, where appropriate, is helpful. However, it requires dialogue; interaction between teacher/leader and students as well as between students themselves is needed. A leader's openness to incomplete student conclusions is likewise required. It includes a reluctance to seek easy answers to complex issues.

Psychoanalytic Development

While cognitive understandings of development focus on the intellect, psychodynamic theories take into account the emotions and their influence on development of personality. The focus of some studies has been on the function of drives and the inner mind, and their effect on behavior. Others have emphasized the social and cultural influences of experience on drives that emerge as an individual matures biologically.

Psychosocial Development

Erik Erikson, building upon the work of Sigmund Freud, identified specific issues at each stage of development which must be resolved if the person is to function effectively.[6] Each issue may be resolved either positively or negatively. For the child, the direction of resolution depends in large measure on the influence of parents and other significant adults. As the child matures, adolescent peers and then the adult self determine whether the issues are handled positively or negatively. Issues which are resolved negatively tend to inhibit healthy functioning in subsequent stages.

Early in the development of a new-born child there is need for *bonding* and *attachment*, particularly to the mother.[7] Attachment is necessary for later development of independence. Without it, the child becomes insecure and clinging, afraid to venture out and express appropriate selfhood. It is in this period of development, birth to one year, that either *trust* or *mistrust* develop. Trust is a sense of security and confidence, while mistrust is a prevailing feeling of apprehension or fear. If the child's primary caretakers provide a supportive, caring environment, trust will be the result. The second stage, 2-3 years, involves the achievement of *autonomy*, on the positive side, or *shame and doubt*, on the negative. Autonomy is a sense of self-control and independence. Shame and doubt, on the other hand, involve feelings of inadequacy and inappropriate dependence.

During ages 4-5 years, the child acquires a sense either of *initiative* or *guilt*. Development of a feeling of mastery over activities and a sense that initiative is acceptable are at stake. Failure to develop initiative results in feelings of anxiety about one's behavior which can lead to overcontrol of self.

In the stage of *industry vs. inferiority* the child may develop either an ability to apply self to a task, or a sense of inadequacy and disappointment with self. This is the age of approximately 6-11 years. Adolescence, age 11-18 years, marks the emergence of the issues of *identity vs. role confusion*. If the search for identity is resolved, there is a sense of congruence between self-concept and the way the youth appears to others. Role confusion, on the other hand, results in doubt and confusion about personal identity.

In young adulthood, ages 18-28 years, *intimacy vs. isolation* are primary concerns. Intimacy is the ability to share closely with others without fearing loss of self-identity. It includes the ability to make commitments and abide by them. Isolation, on the other hand, includes feelings of distance from others and avoidance of contact that requires intimacy. There is also a high level of self-absorption.

Generativity vs. self-absorption are the competing issues of middle adulthood, ages 28-50 years. Concern for others, particularly the next generation, is the issue of generativity. It involves an ability to lose self for the sake of others. Self-absorption, by contrast, is characterized by self-indulgence and self-concern. The final pair of issues, *integrity vs. despair,* are of particular concern during the years 51 plus. A dominant sense of integrity results in feelings of fulfillment and that one's life had order and meaning. Failure to achieve integrity results in despair, or lack of acceptance of and satisfaction with life. Figure 5.2 summarizes Erikson's theory.

Erikson's Eight Stages of Psychosocial Development

	Stage	Age	Developmental Crises
1.	Infancy	0– 2	Trust vs. Mistrust
2.	Early Childhood	2– 3	Autonomy vs. Shame and Doubt
3.	Play Age	4– 5	Initiative vs. Guilt
4.	School Age	6–11	Industry vs. Inferiority
5.	Adolescence	11–18	Identity vs. Role Diffusion
6.	Young Adulthood	18–28	Intimacy vs. Isolation
7.	Adulthood	28–50	Generativity vs. Self-absorption
8.	Old Age	51 +	Integrity vs. Despair, Disgust

Figure 5.2

Implications for guiding spiritual growth: Primary caretakers are essential in development toward the positive trait at each stage in the child's development and provide foundation for similar development in youth and adult stages. When an overly-active conscience is formed, there is a strong tendency toward the negative traits. This may show itself as an underlying feeling of alienation.

An occupational hazard of Christian leaders is to become so involved in the demands of ministry and helping others that personal needs at each stage of adulthood are neglected.[8] One consequence may be the development of negative traits which distort the leader's ministry. Unresolved issues from earlier stages may even cause dysfunctional leadership. For example, a leader still struggling with issues of autonomy may have a deep-seated need to view ministry as a personal possession rather than something to be shared with others. Similarly, a young leader who has unresolved identity issues may tend toward isolation and a "loner" approach to ministry.

Adult Lifecycle Development

Daniel Levinson identified a universal pattern of adult male development that has many variations according to the person and the culture in which one lives.[9] Men pass through eras of development which are alternately stable and transitional. It has been noted by some that while Levinson's research focused on men, many of the same characteristics are true of women as well.

The first stage of adulthood Levinson labeled *early adulthood*, ages 17-40. It involves issues of separating from one's pre-adult world in significant ways. Included is establishing an appropriate adult identity, one equal to the challenges of adulthood. Drives toward achievement and reaching personal potential are strong. In *middle adulthood*, age 40-60 years, most drives of early adulthood continue. But the man is less tyrannized by them. The quality of relationships grows stronger along with greater capacity for intimacy and

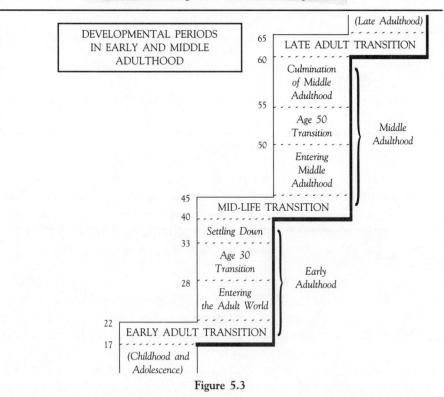

Levinson's Stages of Adult Development

Figure 5.3

tenderness. Personal qualities which were held subservient to the drives of early adulthood now become more obvious. During this period, a fuller, more personal identity is developed. The era identified as *late adulthood*, age 60 and beyond, is characterized by mental and physical changes at the same time in which "the baton" is passed to the next generation. The primary task is to terminate earlier life structures and adopt structures more appropriate for late adulthood. The process can be anxiety-producing. Levinson's stages are summarized in figure 5.3 on page 82.

Implications of psychoanalytic development for guiding spiritual growth: Seeds of faith are planted as finite parents represent the trustworthiness of an infinite God. Each succeeding stage presents an agenda of issues to which biblical truths need to be related. A ministry which helps people work through these issues in light of God's Word prepares them for relationships with God and with each other that are less distorted by unresolved issues. It also results in equipping people for stronger ministries to each other within the body. There is greater freedom for expressing one's spiritual gifts when the issues of life are addressed through the insights of biblical truth.

It also appears that the way in which each stage issue is handled has potential to influence a person's interpretation of Scripture, or at least those aspects of Scripture selectively chosen for emphasis. Unresolved issues serve as "filters" through which Scripture and life are distortedly viewed.

Behavioral Development

Much of the behavioral approach to development has focused on learning theory and is therefore discussed in some detail in chapter 6. It is important for us to note here, however, that gradual changes in behavior that come with age are seen as the result of accumulation of knowledge. Internal structures are not the concern of behaviorists. Rather, focus is placed on the means of learning, particularly reinforcement and conditioning through stimulus-response.

Many learning theories seem to emphasize that the individual is passively involved in his or her own growth. Like a cork bobbing in the ocean, the person is swayed by whatever tide of reinforcing stimuli may be present. Such a view does little to support the biblical concept of individual responsibility. It provides little to help the Christian leader nurture in believers a sense of responsibility for personal spiritual development. Many evangelical churches unknowingly employ a behavioral philosophy in their programming when they encourage children to memorize large portions of Scripture with little concern for understanding or comprehension. Rewards and prizes are given purely on the basis of knowledge learned with little concern given for application.

However, perhaps the greatest benefit to Christian educators has been *social learning theory,* one form of a behavioral approach to development.[10] Going beyond mere conditioning, social learning theory emphasizes processes such as imitation, identification, and modeling. People learn by watching others and noting the consequences of their behavior, a process known as *imitation. Identification* is taking on the values, attitudes, and beliefs of others. The identification process requires a positive relationship with *models* whose values are desired.

Implications for guiding spiritual growth: The process of imitation is powerful and perhaps one reason Christ spent so much time in close relationship with the twelve disciples. Maybe for similar reasons, the Apostle Paul offered himself and his colleagues "as a model for you," instructing the Thessalonians to "follow our example" (2 Thes. 3:7, 9).

Encouraging the formation of relationships must be a priority for Christian educators, even in formal classroom settings. It is largely in the context of relationships that biblical values are passed on, in large part through imitation. Although classroom instruction provides essential content for faith, its effectiveness is limited. Still, even formal teaching can be enhanced by giving attention in the classroom to relationships. Far more powerful, however, are nonformal settings such as camping. In these environments where life is in community, there is opportunity to observe models in situations that more closely resemble life itself.

Principles of Application for Christian Education

An understanding of human development provides us with guiding principles which, in turn, can enable us to experience more effective ministries. Some of these principles include:

1) *Developmental insights serve as agendas for specific life issues to which the truths of Scripture are to be applied.* Developmental issues in students of all ages frequently are unconscious motivators which need the light of God's Word. The wise teacher or leader consciously considers the developmental context of life in which biblical truth is presented.

2) *Developmental awareness influences methodology.* None of the major theories of human development assume that individuals grow best by being passive learners. No developmental approach suggests that we can encourage growth by causing learners to absorb content without thought or personal involvement. In this there is clear agreement with biblical examples of maturing believers.

3) *Developmental theories add to our understanding of spiritual growth.* The biblical process of growth to maturity involves changes toward greater "wholeness." This refers not only to becoming more fully Christlike, but to becoming whole in each aspect of life. All dimensions are to become whole.

4) Faith tends to be shaped, in part, by developmental characteristics. The nature of one's personal development tends to influence the way in which spiritual matters are approached. For example, Scripture indicates that believers must move from a man-centered perspective to one that is God-centered. However, spiritual perspective is shaped by patterns of thought which are characteristic of a particular stage of development. For this reason, a self-centered life may tend to prevail at certain stages over one that is God-centered. Or, for example, failure to experience trusting relationships in early childhood may make it difficult for an adult to place full trust in a loving God. The ways in which development occurs give form to personal faith which may or may not conform to biblical faith.

5) A developmental understanding of human growth toward maturity supports the biblical idea that growth requires thinking and reflection. God has designed us so that we must be reflective if growth is to occur. In short, we must think. Leaders and teachers are obligated to minister in such a way as to stimulate thought.

6) God's Word must be taught in a form appropriate to a believer's level of development. If taught too far ahead, Scripture comes across as unattainable and irrelevant. If taught too far behind the learner's level, the student tunes it out thinking it has all been heard before. God's Word is seen as childish, something that "does not relate to me." Studies show that the optimum level at which instruction should be aimed is a point just ahead of the learners' developmental level. This provides challenge and encouragement to develop further.

7) Developmental approaches acknowledge that in the absence of a community context, growth does not occur without distortion. Individualism does not result in maturity. Only individuals interacting with other individuals in the supportive context of fellowship have potential for growth toward biblical wholeness and completeness.

Summary

Research findings in the field of human development can help the Christian educator understand the complexities of our created nature. Issues and concerns which are evident during one stage of development may serve as a foundation for future development and can have a profound effect on the way we provide ministry support. Each theory of human development, though inadequate by itself to explain all that is involved in human growth and maturation, can together form a lens through which we view our lives. With Scripture as our foundation, we can view human maturation through these various developmental theories and become more effective in our methods of evangelism, curriculum development, discipleship training, program design, counseling, and a host of other ministry elements for church and parachurch ministry.

There is a temptation among some conservative evangelicals to overreact to these theories by seeing them as purely secular and therefore without merit. Such a view limits a minister's ability to understand the individuals whom he or she seeks to reach. For example, if we know from research theories that most men undergo a period of intense personal self-evaluation during the mid-life years, the church can respond by providing opportunities to help them in this time of transition. It can point out the true meaning and purpose of life to these adults when they are eager to find such answers. Such an approach to program design will make us far more effective, and therefore fruitful, than if we had never considered the theory's input at all.

Wisdom is needed, however, not to assume that these theories represent truth, for only Scripture can provide us with such absolutes. However, if viewed in an integrative perspective, these theories can prove to be quite beneficial for those who seek to minister in the name of Jesus.

Notes

1. David Elkind, *The Hurried Child: Growing up too Fast too Soon* (Reading, Mass.: Addison-Wesley Publishing Company; 1981). David Elkind, *All Grown Up and No Place to Go.* (Reading, Mass.: Addison-Wesley Publishing Company, 1984).

2. Benjamin S. Bloom, ed., *Developing Talent in Young People* (New York: Ballantine Books, 1985).

3. Jean Piaget, *The Development of Thought: Equilibration of Cognitive Structures* (New York: Viking Press, 1975); Jean Piaget, *Intelligence and Affectivity: Their Relationship during Child Development* (Palo Alto, Calif.: Annual Reviews, Inc., 1981); Paul Mussen, ed., *Handbook of Child Psychology* vol. 2 (New York: John Wiley & Sons, 1983); Herbert P. Ginsburg, and Sylvia Opper, *Piaget's Theory of Intellectual Development*, 3rd ed. (Englewood Cliffs, N.J.: Prentice-Hall, Inc., 1985); Harry Beilin, "Piaget's Theory: Alive and More Vigorous than Ever," *Human Development*, vol. 33, no. 6 (1990): 362-65.

4. Jerome S. Bruner, *Studies in Cognitive Growth* (New York: Wiley & Sons, 1966); D. R. Olson, "Possible Minds: Reflections on Bruner's Recent Writings on Mind and Self," *Human Development*, vol. 33, no. 6 (1990): 339-43.

5. William G. Perry, Jr. *Forms of Intellectual and Ethical Development in the College Years: A Scheme* (New York: Holt, Rinehart and Winston, Inc., 1970).

6. Erik Erikson, ed., *Adulthood* (New York: W. W. Norton & Company, Inc. 1978); Erik Erikson, *Identity and the Life Cycle* (New York: W. W. Norton &

Company, 1980); J. Eugene Wright, *Erikson: Identity and Religion* (New York: Seabury Press, 1982).

7. M.D. Ainsworth, and M.C. Blehar, *Patterns of Attachment* (Hillsdale, N.J.: Lawrence Erlbaum Associates, Publishers, 1978); Margaret S. Mahler, *Separation and Individuation.* (New York: Jason Aronson, 1979).

8. C.R. Paul, *Passages of a Pastor: Coping with Yourself and God's People* (Grand Rapids: Zondervan Publishing House, 1981).

9. Daniel J. Levinson, *The Seasons of a Man's Life* (New York: Alfred A. Knopf, 1978).

10. Albert Bandura, *Social Learning Theory* (Englewood Cliffs, N.J.: Prentice-Hall, 1977).

For Further Reading

Elkind, D. *The Hurried Child: Growing Up Too Fast Too Soon.* Reading, Mass.: Addison-Wesley Publishing Co., 1981.

_____. *All Grown Up and No Place to Go.* Reading, Mass.: Addison-Wesley Publishing Co., 1984.

Erikson, E.H. *Identity and the Life Cycle.* New York: W.W. Norton & Co., 1980.

Ginsburg, H.P. and Opper, S. *Piaget's Theory of Intellectual Development.* 3rd ed. Englewood Cliffs, N.J.: Prentice Hall, 1988.

Levinson, D.J., et al. *The Seasons of a Man's Life.* New York: Alfred A. Knopf, 1978.

Paul, C.R. *Passages of a Pastor: Coping with Yourself and God's People.* Grand Rapids: Zondervan Publishing House, 1981.

Perry, W.G., Jr. *Forms of Intellectual and Ethical Development in the College Years: A Scheme.* New York: Holt, Rinehart and Winston, Inc., 1970.

Sell, C.M. *Transitions Through Adult Life.* Grand Rapids: Zondervan Publishing House, 1991.

Steele, Les L. *On the Way: A Practical Theology of Christian Formation.* Grand Rapids: Baker Book House, 1990.

Six
Psychological Foundations
of Teaching in the Local Church

It was a terrible, horrible, no good, very bad day. That's what it was for a little boy named Alexander in a popular children's book.[1] His breakfast cereal had no toy prize, his mom forgot to put dessert in his lunch, his teacher did not appreciate his picture of the invisible castle, there was kissing on TV, lima beans for dinner, and he had to wear his railroad train pajamas to bed! It had been a terrible, horrible, no good, very bad day. Some days are like that, even in teaching.

What comes to your mind when you think about teaching? Lesson planning? Classrooms? Lectures? Curriculum materials? Taking notes? A favorite subject? *Who* comes to your mind when you think about teaching? If you had to choose one of your most favored teachers, whom would you select? Pause for a moment in your reading of this chapter and think about that person. What was it about them and their approach to teaching you so enjoyed? Why would you consider them to be effective teachers? Did you learn from them? What did you learn? How do you know learning occurred? What is learning? What is teaching?

Learning can be defined as a change in behavior resulting from experience. These changes are relatively permanent and are not simply the result of growth, maturation, or the temporary effects of factors such as fatigue or drugs.[2] Some behaviors might be mistaken for learning which do not actually reflect an internal and lasting change. For example, memorizing facts without comprehending the material would not be considered learning. Identifying and isolating behavior changes can be a challenging process. In reality, the outcomes of learning — meanings, understandings, attitudes, and behaviors — are multiple and complex.

James Michael Lee has defined teaching as an "orchestrated process whereby one person deliberately, purposively, and efficaciously structures the learning situation in such a manner that specified desired learning outcomes are thereby acquired by another person."[3] Effective teachers know best how to determine learning outcomes and how to structure the learning situation so as to facilitate the accomplishment of those outcomes. This approach to learning is known to educators as educational psychology. In essence, it is the foundation of the entire teacher-learner process.

Educational psychology is one of the subfields within psychology which apply psychological research to teaching and learning. Theories are formulated which help to explain facts and observations related to the teaching-learning act. Application of these theories serves to shape present instructional decisions as well as to predict future instructional responses.

In the same way that secularly gained knowledge has been applied in such fields as medicine and engineering and utilized by Christians to function in daily life, so also can general principles of learning and teaching be gained from study in educational psychology and carefully applied. Three primary theoretical approaches to the instructional process will be summarized in this chapter: the behavioristic approach, the cognitive-discovery approach, and the humanistic approach. The major theorists representing each approach will be discussed followed by a brief critique and application section.

The Behavioristic Approach

Behavioral learning theories focus on how the environment influences and directs simple and overt behavior. Learning is defined as a change in observable behavior. Behaviorists are concerned with the conditions which influence and shape human behavior. The learner is a passive respondent and the teacher becomes the manager of the learning environment. This approach is also referred to as the associationist-connectionist theory because of its emphasis on the associations and connections formed between stimuli and responses.

Background and Major Theorists

Ivan Pavlov (1849-1936) was a Russian physiologist who received the Nobel Prize for his research on the digestive glands. While studying the salivating reflex of dogs in his laboratory, he noticed that the dogs would begin to salivate at the sight of the food or even at the sight of the keepers who carried the food. Intrigued, he explored the phenomena further by ringing a bell everytime food was brought to the dogs. If this procedure were repeated frequently enough, the dogs began to salivate at the ringing of the bell apart from any presence of food (see figure 6.1).

This process is called *classical conditioning*. In classical conditioning a conditioned stiumulus (the bell) is paired with an unconditioned stimulus (the food) and an unconditioned response (salivation) occurs. After enough trials of the bell and food combination, the bell can be rung apart from the presence of food to elicit a now "conditioned" response (salivation) from the dog.

	UCS (food) ----------------	UCR (salivation)
CS (bell) ------------------	UCS (food) ----------------	UCR (salivation)
CS (bell) ------------------	(no food)----------------	CR (salivation)

Figure. 6.1

In addition to contributing the terms of stimulus and response to the study of how people learn, Pavlov's study has several implications for the classroom. It is often through these unconscious processes that learners come to like or dislike the classroom, topics, and teachers. Classical conditioning is occurring all the time in the teaching-learning setting. Fears and phobias are often the result of classical conditioning. Children, youth and adults are forming many of their concepts about God, their faith, and the church on the basis of unconscious positive and negative encounters within the church setting. For example, when asked about early Sunday School memories, some adults recall cold classrooms and chairs that were too big and too hard. What message did they receive about Sunday School and God?

Building on the work of Pavlov, John B. Watson (1878-1958) was a significant force in introducing the components of behaviorism to American psychology. He was a strict environmentalist. His application of behaviorism stressed that behavior can be both predicted, controlled, and shaped if all of the parts making up the larger whole are isolated and subsequently reinforced.

Further examining the relationship between stimulus and response, Edwin L. Thorndike (1874-1949) was one of the primary influences in the development of behaviorism and has been variously referred to as the dean or father of educational psychology. His focus was on the connection or bonds formed between a stimulus and a response and he referred to his learning theory as "connectionism." He experimented with hungry cats in cages. A lever was installed on the floor inside the cage which, when tripped, would open a door leading to a dish of salmon outside the cage. Observing the trial and error approach of the cats to learning to trip the lever, Thorndike formulated three laws of learning:

1. The Law of Readiness. A behavioral response is more apt to be made when the organism is "ready" in an emotional or attitudinal sense.
2. The Law of Exercise. Exercise, or repetition, will strengthen the connection between a stimulus and a response.
3. The Law of Effect. If a behavior is followed by a pleasurable experience, it is more likely to be repeated. A response followed by a dissatisfying state will be weakened.

Although considered somewhat mechanical in nature, these laws and others formulated by Thorndike, have been applied in designing the instructional process in the classroom. For example, it is helpful to wait until children can read before teaching them how to look up verses in the Bible (Law of Readiness). As they are learning this skill, children should practice finding verses on their own for several consecutive weeks (Law of Exercise). Praise the children when they successfully locate the verses (Law of Effect).

Perhaps the most influential and well-known of all the behavioral family of psychologists is B.F. Skinner (1904-1990) (see chapter 5). He is best known for his development of the theory of operant conditioning. In operant conditioning, a voluntary response made by the organism acting upon the environment is strengthened through reinforcement. Reinforcement is any stimulus that will increase the probability that a response will occur.[4] Behavior is the focus and behaviors are the result of the conditions and pattern of reinforcers found in one's environment.

Skinner developed a box-like apparatus to study the behavior of hungry rats. The "Skinner box" contained a bar and a small tray into which a pellet of food would drop under certain conditions when the bar was pressed. Unlike the passivity of the dogs in Pavlov's experiments, the rats in the Skinner box are active. Skinner's theory proposes that all behaviors are accompanied by certain consequences. These consequences then influence or determine whether or not the behaviors are repeated and at what level of intensity.[5] Categories of these various consequences are listed below:

1) *Positive Reinforcement.* When a positive consequence is presented immediately following a behavior, the behavior will be strengthened, increasing the chance that the behavior will be repeated. For example, Johnny receives a candy bar for remembering to make his bed all week.

2) *Negative Reinforcement.* When an unpleasant element is removed from the situation immediately following a behavior, the behavior will be strengthened, increasing the chance that the behavior will be repeated. This is the principle behind the annoying buzzing of a bell in some cars which only stops when the occupants put on their seat belts.

3) *Punishment.* When an unpleasant consequence follows a behavior weaken-

ing that behavior over time, it can be called a punishment. A stomachache after eating two large, fluffy mounds of cotton candy might be a punishment to some individuals and will inhibit indulging in similar behavior in the future. Another type of punishment involves removing something pleasant from the situation, such as a privilege or anticipated activity, as the consequence to behavior. For example, talking in class might mean a reduced recess time for a group of children. It is the goal of punishment to reduce the probability of an undesired behavior being repeated. These consequences are summarized in figure 6.2.[6]

	Pleasant	Unpleasant
Added to the Situation	**Positive Reinforcement (reward)** A book is given to all who memorize fifty verses of Scripture.	**Punishment (Type I)** After hitting another child, Sandy is asked to sit in a chair for five minutes.
Removed from the Situation	**Punishment (Type II) (penalty)** Arriving late to Sunday School, you did not have time to grab a coffee and donut.	**Negative reinforcement (relief)** If we confess our sins, God will forgive our sins.

Figure 6.2

It has been shown that positive and negative reinforcement consequences will improve learning. When reinforcers are chosen which will be motivators to an individual, behavior changes are observed. However, the effects of punishment have not been shown to be as effective in altering behavior in learning situations.

Educators disagree about the effectiveness and appropriate application of punishment in the classroom setting.[7] Ineffectively appropriated, punishment draws attention to the negative aspects of behavior without presenting the positive alternative.

Although not purely behavioristic in all its presuppositions, the social learning theory of Albert Bandura is based in part on a model of operant conditioning. It recognizes the importance of social variables on influencing behavioral change. Change in behavior may occur as people observe other people in their environment and imitate the behavior observed. One observer notes, "Modeling or observational learning is the process within which a person observes the behaviors of others, forms an idea of the performance and results of the observed behaviors, and uses that idea as coded information to guide his future behaviors. Most of the behaviors that people display have been learned, either deliberately or unintentionally, through modeling."[8]

Most of our understanding of appropriate gender roles is the result of social learning. Many complex skill behaviors, such as those involved in learning how to swim, play tennis, or throw a ball are the result of observing other people demonstrating the behavior. Social learning is prevalent in the church as well. New converts will take many of their cues for what is "acceptable and unacceptable" Christian behavior by observing the actions of other believers around them.

Critique of the Behavioral Approach

Behavioral learning theory has received criticism from several directions. Its mechanistic view of people as determined and as equal to animals conflicts with Scripture's teaching of men and women created in the image of God and capable of self-directed behavior and free choice. Many have pointed out that behaviorism denies the worth and dignity of the individual. Behaviorism is also unable to account for aspects of human behavior which seem to arise from maturation, inherited characteristics, and internal motivation. Further, it raises the question of who is to set the standards for selecting the appropriate and desirable behaviors to be reinforced.

Application of the Behavioral Approach

1) Be aware of the subtle ways in which we use conditioning and reinforcement in our churches. Positive application of conditioning principles is useful in creating a warm and inviting learning environment.
2) Utilize reinforcement to help elicit behaviors which are fairly specific; for example, in the memorization of factual information.
3) Repeat key concepts as an aid in the learning process.
4) Create a physically comfortable and appealing learning environment.
5) Strive to utilize positive and negative reinforcement rather than punishment in developing classroom discipline approaches.

The Cognitive-Discovery Approach

As a partial reaction to the mechanistic approach to learning espoused by the behavioralists, a second major theory of learning based upon Gestalt psychology (*gestalt* is German for "pattern," "form," or "configuration") originated in Europe. As its name suggests, the cognitive-discovery approach focused on nonobservable behavior or cognition (thinking). It was concerned with such internal thought processes as insight, problem-solving, and how relationships between concepts develop. Another name used for this theory is cognitive-field. "The word *cognitive* suggests how learners gain understanding of themselves and their environment, and how, using their cognitions, they act in relation to their environment. The word *field* is used to designate the emphasis this theory places on the properties and structure of the setting (the *field*) in which behavior is taking place. In other words the word *field* is the situation or the environment or the context for learning."[9] In this theory, the learner becomes more of an active participant in the process and the teacher is a guide or an arranger of the learning environment.

Background

Gestalt psychology proposed that learning could not be understood simply as a summation of individual parts leading up to a whole. Many things are learned when ideas are arranged into patterns and relationships are discovered.[10] Our perceptions, the way we think about and interpret the stimuli in our environment, are influenced by the arrangement of these patterns.

One of the early Gestalt psychologists, Wolfgang Kohler, conducted a famous experiment with a chimpanzee named Sultan. Sultan was confined to a cage with a variety of objects including a short stick and several boxes. In one of the experiments, a bright yellow banana and a long stick were placed outside the cage beyond his reach. After several unsuccessful attempts to reach the banana and a brief pout, Kohler observed that Sultan picked up the short stick, pulled in the longer stick and used the longer stick to snag the banana. Kohler termed this kind of perception "insight" in contrast to the trial and error learning of the behavioralists.

Kurt Lewin (1890-1947) was one of the primary theorists to bring cognitive-field theory to the United States. Although his field theory was developed more as a theory of motivation and perception rather than as a theory of learning, he did make some applications to the teaching-learning process. The fundamental concept in Lewin's theory is "life space."

Life space has been described by some as similar to the positive and negative forces created by placing two magnets on a table with the north end of one facing the south end of the other. In a similar way, various past experiences and current interests all act together to exhibit alluring or repelling influences on the way in which we organize the happenings in our world. The learner now must be understood as a unique person and consideration must be given to the forces which are acting within and upon the learner throughout the learning process. Furthermore, there is interaction occurring between the life spaces of individuals in the same room.[11] Teaching has now moved beyond simple organization and management of the learning environment. It is far more complex and comprehensive than applying a schedule of reinforcement.

An American who further developed the cognitive theory of learning was Edward Tolman (1886-1959). For Tolman, behavior was purposive, meaningful behavior directed toward goals which would satisfy personal needs. In a sense, it is as if one has a map and is pursuing signs to a designated end and each sign along the way is significant and connected to all the others. Learning, therefore, is not disjointed parts, but a fluid whole and is goal-oriented. Tolman also emphasized that these goals should be within the capacity of the learner to achieve.

You have probably observed by this point that learning has become increasingly learner-focused. The learner is an active component in the teaching-learning process. Jean Piaget is a cognitive theorist who was a strong advocate of active learning. He studied the origins of cognitive structures in children and concluded that children have an innate desire to learn. He formulated his findings into a stage description of cognitive development at different ages. See chapter 5 for a more detailed explanation of Piaget's cognitive structure theory.

Greatly influenced by Piaget and the other cognitive theorists, Jerome S. Bruner is a leading spokesman for cognitive-discovery theory and highly respected for his extensive research and writing in the area. Bruner was primarily concerned with how people actively select, retain, and transform information. He emphasized that learners should understand how fragments of knowledge fit together in a structured whole rather than simply memorize isolated facts.[12] Key concepts in Bruner's approach are cognitive structure, the spiral curriculum, and discovery learning.

Cognitive structure refers to understanding the basic characteristics of objects and events and how they relate to each other. According to Bruner, a person needs to understand the fundamental structure of a subject in order to fully comprehend it. Detail is more easily remembered when it is part of a larger picture.

The *spiral curriculum* represents Bruner's belief that any subject can be taught to any child in some cognitively appropriate form. It involves introducing the subject in its most basic and simple forms to the younger child. As they mature, the same subject is elaborated and expanded in more complex form. For example, toddlers or preschoolers come to "learn" about God's love as they act on their world and receive loving behavior in response from caring adults. This way of representing their world through personal actions is called *enactive* learning. An intermediate stage of representation is *iconic* learning, concrete mental images. This can be seen when elementary children learn about the love of Jesus as they study His concrete actions in the healing of sick people as recorded in the Gospels. Finally, in early adolescent and more likely into the later adolescent and adult years, a person is capable of *symbolic* representation. Symbolic representation is utilized when explaining the love of God as compared in abstract terms to a shepherd seeking after the one lost sheep.

Discovery learning is Bruner's answer to the rote format and step-by-step approach of behavioralists' programmed learning materials. LeFrancois writes, "Discovery learning can be defined as the learning that takes place when students are not presented with subject matter in its final form but rather are required to organize it themselves. This requires learners to discover for themselves relationships that exist among items of information."[13] The teaching process is not a dump truck unloading content into the student. The teacher functions as a guide and facilitator in the discovery process.

Another cognitive theorist, David Ausubel, also advocates presenting new information by linking it to existing cognitive structures. Ausubel's theory focuses on meaningful verbal learning facilitated through expository teaching rather than on the more time-consuming discovery approach. According to Ausubel, "Good-quality expository teaching involves presenting what is to be learned to the learner in more or less final form. That means the information, in a lecture or reading passage, for example, is organized and stated in such a way that it can be easily related to students' existing knowledge schemes."[14]

He encourages the use of advance organizers and logical, systematic presentation of content. Advance organizers are introductory materials which introduce the material to follow by presenting the "big picture." They are more abstract in nature and are used to help the learner find a place to connect the new information to prior knowledge.

Critique of the Cognitive-Discovery Approach

The cognitive-discovery approach assumes a fairly high level of learner internal motivation and persistence. Not all individuals work well when left to themselves. The approach is more autonomous than relational in its view of the teaching-learning process. Some have argued that the discovery method is too haphazard in its communication of necessary content.

Application of the Cognitive-Discovery Approach

1) Design an active approach to the learning process.
2) Utilize problem-solving approaches in the classroom setting as an aid to helping learners solve problems outside of the classroom.
3) Enhance retention by emphasizing meaningful learning of content.
4) Encourage learners to become self-motivated rather than relying on external motivators.
5) Acknowledge the learner as a person capable of reasoning and making meaning of the experiences in his/her world.

The Humanistic Approach
In contrast with the behavioral and cognitive emphases already discussed, humanistic psychologists and educators are concerned with the affective dimension of the learner. Their focus is more individualistic and stresses the humanity and the uniqueness of each individual. Learning does not consist of a prescribed body of knowledge; rather, it is defined as whatever enhances the self-actualization of the learner. Learning depends on self-perception. The learner is self-directed and the teacher acts as a facilitator in the learning process.

Background and Major Theorists
In reaction to the product mentality of behaviorists and an increasingly technically-oriented society, several theorists began to call for a dual emphasis in educational approaches. Agreeing that the learning environment should promote and encourage discovery, they also advocated attending to a learner's emotional needs and orientations.

Theorists who were part of the progressive influence in education reacted against any authoritarian approach in the classroom. They condemned memorization of facts, an overdependence on textbooks, and accused the current school structure of isolating students from reality. Some of the progressive principles which have influenced the humanistic approach include:

1) The child is the central focal point of the school.
2) The child is an active learner and will learn if adult authorities do not insist on imposing their wills upon the child.
3) There can be no authoritative teaching of a particular, "essential" body of knowledge, so the teacher becomes a guide and fellow traveler with the students.
4) The school should reflect the realities of the larger society, rather than being a preparation for "reality to come" after graduation.
5) The teaching-learning process should teach problem solving, rather than particular bodies of subject matter.
6) Cooperation rather than competition, and a democratic atmosphere, should characterize the school.[15]

Three prominent leaders of educational humanism in American psychology have been Abraham Maslow, Carl Rogers, and Arthur Combs. They stressed that the instructional process should be learner-centered. Teachers should seek to build positive relationships with students built on values of trust, empathy, open and honest communication, and personal responsibility. The teaching-learning process should encourage value development, individual decision-making, and choosing, prizing, and acting on beliefs. Curriculum should be adjusted to fit individual needs, encourage exploration of affective elements, and help to clarify personal attitudes and values.

Critique of the Humanistic Approach

Educational humanism has perhaps received its greatest criticisms for its use of vague terminology. Terms such as "real," "genuine," and "authentic," when used by humanists are difficult to interpret and measure. The standards are arbitrary. Its overattention to affective growth neglects necessary cognitive and behavioral objectives. The philosophical assumption that the person is innately good seems to contradict the biblical teaching of the human sin nature (Rom. 3:23).

Application of the Humanistic Approach

1) Create a warm, positive, and accepting emotional climate to enhance the learning environment.
2) Challenge the learners to work to the level of their individual gifting.
3) As a teacher, be personally transparent to facilitate modeling, identification, and the application of principles to real-life situations.
4) Write teaching-learning objectives which include affective, feeling, and attitude components.
5) Utilize a variety of methods in order to appeal to individual learning styles. Effective values clarification methods include role playing and simulation games.
6) Plan activities which appeal to the interests and needs of the learners.

Summary

The three approaches to learning can be summarized for quick evaluation. Trace the major aspects of the three key learning theories in figure 6.3 on page 99.

The Biblical Approach

One of the most complete educational psychology books ever written is the Bible. Although its primary purpose is not to serve as a textbook for learning psychologists or for teachers, God has revealed in His Word hundreds of principles which can be applied to the teaching-learning process. Several of these principles are listed on page 99 (see figure 6.4). As you look over the list, you may be able to identify several areas where behavioral, cognitive-field, and humanistic theories intersect with the teachings of Scripture.

Theory	Key Theorists	Focus	Key Terms	Learner's Role	Teacher's Role
Behaviorism	Pavlov Watson Thorndike Skinner Bandura	Behavior Environment	Stimulus Response Reinforcement Punishment	Passive respondent	Manager of environment
Cognitivism	Ausubel Bruner Gagne Piaget	Thinking Knowing	Cognitive structure Understanding Information processing	Active participant	Guide Arranger of learning environment
Humanism	Maslow Rogers Combs	The person Feelings Attitudes	Self-actualization Values clarification	Self-directed	Facilitator

Figure 6.3

Conditions of Learning

1. Truth is not revealed or learned all at once—it is a maturing and developmental process (1 Cor. 13:9-13).
2. Study of the Scriptures as a source of truth must not be divorced from the experience of the Scriptures as life as well. Scripture study should be alive, energizing, and meaningful! (John 14:6).
3. The Holy Spirit is the One who brings new life and sustains new life (Acts 1; John 3).
4. Each learner will approach God and His Word in a manner all his/her own (2 Tim. 2:15).
5. Each learner is free and able to make choices and is thus responsible, in conjunction with the Holy Spirit, for his/her own growth (Rom. 8:9-17).
6. Learners need to be actively involved in the discovery of relevant truth (John 4).
7. Effective learning begins with the current life situation and needs of the learner (John 4).
8. Learning should be varied in approach and methodology, making provision for various learning styles (the Gospels).
9. Learners need space to be "in process," allowed to move, grow, live, at their own individual pace (2 Tim. 2:20).
10. Learning settings should be both formal and informal (the Gospels).

Figure 6.4

Below (figure 6.5) are a few teaching principles derived from Scripture.

Principles of Teaching

1. The teacher must be a student of God's Word and a lover of God's Word (Ps. 119).
2. The teacher seeks to cultivate within the learner an openness and preparedness to receive the message of truth (Heb. 4:12; 2 Tim. 3:16-17).
3. Some form of systematic study of the Scriptures should be facilitated within the teaching-learning process (Acts 17:11).
4. The teacher can only give away what *life* he/she already possesses (1 Cor. 3:16).
5. Modeling is central to communicating the life and relevance of Scripture (1 Thes. 2:1-12; Heb. 13:7).
6. Teaching is to be built upon a foundation of prayer (Col. 4:2-4).
7. Teachers should be "students" of the learner and strive to perceive the needs of the learner (Matt. 9:36; John 10:3, 27).
8. Teachers should be able to call their learners by name, to know them, to be "connected" with them (John 10:3, 27).
9. Teachers should be transparent and vulnerable (2 Cor. 4:7-18; 5:11-13).
10. Teaching is holistic in approach—thinking, feeling, sensing, and intuiting (soul) (Col. 1:28; Deut. 6:5).

Figure 6.5

Many additional teaching-learning principles can be found in the reading of the biblical text. As you read familiar passages, ask questions you may not have thought to ask like: What does this passage reveal to me about the way people learn? How did God seek to motivate people to respond to what they were learning? What approaches to teaching are demonstrated in this passage? Why was one method chosen in a certain situation over another? Let these questions be the start to a study of your own.

Does a study of educational psychology guarantee the elimination of terrible, horrible, no good, very bad days in teaching? Probably not, but it may provide a few constructive suggestions for improving the effectiveness of the teaching-learning process. Perhaps twenty-five years from now, when asked who was their favorite teacher, *you* will come to the mind of one of your learners!

Notes

1. Judith Viorst, *Alexander and the Terrible, Horrible, No Good, Very Bad Day* (New York: Macmillan Publishing Company, 1972).

2. Guy R. LeFrancois, *Psychology for Teaching,* 7th ed. (Belmont, Calif.: Wadsworth Publishing Company, 1991), 24.

3. James Michael Lee, *The Flow of Religious Instruction.* (Birmingham: Religious Education Press, 1973, 206.

4. LeFrancois, *Teaching,* 37.

5. Robert F. Biehler, and Jack Snowman, *Psychology Applied to Teaching,* 6th ed. (Boston: Houghton Mifflin Company, 1990), 322.

6. Adapted from LeFrancois, *Teaching,* 40.

7. Daniel L. Barlow, *Educational Psychology: The Teaching-Learning Process* (Chicago: Moody Press, 1985), 140.

8. Morris L. Bigge, *Learning Theories For Teachers,* 4th ed. (New York: Harper & Row Publishers, 1982), 163-64.

9. Leon Marsh, *Educational Psychology for Christian Education* (Fort Worth: Southwestern Baptist Theological Seminary, 1982), 165.

10. Robert F. Biehler, *Psychology Applied to Teaching,* 1st ed. (Boston: Houghton Mifflin Company, 1978), 293.

11. Bigge, *Learning Theories,* 225.

12. Biehler & Snowman, *Psychology,* 424-25.

13. LeFrancois, *Psychology,* 93.

14. Biehler & Snowman, *Psychology,* 443.

15. Barlow, *Educational Psychology,* 188.

For Further Reading

Ausubel, D.P. *Educational Psychology: A Cognitive View.* New York: Holt, Rinehart & Winston, 1968.

Bandura, A. *Social Learning Theory.* Morristown, N.J.: General Learning Press, 1977.

Barlow, D.L. *Educational Psychology: The Teaching-Learning Process.* Chicago: Moody Press, 1985.

Beechick, R. *A Biblical Psychology of Learning: How Your Mind Works.* Denver: Accent Books, 1982.

Biehler, R.F., & Snowman, J. *Psychology Applied to Teaching.* 6th ed. Boston: Houghton Mifflin Co., 1990.

Bigge, M.L. *Learning Theories for Teachers*. 4th ed. New York: Harper & Row Pub. Inc., 1982.

Bruner, J.S. *The Process of Education*. Cambridge, Mass.: Harvard University Press, 1966.

Combs, A.W., Blume, R., and Wass, H. *The Professional Education of Teachers*. 2nd ed. Boston: Allyn and Bacon, 1974.

Flavell, J.H. *Cognitive Development*. 2nd ed. Englewood Cliffs, N.J.: Prentice-Hall, 1985.

Gagne, E.D. *The Cognitive Psychology of School Learning*. Boston: Little, Brown & Co., 1985.

Gangel, K. and Hendricks, H. eds. *The Christian Educator's Handbook on Teaching*. Wheaton, Ill.: Victor Books, 1989.

LeBar, L.E. *Education That Is Christian*. ed. J.E. Plueddemann. Wheaton, Ill.: Victor Books, 1989.

Lee, J.M. *The Flow of Religious Instruction*. Birmingham: Religious Education Press, 1973.

LeFrancois, G.R. *Psychology for Teaching*. 7th ed. Belmont, Calif.: Wadsworth Publishing Co., 1991.

Marsh, L. *Educational Psychology for Christian Education*. Fort Worth: Southwestern Baptist Theological Seminary, 1982.

Rogers, C.R. *Freedom to Learn*. Columbus: Merrill Publishing Co, 1969.

Skinner, B.F. *The Technology of Teaching*. New York: Appleton-Century-Crofts, 1968.

Seven
Cross-Cultural Perspectives in Christian Education

Too often teachers expect their students to come from the same background they do. We like to teach persons who can understand our vocabulary, recognize our gestures, follow our logic, smile at our jokes, and cry at our stories. But what should we do if they come from another culture, with a mother tongue different from ours, and who think in patterns quite strange to us?

Cross-cultural education wrestles with such questions. It studies how to teach people from cultures originating outside of North America, or from a special ethnic subgroup within our country. Such study helps the typical North American educator learn how to teach in an unfamiliar cultural situation. Current immigration movements into the United States and Canada require the local church to become sensitive to the relevant issues involved in communicating with members of other cultures.

The purpose of this chapter is to open the reader to the challenge and the opportunity for cross-cultural teaching, to show what it is and what it should not be, and to give helpful insights into what must be learned to become an effective cross-cultural educator.

The Christian Dilemma: Cultural Understanding

Culture is like air; we breathe it but do not see it. Nor do we recognize the values, beliefs, and patterns that shape its norms of thinking and behavior. We begin learning cultural mores from the moment of birth and continue to learn them throughout all of life. Rarely do we think about our culture any more than we think of breathing.

It is this invisibility that makes explaining culture difficult. Everyone else is as oblivious to it as we are. Like fish that do not see the water, or birds the air, so we do not see the patterns by which we live. It is only when we encounter those with different ways of thinking and acting from ours that we notice the strangeness of cultures. Sometimes we act defensively or superior toward persons whose customs seem strange to us. People often criticize or belittle the dress, foods, or actions of others, thinking them weird or ill-mannered. Failing to see our own contradictions, we ridicule other societies out of ignorance or pride.

It is essential for Christian educators to understand what contributes to the formation of a culture before effective educational ministries can take place with persons of other lands and societies. Christian educators must learn to accept people from other cultures for who they are, not for what we want them to become. We must reject the notion that our way of doing something is best simply because it is the way we do it in North America. Simply stated, the Gospel transcends all cultures, though its drama was purposefully acted out on the stage and history of the cultures of the Middle East. The Gospel's essential message is *transcultural*, with equal significance for people of all backgrounds, all places, all languages, and all times. Our major goal as twenty-first century Christian educators is to learn how to cross over cultural barriers so that we may plant the Gospel's essential message in a native soil different from our own.

What Culture Means

Intercultural communication occurs whenever persons of different traditions meet. For example, a message is "transmitted" by a person from one culture, but "received" by a person in another. This message is first decoded by the receiving person through the grid of his or her own cultural system. The last step in the process occurs when it is interpreted. The original message could be taken to mean something radically different from what the sender intended. A display of friendship for one culture may be read as a romantic intention by another, or even as aggression to yet another. A display of silence might be seen as pondering, rejection, ignorance, or deafness. None of these interpretations might in fact be the message the sender intended to communicate. The person who receives words, gestures, and non-verbal signals does so through a cultural lens that has a different tint and focal strength than that of the sender, allowing unintended meanings for them. This is why it is necessary for teachers to learn some of the patterns of culture familiar to their students. For it is in doing so that they will become effective communicators.

Culture comprises the very fabric of our lives. No aspect of life is untouched or unaltered by culture. Our social outlook, how we express ourselves, and the ways we show emotion are all cultural. All we talk about or do not talk about, how we say it, what language and vocabulary we use to do it, and to whom we tell it will in someway be determined by the cultural patterns we practice. How we value things, pattern our thinking, add, subtract, and multiply, and make use of the earth's resources are patterns of our culture. How we perceive skin color, act in public, and treat our parents or grandparents, and discipline our children are also part of our culture. What teachers put into a curriculum, the ways they go about the process of educating in the classroom, and how they manage decorum is also cultural. Culture is a pervasive pattern. These are things you learned from others, passed down to you by observation or instruction.

Culture includes our unconscious and nonverbal behaviors: the gestures we use, whether we cross legs or not, the way we cut and style our hair, the design of our clothes and how we walk are cultural patterns. We have been so immersed in learning them from the family and society in which we were reared that it is almost impossible to recognize them. We just know that certain things seem right and others wrong and that other people who don't practice them seem strange. People strive for what their culture considers proper. But what is correct to one society may be improper or even offensive in another. Christian educators may easily offend the sensitivity of the very ones they are trying to help unless they become sensitive to the cultural patterns of their students.

A Culture Is a Tapestry of Subcultures

Cultures are not monolithic with the same consistency throughout their regions. They comprise a great mosaic with varying but small degrees of change which an outsider might not detect at first. In Anglo-America, Canadians are thought to hold attitudes and values different from their neighbors to the south. Californians tend to possess a carefree lifestyle which seems strange or rude to people in other parts of the United States. A man reared in Boston will have a different accent and attitudes than someone from Texas. If a woman reared in New York City moved to Tennessee she would be immediately impressed by how warm, personable and charming the southerners seem and may, at first, distrust them as being insincere. Inner-city African-Americans are reared in a vastly different subculture than the average middle-class white American. To learn the inner-city subculture, its vocabulary, and its values is the first step toward effective ministry with inner-city individuals.

Subcultural differences may make teaching difficult. Degrees of cultural remoteness even exist between speakers of the same language. Persons who speak English with regional or international accents, as the British, English speaking native Africans, and East Indians, may test the finest of North American instructors who have not learned to be sensitive to dialect differences.

Ethnic units, groups with common cultural or national ties, are powerful subcultural forces within the host culture. These units form submergent societies who feel deep loyalty to other countries, speak other languages besides the dominant one, and often show devotion to a minority religion. They may possess distinct physical (racial) characteristics. They hold subcultural behavioral patterns and strong group values. Most recent migrants from other countries take a long time to mix into the salad bowl of America. Due to this significant challenge some never are able to mix very well. The result is that they feel ostracized and removed from their base of security. The loneliness that results from such a condition can be overwhelming.

This is one reason why churches tend to divide into a mosaic of congregations. African-Americans have developed a certain style of worship and community whether they are Baptist or Roman Catholic. Latin Americans have other preferred worship forms, with guitars, drums, and specific cultural traits. One may observe the same God worshiped differently, with song here, dance there, and meditative stillness over there. Short sermons may be preached in one place, hour-and-a-half messages in another, while several sermons and testimonies joined together into a half-day service might be the norm in another congregation. Customs, music, and emphases reflect ethnicity. Clapping or sedate, the same joy of Jesus abounds in avenues that show our cultural uniquenesses and subcultural preferences. This is not to say that multicultural churches do not or should not exist, but all have to make compromises for them to survive.

The Gospel ties all cultures together. The Christian is in a good position to pass the crest of cultural barriers because the love of God is transcultural. God is beyond culture and time. Finding acceptable ways to transmit and teach that message will take time, patience, and a teachable spirit. It is important for the North American Christian educator to realize that we teach through the lens of our own culture and subculture, our time-bound language, our national, racial, and personal prejudices.

The Bible Encourages Intercultural Relationships

Since the Bible was written in a multicultural arena it speaks forcefully to the mosaic of our age. The biblical world was a diverse world. It's Middle Eastern and Mediterranean settings transected hundreds of nationalities, groups, and languages. One was never far from anyone of a different ethnicity, language, or religion.

1) *It was a geographically small world.* The biblical cosmos extended approximately from the tip of the Black Sea in the north 1,900 miles to the tip of the Arabian peninsula at the south. From east to west it spread from Italy in the western Mediterranean 2,600 miles to Persia. This would fit into North America from Seattle to Boston and from Montreal to Jamaica. Most of the

Bible's story occurred, however, in a much smaller region. The Old Testament region would approximate the area of Minneapolis east to New York City, and from Chicago south to New Orleans. The New Testament region took up a space approximately from Denver to New York City and Baltimore south to Miami. Palestine itself was a territory smaller than New Jersey. Most of this area was dry with a strip of modest rainfall in the north and complete desert in the south. In it intermingled or lived side by side hundreds of ethnic groups. Their commerce depended on peaceful intercultural relationships.

2) *It was a multilingual world.* Almost no one spoke only one language. While one's mother tongue was always primary, the wide mix of languages and dialects used for commercial or governmental purposes forced most people to speak no less than two languages. Everyone was a neighbor to any number of different ethnic groups. An example today would be Europe where citizens, crowded into a small region, have found it necessary to learn two or more neighboring tongues.

3) *It was a multiracial world.* Race, in a classic sense, speaks of physical characteristics in a group which breed true in each generation. Middle Eastern Semites — Hebrews, Arabs, Chaldeans, Arameans and their kin — are at the central core of the Bible's story. But non-Semitic nations bearing different physical features and shades are prominent in the Scriptures as well. Among them the olive-toned Egyptians, Persians, Anatolians, Macedonians, Italians, Greeks, Ethiopians, and other Africans. Each had their own distinct features. Moses' wife was very dark, perhaps black, as was the maiden described in the Song of Solomon. Racial mixing was not unusual.

4) *It was also a multireligious world.* Religious practices of many types are recorded in the Scriptures. Polytheistic cults were the majority with innumerable gods and goddesses made of bronze or trees (see Isa. 44:6-20), spirits, animals, constellations, the glories of the night sky, and phallic symbols. God-forms seem endless to the reader of ancient Greek and Middle Eastern history and mythology. They are readily reflected in the records of the Canaanites and competing nations. It is out of this pagan world, from Noah and Abraham on, that God called His people to follow Him alone, the only true God.

Six Principles of Cross-Cultural Ministry

1) *The Bible shows no ethnically pure "correct" culture.* A very complex cultural milieu comprised the world at the hour Jesus died. It was a multicultural and not an ethnically pure earth, and it should be no surprise that it is to this kind of world to which He sends His servants today. We should consider it the normal and expected thing to cross into other cultures for Christ.

2) *As in the Bible, so today we should accept people from every culture and ethnic group as our neighbors and treat them with mutual respect and dignity.* The

Scripture's example ought to serve as an encouragement for Christians to learn at least one language other than their own for the advancement of the Gospel. Our world is even smaller than the New Testament's as technology brings other lands to us in days, hours, or minutes rather than years, months, or weeks.

3) The Old Testament Scripture is replete with examples of a transcultural Gospel. Several of the Hebrew prophets—Joseph, Elijah, Daniel, Jonah, and Isaiah—are some of the Bible's finer examples of intercultural messengers. David and Isaiah, in particular, provide two notable examples of Old Testament intercultural advocates. David requests the Lord to bless the testimony of His people so that the whole world would come to know Him (Ps. 67). Isaiah says that God invites all nations of the entire multicultural world to come to Him so that He may save them (Isa. 45:22).

4) The New Testament does not show one culture to be the correct one and all others wrong. There was no perfect cultural example on earth. All have the potential for good and bad. The Bible is one endless cross-cultural story in which wherever the reader opens other cultures are encountered. For example, Jesus did this when He confronted cross-culturally the Samaritan woman about her sin and how inadequate her cultural attitudes were apart from God's truth. Jesus never equated Israel's culture as the equivalent of divine truth (often the opposite) nor did the apostles, or New Testament writers. Yet it is such a great temptation for Christians to equate their way of doing and thinking as being right. That will not be until Christ sets His kingdom up on earth. Christians tend to theologize their cultures into a deception that theirs is the most "biblical." Only careful attention to what human culture is can reverse that shortsightedness.

5) The true message of Christianity is a person, Jesus Christ. It is He who transcends all ethnicities and transforms any cultures from within: not by our tampering with structural forms from without, but by transforming mankind from within. Jesus Christ is supracultural, greater than any culture and above all human mores and values. His incarnation implies that God is incarnate through individuals in the cultural mosaics of redeemed humanity.

6) To cross into other cultures is the expected norm for God's people, not the exception. Love is felt in all languages and God expects to love the world through His church. For twenty-first century believers to meet the needs of others we must learn to appreciate the richness of other societies and learn culturally acceptable ways of putting God's timeless truth into time-bound cultural forms. We must become, in a sense, a new translation of the Scriptures.

Culture Distance

In his useful scale of cultural distance, Ralph Winter[1] shows degrees of culture-remoteness in evangelism. Using the Jerusalem, Judea, Samaria and the ends of the earth of Acts 1:8, he categorizes evangelism by the cultural distance between the evangelist and the evangelized. He calls evangelism among persons of the same culture group E-1, working with those who share the same language and traditions like reaching Jerusalem and Judea. If an American leads a neighbor of the same background to Christ, that is E-1. No culture barrier is crossed.

The second level of evangelism (E-2) refers to a setting where people of a somewhat similar but different culture from one's own are reached with the Gospel. This is similar to reaching Samaria as depicted in the Book of Acts. A contemporary example would be the ministry of evangelism with international students in North American universities, for whom English is not their first language but who know it well enough to permit the basic transmission of the Gospel. A second example is white Americans seeking to evangelize African-Americans where similar but subtle differences and prejudices may exist. A third would be people of related languages whom are close enough to communicate somewhat, but not at a profound level (e.g., Swedes communicating with Danes, close but not exactly the same).

The most remote cultural distance, Winter indicates, calls for E-3 evangelism. This form will be needed to reach the peoples "of the ends of the earth." Mutual unintelligibility of languages makes it necessary for cross-cultural workers to learn a new tongue and culture in order to speak, evangelize, and teach freely. This linguist missionary must attempt to attain sufficient fluency to allow the Gospel to be sown in the soil of the native mind so it will sprout native faith in the hearts of the people.

Elements to be Learned for Effective Cross-Cultural Education

To teach persons of a different culture effectively requires the teacher to involve himself/herself in detailed and exhaustive study in another culture. This will cause a paradigm shift and enable the teacher to utilize newly understood traditions, values, and patterns using appropriate and basic terms. Though not a simple matter, the result is rewarding.

Before we can discern patterns in other cultures, we must come to terms with those in our own. The only way you "see" your culture is to compare it with another. All cultures vary in subtle and unfamiliar ways making little immediate sense to the observer. For example, the Asian appears indecisive to the highly organized, logical thinker from the West. When we compare Western and Eastern mind-sets, we find ourselves with a maximum of cultural separation on many issues. By contrast, differences between Mennonites and Baptists may appear amazingly small. So that we may analyze our own culture and begin the pathway of learning how to understand others, we must survey the networking major elements that have a direct influence on the meanings we attach to our patterns. They are beliefs, values, attitudes, social organizations and worldviews.[2]

Beliefs

All cultures assume definite beliefs based on either: 1) direct experience, 2) beliefs gained from inference, or 3) on the basis of authorities. Direct experience teaches us that fire is hot and burns. Inference allows us to conjecture, perform experiments, and discover a logical world. Authority beliefs are generally passed down from one generation to another by the elders of the community. Religious beliefs are of this latter type although Christians also claim that they "work" experientially and that they are logical. In teaching persons of other culture groups one must deal wisely and respectfully with authority belief systems. Their authorities must not be belittled but treated kindly before setting them aside. You cannot help people unless you take their religious background and philosophy seriously. It's important that you present the authority of the Bible in your discussions. As we teach and witness cross-culturally we should hold high the Bible's authority and encourage its reading. As you come to know the teachings of other belief systems, show careful comparisons with what Scripture, our authority, says. Never fear that the Bible will fail you as a teacher. It is attributed to Spurgeon, the British preacher, when asked should one defend the Bible that he replied, "Defend the Bible? Would you defend a lion? No, you would let it out of its cage. You don't need to defend the Bible. Open it up and it will defend itself."

Values

1) Age. It is absolutely necessary for western Christian educators to appreciate the overwhelming importance of age in many cultures or it will be impossible to teach them successfully. Every culture defines what it finds worth living and dying for. The West values youthfulness and the East age and maturity. In the West people tend to put distance between themselves and the elderly. They are apt not to care or show respect for them and their mature wisdom as Asians do. The West's emphasis on youth has little meaning to the Orient, only in the context of age scale. To place the elderly in specialized homes away from the family would be social blasphemy in Asian and African communities.

In this, the Orient seems more biblical than we. Since age is honored among Asians, the more mature the teacher is the more effective the ministry is likely to be. The idea of a young person leading or teaching mature people is culturally out of place in most Asian and African communities. This must be taken into account by Christian educators seeking to work cross-culturally.

2) Individualism. Independence and privacy are hallmarks of Western cultures. While we in North America want to be left alone, most of the world seeks companionship. Privacy is important to us, but not in most other cultures. We also esteem doing things our own way, decided individually. Most of the world expects major decisions to be made by a group. One submits many decisions to social units, clan, extended family, or parents. Issues such as which of the children will go to school, whom one will marry, or what a man's occupation will be may be an elder's or a group's decision, not the individual's alone. Americans value competition and "coming out on top," something of little importance to Asians, Africans, and American Indians who desire group acceptance. It will do the Christian educators little good to criticize social systems of students that are different from their own. In fact, it is quite possible that they might be more biblical than we.

3) *Time.* North American Christians value punctuality and precision more than many other cultures around the world. We venerate efficiency and exactness above all else. In these things we have theologized our culture. Based upon this misconception of Scripture, we carry watches, put clocks in our cars and on our office walls, hang calendars in our rooms, and monitor our lives according to strict schedules. Nothing is to start late in Western culture. Most Christians around the world cannot find any biblical rationale for our attention to such detail. They think it an obsession that gets in the way of joyful living.

Many cultures are *event* oriented and not *time* oriented. They want events to happen when they are ready, all the while mixing with people of the community in the process. North Americans are concerned that events happen when the clock says they are supposed to. They want the day to end, or the week to pass, and their list of "things-to-do" completed. In some cultures, church services or classes start only after the people have all come. Westerners are likely to start "on time" whether everyone has come or not.

4) *Other Patterns.* We are coming to value gender equality while most of the world accepts male dominance as natural and proper. Skin color has consistently been a difficult attitude and value issue among all peoples, as people in some groups strive to overcome stubborn ethnic attitude patterns. Modesty and humility is admired by cultures who see Americans as arrogant and boastful. "The fragrant flower does not have to be announced to the world" they say, while Americans retort, "If you've got it flaunt it."[3] Unfortunately many North Americans possess a sense of superiority, a cultural baggage which weighs them down in intercultural encounters. An unlearning process is necessary for an effective ministry.

Attitudes

Attitude systems teach us to respond consistently to situations in different ways. To a Latin a bullfight may be one of life's richest experiences. In North

America our attitudes cause most of us so to cringe against the thought of bulls being tortured to death. Sushi, a raw fish delicacy, is valued in Japan and Korea. American dietary attitudes have kept this import from spreading quickly across the country, unlike Chinese, Mexican, and Italian foods which have spread rapidly throughout the hemisphere.

Thus, in teaching students from other cultures we must recognize that attitude systems will be different. Ours is not right or biblical, it is just "ours." Happy is the person who can accept that most cultures are basically noble. If we are able to plant the seed of faith in Christ in them, it will spring up as an indigenous sprout, a transcultural incarnation of the Lord Jesus will arise and not a Western transplant. That, after all, is our objective.

Social Organizations

Society determines the manner in which a culture organizes itself. The *family* is one of the most influential organizations. It will decide matters of family authority, male dominance, wife's (or wives') responsibility, child rearing, and male child preference. *Schools* are institutions which help with the responsibility for passing on and maintaining the culture, in a sense assisting or substituting for the family. Similarly, *religious institutions* possess a powerful social tool for maintaining belief systems within a culture.

Worldview

A culture's view of God or gods, the concept of being, origins, the universe, man, sin, nature, the future, and other philosophical issues are part of one's worldview. Worldviews permeate all facets of culture for they are part of our authority/belief systems. For Christian teachers one's worldview answers the most important questions of culture and thus must be addressed in our cross-cultural classroom. We must not get sidetracked and seek to change lesser cultural things today as did some early missionaries and teachers. Records show there were many well-meaning persons who confused the Gospel at times with cultural trappings. Some insisted that clothes be required for indigenous peoples in regions where clothing was neither culturally nor environmentally necessary, only decorative. Paint did that just fine! Others taught European hymns in the musical scale of the West to tribal communities rather than following indigenous expressions, using the native scales and tunes.

This is an important issue for the Christian educator. Just because a person may hold to a differing world view does not mean that such a worldview is biblically incorrect. What is needed is the ability to distinguish between biblical absolutes (e.g., personal purity, honesty, justice) and cultural standards or societal norms (e.g., dress codes, authority systems).

The Teacher's Goal in a Cross-Cultural Context

As Christian educators we should strive to communicate a biblical worldview to our students and one not wrapped in the values and views of our culture. Shirts, ties, short haircuts, and clean-shaven faces have sometimes become synonymous in peoples' minds with the Gospel, for they were imposed along with its preaching. Again, to forbid dancing to students whose culture is expressed by dance is an imposition not from the Scriptures but from one's own culture. To teach culture along with the Gospel carries the danger that students may be led into unnecessary cultural legalism. Converts are tempted to clean up outwardly and act the part expected while their hearts remain unchanged. Our goal is to convince persons of a God-oriented worldview which answers life's deepest questions, founded on the teachings of the immutable Word. We want conversions to Christ, not to our culture. As Christian educators, our objective is to inspire students from other societies to learn the Scriptures. To do this we need to learn to relate to them in a cross-cultural setting.

Summary

This chapter has laid out the challenge of what must be understood for cross-cultural learning to take place. First, we surveyed the implications of culture, an impish, elusive concept, that invisibly patterns the behavior of our lives. Second, we recognized that there is a mosaic of subcultures within the general culture. These exist in North America alongside the vastly different cultures of recent immigrants. Third, we noted lessons from a general overview of the biblical cultural scene. It was a mixed cultural world that Jesus lived in and died for, and the charge given was to go to it with the Gospel. Fourth, there are degrees of culture distance between groups which has an effect upon the way we approach others. This is particularly evident in evangelism where those differences matter in how and by whom the Gospel is presented. Fifth, we reviewed a network of ingredients around which a culture is organized. These included: beliefs, values, attitudes, social organizations, and worldviews.

The greatest transcultural language is love. Students who know that they are loved will be receptive to the message being communicated. A man speaking about his Sunday School teacher said, "First I came to love my teacher, then I came to love my teacher's God." That is the general order. In all cultural contexts love is the master teacher; this is the basic rule for all intercultural ministry.

Notes

1. Ralph Winter, "The Highest Priority: Cross-cultural Evangelism" in *Crucial Dimensions in World Evangelism*, by A. Glasser, P. Heibert, P. Wagner, and R. Winter. (1976), 105-131.

2. Larry Samovar, et al. *Understanding Intercultural Communication* (Belmont, Calif.: Wadsworth Publishing (1981), 23-54.

3. Ibid., 45.

For Further Reading

Brown, I.C. *Understanding Other Cultures.* Englewood Cliffs, N.J.: Prentice-Hall, 1965.

Glasser, A.F., Heibert, P., Wagner, P., and Winter, R. *Crucial Dimensions in World Evangelism,* South Pasadena, Calif.: William Carey Library, 1976.

Hall, E.T. *Beyond Culture.* Garden City, N.Y.: Anchor Books, 1977.

_____. *The Silent Language.* Garden City, N.Y.: Anchor Books, 1979.

Lingenfelter, S.G. and Mayers, M.K. *Ministering Cross Culturally: An Incarnational Model for Personal Relationships.* Grand Rapids: Baker Book House, 1986.

Luzbetak, L.J. *The Church and Cultures.* Rev. ed. Maryknoll, N.Y.: Orbis Books, 1989.

Mayers, M.K. *Christianity Confronts Culture: A Strategy for Cross-Cultural Evangelism.* Rev. ed. Grand Rapids: Zondervan Publishing House, 1987.

Musgrove, F. *Education and Anthropology: Other Cultures and the Teacher.* New York: John Wiley & Sons, 1981.

Nida, E.A. *Customs and Cultures.* South Pasadena, Calif.: William Carey Library, 1975.

Spindler, G.D. ed. *Education and Cultural Process.* 2nd ed. Prospect Heights, Ill.: Waveland Press, 1987.

Eight
Moral and Faith Development in Christian Education

Communication of biblical content is an indispensable goal of Christian Education. If God saw fit to provide us with an inerrant Scripture, it seems logical that one of our responsibilities is to convey knowledge of His Word and an understanding of His plan to others. But God's Word never was intended only for the sake of knowledge or understanding. As Paul says, mere "knowledge makes arrogant" (1 Cor. 8:1). Rather, God gave Scripture for a purpose that encompasses far more than information. It was intended to change lives. Paul reminds Timothy of this purpose when he says that all Scripture is "profitable for teaching, for reproof, for correction, for training in righteousness" (2 Tim. 3:16). There is a dynamic quality to God's Word that does not settle for simple knowledge. Scripture consistently points us toward personal growth.

The New Testament abounds in metaphors of growth. Some, like the botanical images of seeds and soil or vines and branches are explicit. Others, though more implicit, such as the concept of maturity, clearly suggest growth that leads to maturity. One such image is that of becoming "complete in Christ" (Col. 1:28). Such Christlikeness means to have mature perspectives in thinking, emotions, and behavior. It involves a fundamental reorientation of people that produces changes in ways of looking at life.

Clearly, maturation is a process. There can be no credible shortcuts to maturity. Maturity requires a lifetime of growth. A primary element of biblical maturity is a deepening relationship with God in Christ. There is growing commitment to follow His way. This process takes place as a believer engages in the practice of "spiritual disciplines" such as corporate worship, Bible study, prayer, and confession of sin, among others. However, these "behavioral" characteristics of maturity are only the partial picture. All too often these forms of religiosity can have mere head knowledge as their end result. In a more complete biblical sense maturity refers to completeness or wholeness. This form of spiritual maturity in Christ permeates to the core of one's being.

This chapter examines moral and faith development with this latter concept of maturity in mind. It is our belief that merely "a closer walk with Jesus," as essential as that is to spiritual growth, is not an adequate measure of true spiritual maturity. Mature spiritual adulthood is a product of reflective prayer, study of Scripture, and other experiences in which there is thoughtful, intentional application to the issues of life. While Scripture provides us with understanding of Christlike maturity, theories of moral and faith development help us perceive the process of growth to maturity. They supply markers of growth, giving us understanding of changes along the way. They help provide a picture of the kind of maturity that overtakes all aspects of a person's life.

Moral Development

Moral maturity, one dimension of biblical maturity, has been examined from a variety of perspectives. It has been studied as actions which assist someone else. Sometimes it is viewed as internalization of social norms, or as actions which are in conformity with social norms. Reasoning or decision-making has sometimes been the perspective from which moral maturity has been scrutinized. Provoking empathy or guilt or putting others' interests ahead of one's own are other ways in which this aspect of maturity has been studied.

James Rest, who has spent much of his life investigating moral development, defines morality as concern for the influence of actions on others.[1] From a biblical perspective, this is obviously only one dimension of morality. Biblical morality is also concerned with relationships with God and His lifestyle expectations. Rest identifies four components of morality. When faced with the need to make a moral choice, the first component is to *interpret the situation*. Interpretation is based on the ways in which the welfare of others is influenced by the various possible responses to a situation. Emotions such as empathy and altruism are involved at this point. Clearly, not everyone is accurate in this step. In fact, the less accurate the interpretation, the less likely it is that moral behavior will result. However, the ability to interpret situations generally develops with age.

A second component of morality is to *consider the needs of others*. Those needs are then integrated with one's own needs and with the expectations implied in the situation. What ought to be done is then determined. This aspect of morality attempts to identify the appropriate behavior in the midst of what may be conflicting demands. Solomon was faced with this moral component when he was confronted by two women both of whom professed to be the same baby's mother. One of Solomon's tasks was to attempt to resolve the competing needs of two "mothers," exert leadership appropriate for a king, and protect the well-being of the young child.

A third component is actually to *decide what to do*. It is one thing to analyze the situation, as in component two. It is another matter to make a commitment to do what needs to be done. The fourth component that follows is to *implement the commitment in action*.

Moral failure, according to Rest, is a result of failure in any one of the above four components. Failure in the area of biblical morality no doubt includes all of the above. But it begins by looking at the situation from God's perspective.

Major bodies of research or theories of moral development have been developed, each of which examines a different component of morality. Psychoanalytic theory, pioneered largely by Freud, focuses on moral feelings including guilt, shame, inferiority, etc.[2] This theory holds that powerful urges must be controlled by strong internalized values received from parents and others early in life. Psychoanalytic theory provides understanding of the first component of morality, interpreting the situation.

Social learning theory focuses on learned behavior attitudes and values.[3] It emphasizes self-control and resistance to temptation. Insights of social learning theory help us better understand the third and fourth components of morality, making a commitment to do what is right, and actually doing it. Cognitive-developmental theory directs attention to moral thinking.[4] Cognitive research has identified sequential stages of moral reasoning which are universal and not dependent on cultural contexts. The focus is on the form or structure of moral thinking. The content of morality, or specific "rights and wrongs," is not analyzed or considered. The second component of morality, analyzing the situation, is the concern of cognitive-developmental research.

Each of the three major theories (psychoanalytic, social learning, and cognitive-developmental) provides a slice of the moral behavior pie that together give us a more comprehensive view. This chapter will briefly examine the social learning and cognitive-developmental theories of moral development.

Social Learning Theories of Moral Development

Development of Prosocial Behavior

Choosing to satisfy the needs of others rather than merely of oneself is biblical. It involves a range of behaviors that have been given the title "prosocial behavior".[5] Such actions are intended to benefit others without thought of extrinsic rewards. Frequently, cost or personal sacrifice is involved. Examples of prosocial behavior include: helping, sharing, generosity, altruism, and sympathy. Four stages of prosocial behavior have been identified:

Stage 1: Hedonistic: self-pleasure is sought.

Stage 2: Stereotypic, approval-oriented: behaviors are chosen which result in adult attention and approval.

Stage 3: Empathic: able to empathize, desires to help others.

Stage 4: Internalized values and responsibilities: recognizes that internal well-being comes as a result of attending to needs of others, while inner conflict is a result of failure to do so.

Many factors influence development through the above stages of prosocial behavior. But some of the most significant are modeling, role-playing, and induction. The use of induction involves helping a person understand the consequences of actions on others.

Imitation and Modeling

Much of what may be described as moral behavior can be explained in terms of imitation. People often behave morally because of what they have observed in others. Scripture repeatedly refers to imitation of significant models as an important means of shaping one's life. Paul offered himself to the Thessalonians "as a model for you, that you might follow our example" (2 Thes. 3:9).

Social learning theorists emphasize identification and observational learning or imitation which involve patterning one's thoughts, feelings, and actions after a model.[6] Behaviors learned in these ways do not require direct reinforcement, but may be maintained through vicarious reinforcement. This form of reinforcement may come as someone sees others being reinforced for a particular behavior and is then prompted to imitate the same behavior. Actions that continue to be imitated when the model is not present are particularly stable and longlasting.

Copying the behavior of another is one of the most common forms of learning, beginning with the young child, continuing through peer influence of adolescence and into the adult years. Models which are imitated may be real or imaginary. They may involve behaviors that are sanctioned by society and those that are not. Imitation of models can be a potent influence for good or for bad.

Many social learning theorists focus on situational influences on behavior. It is their conclusion that factors influencing moral behavior vary from situation to situation. There are some situations in which they are not as strong, so moral failure is a result. From a theoretical perspective, researchers have identified what Paul noted when he said, "For the good that I wish, I do not do; but I practice the very evil that I do not wish" (Rom. 7:19). Other theorists point to the fact that internalization of external standards increases the likelihood of moral consistency. The greater degree to which an external rule is internalized, the more likely it will be acted upon. This focus is similar to that of the psalmist who said, "Thy word have I treasured in my heart, that I may not sin against Thee" (Ps. 119:11).

Cognitive Developmental Theories of Moral Development

Studies of cognitive moral development focus on development of moral reasoning. It is the conclusion of such researchers that at the root of moral behavior is first a moral decision or judgment. In some respects, cognitive-developmentalists are concerned with issues like those expressed by King Solomon who said, "For as he thinks within himself, so he is" (Prov. 23:7).

Piaget's Moral Judgment

In addition to his work on the cognitive development of the individual referred to in chapters 5 and 6, Jean Piaget is also well known for advocating stages of moral development. This schema is recorded in his classic work *The Moral Judgment of the Child.* Piaget worked out his hypothesis by watching young Swiss children establish and maintain rules of conduct while playing a game of marbles. He noticed that the younger children saw the rules of the game as not being applicable to them. Gradually, they developed internal ownership of rules. Finally, rules were seen as a result of mutual agreement and autonomous or independent conscience. Piaget described growth in moral perspective in three areas:

1) The rules of the game — how rules in games come to be accepted, and how children regard these rules.
2) Moral realism — the tendency to "regard duty and the value attaching to it as self-subsistent and independent of the mind, as imposing itself regardless of the circumstances in which the individual may find himself."[8]
3) The idea of justice — the development from "retributive justice" to "distributive justice."

The development of stages which Piaget finds in these three "areas" do not correspond, and there is no single, simple scheme of developmental stages. There is, however, an underlying developmental progression throughout childhood moral reasoning from "heteronomous" to an "autonomous" attitude or orientation.[9] A brief summarization of his stages of moral development follows:

Children begin under the moral constraint of adults, a condition Piaget described as heteronomy. At this level adult authority is unconditionally accepted and seen as infallible. It is also characterized by moral realism. Duty and rules are regarded as existing in themselves, independent of the child. This understanding of rules demands the letter of the law, not merely the spirit. It is a crude form of Pharisaism or legalism which requires exact conformity with no regard for a person's intent. Good is seen only as precise obedience. Experiences of mutual cooperation and mutual respect are necessary for development to the more mature moral perspective of autonomy. According to Piaget, autonomy is the ability to make independent moral judgments which do not require the presence of an authority figure.

Piaget studied differences between the conception of rules, or how they are understood, and the practice of rules, or how they are lived out. He found that the practice of rules develops along a pattern of four stages. The first stage is *motor* and individualistic, which occurs up to age 4. Personal desires and motor skills determine what is right and wrong to the child. Behaviors that have become ritualized by repetition tend to be considered "right." The second stage, *egocentric*, occurs during the years 4 to 7. The child receives rules from the instruction and example of others. But the child is centered in self and unable to take into consideration the perspective of others. Although the child may not know or follow rules, the child insists that the rules are being observed.

Cooperation, the third stage Piaget identified in the practice of rules, generally encompasses the years 7 or 8 through age 10. There is development toward agreement between children on a common set of rules. Still, ideas regarding rules are rather vague. Finally, between the ages of 11 and 12, *codification of rules* occurs. There is genuine cooperation in developing and identifying rules. Piaget's understanding of growth from a self-centered outlook to one which, in this final stage, takes into account the needs of others is similar to the ideal of selflessness presented in Scripture.

Three stages in the perception or consciousness of rules were identified. In the first stage, rules are not seen as coercive. They are interesting to the child, but not obligatory. The second stage finds rules viewed as inviolable. Since they come from adults they must be taken literally. Rules last forever. Any alterations are seen as trangressions. In the final stage, rules may be set and altered by mutual consent.

Piaget found that rule perception lags somewhat behind practice. An understanding of rules grows out of experiences in living the rules. Perhaps this is in part what Christ meant when He said that, "He who practices the truth comes to the light" (John 3:21). The author of Hebrews spoke in similar terms of practice which leads to the training of the senses "to discern good and evil" (Heb. 5:14).

Due to the brief nature of this chapter, a detailed explanation of each stage, substage, and subset is not possible. The reader who is interested in a more exhaustive discussion of Piaget's stages of moral reasoning is advised to read any of the suggested books regarding moral development listed at the conclusion of this chapter.

Piaget's Two Stage Theory of Moral Development

Age	Stage	Characteristics
4–7	Moral Realism	Focus is on consequences of actions. Rules are unchangeable, and being punished is the consequence of breaking a rule.
7–10	Transition	Slow transition takes place to a second stage level of reasoning.
11 +	Moral Autonomy	Child considers actions, realizes that some rules can be changed and some can even be broken. Punishment is not always automatic or inevitable.

Figure 8.1

Kohlberg's Moral Development

Lawrence Kohlberg examined moral development as changes in internal cognitive structures.[10] Morality, from this perspective, is not merely traits of personality that cause an individual to make appropriate decisions. Nor is it motives or habits learned without thought. Instead, morality is in large measure determined by structures, or patterns of thought, which guide moral decisions. Structures develop in stages from simple to complex, integrated structures. Potentially, they develop toward increasingly effective bases for moral decisions.

Differences between stage structures are primarily qualitative. This means that development to higher, more effective structures is not merely a matter of accumulating knowledge. Rather, the characteristics of thought differ at each stage. The stages are sequential; that is, their order is always the same. There is no stage skipping nor differences in sequence. Responses to moral issues depend on the characteristics of a person's structure at any given stage, rather than on knowledge of the issue. To Kohlberg, differences in perspective between individuals about appropriate responses to a moral issue may be explained primarily by differences in structure. From a biblical point of view, however, differences in thought forms may be only one explanation for perspective differences. Failure to view moral issues from God's outlook is another.

According to Kohlberg, structures are the same from person to person and from culture to culture. In that sense they are universal, but they are not innate. People do not automatically move from one stage to the next. Rather, they develop as they interact with situations, persons, and ideas.

Moral decisions at each stage include a number of factors. First, there is what the person believes is important, his or her moral value. Second is the moral language used which includes such words and phrases as "obeying" or "having duties." Finally, there are value elements, or those reasons, motivations, and attitudes on which moral decisions are made. For example, a teen is faced with an opportunity to cheat on homework. She is committed to honesty (moral value) and believes she has an obligation to obey God's Word (moral language). She may be motivated to obey out of a desire to avoid displeasing her Lord (value element or reason).

Changes in a person's cognitive structures result in changes in the value element, that is in motivations for doing what he or she chooses to do. In the lower stages, each of the above factors is incompletely understood. As development occurs to upper stages, these aspects become more fully integrated into the individual and, as a result, become more powerful.

Kohlberg makes clear distinction between structures of thought and content. While thought patterns (structures) are constant between persons, content may vary according to situation or person. For example, two individuals confronted by the same moral dilemma may have differing values on which to make a decision. One may examine the choices by referring to God's Word, while the other looks at the situation on the basis of family tradition. By isolating structures from content, Kohlberg is able to identify progressive ways in which individuals handle moral rules.

Kohlberg's stages of cognitive moral development, in general terms, involve changes that are much like those in Piaget's conception of moral growth. There is development from heteronomy to autonomy. Heteronomy is based on unilateral respect for authority such as tradition or law. There is a tendency toward making moral decisions on the basis of pragmatism. Whatever brings the best results and the least unwanted consequences is what is chosen. Autonomy involves independent moral decisions. There is reliance on intrinsic motivation to respect moral principles. Each stage in development toward autonomy makes it possible to make greater sense of reality. People are drawn toward higher stages because the next stage is more adequate for making moral decisions than the present.

Development takes place in a context that is social. Interaction with others is essential for movement to higher stages. Involved is a process known as role-taking, or the ability to see things through the eyes of others.

Gender Differences

Research directed toward male and female differences indicates that females tend to be oriented toward caring, concern, and responsibility to others within relationships. There is empathy, connection, and attachment. In contrast, males are characterized by separation and a push toward independence. Dif-

Kohlberg's Six Stages of Moral Reasoning

Stage:	Moral Decision Making Criteria:
Level 1) **Preconventional Morality** (Ages 4-10)	Children determine what is bad based on the degree of pleasant or unpleasant consequences of action.
Stage 1: Concern with obedience & punishment	Good behavior is desired in order to avoid punishment.
Stage 2: Concern with satisfying needs	Good behavior is associated with satisfying one's own needs and desires. There is little consideration for the needs of others.
Level 2) **Conventional Morality** (Ages 10-13) **Stage 3:** Desire for "good boy" or "good girl" image	Rather than obeying to avoid punishment, a child now obeys the authority figures in order to gain their approval. There is a growing awareness for the need to create and maintain rules of conduct.
Stage 4: Concern for law and order, doing one's duty, and showing respect	Unfailing devotion to authority present at this stage. Laws are made to be obeyed, and rules are not to be questioned.
Level 3) **Postconventional Morality** (Ages 13 to young adult) **Stage 5:** Concern for the legitimate rights of the individual	Moral decisions are made based upon the standards agreed upon by society. These laws are to protect one's rights and have been established by vote of the community. These rules can be changed or even broken if necessary. However, the reason for breaking these rules is critical.
Stage 6: Concern for ethical principles	The basis for moral reasoning is now personal convictions and beliefs. These beliefs are deemed of a higher nature than laws created by mankind. For example, it may be appropriate for a person to break a man-made law for a higher good such as saving a life or protecting an innocent person from harm.

Adapted from L. Kohlberg in D.A. Goslin, ed. *Handbook of Socialization Theory and Research;* Daniel L. Barlow in *Educational Psychology: The Teaching-Learning Process.*

Figure 8.2

ferences such as these led Gilligan to claim that Kohlberg's theory of autonomous reasoning about justice is male-oriented and fails to account for female distinctives of an ethic of care and concern.[11] However, Kohlberg refuted Gilligan's claim by emphasizing that his theory integrates justice reasoning and caring.[12] Subsequent research lends support to Kohlberg's claim.

Another important issue is the relationship between moral judgment and moral action. Many studies have investigated the relationship between knowledge of right, the desire to do right, and moral behavior. Little consistency has been found between these factors. Simply knowing what is right and wanting to do it are not adequate to bring about proper behavior.

Considerable evidence supports the conclusion that the higher the stage of development, the greater the degree to which an individual assumes personal responsibility for moral behavior. Similarly, persons at higher stages experience greater consistency between moral judgment and moral action than at lower stages. They are more likely to act in a morally responsible manner. Moral behavior is also more likely when there is congruence between cultural values, institutional expectations, and the individual's stage of moral judgment. Teens, for example, are more likely to follow the moral guidelines of Scripture when their peers share similar commitments to biblical principles and when reasons for such principles make sense to them according to their stage of moral reasoning.

Other Cognitive Developmental Theories

Robert Selman studied the development of interpersonal understanding, especially the ability to take the perspective of another person.[13] In making moral and ethical decisions that involve others, the skill of seeing the situation through others' eyes is important. Selman found five universal, sequential stages:

Stage 0: Egocentric perspective-taking: failure to understand that others have different feelings and thoughts.

Stage 1: Subjective perspective-taking: ability to understand that others' feelings and thoughts may be different from one's own, though limited understanding of how people affect each other.

Stage 2: Reciprocal perspective-taking: ability to put oneself in the shoes of others.

Stage 3: Mutual perspective-taking: viewing relationships as mutual sharing of understanding.

Stage 4: Societal-symbolic perspective-taking: recognition that persons are unique, that they do not always understand their own motivations and that their perspectives on each other may range from superficial to complex.

Like Kohlberg, Selman found that at the higher stages there is greater congruence between a person's ideals and their behavior toward others. The higher levels of perspective-taking allow a person to accept differences in others and likely make forgiveness easier to practice. It is less likely that grudges will be held as understanding of the viewpoints of others develops.

Applying Piaget's cognitive development theory, Jane Loevinger studied the ways in which individuals view themselves.[14] She found a sequence of seven invariant stages that parallel Kohlberg's scheme. Each stage described below represents the means by which behavior is controlled:

Stage 1: Presocial stage. Awakens to differences between self and surroundings.

Stage 2: Symbiotic-Impulsive stage. Impulsive; dominated by fear of retaliation.

Stage 3: Self-protective stage. Fears being caught; externalizes blame; opportunistic.

Stage 4: Conformist stage. Adheres to external rules; shame, guilt when rules are broken.

Stage 5: Conscientious stage. Standards are self-evaluated; guilt results from self-criticism; holds long-term goals and ideals.

Stage 6: Autonomous stage. Copes with conflicting inner needs; tolerance, in addition to characteristics of previous stage.

Stage 7: Integrated stage. Reconciles inner conflicts; puts aside that which is unattainable because of moral values, in addition to characteristics of previous stage.

The experience of empathy was found to be the most important factor in growth from stage to stage.

The Integration of Moral Development Theory and Biblical Morality

Scripture clearly views life in Christ as a process. New believers are not immediately changed into mature saints at conversion. Development is a normal process which Paul refers to as transformation (Rom 12:2). At the heart of biblical morality is developing the character traits of Christ. As Paul puts it, we are to become "conformed to the image of His Son" (Rom. 8:29).

In part, the transformation process calls for the believer to develop concern for an ethic of both justice and love. Micah describes a balance, which is achieved in the context of relationship with God, in this way: "And what does the Lord require of you but to do justice, to love kindness, and to walk humbly with your God?" (Micah 6:8) Cognitive moral development theory helps provide understanding of the process of development toward justice and love. While "justice reasoning" is one characteristic of moral maturity, Kohlberg is clear that a love ethic is also a necessary component of mature moral judgment.[15]

The pattern of growth toward maturity described in Scripture is one of development from being a "babe" in Christ to becoming an adult, or as the author of Hebrews describes it, a teacher (Heb. 5:12-13). Babes are in a dependency role, described as having "need again for someone to teach you" (Heb. 5:12). Adults, by contrast, are able to teach. The development implied in this process is similar to the moral growth described by Piaget and Kohlberg as development from heteronomy to autonomy.

Biblical patterns of growth likewise present a pattern of development from an external orientation to one that is internal, a pattern which many moral development theorists have noted. Paul, discussing the role of the Law, points out that the Law, which is primarily concerned with external practices, should lead to faith, which is an internal orientation (Gal. 3:24). Man's natural perspective is external, while the perspective of God which we are to adopt, is internal (1 Sam. 16:7).

While drawing insights from moral development theory regarding characteristics of the process of development, the Christian leader can never forget the source of moral growth and behavior. "For it is God who is at work in you, both to will and to work for His good pleasure" (Phil. 2:13).

The Application of Moral Development in Christian Education

Christian educational strategies that are effective in nurturing biblical moral development clearly must begin with a knowledge of God and His commandments (Ps. 119:9-16). Here is where we part company with Kohlberg. To Kohlberg, knowledge is not a concern of the moral educator: "Moral education is the leading of people upward, not the putting into the mind of knowledge that was not there before."[16] We would quickly disagree. But at the same time, we would agree that Christian Education should be concerned not only with what students know, but *how* they know it and what they do with it.

Beyond communicating knowledge of God's Word, Christian educators do not need to become moral development experts. To be effective in encouraging moral development does not require sophisticated understanding of theory nor an ability to identify student's moral stages. What is needed is an ability to discern student comments that are more thorough and adequate and build on them.

The use of dilemmas or hypothetical situations tend to provoke interest, dissonance, and higher levels of moral thinking. Dilemmas may be used with probing questions to stimulate development. Many biblical stories present dilemma-like situations that may be explored. Helpful dilemmas focus on what *should* be done rather than on what students themselves think they might do.

The following educational strategies (among others) likewise encourage moral development:

- Involving students in group decision-making about issues that actually arise in the group.
- Interactive teaching styles which promote active student involvement in the lesson.
- Intergenerational education which provides exposure to higher stages and to models of biblical lifestyle.
- Encouragement for taking the perspective of others (role-taking).

Faith Development

It should be obvious that morality and faith are closely related for the Christian. In fact, biblical morality is generally conceived as an outgrowth of faith. Both go hand in hand.

Evangelicals frequently talk about their faith in terms of spirituality. Although there is no term in Scripture that is explicitly the same as spirituality, the term is generally considered to refer to one's relationship with Christ.[17] This relationship serves as a catalyst for integration of all dimensions of one's being into an authentic Spirit-filled life. It can be seen that spirituality (spiritual formation) is in this way both inward and outward in its form and expression.

One aspect of spirituality is the way in which people conceptualize their faith and then act on it. Recent studies have investigated this dimension, examining the ways in which faith progressively develops toward maturity. It should be noted that although these studies have not focused on ways in which relationship with Christ deepens and becomes closer, they have studied one important aspect of growth of faith. Likewise, when faith is described as growing, it is not necessarily referring to larger doses of faith. "More faith," though essential to growth is only one factor in growth. This aspect was not examined as part of the studies described below.

Theories Regarding the Development of Faith

Faith development has been conceptualized in a variety of ways to express progress that occurs toward maturity. Each reveals a pattern of deeper understanding of faith and its implications for life.

Elkind examined the development of religious thinking of children from a Piagetian perspective.[18] He found religious thought to be global and undifferentiated from ages 5 to 7 years. To children of this first stage, people of different religions differ in hair color and other external characteristics. In the second stage, ages 7 to 9, religious identity is determined by birth and participation. Concrete behaviors define one's religion. At the third stage, from ages 10 to 14, religious identity comes from something within, rather than being defined by externals. Elkind's research called attention to development from concern for externals to a more internal outlook.

In another examination of the development of religious thought, Oser studied religious development through the use of Kohlberg-like religious dilemmas.[19] He identified five stages which parallel to some degree the stages of faith identified by Fowler (see page 129). Prior to the first stage, a child is unable to distinguish between events caused by human error and those which are the result of God's actions. The first stage, *determinism*, regards God as a unilateral, ultimate source of power whose actions are a form of rewards and punishments. Human behavior is driven by God. Stage two, *reciprocity*, views mankind's relationship with God as give and take. People do things for the purpose of securing God's favor. God becomes involved only in certain events in people's lives, which for the most part are incomprehensible.

Fritz Oser's stage three, *volunteerism*, sees events as caused by humans rather than God. Both God and man function independently of each other. Conformity to God's will and individual free will are separate issues that the person at this stage holds in tension. *Correlationalism*, the fourth stage, is a recognition that humans are dependent on God and are part of God's unknown plan. God is responsible for human actions as He weaves a plan of goodness and love. The final stage of development, *religious autonomy*, involves a kind of self-fulfillment which recognizes that God is the source of all human autonomy.

An experiential model of faith development was proposed by Westerhoff.[20] He suggested four "styles" of faith, each of which builds on the previous style in developmental fashion. In the first style, *experienced faith*, religious experiences define faith for the young child and the young Christian. In *affiliative faith*, there is a sense of belonging with others of likemindedness. *Searching faith* involves seeking new meaning that goes beyond earlier, more simple conceptions of faith. Finally, the fourth style, *owned faith*, becomes a central, vital part of one's being.

A social learning model of faith was suggested by Gillespie.[21] He identified stages of faith that are more or less chronological. The title given to each form of faith is descriptive of its nature. Gillespie called the faith of early childhood, *borrowed faith*, while middle childhood is *reflected faith*. Early adolescent faith is *personalized faith*, and that of later adolescence is *interior, established faith*. Faith experienced during young adulthood was called *reordered faith*, while middle adult faith is *reflective faith*, and that of older adulthood, *resolute faith*. It is obvious that faith does not naturally follow such a trajectory merely as a function of age. It may become hung at one stage or another.

Fowler's Faith Development Theory

One of the major recent studies of faith development is that of James Fowler.[22] Examining faith from the perspective of cognitive stages, and drawing upon the insights of Jean Piaget, Lawrence Kohlberg, and Erik Erikson, Fowler studied faith as a universal experience. Originally, Fowler did not confine his theory to the Christian faith. Rather, it was his conviction that all faith proceeds through similar structural changes, regardless of the content. Considerable research seems to support the universality of Fowler's theory, that it indeed does relate to any faith, regardless of the content of that faith. Later Fowler discussed his theory's relationship specifically with Christianity.

Fowler identified seven invariant, sequential stages through which faith develops. Each stage is qualitatively different. Faith begins with what is called *undifferentiated faith* (birth-2 years) and is an extremely simple form of faith. Here young seeds of faith are sown through experiences in which the young child develops trust in care-giving adults, and experiences hope and love, all of which are wrapped together and undifferentiated. In these early experiences, the basic characteristic of faith is trust and mutuality with parents and other significant adults.

The second stage of faith development, *Intuitive-projective faith* (2-6 years), is imagination-filled faith. Imitation is strong and is powerfully influenced by examples, attitudes, and behaviors of close adults. It is characterized by fluid thought patterns which ebb and flow with experience. There is little specific content that shapes and gives stability to faith. Imagination is a strong component of this faith stage.

The third stage, *mythical-literal faith* (7-11 years), involves an anthropomorphic view of God. It attributes human qualities to God. Goodness is seen as whatever is rewarded, while badness is whatever is punished. Beliefs and moral rules are taken literally.

The fourth of Fowler's stages of faith development is *synthetic-conventional faith* (12-22 years). This form of faith involves mutual perspective-taking between people. Faith is shaped in large measure by relationships. This characteristic leads to conformity to the expectations and judgments of others. Faith is in large measure shaped by concerns for identity. There is also hunger for a God who knows, accepts, and confirms.

The fifth faith development stage, *individuative-reflective faith* (young adulthood), involves taking greater reponsibility for one's own faith and beliefs. Faith is no longer shaped to the same degree by others. Personal ownership and responsibility have emerged. There are, however, tensions or struggles: individuality vs. faith defined by others, self-fulfillment vs. service to others, and issues of relativism vs. absolute. At this stage the individual is able to examine beliefs critically.

Conjunctive faith (middle adulthood and above) is the sixth stage. There is an ability to look at issues of faith from many perspectives simultaneously. In a sense, it is a bit like looking at a field of flowers through a microscope and a wide angle lens simultaneously. The individual scrutinizes inner inconsistencies and develops a commitment to justice toward others that transcends age and race. Keen interest in developing the faith of others emerges.

The final faith stage, *universalizing faith,* strives to live out ideals of love and justice. There is investment in spending and being spent for the good of others with little regard for self-preservation. Freedom from man-made rules, expectations, and conventions develops. A summary of Fowler's stages of faith are seen in figure 8.3.

In showing the relationship of faith development to Christianity, Fowler indicated that a person's partnership with God's Spirit is the most significant factor in the quality and progress of one's faith. He viewed faith development as a pilgrimage toward wholeness or completeness. Still, the goal is not for all to reach the final stage of faith. Instead, it is for each person to be as open to the Spirit of God as possible, within the structures of one's current stage. In this, Fowler means that faith development does not come automatically with the passing of time.

Fowler identified one particular danger in the development of faith. If an individual becomes "locked" at one of the first two stages and carries this stage through adolescence into adulthood, it will be very difficult to break loose and develop to the next higher stage. This suggests that a well-designed educational process in the first few stages is essential.

The Integration of Faith Development Theory and Biblical Faith

Scripture was not intended to provide an exhaustive analysis of the *process* of faith development. Although Scripture gives a broad outline of spiritual growth, its focus is on the goal of spiritual development. It provides understanding of the characteristics of maturity, the ideals toward which God requires that we grow. Description of the process in reaching maturity is in large measure left unsaid. It is in this latter area that faith development research helps us. Insights are gained that guide the practice of Christian Education in assisting people to grow toward maturity in Christ.

Growth is a biblical word which implies processes that God has built into persons. These processes are not automatic as they require intentional attention. Spiritual growth is growth in relationship with God in Christ. It is becoming "conformed to the image of His Son" (Rom. 8:29). It involves increasing congruence between knowledge and behavior.

It is somewhat confusing that the studies of faith referred to earlier do not use familiar biblical terms. This lack of familiarity might cause us to disregard

Fowler's Seven Stages of Faith Development

Stage:	Title:	Description:	Age:
1)	Primal (Undifferentiated)	Child learns to trust in care-giving adults. Also experiences hope and love. All of which are difficult to differentiate.	0-2 years
2)	Intuitive-Projective	Imagination filled and influenced by examples, attitudes, and also behaviors of close adults.	2-6 years
3)	Mythical-Literal	Attributes human characteristics to God. Beliefs and moral rules are taken literally.	7-11 years
4)	Synthetic-Conventional	Faith is shaped by relationships with others. It involves a level of mutual perspective-taking between people.	12-22 years
5)	Individuative-Reflective	Taking personal ownership in one's faith. Able to take a critical look at one's faith system. Several tensions develop.	Young adulthood
6)	Conjunctive	Able to examine several opposing views simultaneously. Has a keen interest in developing the faith of others.	Middle & above adulthood
7)	Universalizing	Lives out ideals of love and justice. Living one's life for higher ideals with little regard for self-preservation.	Late adulthood

Figure 8.3

their findings. Rather than reject them outright, however, it is helpful to identify aspects of these theories that contribute to our understanding of the development of biblical faith.

Scripture and research alike suggest that spiritual, or faith, development has patterns of growth. It is not haphazard. It is described in general terms of development from being a child to becoming an adult, one who is mature (Heb. 5:12–6:1). The process is not one of merely adding to the quantity of faith. It involves substantive changes in outlook toward God and life. The course of these fundamental alterations of perspective is what research helps us understand.

For example, Fowler's description of faith stages seems to add detail to the developmental process outlined in Hebrews 5 and elsewhere. Fowler describes growth from the simplistic, imaginative faith of a child to more integrated faith in which there is greater congruence between beliefs and behavior. Paul speaks in similar terms of children speaking, thinking, and reasoning like children, while adults are qualitatively different (1 Cor. 13:11). Fowler's concept of development toward wholeness or completeness resembles the biblical ideal of maturity, which likewise is a condition of wholeness.

Facilitating Faith Development

According to Fowler, it is not particularly important that Christian leaders attempt to facilitate growth through the stages of faith.[23] Primary concern should be given to proclaiming God's truths and helping them find deep root in lives. Movement through stages will come when this is done effectively.

No doubt Fowler is correct. However, the history of Christianity suggests that some intentionality needs to be given to faith development. It seems all too easy for believers to become trapped midway along the faith continuum. Unhealthy, sub-biblical Christianity is a result.

Assisting Christians to become actively engaged in thinking through the application of biblical truth to life issues and situations is one essential task of nurturing faith. Considering implications of faith for living promotes growth. This requires an environment that is nonthreatening, one in which there is safety to explore faith-life linkages. Opportunities are needed to recover from failures. Experiences of pain, suffering, and disappointment provide meaningful, powerful influences on faith development, when there is thoughtful reflection on the biblical perspective.

Meaningful fellowship among believers provides essential elements for growth in faith. Without a community of believers that is interactive, apart from multiple models and confrontation in love where needed, development is unlikely. Of particular importance is the family in which early experiences deeply affect growth in faith. Similarly, exposure to older Christians in intergenerational experiences helps provide a longing for the wisdom of mature faith.

Conclusion

Moral and faith development research help us understand the process of growth to maturity. It provides insights for educational and nurturing practices that not only add knowledge, but which also encourage a deeper level of spiritual development. There is much that church educators can learn by examining these relevant theories of moral and faith development.

Obviously, the wise Christian educator must be able to synthesize and critique theories based on man's attempt to understand human nature. The

Bible is clear about the underlying condition of man. However, these theories can provide us with a broader perspective for analyzing how people develop and mature in their moral and faith development.

Notes

1. James R. Rest, "Morality," in Paul H. Mussen, ed. *Cognitive Development*, 4th ed., vol. 3 of *Handbook of Child Psychology* (New York: John Wiley & Sons, Inc. 1983).

2. Sigmund Freud, *Introductory Lectures on Psychoanalysis*, ed. and trans. James Strachey, (New York: Norton, 1966).

3. Albert Bandura, *Social Learning Theory* (Englewood Cliffs, N.J.: Prentice-Hall, 1977); Justin Aronfreed, *Conduct and Conscience: The Socialization of Internalized Control Over Behavior* (New York: Academic Press, 1968).

4. Lawrence Kohlberg, *The Psychology of Moral Development*, vol. 2 in *Essays on Moral Development* (San Francisco: Harper & Row, 1984).

5. Paul H. Mussen and Nancy Eisenberg, *The Roots of Prosocial Behavior in Children* (New York: Cambridge University Press, 1989); Nancy Eisenberg and Janet Strayer, *Empathy and Its Development* (New York: Cambridge University Press, 1967).

6. Albert Bandura, *Social Foundations of Thought and Action: A Social Cognitive Approach* (Englewood Cliffs, N.J.: Prentice-Hall, 1986); Martin L. Hoffman, "Moral Development" in Paul Mussen, ed., *Carmichael's Manual of Child Psychology*, 3rd ed. (New York: John Wiley & Sons, Inc., 1970).

7. William K. Frankena, *Ethics*, 2nd ed. (Englewood Cliffs, N.J.: Prentice-Hall, 1973).

8. Jean Piaget, *The Moral Judgment of the Child* (New York: The Free Press, 1965), 106.

9. Douglas Graham, *Moral Learning and Development: Theory and Practice.* (London: B.T. Batsford, 1974), 202.

10. Lawrence Kohlberg et al. *Child Psychology and Childhood Education: A Cognitive Developmental View* (New York: Longman, 1987); Kohlberg, *Moral Development.* 1984.

11. Carol Gilligan, et al. eds. *Mapping the Moral Domain: A Contribution of Women's Thinking to Psychological Theory and Education* (Cambridge, Mass.: Harvard University Press, 1988); Carol Gilligan, *In a Different Voice: Psycho-*

logical Theory and Women's Development. (Cambridge, Mass.: Harvard University Press, 1982).

12. Kohlberg, *Moral Development.* 1984.

13. Robert Selman, *The Growth of Interpersonal Understanding: Clinical and Developmental Analyses* (New York: Academic Press, 1980).

14. Jane Loevinger, *Ego Development* (San Francisco: Jossey-Bass, 1976).

15. Kohlberg, *Moral Development.*

16. Lawrence Kohlberg, *The Philosophy of Moral Development*, vol. 1 in *Essays on Moral Development* (New York: Harper & Row, 1981), 30.

17. T.R. Albin, "Spirituality," in Sinclair B. Ferguson, David F. Wright, and J.I. Packer, eds., *New Dictionary of Theology* (Downers Grove, Ill.: InterVarsity Press, 1988), 657.

18. David Elkind, *The Child And Society: Essays in Applied Child Development.* (New York: Oxford University Press, 1979).

19. Fritz Oser, "Religious Dilemmas: The Development of Religious Judgment," in Carol G. Harding, *Moral Dilemmas* (Chicago: Precedent Publishing, 1985).

20. John Westerhoff, *Will Our Children Have Faith?* (New York: Seabury Press, 1976).

21. V. Bailey Gillespie, *The Experience of Faith* (Birmingham, Ala.: Religious Education Press, 1988).

22. James W. Fowler, *Stages of Faith: The Psychology of Human Development and the Quest for Meaning.* (San Francisco: Harper & Row, Publishers, 1982); James W. Fowler, *Becoming Adult, Becoming Christian: Adult Development and Christian Faith.* (San Francisco: Harper & Row, Publishers, 1984); James W. Fowler, *Faith Development and Pastoral Care* (Philadelphia: Fortress Press, 1987).

23. Fowler, *Faith Development.*

PART TWO.
Christian Education Ministries Across the Lifespan

Nine
The Christian Education of Children

Designing a ministry to meet the needs of children in the local church brings to mind pictures of crayons, clay, and visualized Bible stories. Sunday School has been the church's traditional vehicle for training children in biblical truth. However, Sunday School, and more broadly, children's ministry programming, is undergoing an identity challenge.

Sunday School was created in the late 1700s as an attempt to meet the basic educational needs of poor and illiterate city children. During the 1800s it grew more evangelistic in its emphasis and extended beyond the poor to include children from the middle and upper class strata. It became tied to the established church and a regular part of its programming. While continuing to espouse evangelistic goals, its primary purpose increasingly focused on the nurture and training of the children of church members.[1] Its strength as an institution was its connection to the values of the traditional family, stability, and the predictable pace of small town living. As the year 2,000 approaches, these values are disappearing.

Figure 9.1 on page 138 illustrates some of the changes that have shaped the family which have a particular impact on the children in the home.[2]

The shifting needs of children are becoming the focus of both the secular and Christian press. Books and articles are reflecting a society increasingly concerned for its children and their future. In October 1990, the United Nations called leaders together for the first World Summit for Children.

Even as world leaders have met, the church too is responding. Sunday School is undergoing examination and redesign to more adequately meet the needs of children today. Children's ministry is expanding to offer innovative programming approaches which take into consideration current trends without sacrificing unchanging biblical truth.

The Changing American Family

☞ Sixty percent of recent first marriages are likely to end in separation or divorce.

☞ Nearly 25 percent of children today live in single-parent families compared to 9 percent in 1960.

☞ Only about half of the children in single-parent families will eventually live in a remarried two-parent family.

☞ Only 40 percent to 50 percent of all children will grow up in a traditional two-parent family.

☞ Fifty-six percent of children under 6 in married-couple families have mothers who work outside the home. That compares to 19 percent in 1960.

☞ Forty-two percent of children from kindergarten through third grade are left alone to care for themselves occasionally, if not regularly.

Figure 9.1

Gaining a Sociological Perspective

Before examining in greater detail several of the social and cultural influences affecting the shape of children's ministry in the church, we need to understand the developmental needs and characteristics of children. These characteristics are summarized in the tables below. In the left-hand column, physical, cognitive, social/emotional, and spiritual developmental characteristics are summarized for each major age grouping. In light of these characteristics, several ministry implications and approaches are suggested in the right-hand column.

INFANCY (birth–12 months)	
CHARACTERISTICS	MINISTRY IMPLICATIONS
• Physical needs predominate	• Childcare rooms need to be bright, cheerful, roomy, safe, and clean
• Requires adequate rest and nutrition	• Cribs, changing tables, and toys require weekly sanitation
• Needs responsive adults to attend to his/her cries	• Utilize quiet background music
• Active sensory systems—learns through touch, taste, attracted to color and movement	• Staffing should be sufficient to provide prompt attention to child's needs
• Progresses from rolling over to sitting up, crawling, and standing up	• Infants can sense care that is gentle, consistent, and loving and will feel the church to be a safe and welcoming environment
	• Ministry to infants is also potential ministry to new parents

TODDLER (13–24 Months)

CHARACTERISTICS	MINISTRY IMPLICATIONS
Physical:	
● Rapid growth	● Provide both cribs and adequate carpeted floor space
● Able to grasp and hold objects	● Large, colorful toys with rounded edges and no loose parts
● Small-motor control not consistent	● Low shelf space for storage at a height toddlers can reach
● Beginning to walk	● Weekly sanitation of toys
Cognitive:	
● Language growth—imitation of adult sounds and words	● Address the child with simple statements
● Five to ten word vocabulary	● Simple, one or two sentence Bible truth statements
● Able to understand simple commands	● Use of Bible story pictures
● Enjoys repetition	● Clapping, finger movement, and simple songs about how Jesus and God love him/her and about creation
● Attentive to stimulation which is novel, surprising, puzzling, and curious	● Utilization of the "teachable moment," natural conversation about God and Jesus as part of their "play," as opposed to extended teaching time
● Short attention span	
Social/Emotional:	
● Form attachment to primary caregivers	● Gentle, calm, and patient teachers will calm the frustrated toddler
● Conscious of adult presence	● Appreciates familiar routine, caregivers, and room environment
● Displays wide and unstable range of emotions	● Feel that church is a safe and happy place to visit
● Distinguishing between "you" and "me"	
Spiritual:	
● Parents and other caregivers are the toddlers' first impression and image of God	● Caregivers in the church who accept responsibility to minister to toddlers as an opportunity to do more than fulfill a "baby-sitting" request

TWOS AND THREES

CHARACTERISTICS	MINISTRY IMPLICATIONS
Physical: • Large muscle control — walking, climbing, running, and jumping • Constant movement • Fine motor skills developing, though not fully coordinated • Limited endurance • Working on toilet training	• Rooms with lots of open space • Toys which encourage use of large muscles (blocks, slides, balls, etc.) • Offer a choice of activities at any given time • Craft supplies tailored to fit — jumbo crayons, large pieces of paper, puzzles with minimal pieces, long-handled paintbrushes with wide bristles and paint smocks, paste rather than glue • Utilize interest centers for most of the session's activities • Provide opportunity for both active and quiet play • Sufficient staff to be alert to the individual needs of the children • Provide healthy, natural snacks in small amounts (fresh fruit, crackers, juices, etc.)
Cognitive: • Time-space world is expanding, though still limited • Elementary reasoning ability • Learns through the senses; loves to explore; highly curious • Short interest span — two–three minutes • Elementary reasoning ability • Vocabulary increasing at a rate beyond comprehension level — enjoy talking. • Loves repetition • Enjoys imitation	• Expect brief participation in activities • Use simple words from the child's limited vocabulary rather than questions to communicate directions • Give one direction at a time • Provide much opportunity for hands-on learning and exploration • Use objects, pictures, and other visual aids to tell simple Bible stories • Children need actively to participate in the Bible stories being told — use movement, songs, rhymes, playacting
Social/Emotional: • Parallel play — playing alongside the other children, but little interaction with them	• Provide opportunities for the children to play alongside and with each other; encourage and demonstrate "taking turns"

• Likes to do things without the help of others	• Learn and use the child's name
• Sense of self and his/her uniqueness	• Attend to the child when he/she is attempting to share personal information
• Sensitive to adult feelings and attitudes	• Provide materials and experiences in which the child can find success
• Desire close physical contact from caregivers in their environment	• Avoid shaming the child
	• Allow child to work at his/her own pace
	• Demonstrate appropriate love and affection — hugs, cuddling, holding on lap while reading

Spiritual: • God loves me, takes care of me, and is with me at all times	• Twos and threes enjoy hearing Bible stories and learning simple Bible words
• God made me, my family, the world and all that I can see and touch	• Lead them in simple prayers to God where they tell Him they love Him
• Jesus is my friend and God's Son	• Teach and sing happy songs about and to Jesus
• Jesus was born as a baby and grew up to be a man who did good and kind things	• Help these children practice simple ways to obey what they hear or read from God's Book
• The Bible is a special book which tells me stories about God and Jesus	
• Prayer means that I am talking to God	
• Twos and threes are beginning to distinguish between right and wrong	

KINDERGARTEN (FOURS AND FIVES)

CHARACTERISTICS	MINISTRY IMPLICATIONS
Physical: • Rapid growth with constant physical activity	• Chairs and tables should fit the body size of the four- and five-year-old
• Developing muscles require exercise	• Provide room to move about
• Beginning to gain control over small muscle movement	• Offer activities which utilize both large and small muscles
• Great variation in rate of growth among children	• Gaining in ability to use more sophisticated toys and art materials (however, do not expect neatness and perfection!)
• Play is becoming more purposeful and directed	

Cognitive:
- Eager to learn and curious

- Asks many questions
- Vocabulary far exceeds their comprehension

- Symbolic function appears—able to put thoughts and ideas into words
- Thinking is concrete and not logical

- Egocentric

- Think from particular to particular, unable to generalize

- Enjoy using imaginative and imitative play

- Primary learning mode is through personal exploration—provide many opportunities for firsthand taste, touch, sight, and smell

- Fours and fives love to hear Bible stories
- Constantly review and check for accurate understanding of verses and Bible stories being used
- Make simple, concrete application points

- Avoid using symbolism and figures of speech—words and phrases should mean exactly what the words say
- Provide concrete pictures and objects of subjects discussed
- Rule learning, for classroom management purposes, is difficult, but can be encouraged with consistency and patience

Social/Emotional:
- Tend to be loving and expressive
- Enjoy opportunity to initiate activity on their own

- Beginning to play in groups with other children
- Fears become more prominent

- Self-centered
- Testing limits
- Gender role socialization is occurring

- Praise the child's efforts
- Need opportunities to play and learn in groups—watch for teachable moments to aid the child in learning to share and work with others
- Allow child to express fears, do not deny their validity
- Children need the security of consistent discipline and behavior guidelines. Look for chances to reinforce and praise the desirable behaviors
- Staff with both men and women

Spiritual:
- God created the world and me

- God is good, powerful, loving, and always with me

- Help the child in choosing and doing simple activities which show his/her love for God
- Practice being kind, sharing, taking turns, saying "please/thank you" during class

• God cares for me and helps me to do right things	• Planned and spontaneous simple worship experiences
• God loves me even when I do wrong things; He will forgive me	• Talk to God in short prayers of thanks and talk to God about matters of concern to him/her
• Jesus is God's Son	• Sing songs which tell about Jesus and God
• Jesus is my friend	• Bring friends to church with him/her
• Jesus died on the cross, arose from the dead and now lives in Heaven with God	• Able to repeat the Bible stories to others
• I can learn about God and Jesus in God's Word—the Bible	• Information should be accurate and truthful

PRIMARY (SIX- AND SEVEN-YEAR-OLDS)

CHARACTERISTICS	MINISTRY IMPLICATIONS
Physical:	
• Increased small muscle coordination, though clumsy at times	• Able to participate in activities using such skills as printing and cutting
• Slower growth period; girls tend to be ahead of boys	• Provide opportunity to change activities and pace often
• Constant movement—need to wiggle	• Provide for physical movement about the room and from activity to activity
• Likes to make things	• Enact Bible stories
	• Create projects relevant to concrete aspects of Bible stories
Cognitive:	
• Eager to learn	• Listen and respond to their questions
• Ask a lot of questions	• Avoid symbolism in telling Bible stories and Bible concepts
• Still limited in time-space concepts	• Avoid object lessons
• Much variation in reading skills	• Use visual illustrations to support Bible story
• Tend to focus on only one or two details of a story or experience at a time	• Plan for active Bible learning involvement
• Attention span limited—seven–ten minutes	• Avoid dependence on a child's ability to read when utilizing printed curriculum materials
• Literal thought processes	• Emphasize one main point—one idea at a time
• Able to use simple categories	• Teach the Bible as a book of true stories, not as a story which might be mistaken for one more fairy tale or fantasy adventure

Social/Emotional:

- Need for adult approval

- Sensitive to criticism

- Testing ability to be independent
- Awkward in knowing how to get along with others
- Beginning to pair up with "best friends"
- Competitive with siblings
- Positive attitudes toward school and church
- Moodiness

- Communicate care to each individual child
- Help children in accepting each other and practicing acts of kindness
- Facilitate group activities
- Need time for solitary activities

Spiritual:

- Creation story

- Stories of Bible people and how they obeyed God and why we should also
- How to worship God

- Jesus is God's Son and my friend and He teaches me how I should live
- Expand on the events in Jesus' life and ministry
- The Bible has two main divisions. It also has different books and chapters and verses
- I can respond in love, worship, and obedience to God
- Desire to live like Jesus did
- Beginning to understand the emotions in Scripture

- First- and second- graders are now able to begin to use their Bibles in simple fashion — looking up a verse and reading it
- Emphasize the truth of the Bible stories

- Provide opportunity for them to experience as much of the Bible story as possible
- Lead them in worship and celebrative experiences
- Praying to God with others

MIDDLER (EIGHT- AND NINE-YEAR-OLDS)

CHARACTERISTICS	MINISTRY IMPLICATIONS

Physical:
- Active use of developing large and small muscle coordination
- Increasing in strength

- Attempt mastery of basic skills

- Provide opportunity for children to work at tasks with little assistance
- Focus on participation and trying one's best, rather than on winning
- Praise children for their efforts at attempting new skills

• Enjoy team sports and other athletic activities • Impulsive in their active pursuits	• Design out-of-class experiences for children to play together • Facilitate activities which require following game rules • Help children learn appropriately to handle the property of others • Challenge children to create projects on their own which illustrate Bible stories and personalities being studied

Cognitive: • Continued eagerness to learn • Growing in ability to understand the viewpoint of others • Concerned with the "why" of events • Time-space concept expanding beyond the here and now • Continued development of writing and language skills • Academic achievement becoming important • Able to comprehend more of the "whole" picture • Highly creative and inventive • Highly curious • Memorization comes easily • Refinement of right/wrong concepts	• Greater use of the Bible in learning activities — able to locate Scripture passages • Beginning to grasp some of the chronological sequencing of Bible events and simple Bible geography — use concrete means to discuss these time-space concepts (e.g., maps, time lines) • Enjoys discussing Bible topics, personalities, and stories • Able to memorize books of the Bible and verses/passages. Comprehension should be checked as memory skills exceed ability to understand all of the words and concepts. Help children to verbalize and practice practical application of biblical truth. • Provide for a variety of Bible learning activities which utilize writing, crafts, drama, music • Able to learn new games and songs at an increased pace

Social/Emotional: • Primary involvement with peer group of same-sex friends • Group influence is strong • More critical in choice of friends • Sensitive to criticism and ridicule	• Allow children to work in same-sex groups if desired • Enjoy camping and "club-type" activities • Facilitate social activities • Provide opportunities to assume responsibilities within the learning environment

• Generally outgoing and self-confident	• Create options from which children can choose learning activities
• Competitive attitudes developing	• Provide a wide assortment of varied and unique learning experiences
• Sensitive to fair play	• Workers with this age-group will become models of what acceptable and Christlike behavior looks like
• Attentive to adult actions and behaviors	• Capitalize on stories of Bible heroes and strong personalities
• Growing in awareness of sex-appropriate behaviors	• Introduce children to more recent Christian "heroes"—include both male and female personalities
• Beginning to separate from family; able to participate in activities apart from the family	• Be transparent with children in the expression and experience of normal human feelings. Give them permission to talk about their feelings. Point out the feelings of fear, guilt, anger, etc. exhibited by biblical personalities.
• Developing a sense of humor	• Turn current events and social issues into possible curriculum emphases. Explore what the Bible says about related topics. Avoid abstract discussions.
• Experiencing range of emotions—fear, guilt, anger, etc.	
• Awareness of current social issues, though not emotionally mature enough to handle all the implications	

Spiritual: • Continued expansion into greater detail of basic concepts studied earlier	• Plan activities to demonstrate God's love and kindness to others
• God is all-wise, all-powerful, all-knowing, and always loving	• Facilitate participation in mission involvements and support activities
• God hears my prayers and answers them	• Provide opportunity to interact with people of other races, nationalities, and social status
• Sin is when I am disrespectful and disobedient	• Design means for children to become more active members of their local church and its ministries
• Jesus died for my sin. When I ask for forgiveness, God will forgive me	• Encourage and help children to begin reading the Bible and praying on their own at home
• Awareness and understanding of need for salvation	• Provide opportunity for children to give financially to needy projects. Include visual aids of how their money will help.
• Awareness of need for God's daily care and help	• Be prepared to talk with interested children on an individual basis about their need for salvation

JUNIOR (TEN- AND ELEVEN-YEAR-OLDS)

CHARACTERISTICS	MINISTRY IMPLICATIONS
Physical:	
• Rapid physical growth	• Structure active learning activities
• Becoming increasingly well adapted to his/her body	• Challenge this age-group with projects requiring greater concentration, inventiveness, and fine motor skills
• Fine motor coordination developed	• Be sensitive to the child who is feeling awkward about his/her appearance
• Boys moving ahead of girls in strength and endurance	• Discuss with parents the possibility of designing a unit on sexuality and the pre-adolescent from a biblical perspective
• Girls often taller and heavier than the boys	
• Tremendous energy and activity	
• Increased appetite	
• Increasing concern and curiosity about sex (especially among girls)	
Cognitive:	
• Becoming rational, logical, and reasonable	• Require tasks suitable to their ability level—they fear failure and despise tasks which seem "childish" to them
• Development of classification, conservation, and reversibility in thought	• Beginning to understand the person and work of the Holy Spirit as Someone who helps and guides the Christian
• Thinking and fantasizing about the future—considering vocational options	• Able to understand the basics about baptism and the Lord's Supper
• Curious, questioning, and challenging	• God's Word is inspired, true, and available for personal advice about daily living
• Prefers material that can be learned easily	• Lay foundation for teaching evidence of biblical creation
• Concrete in understanding, though may "parrot" concepts which sound abstract	• Teach children how to use Bible aids like concordances, encyclopedias, and dictionaries
	• Encourage memorization of Scripture, but continue to check for concrete understanding and practical application
	• Provide opportunity for children to write and create their own response to application of Bible stories and concepts
Social/Emotional:	
• Powerful peer group influence replaces adult influence	• Continue to provide group learning activities
• Eager to "fit in" with peers	• Facilitate time to be with same sex peers—perhaps in out-of-class settings

• Fairly stable emotionally; occasional outbursts — becomes increasingly irritable as puberty approaches	• Be alert for opportunities to engage in conversations with children as communication with adults decreases
• Enjoys organized group activities	• Avoid judgmental attitudes in interacting with this age group
• Working at self-identification and demanding independence	• Become familiar with their social culture — discover what TV programs and games are of value to them
• Desirous of making own choices	• Adult guidance should be of the low profile variety
• Challenged by basic moral questions	• Involve fifth- and sixth- graders in developing creative service projects
• May demonstrate the beginnings of conflicts with parents	• Utilize Bible stories of people "on the move"
• Beginning to challenge authority and becoming critical of adults	• Bring current topics and issues into the curriculum at a level they can deal with — drugs, alcohol, sex, divorce, abuse, violence, war, etc.
• Hero worship is strong — often choosing heroes from the entertainment and sports industry	• Facilitate development of "their own" group identity within the church — their own club, group, room, etc.
• Enjoys competition	

Spiritual:	
• Shares naturally about God with friends	• Encourage them to bring friends to "fun" activities
• Increased sense of responsibility toward church activities and feeling of belonging to the local church	• Able to read and study Bible at home
• Deepening feelings of love for God	• Pray regularly
• Acceptance of Jesus as personal Savior	• Offer Christian reading material appealing to their interests
• Able to seek God's guidance in decision-making	• Facilitate opportunity to plan and lead both social and Bible learning activities for the rest of the group
• Critical of lifestyle discrepancies they may notice in the lives of family members and/or other Christians	• Recruit couples and singles to work with this age-group
	• Discipleship and relational emphasis

Figure 9.2

In addition to the general developmental characteristics listed in the charts above, current social and cultural influences also need to be considered. These trends cannot be ignored if churches desire to design an effective and meaningful ministry to children of the nineties. Five of these trends are discussed in the following section.

Societal Trends

Divorce: As the rate of divorce rises, the number of children who come from divorced and single parent homes also increases. This often results in sporadic attendance patterns for church activities and may be one of several factors leading to possible behavior problems in these children. Some children whose home and family life is in turmoil may experience depression and appear withdrawn during ministry events.[3]

Ministry Application: 1) Make adjustments in the curriculum to aim for a self-contained lesson each week. 2) Recruit adult staff committed to consistency. If the staff turnover is as sporadic as the children's, few significant relationships will be developed. 3) Do not immediately assume problem behavior is rebellion—be alert to explanations which have deeper emotional roots.

Abuse: Reported cases of violence in the home have increased and Christian homes are not immune from the statistics. Children in our ministries are coming with physical and psychological wounds. Often, abused children have difficulty understanding God as a loving father. They may have a hard time concentrating on the activities and may resist even healthy and appropriate expressions of intimacy and affection expressed by adult staff.[4]

Ministry Application: 1) Train ministry staff to identify possible symptoms of abuse and proper channels of reporting suspected abuse. 2) Screen ministry staff to insure a safe environment for children who are being attended by these staff under the auspices of the church. 3) Teach the whole counsel of God, which includes a Jesus who was abused and hurt and expressed His pain and sought comfort and support from others.

Stress: American children are beginning to show physical and emotional signs of stress-related problems. The source of stress can be due to divorce, abuse, family financial struggles, being pushed to perform, and being pressured to grow up too fast too soon, known as the hurried child syndrome.[5]

Ministry Application: 1) Examine your children's ministry for possible factors which add to a child's already stressful life. 2) Ask, "What performance expectations do we consciously or unconsciously place on our children?" 3) Include in your curriculum the Bible stories of people who failed or who needed "time out," or who did not quite perform up to everyone's expectations. 4) Children need at least one caring, patient, and accepting adult in their life, hopefully within the sphere of their church experience, who has time to listen to them and attend to them individually.

Women in the Work Force: More and more women are choosing to enter the work force in both part-time and full-time capacities while their children are still young. The reasons are varied including single-parent homes, family financial needs, and personal vocational goals. As a result, more young children are being raised by caretakers other than their own parents. Parents are often tired and stressed from managing both home and job responsibilities, and both quality and quantity time between parents and children is diminishing.[6]

Ministry Application: 1) Churches need to consider the strengths and weaknesses of providing on-site day care for employees and parishioners. 2) The traditional pool of volunteer workers found in stay-at-home mothers is decreasing. Alternative staffing measures are requiring innovative approaches. One emerging pool is the growing population of older adults. 3) More than ever, children are needing relational approaches in ministry.

Reluctance to Make Commitments: In a constantly changing society with uncertainty at a high level, people are unwilling to make open-ended or long term commitments. There is a resistance to "joining" causes or organizations, including the church. Children may be taken by their parents to different churches or no church at all on any given Sunday.[7]

Ministry Application: 1) Obtaining long-term service commitments from ministry personnel may be difficult. Team teaching and rotation schedules are possible options. However, if staff rotation is on a short-term basis, children will remain strangers to children's workers. 2) Adjustments may be required in working with curriculum materials which build upon concepts taught from week to week. 3) Active and accurate follow-up and contact procedures need to be implemented.

Identification of Relevant Needs

Of all the age-group ministries which exist within the church, children's ministry is one which depends heavily on external support structures. Children are unable to lead and direct a ministry alone. Therefore, in identifying needs relevant to children's ministry it is important not only to discuss the developmental needs of children, but also to consider key issues in designing the infrastructure which will support the ministry.

Philosophical Issues

Referring to the early childhood years of Jesus, Luke records, "And the Child continued to grow and become strong, increasing in wisdom; and the grace of God was upon Him" (Luke 2:40). Of His later childhood years Luke reports, "And Jesus kept increasing in wisdom and stature, and in favor with God and men" (Luke 2:52). An effective and holistic ministry to children will include attention to the same developmental areas as were important in the development of the childhood life of Christ. These four areas are listed in the table below. Alongside each area is a list of suggested questions to consider as you work together with your leadership, seeking God's wisdom in laying the philosophical foundations for your children's ministry.

DEVELOPMENTAL AREA	QUESTIONS
Wisdom (Cognitive)	**Curriculum Questions** 1. What do we want to teach? 2. Which curriculum should we use? 3. Should we write our own? **Methodology Questions** 1. How best do our children learn? 2. How can we facilitate an effective and stimulating learning experience?
Stature (Physical & Emotional)	**Organization Questions** 1. How can we most effectively group our children, considering their age-level and the number of available ministry personnel? 2. What type of support staff might we want to recruit to aid the teaching and leading personnel? 3. What precautionary steps are we taking to safeguard our children from any chance of sexual abuse within the children's ministry of our church? **Personal Ministry Questions** 1. As an extention of our ministry to children, how are we equipping parents to more effectively minister to them at home? 2. How are we preparing ourselves to meet the special needs of some children in our ministry (the abused, disabled, or children of single parents)? **Facility Questions** 1. Are our facilities equipped to handle the varying physical needs of children at each of their developmental age levels? 2. Is the space adequate to accommodate the movement needs of children? 3. How have we made provision for safety and sanitation needs? 4. What additional equipment might we want to purchase to make our children's rooms attractive, inviting and appealing?
Favor with God (Spiritual)	**Foundation Questions** 1. What biblical basis do we have for devoting time and resources to a ministry to children? (Consider a study of the following: Gen. 1:26-27; Deut. 6:4-9; Ps. 78, 139; Prov. 4:1-4, 22:6; Matt. 11:16-17, 18:5-6, 28:19-20; Mark 9:36-37, 10:16; Luke 11:13; Eph. 6:1, 4; Col. 3:21; 1 Tim. 3:1-4; 2 Tim. 2:2, 3:14-15; Titus 1:6.)

2. What is our mission statement?
3. What are our primary goals?
4. How is prayer undergirding the entire ministry?

Worship Questions
1. How are we leading our children in positive experiences of enjoying worship and praise?
2. How can we help our children understand the sacraments?
3. What part can the children play in the worship practices of our church?

Evangelism and Discipleship Questions
1. How have we equipped our children's ministry staff to be prepared to talk with a child about a personal decision to accept Christ as Savior?
2. How are we communicating to the church at large our vision to see our children's ministry fulfill the Great Commission (Matt. 28:19-20) among the children in our church and community?
3. How do our recruitment procedures reflect our commitment to relational ministry?

Favor with Man (Social)	**Service and Outreach Questions** 1. How are we helping our children to put their faith into practical action? 2. What steps are we taking to attract the unchurched child to Jesus Christ through our ministry? **Community Questions** 1. How are we facilitating opportunities for our children to develop meaningful relationships with each other? 2. How are we inviting people from our church body to be exposed to what is going on in the lives of the children?

Figure 9.3

Personnel Issues

In addition to exploring the philosophical questions listed above, thoughtful consideration needs to be given to the people who will be directing the implementation of the philosophy decisions. Personnel issues need to be examined in four areas:

Selection: What qualities do you feel are necessary in someone desiring to work with your children? A written job description, detailing the specifics, is used when interviewing interested candidates. Categories to include might be personal attributes (e.g., a Christian, teachable, love for children), time commitment involved, expected weekly responsibilities, and the church's commitment of support to them (e.g., training, provision of resources and materials). Also recommended is asking each potential worker to complete a personal history form which includes a list of references. Resources to help you develop this form are listed at the end of this chapter.

Recruitment: Who will do the recruiting and what strategy will your church use to recruit potential children's ministry personnel? Some churches publicize the need as they would any other need using the bulletin, or announcements. Other churches choose options which enable them to be more selective such as one-on-one contact, committee nominations, and recruitment by department heads. Many churches have chosen annual recruitment campaigns to put the vision and work of children's ministry in front of the entire congregation utilizing creative slogans accompanied by banners, T-shirts, buttons, and multimedia presentations.

Training: Children's ministry personnel will function at the level of their preparation and training for the task. New teachers should be given time and opportunity to observe and aid an experienced teacher. Basic introductory training should be provided for all incoming personnel. In addition, ongoing in-service training on a quarterly or semiannual basis is recommended. Training topics should include tips for effective use of the curriculum, classroom management issues, personal development concerns, and special need areas such as the legal responsibility to report suspected child abuse or ministering to children under stress.

Deployment: How long is the expected term of service? Will you enter into a contractual relationship with your children's ministry personnel? How does the church plan to demonstrate ongoing tangible support and affirmation for those who are committing time to minister to children? What natural and regular means of evaluating the personal satisfaction and effectiveness of your children's ministry personnel are built into your ministry?

Strategy for Ministry to Children

If your church is interested in beginning a ministry to children or strengthening an ongoing one, consider the following principles to get you started:

1) *Prayer:* Ask God to select a small group of people who are willing to commit to pray for the children's ministry on a weekly basis. These people should be kept informed of specific needs and answers to prayer. Everyone who is serving in your children's ministry needs to be aware of this prayer support group and how to contact them with their ministry concerns.

Pray together regularly as coworkers. Living in a society which values bulk and speed, it's difficult to be consistent and faithful to participate in prayer which is often intangible in its immediate results. However, people are also longing to find meaning amidst the flurry. Praying together invites those who minister to children to recover their vision and discover the depth of God's love and compassion for children.

2) *Exploration:* One of the most valuable resources available to those interested in developing a ministry to children is the experience of those who are already doing it. As a leadership team or task force group, visit other churches in your geographical area who are currently doing children's ministry. If the choices are limited, write to churches outside of your locale. Ask for samples of their programming brochures. Talk to their children's minister or a member of their leadership team. Ask questions about their infrastructure. Realize that their ministry has developed out of their local church context and church resources. Your ministry will be unique and distinct. Contact organizations dedicated to working with, and developing curriculum for, children. Read and study some of the basic handbooks available which detail answers to logistical questions in children's ministry like room proportions, creative methodology ideas, and administrative forms. (Names of organizations and reading resources are listed in the bibliography at the end of this chapter.)

3) *Survey:* Prepare a survey to elicit general information about your church family. Include such questions as: How many potential children for involvement in your ministry exist? What distance must they come to attend the church? Are they from single or two-parent homes? From the perspective of the parents and other adults, what are some of the significant issues the children in your congregation might be facing? What type of programming would be of value to your families? What time of the week would be most beneficial?

4) *Commitment to Shared Leadership and Team Teaching:* The shape of children's ministry needs to accommodate the increasingly transient nature of the population and the multiple demands placed upon families. Staffing your ministry according to a model of shared leadership and team teaching may help alleviate the frustration of weekly scrambling to fill temporary vacancies due to absences. The initial recruitment will require more effort, however, the resulting benefits to your ministry will be worth the investment. Children will sense a greater continuity in curriculum planning, and teachers will not feel isolated and abandoned.

5) *Training:* Make ongoing training and equipping of your children's ministry staff a priority at all levels. Plan to attend local training conferences. Many curriculum publishers offer training by area representatives. Purchase training materials from your local Christian bookseller. Invite professionals in to conduct on-site training workshops. Utilize members in your congregation with expertise in various areas related to ministering to children. Budget funds to ensure participation by all of your ministry personnel.

6) *Openness to Change:* If you want a children's ministry which will be a vehicle for God to use in transforming the lives of your children, be prepared to explore innovative programming ideas and creative methodologies. A marketing research company committed to the needs of the Christian community has observed that:

Today the Christian community in America is coasting, riding on the coattails of the visionaries of the past, struggling to make tired strategies fresh in a new world. Rather than creating new approaches to new problems, or anticipating responses to future conditions, we are generally attempting to fit yesterday's solutions to today's crises. To thrive, not just survive, we must clear the way for the leaders of tomorrow to take risks, to dream big, and to prepare with vigor, intelligence, and wisdom.[8]

Children's ministry will be transformational and relevant if this attitude of openness is brought into the program design stage.

Implications for Program Design

Programs designed apart from need and sheltered from a regular discipline of critical evaluation have a tendency to stagnate and take up space in a handbook. You might consider subjecting programs themselves to a contractual agreement. Contract to run a program for no more than six months to a year and then evaluate its progress in meeting stated objectives.

Experimentation is the focus in current children's ministry programming. Churches are experimenting with alternative names and times for the traditional Sunday School. Published curriculum is being stretched, shrunk, and adapted to fit the unique needs of children in a particular church body. Some churches utilize more than one curriculum publisher, other churches are venturing into writing their own curriculum. They are experimenting with programs which meet at other times of the week in lieu of, or as an extension of, Sunday morning.

One of the "hottest" areas in children's ministry programming today is the 10- and 11-year-old age group (grades 5 and 6). The preadolescent developmental characteristics of this age group set them apart from younger elementary children's programming, yet their emotional immaturity restricts a youth model. Bridging this unique age group has been a challenge for many churches across America. Some of these churches are finding a tremendous responsiveness to a club approach called "Club 56." This club program is seen as a modified youth ministry tactic.

In addition to reshaping current models of children's ministry, many churches are exploring creative outreaches to children in the community. Intentional efforts are being made to design programs which attract and appeal to the unchurched. One approach is to sponsor, or co-sponsor with community agencies, sports events like mini-Olympics, 5-K walk/runs, and other fun day and/or evening events. Pre-evangelistic in nature, there is no overtly "religious" content. The events are designed to be entertaining, however, their appeal is not limited to attracting the unchurched child. George Barna, a trends researcher commenting on life in the year 2000 says,

Church programs should include more entertainment-related activities. Because Americans perceive Christian churches to have a values filter through which all activities pass, many adults (especially those with children) will depend upon the church to provide morally acceptable forms of entertainment—something which will be increasingly difficult to find in the '90s.[9]

Summary

Most Children's Ministry Directors do not suggest that Sunday School is on the way to extinction. The needs of the children within the local church determine the design of the programming. God's transformational work is not bound by format. His Spirit moves freely within our structures, working primarily through the vehicle of available people, able to breathe life into any form.

God has always welcomed the little children. May our personnel, programs, and place of ministry also be a welcoming extension of His grace and mercy and an invitation to children to find the love of Jesus "here," in children's ministry.

Notes

1. Kenneth O. Gangel and Warren S. Benson, *Christian Education: Its History and Philosophy*. (Chicago: Moody Press, 1983).

2. *Los Angeles Times*, 12 May 1991, cover page.

3. E. Mavis Hetherington, Margaret Stanley-Hagan, and Edward R. Anderson, "Marital Transitions: A Child's Perspective," *American Psychologist*, 44: 303-12, 1989.

4. Alice Kohn, "Shattered Innocence," *Psychology Today*, February 1987, 54-63.

5. David Elkind, *The Hurried Child* (Reading, Mass.: Addison-Wesley Publishing Company, 1981).

6. N. Darnton, "Mommy vs. Mommy," *Newsweek*, June 1990, 64-67; and P. Elmer-Dewitt, "The Great Experiment," *Time*, Fall 1990, 72-75.

7. George Barna, *The Frog in the Kettle* (Ventura, Calif.: Regal Books, 1990).

8. George Barna and Barna Research Group, *America 2000: What the Trends Mean for Christianity* (Glendale, Calif.: The Barna Research Group, 1989), 56.

9. Barna, *Frog in the Kettle*, 93.

For Further Reading

Beechick, R. *Teaching Kindergartners: How to Understand and Instruct Fours and Fives.* Denver: Accent Books, 1980.

Beechick, R. *Teaching Preschoolers: It's Not Exactly Easy, But Here is How to Do It.* Denver: Accent Books, 1980.

Beechick, R. *Teaching Juniors: Both Heart and Head.* Denver: Accent Books, 1981.

Beechick, R. *Teaching Primaries: Understanding How They Think and How They Learn.* Denver: Accent Books, 1985.

Bolton, B. *How to Do Bible Learning Activities for Grades 1-6.* Ventura, Calif.: Gospel Light Publications, 1982.

Bolton, B. J., and Smith, C. T. *Creative Bible Learning for Children, Grades 1-6.* Ventura, Calif.: Regal Books, 1983.

Bolton, B., Smith, C. T., and Haystead, W. *Everything You Want to Know About Teaching Children, Grades 1-6.* Ventura, Calif.: Regal Books, 1987.

Brown, L. E. *Sunday School Standards.* Ventura, Calif.: Gospel Light Publications, 1986.

Clark, R. E., Brubaker, J., and Zuck, R. B. *Childhood Education in the Church.* Chicago: Moody Press, 1986.

Elkind, D. *A Sympathetic Understanding of the Child, Birth to Sixteen.* Boston: Allyn and Bacon, Inc., 1974.

Gibson, J., and Hance, E. *You Can Teach Juniors and Middlers.* Wheaton, Ill.: Victor Books, 1981.

Goldman, R. *Religious Thinking From Childhood to Adolescence.* New York: The Seabury Press, 1964.

Harrell, D. and Haystead, W. *Creative Bible Learning for Young Children, Birth Through 5 Years.* Glendale, Calif.: Regal Books, 1978.

Jacobsen, M. B. *What Happens When Children Grow.* Wheaton, Ill.: Victor Books, 1977.

Klein, D. *How to Do Bible Learning Activities for Ages 2-5.* Ventura, Calif.: Gospel Light Publications, 1982.

LeBar, M. E., and Riley, B. A. *You Can Teach 4s and 5s.* Wheaton, Ill.: Victor Books, 1981.

Marion, M. *Guidance of Young Children.* New York: Macmillan Publishing Co., 1991.

Mead, J. J., and Balch, G. M. *Child Abuse and the Church: A New Mission.* Costa Mesa, Calif.: HDL Publishing Co., 1987.

Richards, L. O. *Children's Ministry.* Grand Rapids: Zondervan Publishing House, 1983.

Shelly, J. A. *The Spiritual Needs of Children.* Downers Grove, Ill.: InterVarsity Press, 1982.

Wadsworth, B. J. *Piaget's Theory of Cognitive Development.* New York: Longman, Inc., 1977.

Publishers (for curriculum, teaching resources, and teacher training materials):

Accent Publications, 12100 W. Sixth Ave., Box 15337, Denver, CO 80215, 800-525-5550, (303) 988-5300 (inside Colorado)

David C. Cook Publishing, 850 N. Grove Ave., Elgin, IL 60120, 800-323-7543

Gospel Light Publications, Box 6309, Oxnard, CA 93031, 800-446-7735

Group, Box 481, Loveland, CO 80539 (upper elementary materials)

Scripture Press Publications, 1825 College Ave., Wheaton, IL 60187, 800-323-9409

Standard Publishing, 8121 Hamilton Ave., Cincinnati, OH 45231, 800-543-1301

Ten
The Christian Education of Youth

Several years ago, the catch phrase for part of the feminist movement in the United States was, "You've come a long way, baby!" A study of the history of professional youth ministry shows that the same can be said for youth work in the contemporary evangelical church.

It was not until the late 1950s that churches began to invest significant salary funds in staff positions related to youth ministry. Prior to that time, most, if not all, youth ministry was done by volunteer workers, most of whom were unqualified and poorly trained for such work. It's also true that most evangelical churches grudgingly instituted youth ministry as part of the total church program only because they feared that parachurch organizations such as Youth for Christ, Young Life, and Christian Endeavor would take young people out of local church ministries if they didn't do something to counteract the appeal of parachurch groups.

Gaining a Sociological Perspective
Youth ministry in the 1950s was often little more than an attempt to provide Christian-oriented entertainment as a means of countering the attraction and influence of secular entertainment on Christian youth:

● Christian films were produced in hopes they would be seen as a viable alternative to movies in secular movie theaters.

● High-powered recreational and social programs were developed as an alternative to school dances which were frowned upon by the church.

● Large rallies featuring famous "Christian" entertainers were held in major cities as a means of convincing youth that one could be Christian and still be popular and well-liked.

An historical perspective makes it clear that the focus of youth ministry in the 1950s was on entertainment as a means of retaining youth within the church.

The 1960s proved to be a landmark decade in our country. The local church's approach to youth ministry was greatly affected by the sociological and cultural times. Young people across our nation began to demonstrate that they cared greatly about issues related to the world in which they lived. Those who were involved in youth ministry realized that the young people in their care needed far more from their leaders than mere entertainment. In fact, many rejected entertainment as an unworthy activity for church youth ministry. Instead, they looked to their church youth leaders to provide biblical responses to issues such as war, racial discrimination, social injustice, ecological concerns, and much more. The turbulence of the 1960s taught youth ministry professionals that young people needed wise advisors whose lives were significant role models more than they needed entertainment.

Some forward thinking youth workers in the 1960s captured the activist vision of young people for ministry and missions work, taking groups of high school and college age young people to various mission fields all over the world for short-term experiences and cross-cultural involvement. This activist mentality continued to dominate the youth ministry scene well into the 1970s.

The decade of the 1980s was in some respects a most troublesome one for church youth ministry. Striving for pleasure has been the dominant theme in American culture for the last several years. No population group has been more influenced by the pleasure motif than adolescents. It is a well-documented fact that the young of this country have enormous amounts of discretionary money to spend and they have, in large measure, bought into the idea that happiness, pleasure, popularity, even fame can be bought for a price. They have further demonstrated that they are willing and able in many cases to pay that price to get what they want out of life.

Ministry to youth in the decade of the 1990s is no less challenging. The effects of decades of eroding sexual standards, growing drug dependence, and epidemic violence which is now commonplace on the high school campus have each contributed toward an adolescent culture which is harder to understand and more difficult to reach.

Perhaps one of the most disturbing aspects of this sociological commentary is the way in which adolescents have sought to get their needs met through sexual involvements. The results of this sexually promiscuous lifestyle are alarming. On a typical day in the United States:

- 7,742 teenagers become sexually active.
- 623 teenagers contract syphilis or gonorrhea.
- 2,795 teenage girls become pregnant.
- 372 teenage girls suffer a miscarriage.

- 1,106 teenage girls obtain an abortion.
- 1,295 teenage girls give birth to a child.
- 2,556 children are born out of wedlock.

Further, this bent on obtaining pleasure, wealth, popularity, and fame have led many young people to a life of violence. Again, on a typical day in the United States:

- 135,000 students bring a gun to school.
- 10 children are killed with guns.
- 211 teenagers are arrested for drug abuse.
- 437 children are arrested for drinking or drunk driving.

Some teenagers have given up hope for any meaningful satisfaction in life. Not only are their own lives so void of meaning that they no longer can cope, but the lives of those closest to them, their parents, are also falling apart. Once more, on a typical day in the United States:

- 6 teenagers commit suicide.
- 1,512 teenagers drop out of school.
- 3,288 children run away from home.
- 2,989 children see their parents divorce.[1]

Who Are Youth?

Prior to the turn of the century, children and adults were generally recognized as the only two developmental divisions in the population. A psychologist, G. S. Hall first coined the term "adolescent" to describe the years between childhood and adulthood which he believed to be too important to be seen as a mere transition period from childhood to adulthood.[2] While many definitions and descriptions of adolescence exist in contemporary literature, for the purposes of local church ministry, youth is a term which applies generally to students in junior high and high school years. Traditionally, this designation has represented students between grades seven and twelve. However, recently in some communities, junior high has come to include students between grades six and eight. Many local school boards facing declining enrollment in the junior high grades and increasing enrollment in the elementary grades have solved a school housing problem by moving sixth grade into junior high school and, where it hasn't already been done, moving ninth grade into high school. This trend is presenting some unique problems for local church youth ministry which in some churches must now encompass a ministry to sixth-graders, many of whom are ill-prepared developmentally for junior high life.

Identification of Relevant Needs

The needs of youth which are relevant to a successful ministry to them emerge from understandings of two dominant themes in adolescent development. Much literature exists dealing with the developmental aspects of adolescence, so for the purposes of this chapter, the material must be greatly condensed and this section will focus primarily on cognitive (mental) development, psycho-social development, and the relationships these dimensions have with spiritual growth and development. Physical development has interesting attachments to psycho-social development as will be shown in that section.

Cognitive Development Needs

1) Teenagers need guidance to help them balance what they are learning with what they already know, or accept to be true. Piaget referred to this balancing process as maintaining equilibration between what students know and the new information they are receiving from their surroundings.[3]

2) Teenagers are able for the first time in their lives to think flexibly. They need guidance as they consider solutions to the problems and issues of their lives and as they try to combine these solutions in a variety of sometimes interesting ways.

3) Teenagers are mentally creating what Piaget referred to as a "Created Reality" against which all new and incoming information and data will be tested. They need guidance which will help them develop this "Created Reality" from a Christian perspective.

4) For the first time in their lives, teenagers are able to think abstractly and hypothetically. They will need much help and guidance as they ask many questions beginning with the words, "Why . . . ?" or "What if . . . ?"

Psycho-Social Developmental Needs

Teenagers, according to Erikson, have the primary psycho-social developmental task of forming an identity.[4] As Erikson saw it, the major task of the teenager is the formation of a secure ego identity which includes all of one's perceptions and feelings about self. Failure to reach this ego identity led to what Erikson called identity/self-diffusion, which means that the teenager has a lack of personal definition, commitment, and a loss of a sense of togetherness. Specific needs which arise from this developmental aspect of teenage life are:

1) *Need to accept one's self as God's special creation.* Many young people are struggling with their physical bodies and appearance. They look in the mirror and worry that they don't measure up to the cultural norm. They are too small or too large; too tall or too short; their hair is too curly or not curly enough; they have freckles; they fight with acne, and the list goes on. They especially need to be affirmed that their worth as persons is not related to their physical capabilities or appearance.

2) *Need for balance in self-esteem.* Teenagers need to know that they individually have worth to God and thus are unique persons. Man's sin nature

distorts worth, but does not destroy it. Each teenager needs to have an affirmation of his or her worth in Christ.

3) *Need for clear gender role definition.* We live in a society in which there are legitimate concerns about the roles and functions of women. Special interest groups are working hard to distort legitimate views regarding gender roles. The teenagers need careful instruction and guidance with regard to biblical guidelines for the societal roles of men and women. For far too long the evangelical church has mistaught its people, giving the impression that the Bible strictly limits the roles of women in society. Teenagers have a right and a need for accurate teaching in this matter.

4) *Need for biblical guidance about human sexuality.* North American teenagers grow up in a world which leads them to believe that they are entitled to a free expression of their sexual selves. Culture teaches that a greater sense of identity is to be found in sexual exploration. Teenagers need to be taught the biblical model for human sexuality and how it (abstinence except in monogamous marriage relationships) protects them from the emotional trauma of sexual promiscuity, pain related to disease (and death), and the heartache of unwanted pregnancies.

5) *Need to make appropriate and responsible decisions in the face of peer pressure.* Many Christian young people have a great deal of difficulty going against the flow of their peers when making decisions. They need support to make right decisions and encouragement to feel good about themselves when their decisions are quality ones.

6) *Need for an outlet to contribute to the life of the church.* Teenagers in church ministry today are not interested in sitting and being entertained, taught, and patronized. They seek involvement and opportunities to positively influence the church they attend. Teenagers need meaningful opportunities to serve the Lord and the church. Those opportunities may be found in teaching children, VBS, day camps, counseling at summer or winter camps with children, short-term missions trips, teacher's aides in Sunday School or children's church, or in a host of other ministry opportunities.

7) *Teenagers need to be affirmed in areas where their development is matching biblical patterns.* Too many youth leaders and parents quickly criticize young people when their attitudes and behavior are inappropriate, but are not nearly as quick to encourage and affirm appropriate attitudes and behaviors. Perhaps more than being criticized when they seem to be wrong, teenagers need to be affirmed when they seem to be thinking and behaving in a biblical way.

Developing a Youth Ministry Strategy

Churches often think that all they need to begin or maintain a successful youth ministry is a few adults interested in teenagers and a significant population of teenagers in the community. Many begin a youth ministry program with nothing more than some pressure from parents of teenagers and a minimal recognition of some of the needs associated with youth ministry. Most of these churches discover several months later that they were ill-equipped to accomplish what they set out to do. What are the steps involved in beginning and maintaining a successful youth ministry?

Step 1: First, prayerful consideration must be given to the needs of young people in the community. The temptation must be resisted to think that all teenagers are similar and therefore have similar needs. Using the general need statements listed above will enable one to discover which of those are prime needs among the youth of the community. The needs of teenagers vary markedly from community to community, even in towns of close proximity. Some questions to guide an inquiry might be:

• Is the junior high and high school population of the community gaining or declining in number?

• What ethnic or racial backgrounds are represented in that population?

• What are the pressing sociological problems facing the community's teenage population (e.g., drug addiction, alcoholism, divorced parents, sexual temptations, academic pressures, etc.)?

• What other churches in the community have viable youth ministry programs and how effective are they?

The answers to these and other similar questions will help to determine if starting a youth ministry is the best use of resources for a church in a specific area.

Step 2: The next step is to determine if a church has the necessary resources to maintain a successful youth ministry once it is started. Resources come in three categories. These have sometimes been referred to as the Three Fs: Folks, Finances, and Facilities. The principles below will help one to make a decision regarding the amount and quality of resources available for a youth ministry.

Folks

To maintain a successful youth ministry people are needed. Professors of Christian Education across the United States and Canada could compile hundreds of horror stories of churches who hired a youth pastor thinking he or she would be able to start and maintain a successful youth ministry alone. It simply cannot be done. For a church's ministry to teenagers to be successful, it needs to have an adult staff to student ratio of approximately 1:8 for high school students and 1:6 for junior high students. In addition, churches should plan from the start to operate the junior high and high school groups separately. It's difficult for junior high school students to feel comfortable in a program which also involves older and more mature high school students. So, leaders must ask themselves, "Does our church have enough capable adult volunteer leaders who are willing to be trained for youth ministry to maintain the above ratios effectively?" If a church does not have a significant core of adult volunteers ready to participate, that church is not yet ready to start a youth ministry.

On the other hand, if a church has a group of volunteers who are willing to dedicate themselves to this task, it may be ready to start a youth ministry and not need to invest finances in a professional youth pastor yet. There are several organizations which can provide training for volunteer workers to help them get started without on-site professional leadership (See the partial list of training organizations at the end of this chapter).

Finances

Every so often one of us in the Christian Education Department of Talbot School of Theology gets a phone call from an area church that is looking to hire a professional youth pastor. With some pride and anticipation they tell us that they have set aside enough monies to afford a youth pastor and they are ready to hire one. We usually commend them for their vision and then ask, "Have you also made allowance in your annual budget for a substantial amount of funds for the youth program?" Too often, they have not.

The fact is that a successful youth program in any local church is a rather expensive item. This is especially true if your church is just getting started with a youth program. There are all kinds of resources to be purchased, training materials and conferences to be incorporated, and a whole host of other costs which, if not anticipated, can significantly drain a church's financial resources.

The majority of financing for church ministries comes from contributions from adults and family groups. In some communities, where families are generally strong financially, most programs can be operated on the basis of costs passed on to the students who participate, but that isn't possible in all cases. Unless a congregation is prepared to commit substantial amounts of money to youth ministry and to see that commitment as a significant investment in the future of the body of Christ, many people might come to see youth ministry as an economic liability for the church. One invaluable resource on youth ministry financial questions is the Fall, 1984 issue of *Youthworker* journal (see resources at the end of this chapter). The entire issue is devoted to financing youth ministry and there are several helpful articles which give you the information needed to begin programming.

Facilities

With creative thinking and applications, this is the easiest of the three major resources to provide. The most advantageous situation is one where there is a set room for the junior high and one for the high school group to use routinely. It should be a room large enough to accommodate the largest number of students expected in a weekly program. The room should be open and airy with seating that allows for a variety of groupings and arrangements.

Churches that do not have enough classroom space for a number of small groups should consider having some activities during the week in private homes. An advantage to this is that the atmosphere is more relaxed and students tend to feel more comfortable. Space for large group recreational or evangelistic activities can usually be rented from local schools or halls for reasonable amounts of money. It isn't necessary for a church to invest in a gymnasium or large multipurpose facility to maintain a successful ministry to youth.

One additional issue related to facilities is change. When beginning a new youth ministry and allocating rooms for them to use, there may be some friction at times when other established groups are forced to change locations. Leaders should be prepared to explain to all parties involved why these changes need to take place and how everyone will benefit from them.

Step 3: Next, one is ready to decide exactly what kinds of program activities a youth ministry should involve. Throughout the age group ministry chapters of this text, program activities have been divided into two major groups by function: outreach and inreach.

Outreach

Evangelism: Youth ministry evangelism needs two dimensions. On the one hand, it should be providing what are commonly referred to as "come level" activities designed to be comfortable gatherings for non-Christian or un-churched students to attend. The chart on page 167 shows how a youth ministry structure can be developed to integrate students, who are initially at the "come level," more securely into the fabric of a youth group. Informal Bible studies, small group discussion groups, concerts open to the youth of the community, recreational and sports activities, an active social calendar and, perhaps, a camp or conference experience each year to which your students can invite their unchurched friends are all examples of "entry level" activities which may be popular.

On the other hand, Christian students should be trained with the goal of helping them become comfortable sharing their faith in Christ with friends at school and in the community. Many youth workers encourage their students to share their faith in Christ at school and elsewhere without giving them training in how to do that. This often produces guilt in students who are serious about their faith but who become discouraged over their lack of ability and confidence in witnessing. Numerous simple evangelistic tools are available which students can easily learn to use. Once they have learned how to

LEVEL & ACTIVITIES

LEAD
Student Leadership
Service Projects

DEVELOP
Discipleship
Growth Groups
Bible Studies
Witnessing Activities

COME & GROW
Sunday School, Retreats, Seminars,
Camps, Worship, Evangelism Training

COME & LISTEN
Retreats, Outreach Activities,
Weekly Youth Group Activities
Group Recreational Activities, Topical Studies

COME
Social Activities, Evangelistic Outreaches
Special Events, Campus Contacts by Staff,
Entry Level Activities Designed for New Kids

Figure 10.1

use them, they often become more confident and begin to see results in their personal witnessing.

Service: Churches all over the nation are discovering the untapped potential of many high school students and some junior highers. Youth leaders who involve their students in short-term missions opportunities overseas, or closer to home in inner-city ministry opportunities, are discovering that these students relish the chance to be involved in ministry and perform very well.

Furthermore, these opportunities cause many students over time to consider more serious service and some even are motivated toward full-time professional Christian service, at home or on the mission field, because of these short-term opportunities. Youth groups can also "get involved" by sponsoring a child through a mission agency, regularly visiting a nursing home or convalescent care facility, participating in rescue mission work in cities which have such facilities, feeding the homeless, helping handicapped persons with daily needs, or doing home care chores for elderly and shut-in church members.

Inreach

Teaching: Many high school students are ready to serve in the church education program as teachers' aides, or in some cases teachers themselves. Failure to give students responsibilities equal to their maturity frequently causes them to become complacent and critical of the youth ministry of the local church.

Worship: Christian young people love to worship God every bit as much as their adult counterparts. However, the forms of worship they enjoy may be quite different from those enjoyed by adults. Having a regular worship service on a monthly basis in which the specific worship styles of youth are used can help teenagers become more actively involved in the total worship functions of a church. It might also help adults discover some refreshing new ways in which they can worship God.

Counseling: Church youth have a number of counseling needs and many of those needs can be adequately met by trained adult volunteers who are willing to give some time to listen to a teenager share his/her concerns about life. Ongoing training for youth workers will enable them to be sensitive to those kinds of needs and situations and greatly encourage your teenagers to seek the help and advice of a Christian adult. Many professional youth workers believe that teenagers today can't have too many godly adult models and counselors. This is a need which must be addressed.

Leadership Training: It is little wonder that in many churches there are few adults who are capable and trained leaders. Prior to adulthood, few of them have had any experience in the church as leaders. By providing leadership opportunities with adequate training for the task involved, you are preparing teenagers to take greater leadership responsibility in the future.

Particularly at the high school level, a leadership cabinet or council of qualified students who work with adult leaders to plan and carry out ministry programs gives students a sense of ownership of their own youth ministry and trains them for greater leadership later in adult life. A list of resources at the end of this chapter provides some excellent ideas to help get started teaching youth to lead.

Summary

Ministry to youth should be an effective program element of most churches in America today. But to be effective it must be started and maintained with a great deal of prayer and careful consideration of the needs of youth in and around the church community. In addition, the costs of such a ministry must also be taken into consideration. The best model for beginning is to determine the youth needs and then develop a carefully planned strategy to meet those needs. The youth of America are in need of the message of the Gospel. In a very real sense, the future of America depends on our ability to shape and influence the moral and ethical fabric of this great American resource.

Notes

1. *Chemical People Newsletter,* Nov./Dec. 1990.

2. G. Stanley Hall, *Adolescence* (New York: Appleton, 1904).

3. Jean Piaget, *The Psychology of Intelligence* (New York: Harcourt Brace, 1950).

4. Erik H. Erikson, *Identity: Youth and Crisis* (New York: W.W. Norton & Company, 1968).

For Further Reading

Benson, W. S., and Senter, M. H. *The Complete Book of Youth Ministry.* Chicago: Moody Press, 1987.

Bundschuh, R., and Finley, T. *The Youth Worker's Emergency Manual.* Ventura, Calif.: Gospel Light Publications, 1988.

Burns, J. *The Youth Builder.* Eugene, Ore.: Harvest House, 1988.

Burns, R. and Campbell, P. *Create in Me a Youth Ministry.* Wheaton, Ill.: Victor Books, 1986.

Sparks, L. ed. *The Youth Worker's Personal Management Handbook.* Loveland, Colo.: Group Books, 1985.

Stevens, D. *Called to Care.* Grand Rapids: Zondervan Publishing House, 1985.

Veerman, D. R. *Reaching Kids Before High School.* Wheaton, Ill.: Victor Books, 1990.

————. *Youth Evangelism.* Wheaton, Ill.: Victor Books, 1988.

Yaconelli, M., and Burns, J. *High School Ministry.* Grand Rapids: Zondervan Publishing House, 1986.

Youthworker. Journal for youth workers published quarterly by Youth Specialties, 1224 Greenfield Dr., El Cajon, CA 92021.

Professional Training Resources

Institute for Volunteer Youthworkers (IVY), c/o Dr. Ken Garland, Christian Education Dept., Talbot School of Theology, 13800 Biola Ave., La Mirada, CA 90639. (213) 903-4818.

National Institute of Youth Ministry, 940 Calle Amanecer, Suite G, San Clemente, CA 92672. (714) 498-4418.

Youth Specialties, 1224 Greenfield Dr., El Cajon, CA 92021. (619) 440-2333.

Professional Training Providers

Center for Christian Leadership, Dallas Seminary, 3909 Swiss Ave., Dallas, TX 75204

Evangelical Training Association, P.O. Box 327, Wheaton, IL 60187. Offers a certified program of teacher training for local church Christian Education ministry.

Fellowship of Christian Educators, ON-345 Willow Road, Wheaton, IL 60187.

Greater Los Angeles Sunday School Association (GLASS), P.O. Box 296, Rosemead, CA 91770-0296. Sponsors the annual Greater Los Angeles Sunday School Convention each fall.

Innovations in Learning, 7018 El Paseo, Long Beach, CA 90815. Provides video tape training sessions for teachers and leaders.

Lowell Brown Enterprises, 15500 Telegraph Rd., Suite B-15, Santa Paula, CA 93060. Provides training and materials for use of computers in teaching and leadership development.

Eleven
The Christian Education of Adults

It has been said that you succeed or fail as a Minister of Christian Education as you succeed or fail in adult education. Of course advocates of other age groups and other ministries claim theirs is the most important ministry. But without adult education, from where are the teachers for other age groups going to come? Where are those involved in church or parachurch ministries going to get their training for ministry? If they don't get it in the adult education ministry, they may be nothing more than spiritual children raising other children.

It is adults in the church who make decisions—about what kind of a church it will be, whom to call as pastor, what to do with church funds, which strategies to implement, what resources are needed and how to use them, how to minister to the community and reach out to the world. The quality of these decisions, and many others like them, will to a very large degree, depend on the quality of Christian Education they receive as adults.

It is adults who provide the needed financial resources as well as leadership for the programs of the church. Recruiting people for ministry leadership is one of the most significant challenges. If adults are growing spiritually, they begin investing both money and time. As they invest, they continue growing. Review Matthew 6:19-23 for more insight into this dynamic.

Adults in the church are the source of babies, children, and many of your church's adolescents. Many churches in America have grown numerically by reaching out to children through Sunday School and Vacation Bible School, then reaching the children's families. This strategy still works in some communities. But in many communities it has minimal effects, and even when it does, a church has to recover from the image of being an institution solely for children. Alternatively, when parents are reached, the children and many times the adolescents come along as well.

But success in adult education is not only measured by body count. As adults' needs are met and as they are equipped they grow in grace and in the knowledge of our Lord Jesus Christ. The result is that spiritually mature adults reproduce spiritual fruit. Ultimately, success in adult education and in the church as a body can be measured by how many people are launched into ministry. The alternative is what many evangelical churches are struggling with in communities today—wounded consumers of church services who never heal and never impact their neighbors for Christ.

Gaining a Sociological Perspective

Today's adults are different from the adults that founded most of America's churches. Morris Massey has argued that our basic values are for the most part shaped by the culture we were a part of up until about age 10.[1] So if a church was founded just twenty years ago, and it was founded by people who were in their forties, the values of that church's founders (who may still exert much influence in the church) were shaped in the 1940s. Some people refer to this segment of our population as "Pre-Boomers."[2]

What events were shaping values in the 1940s? World War II generated an intense commitment to win. Women joined the work force en masse for the first time and family structure changed forever. Kindergartens replaced mama and "teenagers" became a phenomenon. Business, especially big business prospered and Joe DiMaggio became a hero. Then the war ended and America's now giant industrial complex shifted to developing consumers then meeting their demands.

In the evangelical world several parachurch organizations were founded in the 1940s—InterVarsity Christian Fellowship, Young Life, Mission Aviation Fellowship, Youth for Christ, and Greater Europe Mission, among others. Billy Graham's Los Angeles Tent Crusade changed mass evangelism. C. S. Lewis wrote *Mere Christianity*, and A. W. Tozer wrote *The Pursuit of God*. We began singing "Heavenly Sunshine," "Do Lord," "Deep and Wide," and "I Have Decided to Follow Jesus."

In contrast, the young adult of today was value-shaped in the '60s and '70s. Demographers and sociologists refers to these adults as "baby boomers" since they were part of the post-World War II demographic bulge. The 1960s changed everyone and everything! We witnessed men on the moon and the assassination of our president. The hippie generation questioned the traditional Protestant ethic and we were introduced to the "New Morality." Everything changed quickly and we saw it all happening on TV. We lost our leaders in Watergate and ourselves in Viet Nam.

The evangelical world changed too in the '60s and '70s. "The Jesus Movement" began as did Right to Life, Prison Fellowship, and Focus on the Family. Francis Schaeffer wrote *The God Who Is There*, and James Dobson *Dare to Discipline*. We began singing "They'll Know We Are Christians By Our Love," "Seek Ye First," and "Our God Reigns."

George Barna makes some fascinating predictions about life in the beginning of the twenty-first century. Children who turned 10 in the '80s and '90s, often referred to as "baby busters," will be as distinct and different when they are young adults as their "baby boom" and "pre-boomer" counterparts. In 1990, one out of four households were single parent homes. The quality of possessions is becoming more important than the quantity of possessions. Satisfaction comes through leisure as opposed to coming through work.[3] No wonder we feel generation gaps!

The values of those in control, both in society and in our churches, are not *normal* (the values of the norm or modal group in a society). They are pre-1950. *Normal* values are post-1960 values. We should also be aware that the values of ethnic minorities in our society are not *normal*. Hispanic family values are considerably different from Anglo family values, and Asian-American family, education, and work values are generally different from modal values as well. Remember, our values pretty much determine our receptivity to messages—including the Gospel.

Where your church is located also makes a big difference. Frank Tillapaugh contrasts rural and urban values in the following table. (I have added the suburban values in my adaptation.)[4]

Values		
Rural	**Suburban**	**Urban**
Status Quo	Protection	Change
Sameness	Complementarity	Diversity
Harmony	Belonging	Managing Conflict
Smallness	Space	Bigness
Established	Accumulative	Mobile

Figure 11.1

What is the predominant target group for your church? Is it pre-boomers, baby boomers, or baby busters? Is it rural, suburban, or urban? What is the make-up of your community? What kind of people are making the church's decisions?

According to the model of ministry presented in chapter 1, contemporary ministry is based upon the needs of the community and those represented in the church. With this in mind, it is essential for those who are making the ministry decisions in the church to be aware of the predominant adult values found in their local community and church home.

Identification of Relevant Needs

The temptation of Christian educators, when identifying relevant needs, is to immediately list principles, doctrines, or Bible truths a new Christian needs to know. Thus, new Christians tend to become Bible knowers rather than Bible doers. We need to claim a far greater domain for Christian Education than the teaching of God's Word, as important as this is. Discipleship and equipping involve knowing, but it also involves doing and being. So what do adults need? Following are eight significant adult needs.

1) *A personal relationship with Jesus.* We often make the mistake of assuming that adults in our evangelical churches have a personal relationship with Jesus Christ. Because we preach and teach the Gospel and people keep coming we assume they are also committed to Christ. So we teach Christian life principles to people who don't have the power to live what we are teaching. How frustrating! Conversely, in some churches the Gospel message is the only thing taught as if the whole congregation has never responded. The result is a church that is stilted in their spiritual formation.

It's in adult education ministries, where communication can be two-way, that a person's relationship with God can be ascertained. Jesus said that we would be known by our spiritual fruit. There is no opportunity to determine the quality of a person's fruit when he or she is always listening. But in interactive adult education ministries we have the opportunity to get beyond appearances and discover whether a person has a personal faith.

2) *A fellowship family.* The most important thing an adult needs after becoming one of God's children is the fellowship of the family of God. Some churches make the mistake of overemphasis on teaching new Christians, thereby forming future legalists. A foundational aspect of ministry to adults needs to be the development of new relationships with God's people. Incorporation into the "body" is completed by the work of the Holy Spirit upon salvation. But the support of the family of God is crucial for further spiritual growth, especially the formation of spiritual values.

Does your church have an intentional way of providing for this need? If there are not leaders specifically developing this ministry whose primary concern is for new Christians, it will eventually disappear. Getting adults enrolled in a Sunday School class is not enough. New Christians need a network of Christians in which to develop long-term fellowship, interaction, and trust.

3) *Healing.* In Jesus' encounters with people, time after time He ministered to them in a dual way. He forgave their sins and He healed them of their disabilities. In modern America, many Christians have so relegated healing to

medical science that until recently they have abandoned it. Other Christians subscribe to instant healing that is often hard-pressed to demonstrate long-term change. Churches are now realizing how truly wounded people are as a result of their own sins and those of others. Lifelong wounding distorts relationships, including people's perception of and relationship to God. For example, an adult who was physically or sexually abused as a child is going to perceive God the Father quite differently from the adult who grew up in a safe, supportive home. Adults need healing. The body of Christ is to be the healthy environment where the healing process can take root not only on the surface, but into the core of people's lives.

All adults bring wounds into their relationship with God and their relationships with others. Some are deep and immobilizing, others easier to heal. Time does not heal all wounds — it rots those that are left unattended. It is part of the job of Christian Education to address "woundedness" (and dress the wounds). This does not mean that all Christian educators have to be trained professional counselors. But the development of ministries to one another must certainly include healing ministries, and equipping the saints for ministry certainly is part of the Christian educator's role.

4) *Discipleship.* Conceptually, at the core of Christian Education, discipleship is often relegated in practice to young people or to a weeknight program with a curriculum purchased from a parachurch organization. A more adequate perspective is that discipleship is lifelong and involves all that a Christian does to grow in his or her faith. Adults need to be discipled, then to be trained to disciple others. Among adults, discipleship needs to include the idea that as spiritual growth occurs within individual believers, adults become more and more responsible for the growth of other, newer Christians.

5) *Ministry Service.* When an adult has been discipled for some time, what then? Jesus chose His disciples to be with and learn from Him for approximately a three year period. Then He commissioned them and sent them out to minister. Adults need to be commissioned and sent out as well. A successful Christian Education ministry to adults is one that regularly commissions its disciples and sends them out into ministry. Some will actually leave their local church as they move to other communities. Some will stay in their church and be commissioned to ministry teams either building up the Body or doing the work of service. (Eph. 4:11-13) This is Christian Education. Without it, the church remains busy but isolated.

6) *A learning laboratory.* Adults not only need a fellowship family with healing, discipleship, and ministry service, but they also need a laboratory for learning the disciplines of the "new life." This also is Christian Education. As they are exposed to Scripture through preaching and teaching, adults become familiar with spiritual concepts. But familiarization is only the beginning. An

adult who can define the term "justification," describe the process of salvation, outline God's redemptive plan in Scripture, or summarize the doctrine of sanctification shows that he or she has been a good hearer of the
Word.

Exploration of familiar concepts takes God's Word from a person's head
into his or her life. Through the process of exploration an adult begins asking,
"What does it mean to me?" The learner relates biblical concepts to behavior,
reassesses lifelong patterns in the light of biblical norms, and practices living
out decisions. In this phase the learner needs support and reinforcement from
the "Fellowship Family." Exploration is the missing ingredient in many church
adult ministries. People are expected to hear and obey. But adults need to
explore, not just accept. If we explore, God's Word gets infused like a meal
rather than applied like a bandage.

On another dimension, Christian Education, especially of adults, ought to
be distinctly different from secular education, and not just in its content.
Secular education seeks the growth of minds. Christian Education seeks the
growth of lives. Some secular educators are beginning to remark on the
importance of education beyond the mind.

> If Allan Bloom is right, that there has been a gradual closing of the
> American mind, then I believe it is due to the closing of the American
> heart. Indeed, the more I listen to college students, the more I come to
> realize that American higher education has focused on the eye of the
> mind to the virtual neglect of the eye of the heart. This has resulted in a
> kind of moral astigmatism and spiritual blindness. To quote Bernadette
> Roberts, "After two years at the university, I suddenly realized I had not
> learned a thing. Despite the influx of information, nothing really hap
> pened. I was the same person with the same mind—I had not grown at
> all. If learning could not bring about change, if it was not a way of
> growth, then the university was a waste of time."[5]

Is a ministry to adults touching minds or hearts? The key to answering this
question is in the relationship between teachers and learners. Strong relationships will open adults' minds as well as their hearts. This is Christian Education. Without it, the church remains busy but undisciplined.

7) *A worship walkway.* Worship is often considered the domain of the
senior pastor or the music minister. But when worship is led but not taught, it
gets confined to weekly "worship services," and adults become passive worshipers, even spectators. If worship is to become a way of walking with God
through life, adults need a walkway modeled and demonstrated. Then we
need to be invited to join other worshipers on the walkway, sometimes follow-

ing, sometimes leading. This is Christian Education of adults. Without it, the church remains religious but impotent.

8) *A witness well.* The injunction to witness is familiar to most adult believers in evangelical churches. But adults need more than injunctions. They need models to watch, companions to witness with, and support teams who will give feedback and keep them accountable. In short, adults need a well of people and resources from which to draw. This is Christian Education. Without it the church remains orthodox but silent.

Strategy for Ministry to Adults

If adults are changing as we suggest they are, and if adults' needs are close to what we've described, what will a strategy for ministry to adults look like? A strategic metaphor might be that we walk on a ridge apt to fall off either side. Obviously, balance is important. Consider the following six strategies.

1) *Ministry to adults must be value driven and market aware.* On one side, the temptation is to be so concerned with our basic biblical values that we lose awareness of the community in which we minister and even the people in our churches. We keep preaching and teaching, unaware that no one is listening or learning. On the other side, we become market driven and, in an effort to appeal to our community, we lose awareness of our basic values. Our ministries take on the shape and sounds of East Coast advertising executives and Wall Street economists.

When we are value driven, our goals for growth come from Scripture and are qualitative. When we are market aware, our goals for growth come from a desire for success and are quantitative. When we are value driven, we focus on unleashing people into ministry. When we are market aware, we focus on attracting people into the ministry. When we are value driven we work with people to assist them in their goal of developing maturity in Christ. When we are market aware we recruit people to help us reach our church goals. When we are value driven we make time for our own growth because it is important to us and to God. When we are market aware we find little time for our own growth; the market is too big to allow us time—for anything but meeting its demands.

When we are market aware our goals for growth are tailored to individual and family needs; we can unleash people to ministries outside our church; we begin to understand why some adults won't respond to the message and others resist growth; we realize people are watching and learning from the way we live and we are conscious of ways we could trip them in their growth. So we need to be both value driven and market aware.

2) *Goal-directed and program aware.* Within the framework of biblical values, we need to be goal-directed and program aware in ministry. We can fall off one side of the ridge by not keeping our goals grounded in our biblical

value system. We achieve appealing goals, but make no spiritually significant difference. We fall off the ridge on the other side by being program directed. In this case, programs are kept running that may have lost their meaning and impact, but are now accepted parts of the church week. If attendance figures sag, we put more emphasis into publicity. Programs are simply ways to get from where we are to where we want to be. Churches need to evaluate their programs yearly with the intention of developing better strategies.

3) *Releasing and handicap aware.* The ultimate goal in ministry to adults is to equip them for their own work, then release them to develop those ministries. But we can fall off the ridge on one side by assuming that adults are healthy and ready for ministry, when in fact they may be spiritually, emotionally, relationally, or morally handicapped and in need of healing. Adults don't need to be in perfect health to minister, but if spiritually handicapped people are recruited, they will damage themselves and others in attempts to get their own needs met.

We fall off the other side of the ridge by never releasing people into ministry. Sometimes churches think that only professional ministers can do it right. Phrases like "preparing for full-time Christian service" are misleading. We are all called to full-time Christian service. So if healthy adults are not ministering, maybe it is because the church is keeping them on a leash. Frank Tillapaugh explains in his book, *Unleashing the Church,* that it is the responsibility of the professional church staff to train and equip its members for ministry within its community. As members identify new avenues for outreach they become empowered for ministry—a process which he describes as "unleashing the church."

4) *Developmental and resistance aware.* A developmental ministry is one that sees individuals at different stages in their growth and with different needs. It might be contrasted with a herd ministry, which sees all adults as one group simply in need of good solid teaching.

Some adults are seekers, normal, still unrelated to God through Jesus Christ and spiritually dead. Others are new Christians, needing a fellowship family and biblical instruction. Other adults need healing; still others need unleashing. There is a flow in developmental ministry. Whereas most churches do almost all ministry at one growth level, hoping that people will mature without seeing how to progress along the path, a developmental ministry identifies a path for growth and the transition points that will help people to move from one level to another. Churches "must also identify when a person has graduated from the training and what is expected of a graduate. The church school is probably the only school in the world that does not identify how to graduate or be promoted."[6] Figure 11.2 on page 179 illustrates how one church conceptualizes a developmental adult Christian Education ministry. All of the church's ministries among its adults fit somewhere onto this chart. Between each column is a key transition event around which an interview is structured.

All-church Yearly Evaluation

COMMISSIONED	
Goal *Exerting team leadership: Leading the church*	Leadership Enrichment Events
	Maintenance Groups
	Leadership Retreats
	In-Service Training

LEADERSHIP

Ministry Initiative: Team Leadership Training

COMMITTED	
Goal *Actively engaged in ministry*	Community Service (Participants) • Casa Youth Shelter • New Life Beginnings • L.B. Rescue Mission • World Impact
	Maintenance Group/Team Member
	Worship/Pulpit Ministry
	Pre-Service and In-Service Training • Stephen Ministries • Teacher Training

ASSIMILATION/CHRISTIAN FORMATION

Second Year Small Group
Spiritual Gift ID/Development

CONVINCED	
Goal *Grasp the basics of Christian living*	Small Groups (first & second year)
	Specialized Ministry ABFs
	Support Groups
	Worship/Pulpit Ministry
	Key Concept Seminars • Marriage Enrichment • Parenting Skills • Dad's University • Marriage Preparation • Financial • Infant Dedication • Intro to Evangelical Christianity • Doctrinal Survey • New Christian Discipleship/Follow-up • Friendship Evangelism

Accepting Christ as Savior

CURIOUS	
Goal *Confronted with the Gospel*	Community Service (Recipients)
	Probe Events
	Specialized Ministry
	Friendship Evangelism (Recipients)
	Support Groups
	Pulpit Ministry
	Sports Ministry
	Services/Events • Marriage Enrichment • Parenting Skills • Dad's University • Marriage Preparation • Financial • Infant Dedication • Intro to Evangelical Christianity

EVANGELISM

Needs met through Christians

COMMUNITY	
Goal *Gain positive personal contact with Christians*	Community Service (Recipients) • Casa Youth Shelter • New Life Beginnings • L.B. Rescue Mission • World Impact
	Friendship Evangelism (Recipients)
	Support Groups
	Sports Ministry
	Contact Events/Seminars • Easter/Good Friday • Christmas Theater • Career/Idak

Figure 11.2

5) *Modeling and person aware.* Everyone experienced in leadership is aware that people look up to leaders. The danger comes when, so aware of being watched, a leader creates a pseudo-self for the watchers to see that is quite different from the real self. All of us probably do this to some extent anyway (see 1 John 1:8), but it is a doubly large temptation for the person in leadership. People want and need models to follow. But individuals get into trouble when they try to model perfection rather than redemption. Knowingly or unknowingly, we model something we are not, then we live a lie trying to keep up with the image. Better to be ourselves, redeemed, imperfect, and in the process of sanctification.

On the other edge of the ridge, people need the kind of program structure that allows them access to models of further growth. The topics being covered in a growth group, weekend workshop, or camp experience are not as important as exposure to the lives of other growing Christians. Strategically, then, adults need proximity to and involvement with other adults who are growing. Adult learners need to be able to watch, not just hear.

6) *Equipping and consumer aware.* In the Christian Education of adults it is crucial to stay on the ridge in the fundamental purpose of leadership. We are called to equip saints for ministry. Christian Education that never equips fails. Inferior quality and poorly targeted adult educational experiences are not effective. Leaders must be able to communicate clear objectives for the time they want people to invest. Educational experiences that have no clear direction will be shunned.

We also need to be aware that adults often perceive the church as a place to have their needs met, a kind of spiritual service station. We are programmed in American society to be consumers. A key need for adult learners is to change from an orientation of wanting to be served to the goal of ministering to others in the church or community. Follow-up and growth must lead to gift identification and service.

Since time is such a precious commodity nowadays, learning experiences must be offered repeatedly and in different formats (e.g., weekly, intensive weekend, different days). Success is better measured in the depth of impact and amount of change in a few individuals, rather than in the number of individuals attending a learning event. The key is not to offer more variety of material, but to offer critical educational material in more time slots and formats.

Finally, as Christians are equipped as ministers they must be encouraged to move out in ministry while staying in proper relationship with church and community authorities. Forming new ministry teams through the initiative of motivated Christians must be a priority for the Christian Education of adults.

Implications for Program Design

Strategic designs are just good ideas unless implemented into actions (pro-grams). The changing needs of adults at the end of the twentieth century and new strategic concerns suggest that we rethink the program design of adult Christian Education. We need to rethink what we *have* been doing as well as what we *want* to do in the future.

Annual Zero-based Planning. It's easy for a church to keep doing what it's always done, assuming that because attendance is up it's being successful. Church leaders need to rethink their church's adult ministries each year, starting from a zero base rather than from what is already going on. This gives leaders the chance to be value driven rather than program driven. Current programs may be good, but may preclude better ones. A program formulated twenty years ago may have been exactly what churches needed then. It may still be exactly what your church needs. But then again, maybe your church needs a new approach—one that will impact adults more deeply and/or reach adults in the community more effectively. A zero-based plan can add ongoing programs when better alternatives have not been created.

A team ministry approach. The basic unit for planning used to be the congregation. It still is in many churches. In some churches it is the class. Building on a strategy that is goal-directed, unleashing, developmental model-ing, and equipping, let me suggest that the basic unit for planning for adult Christian Education be the team. Teams connote teamwork. Whoever heard of teams of consumers? Teams are flexible in terms of size, time, and goals. Support groups, fellowship families, and Bible study groups can become minis-try teams, or such teams can be built out of people who have become accus-tomed to working together as groups. Teams imply mutual accountability and cooperativeness. Each team needs a leader, and team leaders need to be on leadership teams. It all starts with the pastoral staff team.

Adult learning environments. Since church education of adults grew out of education programs designed for children and young people, most adult learn-ing environments are not adult environments at all. Current church adult classrooms, by their design, condition people to expect to sit and listen. This is an area ripe for creative thought. Restaurants, fitness centers, conference rooms, and living rooms are all designed for adults. For the most part they are not designed for learning, but their elements could be adapted to the design of adult learning centers. Lacking funds to create such centers, most churches would be better off using people's living rooms than their adult classrooms.

Resources for exploration. Christian bookstores are full of resources for Bible study, fellowship, worship, and witness. Yet relatively few Christians purchase these excellent resources. Of those who purchase, only 15 percent are men. Groups of adults need resources for Bible study and ministry. Leadership teams need to visit Christian bookstores together, and then adult learning and ministry teams need to be encouraged to do the same. Adult learning centers need to be stocked with Bible study resources so that even new Christians can explore them. Resources need not be limited to books either. Today's church leaders need to be acquainted with video materials and computer software resources for adults.

Yearly evaluation and planning. In our educational endeavors we expect to plan for children and young people. We need to plan *with* adults. One of the hallmarks of truly adult Christian Education is that it is self-directed. The church leadership sees itself as a resource to the learner. This suggests an annual evaluation and planning session with each family unit in the church. A leader might ask what growth goals were set for the year, and were they met? Did the church's ministries contribute toward meeting the goals? What do the individuals and families want to focus on during the coming year? What goals do they have for themselves and for the kids? What parts of the church's program will most help individuals and families meet their goals? What resources are needed? Other questions might also be asked, and both questions and answers need to be documented so progress can be seen each year. This process will also help direct the thrust of adult Christian Education in its awareness of current needs.

New leadership roles. If a church is going to take equipping and releasing seriously, it will have to rethink its leadership roles. In Tillapaugh's description of "transformative leaders" there are some new roles for many church pastoral staffs. In the following chart transformative leadership is contrasted with what Tillapaugh calls managerial leadership, characteristic of many pastoral staff ministers.[7]

Managerial Leadership	Transformative Leadership
Relationships are parental	Relationships are collegial
Leader's role = dispensing information	Leader's role = encouraging action
Leader is problem solver	Leader is problem finder
Leader concentrates on "How?"	Leader concentrates on "Why?"

Figure 11.3

Tillapaugh goes on to suggest that if pastoral staff leaders become "transformative," congregation members can take on new roles as partners in ministry. The church can penetrate the culture rather than focusing all its energies on building a church. A new atmosphere can emerge where everyone is permitted to think, brainstorm, and actually lead the church into its ministry.

Summary

The Christian Education of adults is no longer the same as it was at the turn of the century. Unfortunately, many churches continue to treat their adult learners as dependent children. They give little attention to the contemporary needs and issues facing their adult population. The contemporary church must shake its reputation for being behind the times in its approach to ministry.

The successful Christian educator of the next century will be one who is able to understand the current needs and issues facing adults and integrate changeless biblical imperatives with ever changing ministry methods. Adult Christians must be given opportunities to provide input into the church's adult educational design. Their needs must be considered in light of their developmental stages. Qualitative measures of growth must be considered instead of the temptation to measure success on the basis of attendance alone. Above all, they should be stretched in their spiritual formation and development to explore avenues of service which transcend the relative safety of choirs and Sunday School. They should be taken to the mission field of the inner city and led into situations which test their faith. Pastors who lead their congregations by example will have ministries thriving that never lack for challenge or excitement.

Notes

1. Morris Massey, *The People Puzzle* (Reston, Va.: Reston Publishing, 1979).

2. Gary McIntosh, "Church Growth Network," vol. 3, no. 5 (May 1991).

3. George Barna, *The Frog in the Kettle* (Ventura, Calif.: Regal Books, 1990), 32-43.

4. Frank Tillapaugh, *Unleashing the Church* (Ventura, Calif.: Regal Books, 1982), 26-43.

5. J.D. Lawry, "Caritas in the Classroom," *College Teaching*, vol. 38, no. 3, (1990), 83.

6. P. Sell, "A Proposal Concerning the Philosophy and Strategy of Adult Ministries of Grace Church," Grace Brethren Church, Alomitas, Calif., July 1991.

7. Frank Tillapaugh, Notes from a Vision 1000 Conference, February 1991. For information contact Vision 1000, 2600 S. Sheridan Blvd., Denver, CO 80227. (303) 935-3597.

For Further Reading

Bradshaw, C.O. *Faith Development: The Lifelong Process*. Elgin, Ill.: David C. Cook Publishing Co., 1983.

DeBoy, J.J., Jr. *Getting Started in Adult Religious Education*. New York: Paulist Press, 1970.

Elias, J.L. *The Foundations and Practice of Adult Religious Education*. Malabar, Fla.: Kriegen Publishing Co., 1982.

Foltz, N.T. *Handbook of Adult Religious Education*. Birmingham, Ala.: Religious Education Press, 1986.

Fowler, J.W. *Becoming Adult, Becoming Christian: Adult Development and Christian Faith*. San Francisco: Harper and Row, Publishers, 1984.

Knowles, M. *The Adult Learner: A Neglected Species*. 4th edition. Houston: Gulf Publications, 1990.

_____. *The Modern Practice of Adult Education*. Revised Edition. Englewood Cliffs, N.J.: Cambridge, 1988.

Knox, A.B. *Helping Adults Learn*. San Francisco: Jossey-Bass Publishers, 1985.

McKenzie, L. *The Religious Education of Adults*. Birmingham, Ala.: Religious Education Press, 1982.

Peterson, G.A., ed. *The Christian Education of Adults*. Chicago: Moody Press, 1985.

Sell, C.M. *Transitions Through Adult Life*. Grand Rapids: Zondervan Publishing House, 1991.

Stokes, K. ed. *Faith Development in the Adult Life Cycle*. New York: Sadlier, 1983.

Wilbert, W.N. *Strategies for Teaching Christian Adults*. Grand Rapids: Baker Book House, 1984.

Twelve
Ministry to Families in the Local Church

Family ministry is becoming a rapidly growing avenue of ministry in many churches across the United States and Canada today. The societal factors which threaten the fabric of the family in North America have validated the need for a professionally trained staff member to direct the ministry of the church toward the needs of the family. Long accepted views on marriage and the family are being questioned. People of the United States and Canada are experiencing a change in social attitude toward the family system. Some of these changes include: extensive revisions in divorce laws, individual rights elevated above family rights, unmarried men and women adopting children, marriage no longer being the primary goal of young people, single parent father homes, remarriages creating blended families, parents having only one child or choosing to have none at all, both parents working, and children whose parents have been divorced. What we once considered the "traditional family" with a husband, wife (who is a homemaker) and two children, reflects only 7 percent of U.S. households.[1]

The church can play a key role in society by modeling healthy families that are able to function and relate together. To accomplish this ministry, programs must not be restricted to the traditional family but be broad-based enough to include other family structures evident in our communities.

There are very few resources available for the average parent to use in self-education on parenting skills. Resources such as the public library, community college, and the local PTA have relatively few materials to offer. This is where the church can truly make a significant impact in the community. Education on how to develop a healthy family should be conducted in the local church. Scripture has much to say about the manner in which our homes are to function within our communities. The local church can help provide an understanding of these time-tested principles of family living and assist both members and nonmembers in the application of these principles to daily living.

Biblical Foundations of the Family

The best model for the development of a theology of the family is the relationship between God and the Children of Israel. Myron Chartier has suggested that if God's actions toward Israel are taken as a model, parenting of children will be characterized by loving, caring, responding, disciplining, giving, respecting, knowing, and forgiving.[2]

Balswick and Balswick in their book entitled *The Family* suggest four biblical themes which have a bearing on the nature of the family.[3]

1) Commitment is to be based upon a mature (i.e., unconditional and bilateral) covenant. In Genesis 6:18 God establishes a covenant with Noah. This covenant demonstrates unconditional love from God as parent to Noah. Later in Genesis 15:18, God extends a covenant to Abraham and his descendants. God's commitment was not based on Noah or Abraham's acceptance, rather it was an unconditional commitment as every parent should have with their children. This unconditional love of God is also demonstrated in the New Testament in 1 John 4:19: "We love because He first loved us."

The desire of God in each initiated covenant was that His unconditional commitment would be reciprocal and mutual just as every parent's desire is for their children to respond with unconditional love back to them. This can best be experienced when parents age and become dependent on their children and love is returned.

2) Family life is to be established and maintained within an atmosphere of grace which embraces acceptance and forgiveness. Unconditional love is grace and includes being accepted and forgiven. God's grace is demonstrated in the incarnation. Christ coming in human form made our forgiveness possible. As parents are trustworthy in their love and acceptance, children can trust them to love and direct them. Rules, just as the law, guide the way to God and shouldn't be present to restrict or punish.

3) The resources of family members are to be used to empower rather than control one another. To empower means to be active and intentional in the process of enabling another person to acquire power. Jesus rejected the use of power to control others, rather He demonstrated and affirmed the use of power to serve others, lift the fallen, forgive the guilty, and encourage growth and responsibility in the weak. Empowering is seen by God's work in people's lives. Jesus said, "I have come that they may have life, and have it to the full" (John 10:10). John 1:12-13 says that to those who believe in Him, He gave power to become children of God. Ephesians 4:13 and Galatians 5:22-23

indicate that this power to have the characteristics of God is unlimited. Members of a family applying this truth could give to each other out of their areas of strength whether that be joy, kindness, self-control, peace, or patience in an unlimited way. Successful parenting allows children to gain in personal power while the parents retain their power.

4) Intimacy is based on a knowing that leads to caring, understanding, communication, and communion with others. Intimacy in its perfect state is able to stand completely open and transparent, with nothing to hide. Adam and Eve stood that way before God prior to the Fall (Gen. 2:25). We are encouraged to give our deepest feelings and thoughts to God in prayer and God will understand us (Rom. 8:26-27). Members of a family are intimate when they are fully able to communicate and be known by each other. "These four elements of Christian family relationships are a continual process: intimacy can lead to deeper covenant love, commitment fortifies the atmosphere of freely offered grace, this climate of acceptance and forgiveness encourages serving and empowering others, and the resultant sense of esteem leads to the ability to be intimate without fear. The end product of this process is deep levels of communication and knowing."[4] This is demonstrated in figure 12.1 taken from the Balswicks. It depicts a spiraling inward to represent the potential for family relationships to grow into ever deeper levels of mutual commitment, grace, empowering, and intimacy.

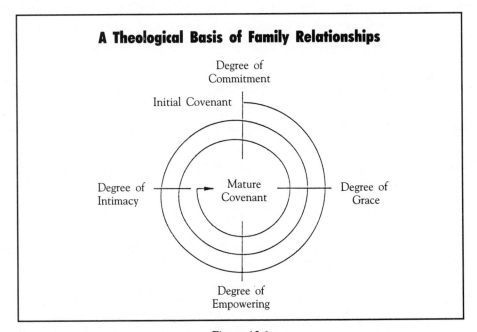

Figure 12.1

History of Family Trends

Historically, the family has had a powerful influence on society. Many of the major problems evident within our society reflect the values and quality of family life. Traditional values such as respect for authority, standards of moral conduct, teachings about right and wrong, are values which should be communicated to a child from his or her parents in the context of their home. Beliefs are taught, attitudes are caught, and values are bought within families (see figure 12.2).

Choosing the Right Key

BELIEFS   are   TAUGHT

ATTITUDES   are   CAUGHT

VALUES   are   BOUGHT

Figure 12.2

Parents need to learn to teach what they believe, model Christian attitudes, and teach and model values that they want their children to have when they are adults.

Figures 12.3 through 12.6 illustrate the types of changes that have taken place in our homes over the past four decades. These changes have influenced the values and trends in our society as a whole.

1950s

Trends:
- Conservative economic patterns
- Focus was on saving money, don't take risks
- Conservative fashions which don't offend others
- Protect youth from harmful effects of:
  - ☐ smoking
  - ☐ alcohol
  - ☐ violence

Values:
- Respect for authority: home, social, judicial
- College was the shaper of dreams and future
- Athletes were our idols, even some politicians
- Family was the primary role of guidance
- Family was the molder of values
- Sexual exploration was limited, according to Kinsey study:
  (14% h.s. females and 25% h.s. males had sex)

Family: (As depicted on TV)

Mother	Father
✎ caregiver, loved children	✎ wise counselor
✎ self-sacrificing	✎ disciplinarian
✎ homemaker par excellence	✎ always home when needed
✎ boundless energy	✎ financial provider
✎ always well kept	✎ wore suits all day/night

Adolescent Rites of Passage:

Boys: Getting drunk, smoking, joining the Army
Girls: Getting married, having children

Figure 12.3

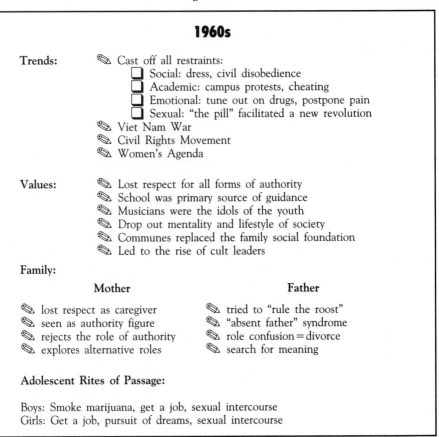

1960s

Trends: ✎ Cast off all restraints:
          ❑ Social: dress, civil disobedience
          ❑ Academic: campus protests, cheating
          ❑ Emotional: tune out on drugs, postpone pain
          ❑ Sexual: "the pill" facilitated a new revolution
       ✎ Viet Nam War
       ✎ Civil Rights Movement
       ✎ Women's Agenda

Values: ✎ Lost respect for all forms of authority
       ✎ School was primary source of guidance
       ✎ Musicians were the idols of the youth
       ✎ Drop out mentality and lifestyle of society
       ✎ Communes replaced the family social foundation
       ✎ Led to the rise of cult leaders

Family:

Mother	Father
✎ lost respect as caregiver	✎ tried to "rule the roost"
✎ seen as authority figure	✎ "absent father" syndrome
✎ rejects the role of authority	✎ role confusion = divorce
✎ explores alternative roles	✎ search for meaning

Adolescent Rites of Passage:

Boys: Smoke marijuana, get a job, sexual intercourse
Girls: Get a job, pursuit of dreams, sexual intercourse

Figure 12.4

1970s

Trends:
- Baby Boomers entered the work force
- Wanted it all NOW!
- Personal debt skyrocketed
- Concern was for credentials and marketability
- Lost urgency to solve the world's problems
- Focus now on "me", self-gratification
- Egocentric materialism as national pastime

Values:
- Material possessions in *all* markets
- Peers are the primary role for values formation
- Most popular TV shows reflect national values:
  Love Boat, Fantasy Island, Gilligan's Island

Family:

Mother	Father
joins Women's Movement	quest for self-identity
wants equal jobs, pay, rights	mid-life crisis literature
going to college in mass	self-absorption
seeks divorce as escape	recreational toys

Adolescent Rites of Passage:

Boys: High school sports, status (car, macho images), drugs
Girls: High school sports, status (clothes, boyfriend), drugs

Figure 12.5

1980s

Trends:
- Major demographic changes in our cities
- Mood: mixture of confidence and caution
  - ☐ Confidence in business growth and economy
  - ☐ Caution due to insecure future
- New hope for future world order
- Patriotism strong once again
- Reliance on computer technology

Values:
- Gender harassment no longer tolerated at work
- High reliance on litigation to solve your problems
- One-half of college students work twenty+ hours per week
- One out of four admit to no use of the library in a week
- Students want benefits without work or effort
- Nielson's top fifteen TV shows reflect national values:

❏ Dukes of Hazard, Muppet Show, M*A*S*H, Sha Na Na, Dance Fever, Happy Days, Mork & Mindy

✎ Anything goes moral and ethical code:
(43% h.s. females & 47% of h.s. males had sex)

Family:

✎ Children run the home
✎ We've created the first filio-centric family system
✎ New phenomenon: the "latchkey generation"
✎ U.S. level of child abuse is a national disgrace
✎ 1980 Census report: 48% of those born in 1980 will
be raised in a single parent home
✎ Discipline problems in school, low achievement

Adolescent Rites of Passage:

Boys: Anabolic steroids in sports, involvement in gang or subculture
Girls: Socially fitting in is a major source of stress

Figure 12.6

In forty years families have moved from conservative to liberal, from saving to spending, from respect to harassment, and from parents heading the home to children leading. Figure 12.7 further illustrates the contrast between the old values (prior to 1970) and current social values.

Old Values/New Values

Quantity of possessions	Quality of possessions
Money	Time
Old traditions	New traditions
Commitment	Flexibility
Group Identity	Individualism
Trusting people	Proven integrity
Satisfaction through work	Satisfaction through leisure

Adapted from G. Barna, *The Frog in the Kettle*

Figure 12.7

Ministry to families in the church is going to have to meet people where they are and move them toward biblical foundations of commitment based on unconditional love, grace embracing acceptance and forgiveness, empowering rather than controlling, and intimacy leading to caring, understanding, communication, and communion.

CHARACTERISTICS OF HEALTHY FAMILIES

1. See individual difference as desirable, as God created each family member unique.

2. See struggle as beneficial. It is through struggle that we grow.

3. See grief and pain as necessary. Loss that creates grief is part of life and growth.

4. Families need to walk toward, rather than push toward change.

5. Each family member receives only what is given with an open hand. What is given with strings attached is refused.

6. Love is seen as a commitment to who they are with each other rather than what they expect the relationship to become.

7. See time spent with each other as desirable and beneficial.

8. When one member urgently needs something from another member, he or she can appreciate whatever is available.

9. See expression of love and appreciation as desirable and necessary.

10. All family members communicate directly with each other and personal language comes from the "I" rather than from "you."

11. Home is shaped by who each family member is, not according to some ideal.

12. Conflict is seen as inevitable, and the process of resolution is experienced by all family members.

13. Spiritual values are taught and modeled and then allowed to be bought in the process of growth.

CHARACTERISTICS OF DYSFUNCTIONAL FAMILIES

1. Parents refuse to speak to each other for extended periods of time.

2. Constant arguing and tension.

3. Battering of spouse and/or children.

4. Abuse of alcohol and/or other drugs (prescribed or illicit).

5. Compulsive behavior such as compulsive eating, working, cleaning, gambling, spending, dieting, exercising, and so on. These practices are addictive behaviors and they effectively disrupt and prevent honest contact and intimacy in a family.

6. Inappropriate sexual behavior on the part of a parent toward a child ranging from seductiveness to incest.

7. Parents who are competitive with each other or with their children.

8. Parents who have conflicting attitudes/values or display contradictory behaviors that compete for their children's allegiance.

9. A parent who cannot relate to others in the family and thus actively avoids them, while blaming them for the avoidance.

10. Parents who deny their feelings and what is really happening.

11. Parents who deny their children's feeling and what is really happening.

12. Extreme rigidity about money, religion, work, use of time, displays of affection, sex, television, housework, sports, politics, and so on. Obsession with any of these can harm contact and intimacy, because the emphasis is not on relating but on following the rules.

Healthy versus Dysfunctional Families

To effectively minister to families, one must recognize both the characteristics of health and dysfunction. Often dysfunction in a family is disguised by the practice of Christian living in front of others. Contrasting health and dysfunction here will be a beginning in discerning when and how to minister to hurting families and whether they are ready to be mainstreamed for ministry in the body. See figure 12.8 on page 192.

Ministry to Families

Since it has been demonstrated that dysfunctional families tend to produce dysfunctional families in the next generation, it is imperative that the church ministers to families in a way that corrects their deficits. This means that churches need to assess families on an ongoing basis to determine how they can provide corrective counseling, family enrichment, and other needed resources. The proverb "An ounce of prevention is worth a pound of cure" certainly applies in the context of local church family ministry. Anything that the church can do to prepare its members for the next developmental stage they encounter will be energy well spent. Using the Balswick's model of family ministry let's look at what it means to minister to families in each of the essential areas: preparation, enrichment, and equipping.

1) *Preparational Family Life Ministry:* Preparational ministry seeks to prepare each individual in the family for the next developmental stage of life. There are physical, social, emotional, cognitive, spiritual, and family transitions that take place with each new development stage in the lifecycle. These areas need to be examined, understood, and discussed before one reaches the next stage. This allows one to prepare to meet and live out each stage to the

---

Preparational Family Life Ministry

Goal:	Rehearsal for upcoming issues
Nature:	Educational, Preventive, Resource awareness
Focus:	Large group, with small group experiences, Age-graded with interstage testimonials
Process:	Input-oriented
Venue:	Classroom, ongoing groups (i.e., Sunday School)
Criteria:	Internalized educational objectives

Figure 12.9

fullest capacity possible in ministry to others in the body. The developmental stages are birth, childhood (early, middle, and late), adolescence (early and late), adulthood (young, middle, and late), and death. Preparational family ministry is seen in figure 12.9.

2) *Enrichment Family Life Ministry:* There are several family life issues that spread over the range of developmental stages. Consequently, individuals need more in-depth understanding and skill to experience them to their fullest potential. This would include such issues as marriage, parenting, career, and singleness. Enrichment ministry is demonstrated in figure 12.10.

The church has often neglected spending time and effort in training and enriching in the areas of marriage and parenting, so these will be discussed in greater detail below.

Enrichment Family Life Ministry

Goal:	Better coping, new patterns, new skills, exploration of alternatives, communality
Nature:	Evaluative, experiential, multi-directional, fellowship-based, experimental
Focus:	Small group, interest-based, open-ended
Process:	Fellowship — Communication — Non-formal structure
Venue:	Dens, interest-response initiated
Criteria:	Feedback on intentional use of new skills, flow to redemptive, evangelistic ministries

Figure 12.10

---

a) Marriage: At the center of a family is a marriage. It has often been said that the best gift one can give to children is a good marriage. But society today has created confusion and chaos by redefining the commitment and definition of marriage. Charles Sell says, "Dedicated and conscientious men and women are caught between society's pressures and proclamations of the church; this dilemma causes sizable amounts of stress and guilt for them."[6] Too often couples in the church are falsely seen as having good solid marriages and when they fail, everyone is surprised.

To begin an enrichment ministry for couples a church must assume that most and probably all couples are struggling in some area of their marriage. It may be conflict resolution, finances, intimacy, parenting, communication, spiritual growth, dual careers, roles, relationships with others, distribution of power, trust, or jealousy. The church should not assume that all in the body is well. Rather, within the church periodic assessments of marriages should occur to determine where resources should be directed. Assessment should be followed by counsel in choosing what method or action would best help any couple who needs to grow in an area of weakness.

b) Parenting: Because conception and birth happen in such a natural way, many believe that being a parent will also come naturally. Adults will parent as they were parented or in reaction to how they were parented, unless they learn skills to do it differently. The natural tendency is to pass to the next generation the dysfunction of the current one. So, the first step in parenting is to understand how one was parented. Separating the positive qualities to hang on to and repeat, from the negatives to let go of is primary but also difficult. Areas to be explored should include:

Love:	Was love felt?
	How was love given? (i.e., thru touch, was it expressed, was time given, thru provision)
Trust:	How protective were your parents?
	How different from your parents could you be? (i.e., in thinking, dressing, feeling)
Power:	How was power distributed in your family? Was more power given with age?
	What roles did you play to get power? (i.e., crybaby, saint, jokester, sinner?)
Self-Esteem:	Were you loved just for who you were?
	Were you special?
	What word pictures were you given?
Identity:	What characteristics did your parents value in you?
	Did they give you the sense that you would have a special future?

Exploring these questions in a safe environment of a small group will help parents separate from the way they were parented to be more objective about their own parenting. The context of a small group which can be trusted is important because no one has been parented perfectly, and there is pain in looking at what was missing. This is an example of an enriching experience the church can provide so dysfunction from one generation isn't passed to the next.

3) *Equipping Family Life Ministry:* Equipping needs to take on a twofold purpose. First, each family member needs to be equipped to carry out his or her individual roles in family life. This equipping is done mostly in the areas of preparation and enrichment. Secondly, equipping needs to be done to carry

out the work of the body. Individual gifts also need to be used to strengthen the body of Christ.

First Peter 2:5, 9 clearly teaches that all Christians belong to a universal priesthood of believers and are called to minister to one another so that each one can achieve maturity in Christ. Ephesians 4 says God created each of us uniquely because diversity is needed to create wholeness in the body. The problem is the church, in most cases, isn't interacting as a family of gifted members. Rather, the church has a few trained leaders who lead and the people follow if and when they feel like it. This is where change is needed. The trained leaders need to see the members as gifted and empower and train them to use their giftedness for the strengthening of the body. This means intimately knowing (as a parent does a child) each member so guidance and training can take place. Figure 12.11 illustrates what an equipping family life ministry would look like.

Equipping Family Life Ministry

Goal:	Congregational leaders in effective ministries
Nature:	Watching — Listening — Exploring — Accompanying — Interning — Practicing — Correcting — Reproducing
Focus:	Small group — Supervised team — Unleashed ministers
Process:	A fellowship-learning group that becomes a ministry team
Venue:	Dens, selected leaders, structured process monthly review and reinforcement
Criteria:	Congregational leaders doing effective ministries redemptive, evangelistic

Figure 12.11

---

4) Remedial Family Life Ministry: There is one more family life ministry, beyond the Balswick's model, that is necessary for a local church body to be functioning as a healthy family. That is a remedial family life ministry. Figure 12.12 on page 197 illustrates the components of such a program.

Figure 12.12 from *Five Cries of Parents* by the Strommens,[7] shows that parents' first choice of preferred help with problems are members of the clergy. This means the church has to have a plan of intervention to assist

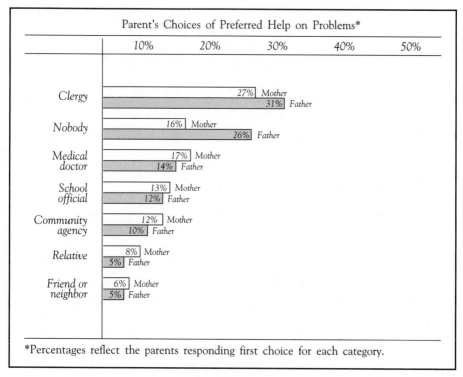

Parent's Choices of Preferred Help on Problems*

	10%	20%	30%	40%	50%

Clergy — 27% Mother / 31% Father

Nobody — 16% Mother / 26% Father

Medical doctor — 17% Mother / 14% Father

School official — 13% Mother / 12% Father

Community agency — 12% Mother / 10% Father

Relative — 8% Mother / 5% Father

Friend or neighbor — 6% Mother / 5% Father

*Percentages reflect the parents responding first choice for each category.

Figure 12.12

families who are struggling. Families may struggle with a wide range of areas, including medical, physical, and emotional. As stated above, the dysfunctions of one generation are passed down to the next unless intervention takes place. As the church helps individuals and families evaluate their needs and strengths for ministry, some people or families will be too dysfunctional to be prepared, enriched, or equipped. Rather, they need to heal by being surrounded with love and acceptance from the body and counseled one on one until they are functioning and ready to be mainstreamed into the family of God.

All levels of help need to be available throughout the network of the body for the church to have a remedial ministry. This network includes Christian counselors, therapists, and social workers—those with the skills to perform intervention, referral, and assistance. This would also include practical helpers, lay counselors, support groups for specific problems, pastoral counselors, psychologists, and psychiatrists who could medicate or hospitalize. When a church doesn't offer a full range of support, a person feels unaccepted and cast out. These feelings of isolation are counterproductive for creating the atmosphere of unconditional love and acceptance desirable in which to drop seeds of faith to be fertilized in these peoples lives.

Remedial Family Life Ministry

Goal:	To mainstream formerly dysfunctional people
Nature:	Relationship — Realization — Responsibility
Focus:	One-to-one, one-to-couple, families, groups
Process:	Therapeutic, Ministerial Counseling
Venue:	Office, as requested
Criteria:	Refunctioning, mainstreamed

Figure 12.13

SUMMARY

The church needs to become a community to play a key role in the reestablishment of the primacy of family relationships. This will require discerning health from dysfunction, discovering strengths and weaknesses, and determining how families can best be met at their points of need and integrated into the church family. Commitment, grace, empowerment, and intimacy need to characterize our church communities so individual families will have a model to follow. Both the church family and individual families should be practicing preparation for new stages, enrichment in the stage they find themselves in, and equipping for ministry to others in areas of strength, while getting remedial help in their areas of weakness. Only in an atmosphere of true love, acceptance, and forgiveness can this begin to take place.

Notes

1. George Barna, *The Frog in the Kettle* (Ventura, Calif.: Regal Books, 1990), 66.

2. Myron Chartier, "Parenting: A Theological Model," *Journal of Psychology and Theology*, 6, 1978: 54-61.

3. Jack O. Balswick and Judy K. Balswick, *The Family* (Grand Rapids: Baker Book House, 1989), 19-33.

4. Balswick, *Family*, 21.

5. Barna, *Frog in the Kettle*, 33.

6. Charles M. Sell, *Family Ministry* (Grand Rapids: Zondervan Publishing House, 1981), 51.

7. Merton P. Strommen, and Irene A. Strommen, *Five Cries of Parents* (San Francisco: Harper and Row Publishers, 1985), 162.

For Further Reading

Arterburn, S. and Felton, J. *Toxic Faith*. Nashville: Thomas Nelson Publishers, 1991.

Barna, G. *The Frog in the Kettle*. Ventura, Calif.: Regal Books, 1990.

Balswick, J.O. and Balswick, J.K. *The Family*. Grand Rapids: Baker Book House, 1989.

Crabb, L. *Men and Women*. Grand Rapids: Zondervan Publishing House, 1991.

Larson, J. *Growing a Healthy Family*. Minneapolis: Augsburg Publishing House, 1986.

Meier, P.D., Minerth, F.B., Wichern, F.B., and Ratcliff, D.E. *Introduction to Psychology and Counseling*. 2nd ed. Grand Rapids: Baker Book House, 1991.

Rekers, G. *Family Building*. Ventura, Calif.: Regal Books, 1985.

Sell, C.M. *Family Ministry*. Grand Rapids: Zondervan Publishing House, 1981.

Skolnick, A.S. and Skolnick, J.H. *Family in Transition*. Glenview, Ill.: Scott, Foresman and Co., 1989.

Stennett, N., Chesser, B., and DeFrain, J. *Building Family Strengths*. Lincoln: University of Nebraska Press, 1979.

Strommen, M. P., and Strommen I. A. *Five Cries of Parents*. San Francisco: Harper & Row Pub., Inc. 1985.

Thirteen
Ministry to Single Adults

Single adult ministry in the local church has taken on unprecedented proportions during the past decade of church ministry. During the 1950s and 1960s the church in North America responded to its ever increasing population of adolescents by providing them with youth leaders, adult sponsors, and eventually their own shepherd: the youth pastor. As these young people grew some of them remained single in order to fulfill important life goals. Many of them married and eventually divorced during the turbulent events of the late 60s and 70s. The result has been a virtual explosion of single adults across the face of North America in the past twenty years. Indeed, this singles phenomenon is by no means restricted to just the Americas. All across the world, adults are choosing to remain single or reenter the singles' world in larger numbers than ever before. Many churches, in turn, have responded by creating a pastoral staff position to specifically address the unique needs and concerns of the single adult.

Gaining a Sociological Perspective

During the 1700s in Colonial America approximately 3 percent of the adults were not married. There was great economic and social pressure to marry. Managing the responsibilities of a farm required a great deal of manpower and single adults found it nearly impossible to cope without a family to help. The average age for first marriage was 13. The chart on page 201 illustrates some of the demographic changes that took place in America over the past 100 years.[1]

As America expanded, so did its population and social structure. Many people began to move into the cities from their rural communities and establish homes near the center of town. Families did not require as many children and single adults, feeling less social pressure to marry, pursued their dreams of

Development of America's Single Adult Population During the Twentieth Century

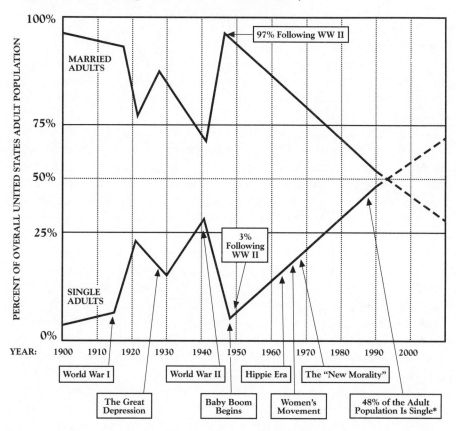

going to school, starting a business, or other personal goals. Eventually, the events of World War I, the Great Depression, and World War II had a profound impact on the demographic composition of America. The population of single adults increased dramatically. However, once the troops returned from fighting overseas America experienced a dramatic rise in the marriage rates, which in turn, led to the subsequent birth of the baby boom generation.

The disillusionment of the 1960s and 1970s brought about the fastest divorce rate in the world. The United Nations recently reported that the United States has the highest divorce rate in the world. The result is an ever increasing rise in the number of single adults.[2] The single adult population in America as of 1990 is approximately 70 million. This represents a significant rise in the age of first marriage which now stands at 26.2 years for men and 23.8 years for women. Times have certainly changed since Colonial America!

Types of Single Adults

Before ministry can be focused to single adults one must consider the diversity of singles that are evident in our society. In essence, there are four different types of singles, and each has their own unique set of characteristics, needs, and issues.

1) *The Never Married:* Adults who never marry are single by choice or by circumstance. In the year 1989 approximately 58 percent of all single adults were never married singles. They represent a large proportion of the young adult/college age population. Although many are young career singles who have chosen to postpone marriage in order to complete numerous years of college and graduate school, there is also a significant percentage of older singles who have chosen to always remain single.

2) *The Divorced Adult:* Divorce rates across most of North America have skyrocketed in recent years. The numbers are overwhelming. Between 1960 and 1978, divorce increased 83 percent for those ages 45-68. The increase was 296 percent for those under 30. According to Dr. Armand Nicholi of Harvard Medical School, divorce in America has increased 700 percent in this century alone. In addition, the number of remarriages has also increased by 63 percent since 1970, to more than one million a year. In fact, the National Center for Health Statistics reported in the summer of '89 that nearly half of all recent marriages are remarriages for one or both spouses. They associate the growing independence of women and fading social stigma of divorce with the creation of a pool of 14.5 million divorced single adults in America today. Some other interesting statistics include:[3]

- More than 70 percent of those who divorce will remarry.
- Only four out of ten adults are married to their first spouse now.
- About one third of all Americans will remarry at least once.
- There is a 60 percent divorce rate among remarriages.

3) *The Widow:* There are currently 13.7 million widowed single adults today, or about 20 percent of the overall population of singles. These individuals are not single by choice but usually by circumstances beyond their control (e.g., death of a spouse through illness, accident, or war). These who become "suddenly single" are probably the least prepared for their new state

and most find the transition into single living to be a painful process.

4) *The Separated Adult:* Exact figures on the number of separated singles in America are hard to find. This can be one of the most painful periods of adult life. This is because the separated adult is caught in two worlds. While still being legally married, this person may be emotionally divorced, or they may be emotionally divorced but still carrying the hurts and pains of their marriage experience with them. Some are perhaps estranged from their spouse for their own safety, for financial reasons, military service, job reassignment, abandonment, or many other possibilities.

Because there are four different types of single adults it's important to realize that no two single adults are alike. Each is characterized by the reason and condition of their single status. The needs of the never married single will be far different from the recently divorced single parent. In addition, the widow who suddenly finds herself in a new set of life circumstances may find single living to be a bewildering experience. In addition, the age of the single adult is an important consideration. A never married single at age 25 will obviously have far different needs than the never married single at age 55. There is much the church can do to minister to the needs of each of these types of single adults, but the first step is to identify the type and then from there design a ministry program to meet their needs.

Identification of Relevant Needs

A survey of 1,400 Christian single adults was recently taken from across the United States. One of the purposes of this survey was to determine their most critical needs.[4] The results of this survey confirmed the findings of other social scientists who have researched other non-Christian singles. In essence, single adults, whether Christians or not, have some of the same basic human needs. Some of these would include the need for:

1) *A sense of bonding with other human beings.* The number one disadvantage of being single, according to numerous national surveys, is loneliness. It's the feeling that one is all alone in the world, drifting without a sense of interpersonal security or attachment. Single adults need to feel a connection to other people around them. Whether with married friends or with other singles, most single adults want to feel a sense of bonding with another human spirit.

2) *Constructive social activities.* Many single adults complain about the lack of opportunities for socializing with other singles. The "dating game" can grind on endlessly. Christian singles don't feel that the popular "singles bar" lifestyle portrayed by the media is appropriate for them and are left wondering where else they can go to meet others with similar needs and interests. Some turn to the church, health clubs, schools, and work for alternative locations.

The basic human desire for social contact with other singles is a strong need.

3) *Opportunities to experience service projects.* Whether short-term assignments such as a holiday weekend or a summer vacation, or a long-term assignment of several years, single adults are in need of developing a broader worldview. When asked to rank order the disadvantages of being single, the number 3 response for these 1,500 Christian single adults was "It makes me self-centered." Many single adults are intent in their quest to climb the corporate ladder of success. Some feel the need to compensate for insecurities through materialism. Still others get so wrapped up in their own problems that it's often difficult to get them to see the opportunities that await them. Since they are single they have greater mobility. In many cases they have fewer restraints and responsibilities that would inhibit their involvement in short-term service projects. The growing single adult population has been one of the reasons why short-term missions has seen such dramatic increases recently.[5]

4) *Encouragement to maintain biblical standards of sexuality.* We live in a world that bombards single adults with the message that it is alright to go to bed with your girlfriend or boyfriend, especially if you love them. The world promotes a sexual ethic that seeks to compromise our faith and counterfeit our values.

Those who were previously married (divorced, widowed, separated) may have established sexual patterns which are now hard to sever. Thus, reevaluating one's ethics, morals, and values is a natural response. However, the moral and ethical standards demonstrated by prominent religious, political, and movie personalities does little to offset this downward social trend of sexual compromise. The church must continue to hold high the banner of abstinence as the only biblical alternative for sexual expression outside of marriage.

5) *Positive self-esteem.* Many Christian singles seem to struggle to find a positive personal identity. In general, society does not cater to the needs of single adults, often leaving them feeling left out and unwanted. This, in turn, contributes to a lower self-concept. Singles need to be reminded of who they are in Christ and of their value as members of the body of Christ.

6) *Financial counsel and advice.* Unlike the popular media image of the "swinging single," most single adults do not possess endless amounts of money. They struggle to make ends meet and find it hard to balance the demands placed upon them by others' expectations. For the single parent, the problem is even more critical. Government statistics reveal that only half of the mothers who are awarded child support by the courts ever receive the full amount. In fact, a quarter receive no payment at all.

Strategy for Ministry to Single Adults
Churches interested in starting a single adult ministry are always wise to follow a few simple steps. Each one is important and needs to be considered wisely.

1) Pray about the desire to minister to single adults and search the motives. If the reason for starting a singles ministry is simply to better compete with the church down the road then those are the wrong motives. Don't expect God's blessing on a church program that is not first of all covered in prayer.

2) Determine the church's climate for a single adult ministry. Ministry always takes place within a certain cultural and social climate. Each church will have a different attitude toward single adults. Some churches view singles as unfortunate souls who have missed God's will for their lives. Other churches see them as equal members of society and of the body of Christ. Knowing how your church feels about single adults is important for laying a foundation for single adult ministry.

3) Consult with the senior pastor and governing church board. Proverbs 15:22 says, "Without consultation, plans are frustrated, but with many counselors they succeed." The leadership team of the church should be consulted and their support should be received before a ministry to single adults is begun.

4) Identify the target area. Realize that with very few exceptions no one church can address all of the needs for all four types of single adults, especially for all age groups. Focus should be on one particular type of single adult and beginning to address their unique needs. Some churches may be able to provide safe haven for embattled single parents. Others may be located close to a university so they will appeal to the younger, never married single. The atmosphere of one church may be more conducive to a particular type of single adult. If so, identify that type and specialize in it.

No church can provide a balanced program for every type of single adult ministry available today. Some may be limited by financial or physical resources. Still others may be going through a transition in leadership.

5) Be a healing ministry. As a strategy for program design, seek to heal the hurts that many single adults possess. Some need healing from a painful divorce, some are going through grieving after the death of a spouse. A few women may be suffering from the consequences of physical abuse, while others are searching for meaning and purpose in life. The most effective single adult ministries are those that are marked by an atmosphere of unconditional acceptance. Singles want an environment where they can be authentic. Many are weary from past broken relationships and need time to regain their focus on life. Their spirits are tired, and they are in search of a place to find peace.

6) Involve as many single adults as possible in their ministry. When single adults own their ministry it will be fruitful and purposeful. The New Testament model of ministry was never designed to be done by just one person. God dispersed numerous spiritual gifts throughout the body to illustrate how much we need each others contribution. An active singles ministry will take a great deal of input from its membership and require a great deal of involvement from its leaders.

Many singles ministries select a leadership council which rotates annually. This council is comprised of leaders who will assume duties such as welcoming visitors each week, calling those who are sick or unable to attend, planning special events and social activities, publicity, coordinating small groups, or directing service projects. Single adults are capable of assuming leadership roles in the church. They handle significant responsibilities during the week in their places of employment and do not want to be treated as dependent children by their local church on weekends.

See the recommended reading section at the conclusion of this chapter for additional resources that are available for churches who desire to start a ministry to single adults.

Implications for Program Design

Once one has identified the type of singles to be targeted and realized the issues involved in such a ministry, it's imperative to think through the philosophy of ministry that the church will use. No successful ministry just happens. The chart on page 207 helps illustrate the various components of a successful single adult ministry and the many program activities for each component.[6]

A balanced program for a healthy single adult ministry requires both "outreach" and "inreach" activities which include: evangelism, social activities, teaching, building community, support groups, counseling, leadership training, etc. Every church cannot provide a comprehensive program that will meet all of these outreach and inreach elements. However, the more balanced a church can become in their programming, the more successful and fruitful they will be.

Outreach

Evangelism. A variety of activities will enable the church to reach out to a lost and needy world. These should reach those who walk through the front door on a weekly basis as well as those in the surrounding community. A partial list of such activities would include: sports events, socials, Friday evening outings, community events, a singles visitation team, and special workshops. Although the Gospel need not be presented every time the singles group gathers together, care should be taken that this important element is not overlooked completely.

Service. The word *minister* means "to serve." No believer can minister in the name of Christ if not actively involved in serving the needs of others. Service projects which a single adult ministry can sponsor include: visiting a convalescent hospital, being a big brother or big sister to a needy child, supporting a third-world child through an organization like World Vision or Compassion, working at an inner-city rescue mission one day a month, having a handicapped

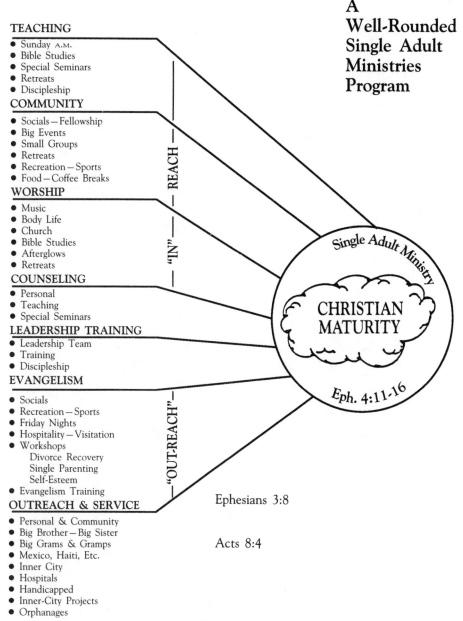

TEACHING
- Sunday A.M.
- Bible Studies
- Special Seminars
- Retreats
- Discipleship

COMMUNITY
- Socials — Fellowship
- Big Events
- Small Groups
- Retreats
- Recreation — Sports
- Food — Coffee Breaks

WORSHIP
- Music
- Body Life
- Church
- Bible Studies
- Afterglows
- Retreats

COUNSELING
- Personal
- Teaching
- Special Seminars

LEADERSHIP TRAINING
- Leadership Team
- Training
- Discipleship

EVANGELISM
- Socials
- Recreation — Sports
- Friday Nights
- Hospitality — Visitation
- Workshops
    Divorce Recovery
    Single Parenting
    Self-Esteem
- Evangelism Training

OUTREACH & SERVICE
- Personal & Community
- Big Brother — Big Sister
- Big Grams & Gramps
- Mexico, Haiti, Etc.
- Inner City
- Hospitals
- Handicapped
- Inner-City Projects
- Orphanages

REACH — "IN" — "OUT-REACH"

A
Well-Rounded
Single Adult
Ministries
Program

Single Adult Ministry

CHRISTIAN
MATURITY

Eph. 4:11-16

Ephesians 3:8

Acts 8:4

Figure 13.2

ministry, promoting short-term mission experience overseas, or helping a needy person within the church by spending the day giving them a hand.

Inreach

Teaching. The teaching emphasis of one's ministry should be balanced and focused on issues that are practical and down to earth. Activities which are conducive for teaching include special seminars and conferences, small group fellowships, retreats, and discipleship groups.

Building Community. Single adults need to feel a sense of belonging. Christian single adults want to feel as though they belong in their church. It becomes difficult for many single adults to feel motivated to contribute in their church if it does not acknowledge their existence or puts minimal resources into reaching out to them. Building a sense of community can be achieved by putting on special social events for singles, having small group fellowship meetings, hosting special speakers for singles, going on weekend retreats, or hosting a large event such as a concert or special speaker.

Worship. All believers enjoy worshiping their Creator. People with common interests can enjoy expressing their worship to God in a similar manner. For this reason, meetings after the evening service, known as "afterglows," have been popular among single adult groups. Single adult groups across the country enjoy contemporary music in their worship meetings. Much can be done to make the worship experience of singles creative and personal at camps, retreats, and small group fellowships.

Counseling. According to one national survey of Christian single adults only 20 percent of the single adults would go to a professional counselor if they needed help.[7] The majority of them consult the advice of friends and relatives. For that reason it would be helpful for single adult leaders to offer some form of counseling training. It might be helpful to bring in a professional counselor for a special series of seminars on introductory counseling issues. A teaching series on important issues facing single adults would be beneficial, as would small group counseling sessions for single adults by a professional counselor.

Leadership Training. As noted previously, ministry must be a team effort when working with single adults. They like to feel as though they have some degree of control over their program design. The more input you can receive from them, the better will be the success rate of your programs. To do this it's essential to conduct some form of leadership training. The leadership council that is involved in the decision-making of the group, and those who will be responsible for implementing their decisions should receive quality training for their assignments. This training can take the form of a semiannual leadership retreat, special training conferences, seminars, and small group or one-on-one sessions with the single adult leaders.

Summary

A ministry to single adults should be *considered* by every church in North America to determine what part they can play in fulfilling the Great Commission. Single adult ministry is a specialized field today because of the unique needs of singles in our culture. No longer can we "graduate" the senior high pastor into the position of Minister to Singles just because he is getting too old to relate to kids. Such a mentality will lead to the inevitable demise of the single adult in the church. They will simply move on to other churches where they will be treated like the adults they are.

The biblical model for designing a ministry is always to first identify the needs, and then plan a strategy to meet those needs through the resources that are available. No church can do it all. Some churches are smaller with limited resources, unable to meet all the needs of diverse groups represented in the church today. But for those churches who have identified a group of single adults to whom they want to minister, then every effort should be taken to ensure quality programming by leadership that is trained to share the responsibilities of the ministry with the single adults themselves.

A balanced program is the goal. Outreach activities will help the single adults keep a focus on their calling to be lights in the world. The inreach activities will help fulfill the mandate of Ephesians 4:11-16 to build up and equip the members of the body of Christ for the ministry. Both must be done to have a healthy ministry to single adults.

Notes

1. Carolyn A. Koons, and Michael J. Anthony, *Single Adult Passages: Uncharted Territories* (Grand Rapids: Baker Book House, 1991), 43.

2. Jerry Jones, *Single Adult Ministries Journal*, vol. 8, no. 3 (Jan. 1991): 3.

3. Jerry Jones, *Single Adult Ministries Journal*, vol. 7, no. 6 (April 1990): 2.

4. Koons and Anthony, *Passages*, 30.

5. Jerry Jones, *Single Adult Ministries Journal*, vol. 7, no. 9 (May 1990): 1.

6. Douglas L. Fagerstrom, ed., *Singles Ministry Handbook* (Wheaton, Ill.: Victor Books, 1988), 239.

7. Koons and Anthony, *Passages*, 204.

For Further Reading

Cavanaugh, M. *God's Call to the Single Adult.* Springdale: Pa.: Whitaker House, 1968.

Fagerstrom, D. ed. *Singles Ministry Handbook.* Wheaton, Ill.: Victor Books, 1988.

Hershey, T. *Beginning Again: Life After a Relationship Ends.* Nashville: Thomas Nelson, Inc., 1986.

Hershey, T. *Young Adult Ministry.* Loveland, Colo.: Group Books, 1986.

Karssen, G. *Getting the Most Out of Being Single.* Colorado Springs: NavPress, 1983.

Peppler, A. *Single Again — This Time with Children: A Christian Guide for the Single Parent.* Minneapolis: Augsburg Publishing House, 1982.

Reed, B. *Making the Most out of Single Life.* St Louis: Warner Books, 1980.

Richards, L. *Remarriage: A Healing Gift from God.* Waco, Tex.: Word Inc., 1981.

Simenauer, J., and Carroll, D. *Singles: The New Americans.* New York: Simon & Schuster, 1982.

Smith, H. *Help for Parents of a Divorced Son or Daughter.* Minneapolis: Augsburg Publishing House, 1981.

Smith, H. *Positively Single.* Wheaton, Ill.: Victor Books, 1987.

Smoke, J. *Growing Through Divorce.* Irvine, Calif.: Harvest House, 1979.

Smoke, J. *Living Beyond Divorce: The Possibilities of Remarriage.* Eugene, Ore.: Harvest House, 1984.

Weiss, R. *Going it Alone.* New York: Harper & Row, Pubs. Inc., 1981.

PART THREE.
Organization and Administration of Christian Education

Fourteen
Organizational Structures
for Christian Education Ministry

Christopher Robin in *Winnie-the-Pooh* once said, "Organizing is what you do before you do something, so that when you do it, it's not all mixed up."[1] Perhaps you can relate to this simple yet concise definition of organization. The benefits of organization and administration in business are obvious. Corporations spend small fortunes on seminars and consultants to make their business more efficient and effective. It's easy to measure the results as well. Since the purpose of a corporation is to make a financial profit, one simply needs to look at the "bottom line." If the profit has increased, then the efforts have been worthwhile.

But in a church, the results are not quite as tangible or easily measured. If we practice good organization and administration, what can we measure to see if it worked—and how will we measure it?

Measuring success must always begin with a clear sense of purpose. Ellis refers to purposefulness as "the clear and dominant sense of what one is seeking to accomplish."[2] It's impossible to measure the distance between two cities until the cities have been identified. In the same way, it's impossible to measure the impact of programs and policies in a church if there is not a clear picture of what the church is trying to accomplish.

Two Purposes for the Church
Many excellent volumes have been written which detail the purpose of the church. The recommended reading section at the end of this chapter will provide the interested reader with a suggested list. The majority of these resources could be summarized in a two-dimensional purpose: evangelism and edification.

Evangelism is the process by which a believer allows the Holy Spirit to use him or her to reach an unbeliever with the message of the Gospel. God could have chosen to use many different ways to speak to people about Himself. But in His sovereignty, He has chosen to use people to reach others.

Four lepers sat outside the famine-stricken city, devising a last-ditch plan for survival. They would visit the camp of the enemy, where they would either be taken prisoner and live, or be killed — which would happen soon in any case through starvation. Upon arriving at the enemy camp, they found the people had fled, leaving huge stores of food — enough to end the famine. The lepers hid much of the food for themselves, but then realized the impact it could have on their starving nation. Second Kings 7:9 records their action. "Then they said to one another, 'We are not doing right. This day is a day of good news, but we are keeping silent; if we wait until morning light, punishment will overtake us. Now therefore come, let us go and tell the king's household.' "

This passage implies one of the simplest definitions of evangelism: One beggar telling another beggar where to find bread. God is the One who does the actual work of convicting and bringing people to Himself (John 16:8). People are the instruments through which this work takes place. The church, then, is in the business of developing people through whom God can do His work freely.

Edification describes the process by which a believer is encouraged to become more mature in his or her walk with Christ. The local church provides the primary environment for this to occur. Since the church is seen in Scripture to be the "bride of Christ," the WIFE acronym simply describes the four aspects of edification:

Worship	— Responding in love to God.
Instruction	— Learning about God through His Word.
Fellowship	— Relating to others because of Christ's love.
Expression	— Exercising our growing faith.

How then can a church measure its effectiveness? By beginning with a solid understanding of its purpose. Once the purpose is clearly in mind, each program and structure in the church can be evaluated in light of how well they support that two-fold purpose — evangelism and edification.

Christian Education will be concerned with both areas, but the focus is more specifically centered on edification, with evangelism being a by-product. Ted Ward suggests two purposes of Christian Education in particular: facilitation of spiritual development and encouragement of the gifts of the Spirit in such ways that the people of God become effective in ministry.[3]

But Is It Biblical?

Our original question asked if it was right to apply business structures to a spiritual organization, such as a church. The question could also be reversed — do biblical principles work in a business setting? In other words, are there certain biblical principles that are applicable in any organization? Can these biblical absolutes apply to other areas outside of spiritual ministry? A number of principles in Scripture can be studied:

1) *Design.* No one goes to bed at night worrying about whether the sun will come up in the east the next morning. Likewise, you would be hard-pressed to convince someone that the sun would reverse its course tomorrow. Why? Because God has created the universe with order, fulfilling the *principle of design* and purpose. The seasons coincide with the growth cycles necessary for agriculture to flourish. Even science is based on the orderliness of God through His creation. Take away that order and science would lose its ability to make predictions based on consistent events.

2) *Organization.* God sees the end from the beginning. When He wanted to lead His people into the Promised Land, He knew what it would take to get them there, and He had an orderly plan in mind. He chose Moses to carry out — *to organize* — that plan. Exodus records the many organizational principles of leadership and delegation that are practiced today in both secular and church settings. Exodus 18:13-24 is a primary example of the principles of delegation, when Moses' father-in-law, Jethro, counseled him concerning ways to lessen his work load by dividing the responsibilities with others.

3) *Administration.* Acts 6:1-8 records the administration that took place in response to a need — the fact that certain widows were not receiving their daily allotment of food. The breakdown took place because the apostles were overworked as responsibilities increased. In response, new structures of organization were put into place to see that the distribution of food was properly administrated.

These and many others are principles that apply in any organizational situation — secular or sacred. It demonstrates that God is a God of order, and that both organization and administration are biblical concepts that come from the very nature of God.

Should a church be run like a church or a business? The answer is *yes.* The church is an organization, much like the governments, kingdoms, families, and other institutions found in Scripture. As such, it can and should be structured and operated using those solid principles that come from God. But it must also be remembered that the church is not a business. It's purposes are entirely different, and alternative standards and measurements must be used to evaluate its effectiveness.

In the analogy of the vine and the branches, Jesus said, "Apart from Me you can do nothing" (John 15:5). A church can be as organized and well-administrated as any secular organization, but if it's not founded on a deep sense of dependence upon God, the organization is functioning apart from its source of life.

Definitions

The discussion in the paragraphs above becomes clearer when we realize that the church is both an *organization* and an *organism*. An organization has structure, design, and purpose. It's designed to work toward a common end. An organism can be exactly the same except for one primary distinctive: life.

A church with structure but no life is well-organized, but dead and ineffective. A church with life but no structure is well-meaning and enthusiastic, but unwieldy and ineffective—like a body without a skeleton.

Organization, then, is critical to the effectiveness of a church. Organization refers to the plan—the conceptual framework that holds the organization together and provides strength. Stemming directly from the organizational purpose, it's the structure that determines how people can work together in relationship to effectively accomplish that purpose.

Administration is often simplistically defined in business textbooks as "getting things done through people." In a strict sense, it involves the "fleshing out" of the organizational structure—placing people in each of the organizational positions to carry out the plan.

The concept has become popular in ministry organizations as well, which works fine if the ministry is simply viewed as an organization. But it breaks down when you view ministry as an organism. Administration is more than simply using people to accomplish a goal. It involves meeting the needs of people through servant leadership, which allows the "body" to work together effectively. This in turn causes organizational purposes to be met. The difference is one of *focus:* for an organization, the focus is goal attainment; for an organism, the focus is serving people.

Getting things done through people is a view that causes people to be extrinsically motivated. Meeting the needs of people causes them to be intrinsically motivated. Biblically, administration must be characterized by the latter view.

Most Christians have learned their views on organization and administration from secular sources and often develop a philosophy that is contrary to the standards of Scripture. Yet as Christians, we believe that God's Word is the resource that gives us understanding in every part of our lives, including how to run a church. Hind emphasizes the importance of a biblical perspective in developing our views of management:

Christ was the most effective executive in the history of the human race. The results He achieved are second to none. In only three years, He defined a mission and formed strategies and plans to carry it out. With a staff of twelve unlikely men He organized Christianity, which has grown to have 1.5 billion proponents today, is international in scope, and has branches in all the world's 223 countries. Christianity has a 32.4 percent share of the world's current population—twice as big as its nearest rival. He recruited, trained, and motivated twelve ordinary men to become extraordinary. He is the greatest manager and developer of people ever."[4]

Biblical Success

A church will realize its greatest effectiveness when it builds a biblical organization and carries that organization out through biblical administration. Each of the organizational structures that we develop must be set up and administrated in biblical ways if they are to lead to success in God's eyes.

Church structures must involve a balance between organization and administration, agreement on common goals, and good communication between members. With this criteria in mind, we can move our focus to the structures themselves.

Where Does Christian Education Take Place?

More than ever before, we live in a changing world. Newspapers constantly present statistics showing the rapid rate of the increase of knowledge. Corporations compete to have a reputation as the most technologically advanced. Nations proudly present their scientific advances as documentation that they are on the "cutting edge." People can look at organizations in the corporate world today and see aggressive attempts to meet the needs of a changing society.

That's not always true in the church. Right or wrong, churches are not usually known as hallmarks of relevance. It's true that we should not let society dictate the way the church should be run. We don't have to use the same organizational and administrative structures as the business world. But it's also true that if our goal, as a living church, is to meet the needs of people around us, then the church must be responsive to those needs when they change.

Gene Getz describes the biblical perspective as a balance between three lenses—Scripture, history, and culture. In developing a ministry, Getz suggests looking first through the lens of Scripture to build a solid biblical foundation for ministry. Second, a look through the lens of history will help develop a relevant ministry by learning from events of the past. Finally, one

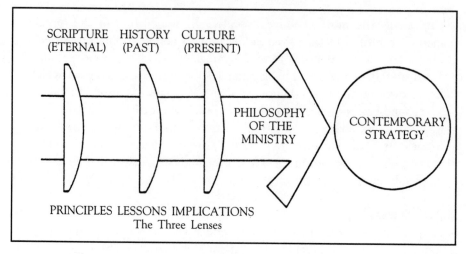

Figure 14.1

must look through the lens of culture to make the organizational structures relevant in terms of effective ministry to the current generation.[5]

Too often, churches focus only the first two lenses—Scripture and history—and ignore the changes taking place in the culture. The church doesn't necessarily always need to be on the cutting edge of technology and innovation, though progress in these areas is admirable. However, the church should be on the cutting edge of how to meet the real needs of people. People look in awe at corporations that set the standard for current technology. People should look in awe at the church as it reaches out to people in relevant ministry. Whatever structures will assist the church in this objective are then appropriate.

Jesus addressed the same problem in His day. Throughout the Gospels, He pointed out the danger of ignoring current culture, evidenced by holding onto traditions that have outlived their purposes. Christ emphasizes the need to have relevance in our structures, "Nor do men put new wine into old wineskins; otherwise the wineskins burst, and the wine pours out, and the wineskins are ruined; but they put new wine into fresh wineskins, and both are preserved" (Matt. 9:17).

New wine was stored in new wineskins. As the wine would ferment, the flexible wineskin would allow for expansion. But in time, the wineskin would become brittle. If new wine was placed in brittle wineskins, the skin would burst from the expansion. Wineskins were not discarded because they were old, but only when they were too brittle to handle what was happening inside of them.

In the same way, the structures of Christian Education are the vehicles by which ministry is accomplished. As a church responds to the surrounding culture, these structures should be evaluated for effectiveness. The structures (often called traditions) need not be discarded simply because they are old; they should only be revised if they are no longer suitable for meeting the current needs of people.

Variables in Contemporary Ministry

Twenty years ago, Christian Education was predictable. Most churches had Sunday School on Sunday mornings, an evening service, and a mid-week program. Curriculum was biblical and appropriate for the people under the church's ministry. Families were relatively stable in terms of roles and relationships.

Since that time, there have been rapid changes in culture worldwide, and the church has tried to be responsive. In the last few years, life has taken on a much more global world view (it's not uncommon to hear children comparing airports they have visited around the world). More Americans than ever hyphenate their nationality, indicating a broader mix in society. Congregations in most areas, both urban and rural, are becoming more multicultural than before, a mix found in the community as well.

Ministry has been impacted as well by such changes. In an attempt to become more relevant, many churches are writing their own curriculum rather than purchasing prepackaged studies. Other churches have shifted from a weekly through-the-Bible type of study to an elective approach for adults. Many churches have eliminated the mid-week service to help families find more time to be together. A lot of churches have experimented with Friday and Saturday evening services to accommodate the diverse needs of their membership. In essence, their structures have adjusted to the needs of those in their communities.

Churches across the world vary in size from the very small to the very large. Both have unique challenges in developing viable ministry. But in each case, organization and administration take place in structures that blend people, resources, and programs for the purpose of accomplishing the work of ministry in the community.

Christian Education as a Whole

Riding a motorcycle is different than driving a car. They both share the same road and accomplish the same purpose, but each operates by different principles. Likewise, churches are structured in different ways. Small churches and large churches, rural ministries and urban ministries, Western culture and foreign culture — all attempt to pursue a biblical mandate for ministry. The goals are common, and the objective is shared. But the structures will differ to meet the needs of the people involved.

The organizational structure of Christian Education is best seen in any particular setting by developing an organizational chart. The purpose of such a chart is
to give a graphic representation of the structure of relationships within the body.
A smaller church will have a less-detailed organizational chart, while a large
church presents a more detailed breakdown of relationships.

In a small church, the person coordinating the Christian Education program is usually a volunteer or part-time person. A medium-sized church will
hire a part-time person, or combine the position with another area of ministry
(e.g., C.E./Music, C.E./Youth). Larger churches generally hire a full-time, paid
professional.

The Christian Education ministry will be divided into a number of areas,
depending on the scope of the program. Each division will be led by an
individual who is directly responsible to the Christian Education Director.
The D.C.E. (or Minister of C.E. if ordained) oversees the entire ministry,
evaluating and coordinating the plans of these individual programs. Each of
those programs may be divided further, depending on the size of the ministry.
Large churches may hire full-time professionals over individual departments,
such as Minister of Early Childhood Education or Minister of Senior Adults.
The following organizational charts will detail the relationships between those
individuals.

This sample organizational chart (figure 14.2) shows the simple divisions of
ministry for a small church (under 250 members):

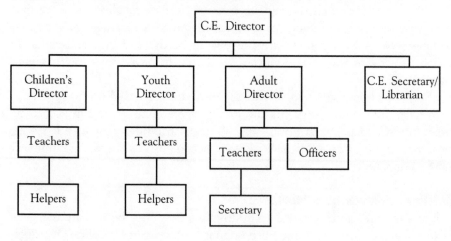

Figure 14.2

The basic structure remains the same (figure 14.3) in a medium-sized
church (250-800 members), but additional levels of leadership are inserted to
accommodate the increase in numbers:

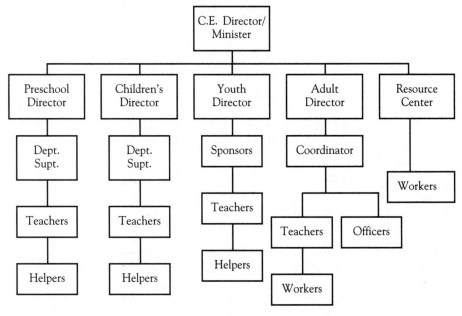

Figure 14.3

A large church (over 800) needs extensive coordination, because of the number of people involved in the program (figure 14.4, see page 222).

Internal Christian Education Structures

Depending upon the part of the world in which the ministry is located, a variety of agencies and programs will make up the details of the organizational chart. Though the church is the central focus of Christian Education, the field can extend to include three primary areas: the church, family, and the Christian school. These areas will often overlap in terms of description, because they are interrelated through the relationship of people.

1) Sunday School. Contrary to popular belief, Sunday School is not mentioned in the Bible. It began in eighteenth century England when Robert Raikes taught children to read on Sunday, the only day they were not working. The Bible was the primary text, and biblical teaching was part of the process.

Today, the institution of Sunday School still exists, but the purposes have changed. Most Sunday Schools do not exist to teach literacy, but the traditional focus is Bible knowledge in a classroom environment. Sunday School is usually the first thing people think of when they hear the term "Christian Education." It crosses denominational lines and has generally been taught by non-professional volunteers.

Sunday School has been an evangelistic tool for many churches throughout

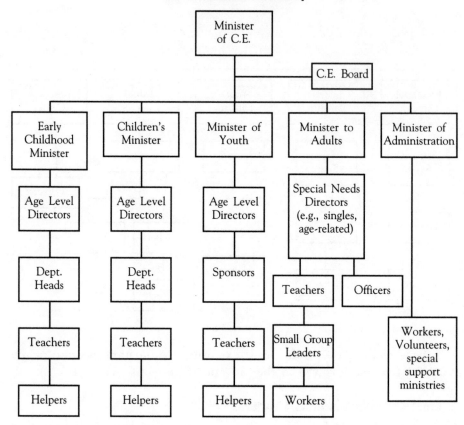

Figure 14.4

recent history. Many adult Christians point to a Sunday School teacher who led them to Christ early in life. Today, Sunday School is the most common Christian Education agency in the context of the church and still claims evangelism as one of its key accomplishments. Instruction and worship can be found in a variety of settings, and expression takes place in various church programs. But Sunday School offers the opportunity for relationships to occur in distinct ways. People who are unimpressed or unaffected in a worship service will often make a commitment to Christ after seeing Him in the lives of the friends they have made.

Sunday School is not sacred, in spite of its advantages. It's similar to the wineskin mentioned earlier. It is an agency that traditionally fulfills the purpose of Christian Education. In recent years, as culture has been changing, many churches have used variations of Sunday School to meet specific needs — moving it to a different day of the week for adults, offering elective topics, or meeting in different locations. The key is to see if it is fulfilling its objective. If it is, then keep the "wineskin." If not, revise it or replace it. As Chuck Swindoll says, "We must be willing to leave the familiar methods without disturbing the essential message."[6]

An example of this "new-wineskins" approach to traditional ministry is found in those churches that have modified the structure and curriculum of the traditional Sunday School program by creating a Lay Bible Institute format. In this contemporary approach to adult Bible teaching the curriculum is planned according to two-year cycles, with each cycle building upon the previous one. After a student has completed three or four cycles, depending on the extent of the program, the student receives a lay institute certificate designed by the church to signify successful completion of a six or eight year program.

Hartman has found five separate types of audience groups in Sunday Schools, each having its own distinctives: the fellowship group, the traditional group, the study group, the social concerns group and the multiple interest group. Each group has different priorities in terms of the types of teachers they prefer, and he suggests a more concentrated effort to match the teacher and the group for a good blend. For example, the traditional group is high on content, but not as interested in the teacher's methods, while the social concerns group wants a teacher who is primarily concerned about class members. Hartman states: "The traditional manner of forming Sunday School classes and assigning persons to them on the basis of age, sex, or marital status is called into question by the above data. Perhaps other criteria such as teaching style, subject matter, and group life expectation should also be considered."[7]

2) Age Group Programs. God designed people to need each other. It's the whole concept of body ministry found in the New Testament. It's also true that people who meet with others who have similar characteristics or interests can learn from each other in a group setting. For that reason, Christian Education has generally taken place in age groups. For example, children's ministry is often divided into:

Nursery (birth–2)
2s and 3s
4s and 5s
Primary (Grades 1–2)
Middlers (Grades 3–4)
Juniors (Grades 5–6).

Many churches eliminate middlers, making primary cover grades 1-3 while juniors cover grades 4-6. Many adults determine their choice of a church by the type of treatment their children receive there. This ministry can take place in a Sunday School setting, children's church (discussed later), or a weekday club program.

Youth have special needs and need a program that allows them to find some solid interaction with adults and other teens in an attempt to find relevant application of biblical truth. Junior high includes grades 7 and 8 (sometimes 9), while high school goes from the end of junior high until graduation from high school. Some churches include college in the youth category, but most include them under the adult department. The challenge of this rewarding ministry is to find relevant connections between the things they're learning in the context of ministry and their day-to-day existence at school, work, and social situations.

Adults can begin at college age and include young adults, middle adults, senior adults, and singles. Recent research has shown the distinct needs of each adult stage and programming should reflect those needs. Larger churches may have a paid staff member in charge of each of these areas. Even smaller churches are emphasizing singles ministry because of the growing number of singles in the church community (see chapter 13 for a detailed discussion on single adult ministry). The focus of Scripture is that the "older" should teach the "younger" (Titus 2), so adult ministry should encourage adults to become more involved in serving those who are younger than themselves. Traditional senior adult ministry is ministry to adults, when the biblical pattern is for ministry to be originating from senior adults. Many churches are beginning to recognize adults as a key resource for meeting the needs of people.

Peterson describes the differences in teaching children (pedagogy) and teaching adults (andragogy) in the following chart. Notice that youth would be in various stages of transition between the two columns:[8]

	Pedagogy	Andragogy
The Learner	Dependent	Interdependent
The Goal	Acquire knowledge	Solve problems
The Process	Teacher-directed	Self-directed
	Teacher determines need	Student determines need
	Authority oriented	Mutually respectful
	Formal	Informal

Figure 14.5

Nichols suggests that balance is needed when approaching different age groups, "Christian educators cannot be satisfied with the overemphasis on ministry to children and youth. This concept is reinforced by Scripture where we notice that in both the Old and New Testaments the emphasis seems to be on adults."[9]

Though many churches continue to hold Sunday evening programs for various age-levels, the trend is moving slowly away from this set program to a more relational setting that meets the needs of today's children, youth, and adults. Again, the key is to ask: is this program meeting needs? Traditional ways of ministry are effective and right as long as they are a balanced blend of scriptural, historical, and cultural considerations.

3) *Children's Worship.* "Children's church" is usually held after Sunday School, during the time of the regular morning service. The purpose is to provide a worship service that is similar to the adult service, but geared to their own age-level. It serves as a training ground to help them know what to expect when they are old enough to attend the adult service. Usually, it is a blend of songs, Bible reading, prayer, storytelling, crafts, and other age-appropriate activities.

4) *Vacation Bible School.* This agency is an opportunity to reach children during their vacation from school. This usually takes place in the summer, though it can happen during other holidays. It tends to be a more informal environment, providing a concentrated time for Bible learning, activities, and fellowship. Many parents who would not send their children to any other church function welcome the chance to get one or two weeks of "freedom" during the summer, knowing their children are in a safe, moral environment. In many parts of the United States and Canada, school districts are opting to save money by going to year round school for children. In neighborhoods where this is the case, creative programming can allow a church to take advantage of other seasonal holidays besides just the summer vacation.

5) *Camping.* The opportunity to be away from the telephone, the television, and the distractions of life are afforded those who participate in camping activities. The payoff is the chance to involve people in a twenty-four-hour-a-day discipleship experience in an outdoor setting, where their focus can be more directed toward spiritual things. It's appropriate for all ages as well. Many centrally located camps have programs that churches can take advantage of, while some larger churches (or denominations) run their own facilities and programs. Many smaller groups within the church plan retreats for classes, staff or leadership groups as a time of refreshment and renewal.

6) *Seasonal.* A church's location will provide opportunities for Christian Education to take place in unique settings. This can involve snow trips and retreats in colder climates, desert hikes and beach trips in warmer climates. Missions trips to other cultural areas, both in and out of the country, are often most appropriate during certain times of the year.

7) *Boards and Committees.* The Board of Christian Education works with the Director or Minister of Christian Education to provide oversight of the C.E. program. Scheduling, budgeting, purchasing, and facilities arrangements are all under the control of this board. In addition, decisions related to teaching standards, content, and curriculum are a part of this board's jurisdiction. A position on the C.E. Board should be viewed as a viable ministry, on the same plane with the teachers of individual classes.

8) *Family Ministry.* Deuteronomy 6 indicates that the primary training ground for Christian Education should be the home. The family structure should surround a child with an environment of God-consciousness from infancy. Unfortunately, today's widespread dysfunctional families have produced a generation of parents who simply do not know how to provide this environment for their own children. The church's role, then, is one of support and education — providing tools and training to make the home the center of Christian Education.

9) *Christian Schools.* Christian Education in the elementary and secondary level is provided as an alternative to the influences of secular educational settings. Privately funded, such institutions are effective to the degree that they provide a strong educational program taught by qualified, committed teachers while genuinely enhancing the student's commitment to Christ. Since the costs of Christian schooling are often prohibitive, home schooling has become the norm for many Christian families. Recent development in curriculum have provided home schooling families with more "user-friendly" resources. Higher education provides the opportunity for college students to study in a Bible college (training primarily for vocational Christian ministry) or a Christian liberal arts college or university (training in a Christian environment for a variety of professions). See chapter 25 for a more detailed discussion of this subject.

Administrative Concerns

Some Ministers of Christian Education lament, "I could get so much work done if I didn't have to deal with so many people." It's great to have well-coordinated, laser-printed organizational charts, but people are at the heart of administration. John Cionca states that the biggest problem pastors face is a people problem: "finding enough people to accomplish the educational program."[10]

Many books have been written that deal with recruitment and personnel issues. But the key to organizational structures that work focuses on placing the right people in the right jobs. It's a biblical concept, as well as a logical one. God has gifted different people in different ways, because He wants them to minister according to those gifts. The degree to which a person is able to exercise his or her God-given abilities in ministry will determine his or her success, interest, and results in that ministry. That doesn't mean that a person should never teach if he doesn't have the gift of teaching, any more than a person without the gift of giving would never place anything in the offering. It means getting close enough to people to know where they would best fit into the ministry, equipping them to do the job, and supporting them through the process.

Organizing for Results

Organizing a ministry is one of the greatest challenges a ministry faces. The structures a ministry chooses to carry out its purpose will determine the effectiveness of the endeavor. With the purpose of the ministry firmly in mind, the organizational structures must find that delicate balance between operating as a business and operating as a church.

Organizational structures must be biblical, but they must also meet the needs of people in the culture around which the ministry is focused. The ultimate mark of success in a ministry is not the number of people which attend, but the percentage of people who are genuinely maturing in their Christian life. People on the "outside" should be able to walk into the church and know that they've genuinely encountered God.

Notes

1. A.A. Milne, *Winnie-the-Pooh* (New York: E.P. Dutton, 1961), 41.

2. Joe Ellis, *The Church on Purpose* (Cincinnati: Standard Publishing, 1982), 17.

3. Ted Ward, "A Standard of Excellence," *Christian Education Today*, Fall 1988: 10.

4. James F. Hind, *The Heart and Soul of Effective Management* (Wheaton, Ill., Victor Books, 1989), 13-14.

5. Gene Getz, *Sharpening the Focus of the Church* (Wheaton, Ill., Victor Books, 1984), 16.

6. Chuck R. Swindoll, "Doing Ministry the Right Way—For the Right Reasons" Sermon given at First Evangelical Free Church of Fullerton, Calif., 26 May 1991.

7. Warren J. Hartman, "Research on the Sunday School Mosaic," in *Renewing the Sunday School and the CCD*, Religious Education Press, D. Campbell Wyckoff, ed. (Birmingham, Ala., 1986), 46-51.

8. Gilbert A. Peterson, *The Christian Education of Adults*, (Chicago: Moody Press, 1984), 74.

9. Charles H. Nichols, "Building the Philosophical Foundation," *Christian Education Journal*, vol. 11, no. 3 (Spring 1991): 24.

10. John R. Cionca, *Solving Church Education's Ten Toughest Problems* (Wheaton, Ill.: Victor Books, 1990), 11.

For Further Reading

Borst, D. and Montana, P. eds. *Managing Nonprofit Organizations*. New York: AMACOM, 1977.

Barna, G. *The Frog in the Kettle*. Ventura: Calif., Regal Books, 1990.

Bryan, C.D. *Relationship Learning*. Nashville: Broadman Press, 1990.

Cionca, J.R. *The Trouble-Shooting Guide to Christian Education*. Denver: Accent Books, 1986.

Hind, J.F. *The Heart and Soul of Effective Management*. Wheaton, Ill.: Victor Books, 1989.

Kilinski, K. and Wofford. J. *Organization and Leadership in the Local Church*. Grand Rapids: Zondervan Publishing House, 1973.

Koontz, H. and Heinz, W. *Essentials of Management*. New York: McGraw Hill Publishing Co., 1990.

Peters, T. *Thriving on Chaos*. New York: Alfred A. Knopf, 1987.

Rush, M. *Management: A Biblical Approach*. Wheaton, Ill.: Victor Books, 1983.

Westing, H.J. *Evaluate and Grow*. Wheaton, Ill.: Victor Books, 1984.

Fifteen
The Roles and Responsibilities
of Christian Education Personnel

A committee is a group of people who individually can do nothing but collectively can meet and decide that nothing can be done.

Ministry today is different than it was ten years ago. Changing work ethics, a new economic outlook, and non-traditional family structures have caused ministry, as well as business, to become more task-oriented than ever before. It's not that the basic needs have changed; we just feel the need to get more done in a shorter period of time. It sounds legitimate. After all, the more "ministry" we can pack into our day, the more "successful" we will feel.

Feeling this performance pressure some ministers are tempted to respond, "I could get so much more done if it weren't for people." Someone quipped that 80 percent of people in ministry admit to making this statement at regular intervals; the other 20 percent are lying. Most experienced ministry professionals recognize the danger of being too task-oriented, as opposed to focusing on people. They also understand the feeling of being out of balance with the two.

Depending on one's perspective, working with people can be the greatest frustration in ministry or the very source of fulfillment. The purpose of this chapter is to focus on *people* — the key players in Christian Education, their roles and the responsibilities, and how they fit into a truly effective ministry.

People and Christian Education

Ministry involves people, and all of the dynamics found in human relationships impact every part of ministry. An essential part of effective ministry, then, is a clear understanding of where people fit into Christian Education. Figure 15.1 adapted from Koontz and Weihrich shows the importance of human skills at every level of an enterprise:[1]

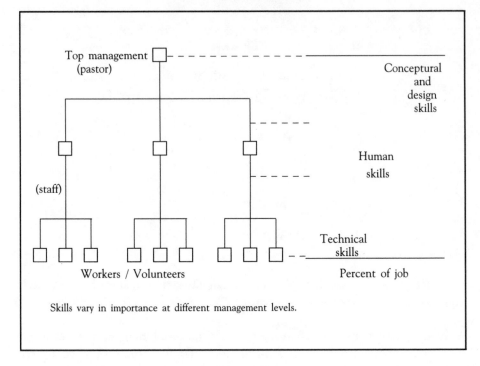

Figure 15.1

Technical skills refer to those proficiencies needed when working with methods, processes, and procedures — how to use the tools involved. *Conceptual and design skills* involve seeing the "big picture" and solving problems in ways that will benefit the organization. *Human skill* is the ability to work effectively with people. As the preceding chart indicates, there is variance between the amount of technical skills and conceptual/design skills needed in differing levels of management. But human skills are necessary at all levels of the organization.

The integration model of Christian Education spoken of in chapter 1 identifies some benefits of business management for church ministry. Studies in leadership training and development, financial management, and stewardship of resources all come from the field of business administration. Indeed, there are many similarities between a church and a business. An outsider could look at the church and see similar structure, motivation techniques, budgets, promotion, and staffing. Decision-making and long-range planning are involved in both organizations.

But there are also many differences. From the outside, the structure may look the same. But a closer look shows that the church is not only an organization, but an *organism*. A business exists to produce a product or provide a service while making a profit for its owners and employees. A church exists to meet the needs of its members. Programs and structures are vehicles by which this meeting of needs (e.g., ministry) takes place.

One of the key differences is that there are no paid congregations. The person who administrates a program of Christian Education will primarily work with volunteers. He or she can't withhold pay for inferior performance. The focus must primarily be *intrinsic* motivation (inner desire) rather than strictly *extrinsic* motivation (rewards and pay). Gangel and Hendricks point out Christ's recognition of this emphasis by stating, "Jesus did not resort to a storage-tank approach to education: 'Take this down because someday you will need it.' He was under no compulsion to teach His disciples everything they needed to know right then, even though He was the personification of truth (John 14:6). We never see Him rushing to cram spiritual content down people's throats. He never asks people to memorize and repeat answers back to Him. . . . The Savior always began where people were—with their questions, needs, hurts, and concerns."[2]

Why Do We Need to Understand Roles and Responsibilities?
God is a God of order (Gen. 1; 1 Cor. 14:40). Organization is evident in creation, in government, even in our human bodies. *Organization* refers to the structure or plan—the way different parts work together. When we set that structure in motion through people, we're practicing *administration.* So in leading people in Christian Education, we're actually carrying out the organizational structure through those people.

It's a biblical concept, as well. First Corinthians 12 and Ephesians 4 talk about the importance of *body ministry.* The church is more than an organization—it's an organism. As mentioned earlier, both have structure, but an organism also has life. These passages indicate that the picture of the church as an organization doesn't go far enough; it can have perfect structure, but no life. A body has intricate structure, but the various body parts also relate to each other. Whatever happens with one part of the body automatically has an impact on every other part of the body. God's design is that the church functions as people minister to people. Our job is to equip them to do just that.

Exodus 18 documents the results of poor organization and administration. Jethro, the father-in-law of Moses, counseled Moses concerning his ineffectiveness in leadership. Because of poor delegation skills, Moses was wearing himself out (cf. 18:18). When he took steps to let people fill appropriate roles and responsibilities, he gained the needed balance in his life, while his purposes were fulfilled even more effectively.

By contrast, the Book of Nehemiah is a study in the effective use of people to accomplish a task. Nehemiah had a clear understanding of his purpose — to rebuild the wall of Jerusalem. But his effective administration of people enabled him to accomplish the task. He realized that purpose and people were closely related.

The focus of Christ's ministry was people. But He didn't focus so completely on the felt needs of people that He overlooked the *task* that God had sent Him to do. Rather, He structured His ministry around the single, focused purpose God had for Him and then focused on people in order to carry out that task. Christ saw *people* as integral to the task. He made the connection between people and purpose.

Understanding the Purpose

Effective organization and administration comes through a clear understanding of the purpose of Christian Education. If the purpose is not clear, programs become simply activities for their own sake. People get caught up in the day-to-day details of running their part of the organization, losing focus on why they're involved. Each person involved in a ministry should see how their role helps the church accomplish its purpose. Many of the frustrations felt by volunteers in ministry could be eliminated if they really understood why their job was important.

As we discussed in the last chapter, the purpose of the church is two-fold: edification (worship, instruction, fellowship and expression) and evangelism. Christian Education, then, should provide the structure in which these two purposes can take place.

The first step in eliminating frustration in ministry is to understand clearly how one's job fits into the overall purpose of the church. Christ was able to focus on people in His ministry *because* of a clear sense of mission, not in spite of it. As Christian Education workers grasp a firm sense of both their purpose and that of the church, their motivation will tend to be intrinsic rather than extrinsic.

Organization considers the structure that is necessary for any purpose to be carried out. This can be demonstrated in a survey of the roles of Christian Education. *Administration* involves the relationships and dynamics between people that make the fulfillment of the purpose possible — demonstrated by looking at the qualifications of those in ministry.

Who Are the Key Players in Christian Education?

Since Christian Education impacts so many different areas of ministry, the potential positions could seem almost infinite. Changing times, changing cultures, and differing philosophies of ministry would make a single list of positions obsolete in a matter of months. For example, a textbook from the early

1980s would probably list only five or six C.E. positions.

Today, it is impossible to make an exhaustive list. Yet the positions listed below are representative of the types of ministries available for both the Christian Education professional and the volunteer.

The *Pastor* is the key to effective Christian Education in a church context. As a general rule, churches tend to take on the character of and emphasize those areas that are most important to the pastor. Thus, the pastor's support of and involvement in Christian Education sets the tone for the success or failure of the program. In many churches, the pastor is the only professional staff person trained in Christian Education, which makes that role even more crucial. The wise pastor will see the pulpit ministry and C.E. as partners in meeting the needs of the congregation. The role is one of inspiration and motivation and often one of personal direction.

The *Christian Education Director (or Minister of C.E.* if ordained) can be either a full or part-time person, depending on the size and scope of the church, and is responsible for the educational ministry of the church. His or her responsibilities can be wide and varied, but the main focus will be managing the Christian Education ministry. This person takes the mission of the church and translates it into structure through people, programs, and resources. The job is heavily people-centered, as the minister coordinates the involvement of a large percentage of volunteers from the congregation. This will include staffing, motivating, resolving differences (involving frequent counseling situations), training teachers and workers, administrating programs, and supervision of workers. One of the most time consuming responsibilities will be the recruitment and training of volunteers for service.

The *Youth Pastor (or Director)* is often the next position added to a church staff because of the specialized needs of this age group. Full-time, part-time or volunteer, the leader of youth generally coordinates with the C.E. Pastor to make sure the youth programs accomplish the basic purposes of the church. Because of the nature and needs of teenagers, this person will generally be heavily involved in both planning and attending the activities of the youth. Often, interns or other volunteer staff will bring him or her into the role of manager, as he trains those workers in effective ministry with teens. A key role for this minister will be communication with parents, as well as working in a staff relationship with other adults. The youth leader must have a strong sense of commitment to the task, as well as to balance in his/her personal life. Youth ministry generally covers junior high and high school (grades 7-12). Some churches may include college age in the Youth Pastor's job description as well. Whether or not this is realistic depends on the size of the groups involved and the extent of the programs.

The *Minister to Children (or Children's Director)* focuses on the administration of the ministries from birth through sixth grade. The responsibilities are similar to the youth director in terms of program, and can involve everything from children's Sunday School to weekday clubs and children's music. Relationships will vary, however. While the Youth Director works directly with the youth and key leaders, the Children's Director will spend a large portion of time training, coordinating, and motivating adults who work with the children. Staffing and recruitment is one of the primary roles of the Children's Director. In a practical sense, adults want to attend church and adult Sunday School with the freedom of knowing that their children are in good hands during that time. The Children's Director is responsible to see that children are not only taken care of, but ministered to at their point of need.

The *Minister to Families* is a fairly recent position, found primarily in larger churches. These churches tend to have a strong emphasis on family ministry, and strive to keep a balance in activities that keep the family together as much as possible. This person's responsibilities can include education, special events, and administration, as well as counseling families. The need for this type of position has increased in the last few years as dysfunctional families, abuse, and economic pressures have threatened the health of today's family. This ministry position is responsible for helping families come back to a healthy way of functioning together.

The *Church Business Administrator* is found in large churches. This position places an individual gifted in administration in service. He or she will coordinate the "business" end of all ministries and is responsible for the smooth operation of the church or organization as a whole. This position frees other ministers to focus on areas of strength without the concern over business-type details such as custodial services, facilities, maintenance, transportation, insurance, purchasing, inventories, and budgeting.

The *Minister to Adults* is trained in the special needs of adult learners and customizes the church's educational activities to those special needs. This position usually covers all ages above (and sometimes including) college age. Many churches also have a separate Minister to Senior Adults, enabling the seniors to have special consideration for their specific needs of ministry. Biblically, since the "older" are supposed to teach the "younger," ministry to senior adults should also be ministry *from* senior adults. With this pattern in mind, adult ministry in many churches is structured around small group ministry or elective Bible studies, rather than strictly traditional educational settings. This minister will focus on training, coordinating, and motivating leaders for these specialized group ministries.

The *Minister to Single Adults* makes a significant commitment of time and energy, since singles have such specialized needs, desires, and resources.

Without the ties of marriage and children, singles tend to be freer for involvement with others. This staff person will utilize a wide variety of opportunities to impact these adults. Usually, the minister's time will be heavily people-centered and will often include more counseling time than other situations. (See chapter 13 for more details concerning singles adult ministry.)

The *Minister of Counseling* enables larger churches to have an in-house resource for people who hurt or who need quality time for specialized needs. Though most staff ministers find counseling to be a regular part of their ministry, many are not equipped to handle some of the "tougher cases" that come their way. This enables the staff person to have a place to refer those needing special attention. This person will generally have specialized advanced training and experience in a variety of counseling situations.

The *Minister to the Hearing Impaired (or the Minister to the Physically Challenged)* is a focused ministry in those congregations with members in these categories. Society has become more aware than ever of the special needs of these individuals, and the church has recognized their special needs in ministry. As churches become aware of the presence of these people in their congregations, special emphasis can be given to their needs by one with special training in these areas.

The *Minister of Recreational Leadership* is usually a part-time or volunteer position, who provides special events, socials, and other activities for either the church as a whole or individual ministries. They are also responsible for the safety of all-church sporting activities, equipment, and supplies. This frees other ministry leaders from concern over coordinating all of the intricate details that might otherwise be overlooked.

The *Camping Director* oversees off-campus seasonal ministries, either for a church in particular or as an on-site camp director. This can involve the planning and execution of camps, retreats, and special outdoor events. Chapter 20 specifically addresses the ministry of Christian camping and camp personnel.

The *Preschool Administrator* and the *Day School Administrator* coordinate educational ministries to children during the week. Schooling of children generally takes place in church-sponsored schools, independent schools, or home schooling situations. The administrator of a church-sponsored school is responsible to fulfill the requirements of the state concerning education and certification of teaching staff, administrate the program, coordinate with the church board, and meet the educational needs of children in that setting. This will almost always be a full-time position and generally requires specific education in early childhood or elementary education.

The *Church Secretary* is usually considered by staff members to be the most important person in their ministry. This person is usually a full-time employee who oversees the execution of the details of ministry, freeing the staff members to focus on ministry without the "busywork."

The *Combination Minister* wears two or more hats in ministry. This person is usually full-time and is responsible to coordinate and oversee all activities in more than one area. Frequent combinations include Youth/Music, C.E./Music, or C.E./Evangelism.

The *Christian Education Board Member* is a volunteer, usually voted into office for a specified period of time by the congregation (or sometimes appointed by the Elder/Deacon board). The Board works with the D.C.E. in the administration of the educational ministry of the church. Board members are a liaison with the congregation and thus can pick up the "heartbeat" of the people concerning needs and directions. This information can be used by the board to set the educational policy and program for the church. Curriculum selection is approved at the board level, as well as staffing and finances. Facility development and use are also under the auspices of this board.

The *Sunday School Superintendent* is invariably a volunteer position found in both large and small churches. The position is delegated by the D.C.E. and involves the oversight and coordination of the Sunday School program. This gives continuity and focus to the program while freeing the C.E. Director to give more balanced attention to his or her other tasks. It is a "hands-on" position, and the superintendent will generally be available and accessible during Sunday School to meet specific needs of teachers as they arise during that time.

What Do Christian Education Workers Do?

As listed above, each position has its unique tasks. But each person will tend to go through certain stages in his or her leadership position. Tead suggests ten facets of administration which generally apply to organizational objectives: planning, organizing, staffing, initiating, delegating, directing, overseeing, coordinating, evaluating, and motivating.[3]

1) *Planning* is the initial process by which the purpose of the organization is quantified. Knowing what needs to be accomplished, planning focuses on goal setting, strategizing, programming, and budgeting.

2) *Organizing* takes the plan and builds a structure in which the plan can become a reality. It takes the purpose and translates it into a blueprint involving departmentation, authority relationships, multi-staff relationships, and job descriptions.

3) *Staffing* is when the organizational structure is fleshed out with people. Individuals are selected according to their gifts, interests, and abilities.

4) *Initiating* sets the wheels in motion. It involves the process of taking the structure which has been developed and bringing it to a point of initial action.

5) *Delegating* involves the distribution of tasks among various people, building in a system of follow-up, and providing adequate training for the task.

6) *Directing* takes place once the people are functioning on the job. It is a constant process of motivation, delegation, affecting change and, if necessary, resolving conflict.

7) *Overseeing* is the job of comparing the process as it takes place with the objectives established initially.

8) *Coordinating* takes that information and makes "mid-course corrections" as necessary to insure the outcome.

9) *Evaluating* is the process by which the progress of the organization is studied and refined. Current performance is charted on records and reports; new procedures can be implemented as needed.

10) *Motivating* is the "lubrication" that makes the organization work. It involves encouragement, direction, and involvement with the people for the purpose of helping them reach a common goal as effectively as possible.

In all ten of these areas, the purpose must be the focal point. The organization can be well-run and highly productive; but if it is not accomplishing the purpose for which it was intended, it is efficient, but not effective.

The Context of Christian Education

When a church is looking for a staff member, one of the first steps is to prepare a job description. In many cases, these documents become rather idealistic, as if they were searching for the perfect staff member. As interviews take place, search committees often tend to de-emphasize their requirements for skills and raise their emphasis on attitude. Cionca cites this emphasis when he says, "As I have worked with people, I have become less impressed with their backgrounds and credentials, and more impressed with their attitudes and performance."[4]

A common problem in Christian Education is people working outside their area of giftedness or interest. If a person takes a position for which he or she has neither the skills nor the interest, the task will become a burden rather than a fulfilling ministry, leading to frustration and burnout. In contrast, people find great joy when they are able to exercise their gifts and abilities in a chosen ministry setting.

A person who is gifted in one area may not be suitable to exercise that gift in every setting. First Corinthians 12:4-6 states that different gifts are exercised in different ministries with different effects. A person who has exercised an administrative gift in a small rural church may be unable to use that same gift effectively in a large urban setting. Some individuals are powerful in front of a large group, but less effective leading a Bible study with four couples. A teacher who is frustrated teaching high schoolers may be the perfect person for a kindergarten class.

Every Christian is gifted and needs the opportunity to exercise his or her gifts in some type of ministry to others. In some cases, this will be a volunteer situation, while for others it will constitute a career. The latter will often focus on equipping the former for ministry, according to the pattern described in Ephesians 4:12: "Equipping of the saints for the work of service to the building up of the body of Christ." Leadership will involve the task of taking people, resources, and programs and bringing them together in a way that will utilize all three most effectively.

The Qualifications for Ministry

The qualifications needed for each position will depend on the specific responsibilities of the job and could vary widely between different settings. Many desirable characteristics could be listed, but six specific areas could be considered requirements for any position.

1) *The worker is a Christian.* A person who has not come into a personal relationship with Jesus Christ cannot approach ministry from the same perspective and motivation as one who has. Romans 8:5-6 makes a clear distinction between the flesh and the Spirit—those who are responsible for the work of God must be filled with His Spirit.

2) *The worker is maturing in his or her Christian life.* Age is not an issue here; neither is the number of years the person has been a Christian. But the one who would minister effectively must be progressing in his or her walk with God in order to minister with vitality. It's ministry from an overflowing life that is constantly being replenished by God, instead of spooning out the last few drops of what God did in the past. The worker may not have "arrived" spiritually, but should be moving forward.

3) *The worker is teachable.* Most corporate executives today have learned, through hard experiences, that it is better to hire someone with fewer skills and a good attitude than many skills and a poor attitude. Skills can usually be learned; attitudes come from character that has been developed over a period of years.

4) *The worker has a love for people.* Ministry is people. A person who does not possess an inner drive to help others will face serious frustrations when the demands of other people's needs becomes the focus of the ministry.

5) *The worker should be a team player.* Cooperation is a crucial aspect of any team effort. Many sports events have been sacrificed by an individual who insisted on doing things his way. Yet a cooperative effort allows the entire team to share the victory—including those temporarily on the bench. It's the principle found in 1 Corinthians 12:26—"If one member suffers, all the members suffer with it; if one member is honored, all the members rejoice with it."

6) *The worker is dependent upon God.* "Apart from Me you can do nothing"

(John 15:5). Not some things, or a few things, but *nothing*. The more skills and abilities and even gifts a person has, the easier it is to function independently with seeming success. But real change in people's lives comes through God working in their life, not through our cleverness. Walter Ungerer says, "We, the people of God, are enabled by the Spirit in order to carry out the tasks God has given the church. For a pastor or lay people to believe that such undertakings, whatever they might be, can be accomplished for any length of time without Spirit empowerment is to misunderstand what it means to be the body of Christ."[5]

What Should Be in a Job Description?

Many people enter a ministry without seeing a written job description. The feeling is that it is unnecessary, since it is a Christian organization. Unfortunately, many people in otherwise fulfilling ministries find themselves frustrated by unstated expectations which cropped up after the commitment to the position was made. When questioned about the new responsibilities, the lack of a clear-cut job description leaves the worker defenseless. Tornquist writes:

> Job descriptions are wonderful tools. A document which is well-written and carefully conceived can clarify such things as responsibilities, authority, deadlines, lines of accountability, and a dozen other useful items. However, no job description in and of itself, no matter how lengthy, can ever completely deal with the potential powder-keg which lies at the heart of many staff positions in a local church. That simmering cauldron consists of role expectations and duties which are nowhere to be found on any piece of paper; these are commonly known as unwritten expectations.[6]

Job descriptions vary in format and content, depending on the type of position and organizational distinctives. Many books and resources have been developed to assist in the formulation of these documents. In general, most have five specific sections:

1) Position title — The official name of the position.
2) Qualifications — Educational background, experience and other skills necessary for the person applying.
3) Requirements of the position — The objectives and purposes of the position — what should happen as a result of this position being in existence.
4) Relationships within the position — How this position fits into the organizational structure; who the individual is responsible to, and who the individual is responsible for.

5) Responsibilities of the position—The specific tasks that the person is being paid to personally accomplish.

A clearly written job description will go a long way in lessening misunderstandings from people in various positions, whether full or part-time, whether paid or volunteer. People have a clear understanding of what their job is, but more importantly they understand what their job is not.

Summary

The starting place for effective ministry is a clear understanding of the purpose of the organization. That clearly defined purpose can then be translated into a structure—a plan that shows how the organization will accomplish the purpose. Then the structure is fleshed out with people who will work together to accomplish the purpose. Administration is the task of coordinating and managing people in the accomplishment of group goals.

Workers should be serving in areas related to their interests, abilities, and spiritual giftedness. Many frustrations in ministry come from people working outside their areas of strength. Qualifications vary, but all should be growing Christians who are teachable, who love people, who work well with others, and who sense their dependence on God for success in ministry.

Christian Education personnel hold a wide variety of positions because of the broad nature of the field. The array of positions available are increasing on a regular basis as ministry becomes broader in scope. Though their responsibilities will vary, most personnel follow ten sequential steps in the execution of their jobs: planning, organizing, staffing, initiating, delegating, directing, overseeing, coordinating, evaluating, and motivating. The specific responsibilities should be concisely but thoroughly outlined in a job description.

Christian Education is *people.* Our success in ministry will be the direct result of our success with people. After all, Christ didn't die for programs—He died for people.

Notes

1. Chart adapted from Harold Koontz and Heinz Weihrich, *Essentials of Management* (New York: McGraw Hill, 1990), 7.

2. Howard G. Hendricks, *"Following the Master Teacher,"* in Kenneth O. Gangel and Howard G. Hendricks, eds. *The Christian Educator's Handbook on Teaching* (Wheaton, Ill.: Victor Books, 1988), 26-27.

3. Ordway Tead, *The Art of Leadership* (New York: McGraw-Hill, 1963), 140-41.

4. John R. Cionca, *The Trouble-Shooting Guide to Christian Education* (Denver, Colo.: Accent Books, 1986), 13.

5. Walter J. Ungerer, *"The Barnabas Project"* (D. Min. diss., Princeton Theological Seminary, 1983), 40-41.

6. Chris W. Tornquist, "Reading Between the Lines: The Problem of Unwritten Expectations," *Christian Education Journal,* vol. 10, no. 2 (Winter 1990): 17.

For Further Reading

Bryan, C.D. *Relationship Learning.* Nashville: Broadman Press, 1990.

Cionca, J.R. *The Trouble-Shooting Guide to Christian Education.* Denver: Accent Books, 1986.

————. *Solving Church Education's Ten Toughest Problems.* Wheaton, Ill.: Victor Books, 1990.

Gangel, K.O. *Building Leaders for Church Education.* Chicago, Ill.: Moody Press, 1981.

————. *Feeding and Leading.* Wheaton, Ill.: Victor Books, 1989.

Hind, James F. *The Heart and Soul of Effective Management.* Victor Books, Wheaton, Ill., 1989.

Hummel, C.E. *Tyranny of the Urgent.* Downers Grove, Ill.: InterVarsity Press, 1967.

Koontz, H. and Weihrich, H. *Essentials of Management.* New York: McGraw Hill Publishing Co., 1990.

LeBar, L.E. *Focus on People in Christian Education.* Old Tappan, N.J.: Fleming H. Revell, 1968.

Rush, M. *Management: A Biblical Approach.* Wheaton, Ill.: Victor Books, 1983.

Senter, M. *Recruiting Volunteers in the Church.* Wheaton, Ill.: Victor Books, 1990.

Westing, H.J. *Evaluate and Grow.* Wheaton, Ill.: Victor Books, 1984.

Wortley, J. *The Recruiting Remedy.* Elgin, Ill.: David C. Cook Publishing Co., 1990.

Sixteen
Organizing Christian Education Ministry in the Small Church

Churches of all sizes periodically struggle with effectively organizing their Christian Education ministries. The small church which desires to conduct a quality Christian Education ministry must deal with two major issues. The first is how to organize a Christian educational leadership team which will be able to give efficient and effective leadership to its C.E. ministry. The second is working with that team to decide which C.E. ministries to conduct and how to implement them.

The goal of any church in organizing the Christian Education ministry, regardless of its size, should be to meet as many needs as possible given the available resources. This is especially crucial for the small church of fewer than 200 members. Most of the churches in this category don't have the financial resources to call a Director of Christian Education and must rely on voluntary leadership to accomplish their C.E. ministries.

This chapter will describe two basic approaches to the organization of a Christian Education ministry and help to determine which approach will likely offer the best possibility for helping the church identify and meet those needs which are apparent in the community as well as in the congregation. From there we will discuss implementing new Christian Education ministries and some principles involved in making those decisions.

The Traditional Organizational Pattern
For many years, churches have organized their education ministries along agency or program lines. This means that they have an administrator for each ministry program they operate, (e.g., Sunday School, children's church, youth groups). Figure 16.1 shows how most churches have historically organized their C.E. ministries for administration purposes along these agency lines.[1]

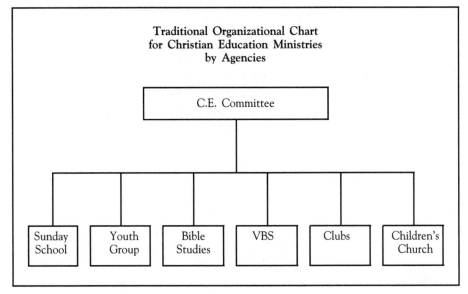

Figure 16.1

There are several disadvantages of this type of organization, particularly as it is used in small churches. First, the Christian Education Committee typically consists of people who are selected from the congregation to oversee the education ministries of the church and are, themselves, not involved directly in C.E. ministries. It's difficult for such people to understand the issues related to the decisions they must make if they aren't involved in teaching or leading one of the departments. Most of these people are well-intentioned, but don't have the background or knowledge to make intelligent decisions regarding the church's Christian Education ministry.

Second, there is built-in conflict of interest. The volunteer staff needs of the small church Christian Education ministry are great. Because the congregation is small in number, there are fewer qualified people to choose from when selecting teachers, leaders, and other volunteer workers. Sunday School leaders, youth group sponsors, children's church coordinators, VBS, and club leaders often are all competing with each other to recruit teachers and workers for their various programs. This leads to great frustration among the congregation which sometimes feels overwhelmed with requests for its time and volunteer service from several Christian education agencies. Often, skilled individuals simply decline involvement because they are being pursued by several leaders at once and don't want to offend one leader by accepting a responsibility from another.

Third, there is duplicate and redundant administration. There is an administrator for the children's department (usually called a superintendent) in

Sunday School, one in club ministries, one in VBS, another in children's church, and still others in further ministries which the church may be conducting for children. The same is true for the youth and adult divisions of the church's educational ministries. This wasteful use of the few skilled administrative persons available in a small church is very difficult to overcome. This approach usually results in individuals being recruited and placed in a volunteer ministry for which they are unsuited or unskilled. In my involvement over 15 years with the Greater Los Angeles Sunday School Convention, I have met literally hundreds of volunteer workers who are frustrated because they have been recruited for management positions for which they are unsuited. Their frustration is further compounded by the fact that there seem to be leaders in other C.E. agencies in their church who are duplicating their efforts. Such people often resign their volunteer ministry positions within a short period of time, and their disappointing experience frequently keeps them from volunteering again in the future.

Fourth, there is often conflict between the various agencies over how facilities are to be used. The high school department uses a large room for Sunday School, but the same room has to be made suitable for a children's club program for one weekday afternoon, and for an adult Bible study on another weekday evening. The various program leaders feel frustrated because the room is never in the condition they need for the ministry they lead. There is often ongoing conflict over how a room should be decorated, what type and size of furniture should be placed in the room, who is responsible to set the room up for the next usage, what that usage will be, and much more. Frequently, the Christian Education Committee members are not trained in efficiently using the church's facilities, so these problems linger and cause problems among the teachers and workers assigned to use the room.

An Alternative Organizational Approach

The Christian Education Leadership Service (CELS) is a California organization dedicated to providing quality advice and expertise to small churches which cannot afford a Minister of Christian Education. The late founder of CELS, Rev. Larry Hutt, devised an alternative organizational approach for Christian Education ministry in the local church which has provided much relief from the conflicts mentioned above. This approach to organization has replaced the traditional organizational chart in more than fifty smaller churches in California with great success. The philosophy of the CELS approach is simple: organize a church's Christian Education ministry around age groups; children, youth, and adults rather than educational agencies such as Sunday School, youth groups, children's church, VBS, and the like. Figure

16.2 illustrates how a small church might structure its beginning Christian Education ministry.

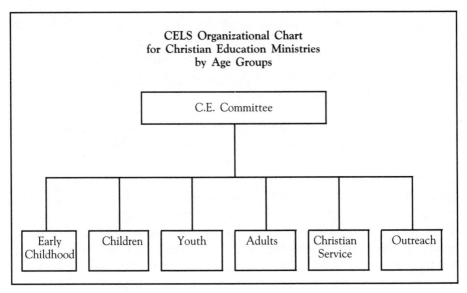

Figure 16.2

In the CELS model, the chairman of the Christian Education Committee is a member of the official church board who is designated to be the overseer of the church's C.E. program. The other committee members are the rest of the administrators or managers of each of the ministry areas. A brief description of the tasks of each of these leaders will be given below. This chapter con-cludes with a *complete* job description for each of the committee positions.

The Christian Education Committee Chairperson. This person should be a member of the official church board. It is this person's responsibility to ensure that the committee leads according to the constitution and policies of the church and reports back to the church board on its progress and needs. The chairperson doesn't need to have teaching skills, but he or she should be one who loves Christian Education and has a strong desire to work with the committee to build a strong ministry within the church. This leader works closely with the church board to help them provide for all the needs of the various Christian Education departments as the church is able to do so.

The Age Group Coordinator. Initially, there are three or four of these age group coordinators on the committee. When a church has a very small group in the early childhood and children's departments, one coordinator can manage both groups. As these groups grow, it is advantageous to split them into early childhood and middle childhood, each having its own coordinator on the committee. Additionally, there is an age group coordinator for youth and one for adults.

Each of these coordinators is responsible to manage or administer all the educational ministries the church desires to develop for a particular age group. It's important that these age group coordinators refrain from being teachers or workers in individual departments. This is important for two reasons: 1) they will not have time as volunteers to do their managing tasks and handle additional teaching or work as well, and 2) they should be people with management skills, not neccesarily teaching skills. Good teachers should be left in the classroom to teach. In many of the CELS churches, these coordinators are people who really cannot teach. That's good because it keeps them from being tempted to fill in when a teacher is needed and free to do the management of their area of responsibility.

The Christian Service Coordinator. Another member of the Christian Education Committee is the Christian Service Coordinator. This person is responsible for surveying the talents and interests of the congregation and keeping a file of persons who have skills in a variety of ministry tasks. All recruitment of volunteer workers is channeled through the Christian Service Coordinator who makes sure that no more than one leader is pursuing a potential recruit at any given time. Age group coordinators take their departmental staff needs to the Christian Service Coordinator and get a list of potential workers to fill the need and begin recruiting only when the Christian Service Coordinator has approved the recruitment. This insures that no single individual will be under recruiting pressure from more than one department at a time. It also limits greatly the "turf war" problem of several program leaders trying to recruit a potential worker at the same time.

The Christian Service Coordinator performs a vital fourfold ministry to the entire church congregation:

1) This person attempts to reduce the work load for those in the church who are carrying more than their share.

2) He or she attempts to get those who are inactive to become involved in the ministry of the church.

3) He or she tries to identify workers who are misplaced in a ministry and help them find a ministry more suited to their gifts and abilities.

4) This person encourages those who are not using their gifts and abilities to the maximum potential to become more significantly involved in the church's ministry.

The goal of this fourfold ministry is to better balance the work load of the church's Christian Education program among as many members as possible.

The Outreach Coordinator. The final member of the committee in the CELS model is an Outreach Coordinator. This person works closely with the teachers in the early childhood, children's and youth departments, and with designated outreach workers in the adult classes to see that adequate follow up is done with those attending the various church Christian Education programs. Two groups of people, visitors and absentees, are very important to the Outreach Coordinator. It is the task of this person to devise a plan, with the committee, which will insure that all visitors and absentees are adequately followed up. In several of the CELS churches in California, the adult attendance in Sunday School, for example, has been significantly increased almost immediately simply by making quality contact with those who have dropped out or are inconsistent in attendance. The Outreach Coordinator does not make the visitor and absentee contacts; he or she works with the teachers and adult class workers to make sure the contacts are made. There is a plan in place to hold the teachers and workers accountable to make the contacts.

Enlarging the CELS Plan
The question is often asked, "What happens when our church grows to the point that some of these individuals can no longer handle the oversight of their department?" The solution is simple. Each of the age group areas can be subdivided easily. Figure 16.3 illustrates how the basic CELS model can be expanded in a church where the youth and adult areas have grown significantly. The youth department has been subdivided into a junior high and a high school department, each with its own coordinator on the committee. The adult department has been similarly divided into young, middle, and older adults, each with its own coordinator. A children's department might be divided into primary and junior departments, if that is where growth has taken place.

What About Professional Christian Education Staff?
There are a number of issues related to expanding the pastoral staff of a small church. Typically when a congregation reaches about 200 in regular attendance, that is an indication that it is time to consider calling a second full-time staff person. Many churches in this position opt for an age group specialist such as a youth pastor or children's director but that's really not the best approach to staffing. A church faced with such a "growing" problem should seriously consider calling a person skilled in giving overall administration to the church's Christian Education ministry. This person may be given one of a variety of titles. Director of Christian Education or Pastor of Educational

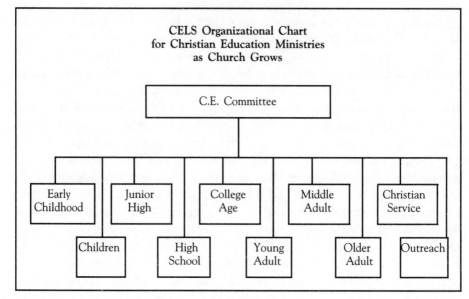

CELS Organizational Chart
for Christian Education Ministries
as Church Grows

Figure 16.3

Ministries are popular titles which specifically describe the position. The various age group ministries can still be conducted quite effectively in a church of this size by volunteer workers if they are managed by a skilled professional who will oversee recruitment, training, and function of a volunteer ministry team. For more information about professional Christian Education staffing in the local church as it grows, see chapter 15.

A skilled C.E. professional will keep the Christian Education Committee structure of the church intact and functioning. The coordinators and committee members, as they have been described, will be a significant asset to the professional who, working closely with the C.E. Committee, will oversee the educational ministries of the church.

Which Christian Education Ministries Should We Conduct?

The types of Christian Education ministries a church should offer depend greatly on the age range, ethnic makeup, location, attendance, and other factors which describe a congregation. The traditional C.E. agencies of the local church have been Sunday School, children's church, youth groups, vacation Bible school, children's clubs, camps and conference ministries, small groups, discipleship programs, and various recreational activities. Newly-planted churches are often replacing some of the traditional Christian Education agencies with alternative programs, because the needs and makeup of their congregations differ from the norm.

A good rule for the small church today is to build the Christian Education ministry initially by using the basic agencies which have proven successful over the years, replacing them only when it is clear that some alternative program will be more effective in meeting the needs of the congregation. Some churches in the United States and Canada are discovering that there is increasing resistance among their members to having Sunday School early on Sunday morning. In some cases, these churches are experimenting with church school at an alternative time, such as a weekday evening or even on Saturdays. The function is still the same as the traditional Sunday School, but the time is different. Such experimentation in a small church, especially one that is a new church can be healthy. However, congregations need a sense of stability, and too much experimentation with programming can cause them to feel unsettled and lead to a lack of participation.

For the small church, starting a new ministry needs to be done carefully and with an adequate amount of research regarding the need for it, the resources available to conduct it, the facilities needed to operate it, and the personnel needed to make it successful. Realistically, a congregation smaller than 200 people will not be able to compete with the kinds of ministries a church of 500 or 1,000 members might have. The pastoral staff, church board, and Christian Education Committee should work together to make long-range plans regarding the implementation of new ministries. If a church lacks the resources, facilities, or personnel to accomplish a suggested new ministry, the Holy Spirit may be working to let the congregation know that it simply is not ready for that ministry right now. It is far better to exercise patience and delay the implementation of new ministries than to begin them prematurely, only to have them quickly cancelled because a church does not have the resources necessary for success.

So, how does one decide which Christian Education ministries a church should conduct? It should be done with a great deal of prayerful consideration of the needs of the local community and congregation (as discussed in chapter 1). Does the church have a large number of young families with small children? It may want to put a strong emphasis on children's ministries, with a long-range plan for youth ministry five to six years in the future when these children reach junior high school age.

Is the local community or church populated with a large number of middle-aged adult families with teenage children? Youth ministry might be an area to emphasize immediately, with a long-range look toward ministry to college students and single adults as these teenagers get older.

Perhaps a church is located near a community college or university. In such a setting a church might want to look into starting a college ministry to take advantage of the students attending school nearby. Or maybe a church is located in a community which is popular as a retirement area. In this case, the focus might be on the needs of retired and elderly adults to guide in building a Christian Education ministry.

In summary, churches should not attempt to implement new ministries when there is not a significant need in their congregations. Beginning super-fluous programs only takes skilled and talented people away from involvement in ministries essential to a congregation. Even when there seems to be a need, one must still deal with the questions of facilities, resources, and personnel needed to conduct the ministry successfully. If a church doesn't have the facilities, resources, or personnel, it should probably wait before attempting to conduct new ministry programs.

A Final Word for Small Churches
Small doesn't mean insignificant. Small doesn't mean unimportant. Small certainly doesn't mean unsuccessful. If you are attending or ministering in a small church, try to concentrate on the educational ministries you know your church can do well. There are still many Christians who prefer a smaller church to a larger one for a variety of reasons. Perhaps it is easier to get to know people. Or maybe it is easier to get more meaningfully involved in ministry in the small church. Some might feel more "at home" in the small church than in a large one. The small church, along with its church board and staff, should concentrate on the advantages it offers, regardless of its size and concentrate on building educational ministries which will enhance those advantages.

Notes
1. All charts in this chapter are from Christian Education Leadership Service, P. O. Box 706, Palo Cedro, CA 96073. Used by permission.

For Further Reading

Cully, I. *Education for Spiritual Growth*. San Francisco: Harper and Row, 1984.

Gangel, K.O. *Building Leaders for Church Education*. Chicago: Moody Press, 1981.

Graendorf, W.C. *Introduction to Biblical Christian Education*. Chicago: Moody Press, 1981.

Messner, R. *Leadership Development Through S.E.R.V.I.C.E.* Cincinnati: Standard Publishing, 1989.

Pazmiño, R.W. *Foundational Issues in Christian Education*. Grand Rapids: Baker Book House, 1988.

Job Description:
Christian Education Committee Chairperson

1) Working with church board and pastor, schedule and lead all meetings of the Christian Education Committee.

2) Develop the agenda for each meeting.

3) At least monthly, contact each member of the Christian Education Committee to consult with them concerning problems, needs, and progress.

4) Be the primary communication link between the Christian Education programs of the church and the church board.

5) Be the primary communication link between the Christian Education programs of the church and the pastor.

6) Pray daily for the Christian Education Committee members.

7) Keep the Christian Education ministries and programs of the church in front of the congregation through bulletin articles, announcements, and the church newsletter.

8) Provide overall management and guidance for the various Christian Education ministries of the church.

Job Description:
Age-Group Coordinator

1) Work toward the goal of seeing that your department is fully staffed with approved and trained teachers and workers.

2) Set the agenda for the regular departmental staff meeting of your department and lead that meeting.

3) Be a source of encouragement and expressions of appreciation for the teachers and workers in your department.

4) Work with teachers and workers in your department to set goals, objectives, and high standards of conduct of ministry for the department.

5) Pray daily for the teachers and workers of your department.

6) Contact each teacher in your department by phone at least once per month.

7) Working with the Christian Education Committee, provide for the curriculum needs of your department.

8) Be the channel of communication between the teachers and workers in your department and the Christian Education Committee.

9) Visit the classrooms of your department regularly to insure the learning environment is being appropriately maintained.

10) Take the needs of the teachers and workers in your department to the appropriate group for resolution.

Job Description:
Christian Service Coordinator

1) Maintain updated file of talent survey forms. Weed out those who no longer attend, and add those who are new.

2) Work with pastor to get talent survey from those attending a new members' class.

3) Build a list of those who are interested in teaching and keep it accurately updated.

4) Work with Christian Education chairperson, church board, and pastor to schedule training classes for potential new teachers as groups of them are formed.

5) Work with age group chairmen to help them fill staff needs as these develop.

6) Keep congregation aware of staff needs in the Christian education program of the church through means such as announcements, bulletin articles, or church newsletters.

7) Help dissatisfied workers find a more satisfactory form of ministry.

8) Work with the Christian Education Committee to reduce the work load for any overloaded C.E. worker.

9) Become the "clearing house person" through whom all staff needs are funneled so that no person is being recruited by two or more departments at the same time for a task.

Job Description:
Outreach Coordinator

1) Recruit a person in each adult class to function as the outreach coordinator for that class.

2) Communicate to the teachers of the youth and children's departments that they are expected to conduct the outreach tasks for their classes.

3) Develop a simple but effective way to keep records on all Christian Education class follow-up.

4) Lead the Sunday School in a focus on two groups (absentees and visitors) for regular follow-up.

5) Hold the teachers (children's and youth departments) and the outreach coordinators (adult department) accountable to follow up visitors and absentees during the first week after a visit or absence.

6) Maintain regular contact with the adult outreach coordinators and children and youth teachers to encourage them and exhort them to maintain steady contacts with visitors and absentees.

7) Obtain names of visitors and regular church attenders who do not attend Christian Education ministries and distribute them to the appropriate classes for follow-up.

8) Communicate to the pastor any needs encountered which you believe merit a pastoral visit to any absentee or visitor.

9) Make sure no person is dropped from any Christian Education class roll who has not been personally contacted for the purpose of getting that person to return to Sunday School.

Seventeen
Leadership Recruitment and Training

The life force of Christian Education ministry in a local church is people. The most innovative or creative Christian Education program cannot survive without people to administer, teach, and lead the various activities. Several years ago as a college student training for youth ministry, I once spent a summer on staff at a Christian camp working with junior age children. At the beginning of the summer season the director of the children's program said to us, "Facilities and creative programs don't love children. People love children, and this summer at Indian Village will only be as successful as each of you are in your ministry to the children in your various village programs."

There are examples nationwide of churches which have started with minimal finances, limited resources, and inadequate facilities. Some of these churches have grown into very successful ministries because they concentrated on people ministering to people. The most skilled and able Christian Education professional cannot develop and maintain a successful ministry alone. He or she must have a team of volunteer leaders, teachers, and helpers who are highly motivated and well-trained for their tasks. Building this volunteer team involves two crucial areas of Christian Education ministry: recruitment and training.

Recruiting Volunteer Leaders: Answering the Questions
The recruitment and retention of a team of quality volunteer leaders has become a primary concern for a Christian Education professional in the contemporary local church. While this recruitment and retention has always been a concern, there are several indications in recent years that it's becoming increasingly difficult in many churches to motivate people to volunteer for Christian Education ministry.

In spite of the difficulties, however, the recruitment of a quality volunteer staff team is essential to successful Christian Education in any local church, large or small. There are four issues in recruitment which, if followed, can aid the C.E. professional in developing a good volunteer staff team.

Where Do I Find Volunteers?

In a typical local church, there is a congregation full of potential volunteers, people who are skilled in needed ministry areas and gifted by the Holy Spirit to minister. The question is not so much where do I find volunteers, as it is, how do I motivate some of these talented and gifted people to commit themselves to ministry.

Christian educators should invest a significant amount of time staying acquainted with the members of the congregation of the church. Constant updating of information about church members is an essential ingredient in knowing who is qualified and available for a particular ministry assignment.

If the church is growing, there is a somewhat constant stream of new people from whom to choose volunteers. The Christian educator needs to stay up to date on who these people are and what their skills and interests in ministry might be.

Some of the people who previously were neither able nor available for ministry at some previous time may now be ready. Personal issues which interfered before are now resolved. Perhaps a person who a year or more ago was not mature enough in some aspect of life for volunteer service has matured now to the place where volunteer ministry is possible. This requires regular reassessment of people who earlier were not considered candidates for volunteer ministry.

Who Is Qualified?

This is a difficult question to answer because there is such a wide range of volunteer ministries available and obviously different levels of maturity and skill necessary at different levels. One thing that is generally certain from Scripture is that people should be recruited initially for involvements which are less significant and then moved to higher responsibilities as they prove themselves faithful (1 Tim. 3:10).

In order to determine who is qualified, the church should have a brief and clear job description for each volunteer ministry position, spelling out the skills and gifts necessary for one to do that task successfully. Every attempt at recruiting a person for volunteer ministry should include matching his or her skills and gifts to see if they match the job description.

Generally speaking, one who would like to serve in a ministry position in the church Christian Education ministry should have the following characteristics:

- A love for the Lord.
- A dynamic and growing Christian life.
- An unqualified love for people.
- Some basic communication skills.
- A patient and forgiving spirit.
- Basic relationship building skills.
- Presence of one or more spiritual gift(s) which is (are) compatible with desired ministry.
- A willingness to work hard, often with small amounts of appreciation or recognition expressed.
- A commitment to the vision and direction of the local church.

How Do I Recruit Successfully?

There are at least two principles found in 1 Timothy 3 which should be considered in any ministry recruitment. As was stated in the previous section, persons should be recruited for lesser tasks first and then, as they prove themselves faithful, be moved to more responsible tasks. Secondly, Paul told Timothy not to recruit novices or people who were too new for responsible positions of leadership (1 Tim. 3:6, 10). Implied in this instruction is that a Christian educator should not recruit a person for volunteer ministry until he or she has had ample opportunity to observe the potential recruit — to make sure his or her lifestyle supports the position of ministry or leadership being offered.

With those biblical instructions in mind, following the simple steps listed below can make the task of recruitment more satisfying.

1) Recruit a recruiter. Not every person in professional ministry is a skilled recruiter. Recruiting is a lot like selling. Instead of selling a product or service, the recruiter is selling the idea of becoming involved in volunteer ministry. Very often the way in which a potential volunteer is approached makes all the difference in whether he or she accepts or rejects the ministry position. Many Christian educators have found that assigning a person who has strong recruiting skills makes the searching task much more successful.

2) Develop a clear job description for each volunteer task. Often, the volunteer ministry position offered is rejected because the recruit simply doesn't know what will be expected if he or she accepts the position. The sample job descriptions at the end of chapter 16 are provided as models to follow. A good job description for volunteers contains four basic elements:

- a list of the qualifications needed to perform the task;
- a list of the various responsibilities involved in doing the task;

• some estimate of the amount of time which will be needed each week to perform the task;

• a description of where this person fits in the organizational structure of the department or organization, including the person to whom he or she will be responsible.

3) Pray for names of potential recruits. At this point, churches need to avoid frequent recruiting faux pas. Some churches advertise openly to the whole congregation about leadership positions and then have to try to explain to an unqualified volunteer why he or she is not acceptable for the position. Other churches, with a particular task in mind, will begin calling through the church directory accepting as a volunteer the first person who agrees to accept the position.

Rather, church leaders should pray and ask God to lead them to individuals He wants the church to approach for this volunteer ministry. No church pulpit or search committee would ever seek a pastoral staff person by simply calling all of the names of available pastors, settling on the first one who agreed to accept the position. Yet many of these same churches approach the appointment of teachers, leaders, and volunteer workers that way.

4) Approach the prospect. Having prayed to be lead to the right person, with job description in hand approach the prospective worker. Lead time is critical. An answer from the prospective worker at this point is not necessary, the goal is simply to inform the potential recruit. Allow as much time as possible for the prospective worker to respond. Give the prospect the job description, answer any questions he or she has, and establish a date by which a decision should be made. You may want to invite the prospective worker to observe the job for which you are recruiting. Assure the candidate of sincere prayer about his or her response and then trust God to move.

All this should be done in anticipation of a positive response. Think about past recruiting experiences—both as a recruiter and target. When was the last time you witnessed a positive expectation on the recruiter's part? All recruiting should be done with the expectation of success.

5) Install the new recruit in ministry. Begin the new volunteer in his or her ministry position as soon as possible after recruitment is completed. The sooner the volunteer starts, the sooner he or she will be able to perform according to the church's expectations. It's at this time that the training phase also begins. Whether the new volunteer needs to be trained from the basics forward or is an experienced veteran in need only of training updates, education is essential to keeping the volunteer motivated to remain in the position for an extended period of time. We'll discuss more about that training later.

What if the prospect turns the recruiter down? That, of course, sometimes happens. The recruiter simply returns to step 3 and repeats that part of the process until a volunteer is secured.

How Do I Keep My Volunteers in Ministry?

The fourth issue in recruitment is, now that volunteers are in place and serving, how to keep them there for a reasonable length of time. Figure 17.1 helps illustrate the process of keeping volunteers in place.

Observation. Any prospective recruit needs to be observed in a variety of situations in the church. Do they get along well with others? Are they exhibiting spiritual maturity? What gifts and abilities are observed in them? With what age group or groups do they seem to be most comfortable? These and other questions will be answered in time as you observe your potential recruits in normal church life situations.

Limited involvement. After a period of observation, candidates may be recruited for limited levels of involvement in roles such as temporary committee members, substitute teaching positions, teachers' aides, attendance monitors, etc. After a time to prove themselves faithful in these limited involvements, they can be promoted to higher positions as their service merits. In the pyramid of the diagram on page 260 (17.1), a volunteer starts at the tip of the pyramid as a helper (H). After a time of observation, this person proves worthy of a position as teacher and after further review is finally recruited to be a program or age-group sponsor, which is seen as a deeper level of involvement.

Limited time. Experts on recruitment in church ministry agree that many members turn down volunteer positions because they fear they will have to serve until death or the Lord returns, whichever comes first. This objection can be easily overcome by establishing a length of service time for each volunteer position in your church's ministry. Most churches have terms of office for elected or appointed officers and board members, but expect Sunday School teachers and other Christian Education workers to labor with an indefinite and undefined term of office.

Newly recruited volunteers should begin their service with an abbreviated trial time after which they can evaluate their own satisfaction with the position and be evaluated as to their effectiveness. A six-month trial period is recommended. Three months is too short for any deep meaningful evaluation to take place, and a year is too long for the volunteer who is chafing in a responsibility for which he or she has proven to be unsuited.

After the initial evaluation, if everything is generally positive, a reappointment for a one year term might be considered appropriate. If the initial evaluation indicates that the volunteer is not going to work in this position, the most desirable alternative is to work with the volunteer toward some kind

RECRUITMENT OBJECTIVES

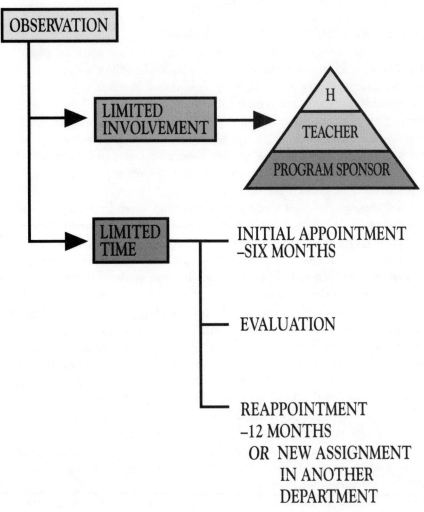

Figure 17.1

of reassignment to another area of ministry. If the unhappy recruit is allowed to simply step aside, he or she will find it very difficult to volunteer again in the future for another ministry position.

Training Volunteer Leaders

There are two major categories of training for church volunteer workers. The first is *foundational* training for new recruits who have little or no formal experience in ministry. The second is *ongoing* or *in-service* training for church volunteers currently involved in ministry who need their training regularly updated to insure continued growth in their ministries. A good C.E. professional can usually provide the foundational training that new volunteers will need to get started in their ministries. Most training problems concern volunteers already in place who either don't accept the need for continuing training to remain effective, or are frustrated because they know they need help, but it isn't being provided and they don't know where to get it.

Dugan Laird has a very helpful sequence which, if followed by a local church, could greatly enhance the church's training of its volunteers.[1] An adaptation of Laird's sequence making it suitable for church ministry is given on page 262 (figure 17.2).

Volunteer Leader Training Needs

Volunteer leaders and workers need to be trained in a variety of areas to be completely competent in their areas of ministry. Traditional thinking has argued that if volunteer workers understood the Bible and how to teach and use it in ministry, they would be competent to be involved in ministry leadership. The experiences of many churches over the years has shown this line of thinking to be very short-sighted. Volunteers need to be trained in nine basic skill areas to assure full competence in ministry:

1) *Bible Knowledge and Theology.* Volunteer leaders need to be taught how to study and apply biblical principles to their areas of ministry. They also need help in knowing the theological distinctives of their church and how those have been determined from Scripture.

2) *Human Development.* Volunteer leaders also need to understand some basic principles of human development. They need to know how people learn at different age levels, how social relationships develop at different stages of life, how moral and ethical decisions are made, how physical growth issues effect other developmental areas of life, and how all these come together to effect the development of faith and spiritual growth.

It isn't necessary for volunteers to have a professional competency in the field of psychology, but it is essential for them to have a working knowledge of the basic assumptions in these developmental areas.

3) *Home and Environmental Concerns.* Volunteers need to learn how home life and the church environment affects the ways in which members learn and apply biblical principles to their lives. A volunteer who teaches children or youth may have a difficult time explaining the concept of God as Father to students whose fathers are abusive, absent, or have in some other ways aborted their parental responsibilities. The volunteer who is aware of creative ways to learn about home life of students will be more successful in ministry.

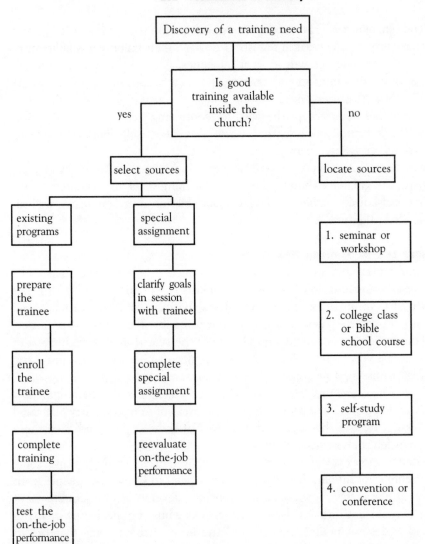

Figure 17.2

4) Working with Goals and Objectives. Volunteer leaders who understand how to develop long-range goals and specific short-term objectives for their ministry will be much more successful in accomplishing meaningful change in the lives of the people with whom they work. Volunteers who don't know how to use these important tools in ministry will labor long and hard sometimes with no real awareness of what they have accomplished. This leads to discouragement in volunteers, and those who are discouraged eventually drop out of volunteer ministry completely. The knowledgeable Christian Education professional will not only teach his or her volunteers how to build goals and objectives, but will model this practice by developing his or her own goals and objectives and regularly communicating them to the volunteer staff team.

5) *Developing Communication Skills.* Communication is one of the most essential skills in volunteer ministry. Volunteers who work for supervisors who regularly communicate to them about their ministry and who are encouraged to regularly communicate to their own workers and students are far more satisfied in their ministry than those who receive no information about how they are doing in ministry.

One of the most important things a C.E. professional can do for his or her volunteer staff team is regularly communicate appreciation for their work. One denominational leader regularly taught that it's never wrong to say "Thank you!" to the volunteer staff. The truth of that statement has been verified many times over the years in local churches.

Volunteer leaders need to learn the most effective ways to communicate to their workers or students. They also need to be taught new ways of communication as these develop in society. For years, after the availability of television in most homes in America, many Sunday School teachers were still communicating visually primarily with flannelgraph boards and still figures. Communication has become a highly technical skill in modern times, and volunteer leaders must be brought up to date with some of those technical skills if the church is to continue to capture the attention of the people who attend.

6) *Program Planning Skills.* Volunteer leaders need to learn how to successfully plan and carry out programs. Successful programs rarely happen on short notice. That very successful banquet, retreat, seminar, or worship activity probably began months before it was actually carried out. Some group of leaders met and thought through the various options and activities and planned carefully allowing adequate time for program development, gathering of necessary resources, and developing publicity for the program. These upfront activites of planning and publicity make all the difference when it comes to numbers involved in participation.

The Greater Los Angeles Sunday School Association (GLASS) which sponsors the very successful GLASS Convention each year in November now appoints its convention chairpersons at least two years in advance so there is adequate time to plan the convention schedule, secure speakers and workshop leaders, and publicize the convention to local churches. Davis Weyerhauser of the well-known Weyerhauser family of companies once said, "My company is planting trees in Oregon today which will not be harvested for at least 100 years, yet I am on the boards of some Christian organizations which do not know what they will be doing five years from now." This is all too true of many leaders in church ministry. Planning for successful programming is a learned skill, and many churches need to train both their professional and volunteer staff teams to plan much farther ahead than they now do.

7) *Selecting and Using Curriculum.* It has become clear over the years that most volunteers who struggle with Sunday School and other C.E. materials do so because they either made a poor choice of curriculum for their church or have not been trained to use their curriculum correctly. This is especially tragic since there are a number of good curriculum companies marketing quality materials and since most of them, including Scripture Press, have a local team of skilled consultants who will spend time with a local church helping them select the best curriculum for their needs and teaching them how to use it.

8) *Biblically Based Counseling.* Volunteer leaders are often asked by a student or worker to give advice related to a ministry or personal problem. These volunteers need to be trained so that they can relate biblical principles accurately to these problems. They also need to know when they are faced with a problem which is beyond their ability and skill to solve. Further, they need to know to where they can refer a person when they recognize a problem is beyond them.

The Bible and prayer are powerful tools available for solving life problems. However, there are times when people are confronted with problems so complex that they can't clearly see the biblical answer. At these times the volunteer needs to know how and to whom to refer the person for more expert counsel.

9) *Program and Ministry Evaluation.* In far too many situations volunteers, and even professional church leaders, don't spend time evaluating the success or failure of ministry activities. But without clearly defined goals and objectives, evaluation cannot be complete. If a group of volunteer leaders doesn't know what they set out to accomplish, they can't adequately evaluate their success or failure.

Volunteers need to be taught how to evaluate each activity carefully. What constitutes successful completion of this activity? What were we trying to accomplish with this ministry? Of those involved, who performed well and who did not? Why did some perform well and others not? Was this ministry adequately publicized? If we do this activity again, what would we do differently and why? These are just a few of the questions to guide an evaluation.

One more thing about evaluation: volunteer leaders need to be encouraged to keep accurate written records of the ministry activities they conduct. It's often difficult after an activity is over to reconstruct exactly what happened without some written record of the event. Volunteer leaders should be given a standard report form following each activity and encouraged to fill it out as soon as possible before they forget important details.

10) *Training Resources.* Where does the Christian Education professional go

to get the necessary resources for the training needs of his or her volunteer staff team? Below are a list of suggestions which might prove to be helpful:

- *Curriculum publisher.* As noted earlier in this chapter, many publishing companies make consultants available, at no additional cost, to churches using their curriculum. Check with individual curriculum publishers to see if this kind of support is available.

- *Sunday School and Christian Education conventions.* There are scores of church education conventions held annually across the country. Most major states have one each year.

- *Denominational leaders.* Denominational offices usually are staffed with ministry professionals who will work to provide leadership training for local churches. Frequently, when churches in a denomination have similar needs, the leadership can provide conferences to train church leaders for those specific needs.

Conclusion

Recruiting, training, and maintaining volunteers in church ministry is one of the most crucial tasks of the Christian Education professional. All social indicators point to the fact that this task will become even more difficult in the days ahead. The goal of the C.E. professional should be to recruit the best possible people for each ministry position, train them with the finest tools available, and keep them in place by providing motivational support services. The key to successful recruiting is keeping volunteers satisfied in their area of ministry.

Notes

1. Dugan Laird, *Approaches to Training and Development* (Reading, Mass.: Addison-Wesley Publishing Co., 1985, 67.

For Further Reading

Fine, E., and B.J. *Teachers Are Made, Not Born.* Cincinnati: Standard Press, 1990.

Friedeman, M. *The Master Plan of Teaching.* Wheaton, Ill.: Victor Books, 1990.

Gangel, K.O. *Twenty-four Ways to Improve Your Teaching.* Wheaton, Ill.: Victor Books, 1986.

Johnson, D.W. *The Care and Feeding of Volunteers.* Nashville: Abingdon Press, 1978.

Senter, M. *Recruiting Volunteers in the Church.* Wheaton, Ill.: Victor Books, 1990.

Shawchuck, N. *How to Be a More Effective Church Leader.* Irvine, Calif.: Spiritual Growth Resources, 1981.

Smith, F. *Learning to Lead.* Waco, Tex.: Word Books, 1986.

Willis, W.R. *Make Your Teaching Count.* Wheaton, Ill.: Victor Books, 1985).

_____. *Developing the Teacher in You.* Wheaton, Ill.: Victor Books, 1990.

Eighteen
The Role of Women in Leadership

One of the most difficult theological issues facing the twentieth-century church is the role of women in ministry. A number of denominations, who in the past would never have considered ordaining women to leadership roles, have recently begun doing so. Increasing numbers of women are enrolling in seminary education all across the United States and Canada. It has been a divisive issue in many denominations, resulting in heated debates generated in ministerial associations, denominational conferences, seminary classrooms, magazines, and across the whole spectrum of Christian leadership.

Godly scholars of the Old and New Testament, who are committed to biblical inerrancy, are divided on this subject. Those on both sides of the issue feel strongly about their view. This chapter will present both sides of the argument with the hope that the reader will be able to clearly understand the presuppositions of each side and, in turn, be able to make his or her own informed decision. No attempt will be made to argue conclusively or exhaustively for either side, since no such argument is possible given the space limitations of this chapter.

Background Factors and Considerations

Before presenting the various paradigms of women's roles in church leadership, it's important to first consider some of the background issues that have helped shape this discussion. These factors help us understand why this topic has become more critical to twentieth-century believers than at any other period in our church history.

1) Society's double standard. Throughout history society has operated on a double standard concerning the privileges given to women. Many cultures around the world continue to operate on the belief that women are not worthy of the same rights, privileges, and protection that men have. As far as our records can be traced back, to the history of early civilization, women have been seen as being inferior to men. Girls were not given the same opportunities as boys for education, career, health care, and employment benefits. Throughout history women were not given the same educational opportunities as men because their role was to remain in the home and train girls in domestic chores such as cooking, sewing, and cleaning. Boys went to school to learn a trade, become literate, and advance themselves in society.

2) *Changing demographic trends of women.* One of the major factors causing the church to rethink its position on women in church leadership roles has been the demographic changes that have taken place in recent years. In 1900, American women had a life expectancy of about 40 years. In 1990 a female infant can expect to live to experience her 80th birthday. This increased lifespan, especially when combined with smaller families and an urbanized technological culture, contributes to the discussion. If a woman becomes a mother she still finds herself in that role for perhaps twenty years. Once the last child leaves home she will still have thirty to forty years of life expectancy remaining.[1] They will naturally be looking for ways to be of service to the church and other Christian ministries during that time. Furthermore, since it has been estimated that over 75 percent of the overall work in the local church is done by women it seems obvious that the role of women in leadership is affected by this changing trend.

3) *Changing demographic trends of men.* Men have traditionally served in high risk occupations (e.g., coal mining, commercial building construction, military, etc.) during the past 100 years of American history. This is changing today, but a look back tells us that the life expectancy for men has rarely been as high as it has been for women. Take for example military service: 52,000 people were killed in the Korean war, 58,000 during the Viet Nam war. Some of those killed were women but the vast majority were men. Combine those figures with the number of men killed each year due to industrial accidents, heart and lung disease, or cancer, and it becomes increasingly apparent why, by the age of 60, there are far more women than men living in our communities. Such a demographic reality affects the number of men available to fill leadership roles in ministry today.

4) *The influence of the women's movement.* No one can deny the vast benefits that have come to women during the past fifty years of American history. Women have received voting rights and opportunities for college and graduate education; career and professional openings are seemingly endless, and the horizon of opportunity is bright. Some will argue that many more benefits are still needed. The women's movement has been credited with providing an atmosphere conducive to the dialogue necessary to achieve many of these

changes. It's expected that this dialogue will continue in the years ahead and as such is a factor to be considered.

It's important to note that many contemporary Christians confuse the hopes of the women's movement with the agenda of the militant feminist movement. Speaking of this issue, Roberta Hestenes comments, "There is no question that some of the more radical feminists with their agendas of lesbian advocacy and abortion on demand attack many of the things that Christians value highly. Yet, some conservative Christians have reacted so strongly against the feminist movement that they have created a backlash."[2] What is needed is the ability to reject the unbiblical agenda of the radical feminists while at the same time accepting the invitation for open dialogue from the more moderate representatives of the women's movement.

The Leadership Roles of Women in the Old Testament

There are numerous Old Testament examples of women who assumed leadership roles. In some cases these roles were familial or prophetic, some were military, others were civic in nature. All of these women felt called to lead and did so as an outgrowth of their Jewish faith.

Examples Of Familial Leadership

Sarah. Although normally in subjection to her husband Abraham (1 Peter 3:6) there is an account in Genesis 21:12 of Sarah giving leadership to Abraham regarding an important family matter. Abraham was uncertain what to do when he had two sons vying for family control. Sarah told Abraham to dismiss their family slave Hagar so as to avoid further tension in their home. God instructed Abraham to "listen to her" for Abraham's seed would pass through Isaac. The same Hebrew word translated "listen to" is translated "obey" in Genesis 22:18 and in almost ninety other places in the Old Testament. This occasion in the life of Abraham reminds us that at least at one point Sarah provided God's direction in instructing her husband.

Abigail. This noble woman risked the wrath of her husband Nabal by providing a sizable peace offering to appease the anger of David. Without her husband's knowledge or consent, Abigail took the initiative and successfully entreated David for the life of her impetuous husband (1 Sam. 25:1-35).

Examples of Prophetic Leadership

Miriam. Born in an Israelite home during the bondage of Egypt, Miriam was the older sister of Aaron and Moses. After the deliverance of the people through the Red Sea, Miriam led the nation in celebration. Exodus 15:20-21 records "And Miriam the prophetess, the sister of Aaron, took the timbrel in her hand; and all the women went out after her with timbrels and with dances. And Miriam answered them, 'Sing to the Lord, for He has triumphed gloriously! The horse and its rider He has thrown into the sea.' " In this capacity she acted as a public worship leader, with the full knowledge and approval of those men who were currently serving in leadership.

Hannah. Hannah's prayer in the house of the Lord and her commitment to God (1 Sam. 1:8–2:10) serve as a role model for Christian women today. After years of anguish due to her barren condition, she received the news that she was pregnant. So thankful was she to the Lord for the blessing of a child that she burst into a chorus of inspired praise and thanksgiving. Her song became the basis of the Magnificat—Mary's psalm of praise eleven centuries later (see Luke 1:46-55). Notice that the High Priest Eli neither interrupted nor reproved her. She was not forbidden from expressing her prophetic gift.

Huldah. This striking example of prophetic utterance clearly indicates God's sovereign guidance of a nation. During this period of Jewish history the temple had fallen into disrepair. Shapan, the scribe, discovered the book of the Law and brought it to young King Josiah. Upon hearing of the impending judgment of God, the king sought the counsel of Hilkiah the priest and four other principal men to know what he should do. Although the prophets Jeremiah, Habakkuk, and Zephaniah were available, Hilkiah went to the prophetess Huldah to seek the counsel of the Lord. Huldah sent word back to King Josiah using the phrase "thus says the Lord" four times in five verses (2 Kings 22:15-19). Huldah was God's mouthpiece, providing instruction and guidance to a nation in desperate need of redirection.

Examples Of Military Leadership

Deborah. Deborah is another remarkable character in the Old Testament who demonstrated competency in leadership. It's recorded that she was a prophetess and a wife at the time of her leadership (Jud. 4:4). She served as a judge in a public location (under the palm tree) so people could seek her wisdom to solve their civic and legal disputes. During one crisis point in the history of Israel, Deborah tried to enlist the support of Barak to lead the nation in defense of an approaching army. Barak was reluctant to lead the nation, and only after Deborah agreed to assume the primary leadership role did Barak agree to assist. "Barak's obvious dependence upon Deborah indicates the degree of leadership which she had attained in Israel at the time. The whole initiative of the campaign lay in the hands of this female warrior-leader, judge, and companion in battle."[3]

Examples of Civic Leadership

Esther. In addition to the obvious example of civic leadership found in Deborah, Esther also serves as an example of a woman who provided her nation with civic leadership. She rose in public leadership and prominence in the Persian empire at a critical time in history. As queen, she was able to steer the events of humankind to provide safety and deliverance to an entire nation of Jewish believers living in Persia. She was a courageous and skillful diplomat who rose reluctantly to a position of power, but was willing to serve as a vessel to fulfill the ultimate will of God.

These personalities from the Old Testament serve as examples of women who demonstrated godly leadership characteristics. Those who were used in roles of leadership saw themselves as God's divine instruments. God did not cease to use women at the close of the Old Testament period either, for the New Testament records numerous examples of women who were used for His divine purposes.

The Leadership Roles of Women in the New Testament

In the New Testament era women became increasingly prominent in service to the Gospel ministry. Examples abound of women who contributed to the ministry and as such were referred to by the apostle Paul as "fellow workers" in Christ (Rom. 16:3; Phil. 4:3). A few of these women are highlighted below.

Examples of Prophetic Leadership

Mary, Mother of Jesus. After Mary received word that she had been chosen for the supreme honor of bearing the Jewish Messiah, she departed and went to stay with Elizabeth, the wife of the priest Zacharias. Upon entering the house Elizabeth was filled with the Holy Spirit and began praising God for the blessing of the Messiah that Mary would one day conceive. Mary responded with prophetic words of praise, filled with declarations of Old Testament prophecies which would one day be fulfilled in the life of her Son. In this we see Mary's prophetic gift being used. "Mary belongs to those grand majestic females inspired with the spirit of prophecy, who are capable of influencing those who would become rulers of men and also the destiny of nations."[4]

Anna. As a prophetess who served in the temple day and night with fasting and prayers, she proclaimed the good news to all who were assembled that the Messiah had come to His chosen people. She prophesied with boldness before the many people who were gathered together for temple prayers.

Philip's four daughters. While traveling through Caesarea Paul and his companions stayed with Philip, an evangelist who had four virgin daughters who prophesied (Acts 21:8-9). Nothing is said in the text regarding any limitations being placed on their ministry so it is assumed that they exercised their gift of prophecy in public gatherings. It is interesting to note that the prophet Joel predicted that one of the characteristics of the church age will be that women would fulfill this prophetic role (Joel 2:28-32).

Examples of Ministry Leadership

Dorcas. In the small seacoast town of Joppa lived a humble woman by the name of Dorcas who was known for her acts of kindness and compassion. She had developed a reputation in her community as one who came to the assistance of the homeless, poor, and needy. It was at her funeral that many of the widows who had been her friends were weeping while showing Peter the garments that Dorcas had made for them. Moved with compassion, Peter raised her from the dead thereby causing many to believe in the Lord Jesus Christ (Acts 9:36-42).

Lydia. A successful businesswoman and charter member of the church in Phillipi, Lydia converted to Christianity along with her entire household. As a God-fearing Gentile this woman was seen as a community leader, who after conversion, provided Paul and his companions with assistance in their Gospel ministry (Acts 16:13-15).

Phoebe. The epistle written by Paul to the believers in Rome ended with a series of good wishes to his friends. Before sending his greetings, Paul added a few sentences, by way of a postscript, to introduce to the church of Rome a deaconess *(diakonon)* located in the eastern seaport town of Cenchrea by the name of Phoebe. Such letters of reference were widely used in the early church to help establish one's credibility.[5]

A controversy exists today regarding the translation of the noun used to describe her. Some versions translate this word "servant" when referring to Phoebe but then translate it "deacon" or "minister" when referring to Apollos (1 Cor. 3:5); Tychicus (Eph. 6:21; Col. 4:7); Epaphras (Col. 1:7); Timothy (1 Thes. 3:2); or Onesimus (Phile. 13). When used in a general sense (Matt. 22:10), the term servant may be acceptable but when used in the context of a church position the term deacon or deaconess is most appropriate.[6]

Euodia and Syntyche. While writing to the church in Phillipi Paul acknowledged the contribution that two of the women in the church had made in his ministry (Phil. 4:3). Paul spoke of Euodia and Syntyche as two women who labored with him in the Gospel (literally "shared my struggle"). These women had evidently performed significant responsibilities for the cause of Christ with Paul.

Priscilla. Priscilla, and her husband Aquila, pulled Apollos aside one day and explained to him the way of God more accurately (Acts 18:26-28). It's significant to note that in almost all references to this husband-wife ministry team Priscilla's name is given first. Some feel that this was an indication of the leadership role that Priscilla had in the teaching aspect of their shared ministry. "This couple," said Paul, "risked their own necks" for the sake of the Gentile church (Rom. 16:4). Clearly this evangelist/teacher team had a public Gospel ministry that was known throughout the early churches of their day.

Paul was truly thankful for them and for the assistance that they had provided for him on occasion and were continuing to provide for the Gentile church as a whole.

Principles of Female Leadership in Ministry

The following passages of Scripture from the Old and New Testament, and many others not cited, help us formulate a series of principles from which we can draw application for the church today.

1) *The ministry of women was prophetically declared to be characteristic of the church age* (Acts 1:13-15; 2:3-4, 16-18; Joel 2:28-32). This was no surprise to the early church leadership. It was clearly predicted many years before that women would demonstrate their prophetic, evangelistic, teaching, or leadership gifts.

2) *The gifts of the Spirit are given to women as well as to men.* In Paul's lengthy discussions about spiritual gifts, he never indicates that they are related to one's gender. In fact, Paul teaches that the Holy Spirit provides gifts to believers without regard to race, economic status, or gender (1 Cor. 12:11-14,18; Eph. 4:7).

3) *Women had a ministry of prophecy in both the Old and New Testament which was recognized by the spiritual leaders* (priests and apostles). References to their prophetic role are given without any indication that the religious leaders prohibited their involvement (Ex. 15:20-21; 2 Kings 22:15-19; Acts 21:8-9; Joel 2:28-29).

4) *New Testament women participated in public prayer services.* In some cases the prayer service was led or sponsored by a woman (Acts 12:12, 16:13; 1 Cor. 11:5).

5) *New Testament women engaged in teaching and other forms of Gospel ministry with apostolic approval.* In Romans 16, ten out of the twenty-nine people commended for loyal service were women. Paul instructs older women to teach younger women and children (cf. 2 Tim. 1:5 with 3:14-15; Titus 2:3-5).

6) *It is apparent that some women held significant leadership roles in the early church.* A few examples of these women and their positions would include: Lydia (Acts 18:2,18); Damaris (Acts 17:34); Priscilla (Acts 18:2,18; Rom. 16:3-4; 1 Cor. 16:19 [It is interesting to note that Aquila is never mentioned apart from his wife. In Paul's writings Priscilla is almost always mentioned first]); Phoebe, the servant [deacon] from the church in Cenchrea (Rom. 16:1-2).

It is important to note that there is considerable debate about how to render the name "Junias" in Romans 16:7. Some say it could be translated "Junia," a feminine form, instead of the traditional "Junias" which is the masculine form. If it is feminine, then this is one instance where the term apostle is used of a woman.

7) *Teaching and spiritual ministry are synonymous with Christian maturity.* As part of Christian growth Scripture indicates that leadership in ministry is characteristic of spiritual maturity (Col. 3:16; Eph. 4:15-16; Heb. 5:11-14). To deny women a teaching role in ministry would be to deny them a vital component of their Christian growth. Furthermore, it would contradict the teaching of Paul in Titus 2:3-4).

Principles of Male Leadership in Ministry

1) *Only a man could serve in the capacity of priest in the Old Testament.* Although women were also represented in the tribe of Levi, God only allowed a man to hold the office of priest (Lev. 3:9-10).

2) *Jesus selected only men to serve as His apostles.* Scripture tells us that many women followed Christ during His ministry travels. In spite of their presence, He chose only men to carry on the apostolic tradition (Matt. 10:2-4).

3) *Men in pastoral leadership was the established pattern of the apostolic church.* One of the requirements for Judas' replacement (Acts 1:21) and of the first deacons that were selected (Acts 6:3-5) was that they had to be men. The apostles apparently recognized the imperative of selecting men for this new church position.

4) *The teaching of the epistles indicates the value of male leadership in pastoral roles.* First Corinthians 11:3, 1 Timothy 2:11-12, and 3:1-12 seem to indicate a strong preference toward male leadership as it relates to pastoral positions. There are differing views regarding this principle today. Some view it as a requirement, a few see it as simply an "ideal" where possible, and still others reject it completely as a cultural limitation applicable only to that historical period of time.

Problem Passages

Simply citing examples of women who were used in Scripture as significant leaders in ministry does not fully justify their involvement in ministry today. Past experience is not always the best way to determine the future will of God. The clearest way to understand the teaching of God on this subject is to review the specific verses of Scripture which address the issue. Although such a method is hermeneutically sound, it is obvious to all who have studied this subject that differing explanations are used to interpret the same passages. The primary Old Testament passage which is used in this discussion is the creation order recorded in chapters 1–3 of Genesis. Following are the New Testament passages most often used in the discussion:

1 CORINTHIANS 11:2-16

Now, I praise you brethren, that you remember me in all things, and keep the traditions, as I delivered them to you. But I want you to know that the head of every man is Christ, and the head of the woman is man, and the head of Christ is God. Every man praying or prophesying, having his head covered, dishonors his head. But every woman that prays or prophesies with her head uncovered dishonors her head; for that is one and the same as if her head were shaved. For if the woman is not covered, let her also be shorn. But if it is shameful for a woman to be shorn or shaved, let her be covered. For a man indeed ought not to cover his head, since he is the image and glory of God; but the woman is the glory of man. For man is not from woman, but woman from man. Nor was man created for the woman; but woman for the man. For this reason the woman ought to have a symbol of authority on her head, because of the angels. Nevertheless, neither is man independent of woman, nor woman independent of man, in the Lord. For as the woman was from the man, even so the man also is through the woman; but all things are from God. Judge among yourselves. Is it proper for a woman to pray to God with her head uncovered? Does not even nature itself teach you that if a man has long hair, it is a dishonor to him? But if a woman has long hair, it is a glory to her: for her hair is given to her for a covering. But if any one seems to be contentious, we have no such custom, nor do the churches of God.

1 CORINTHIANS 14:34-37

Let your women keep silent in the churches, for they are not permitted to speak; but they are to be submissive, as the law also says. And if they want to learn something, let them ask their own husbands at home; for it is shameful for women to speak in church. Or did the Word of God come originally from you? Or was it only you that it reached? If anyone thinks himself to be a prophet or spiritual, let him acknowledge that the things which I write to you are the commandments of the Lord.

GALATIANS 3:26-28

For you are all sons of God through faith in Christ Jesus. For as many of you who were baptized into Christ have put on Christ. There is neither Jew nor Greek, there is neither slave nor free, there is neither male nor female; for you are all one in Christ Jesus.

1 TIMOTHY 2:11-12

Let a woman learn in silence with all submission. And I do not permit a woman to teach or to have authority over a man; but to be in silence.

Two Paradigms for Determining Women's Leadership Role

A paradigm is a predetermined way of looking at something. In essence, it's one's point of view. The paradigm that one brings to these problem passages will influence the way one interprets and applies them to life and ministry. When studying these passages some consideration must be given to the culture of the biblical author and the reader, the historical time and setting of the writing, and other pertinent factors. How much emphasis is placed on each of the these variables will determine which paradigm the reader prefers. There are two primary views regarding women's leadership role in ministry: the Traditional and the Egalitarian.

The Traditional view. This conservative perspective is chief among the views and sees the culture of the author and the reader, and the historical context of the passage as having little, if any, influence on the interpretation of the Scripture.

The traditional position uses a universalizing argument based on the creation order (Gen. 1–3; Eph. 5:22-23) and its correlates of headship and subjection, to argue for a hierarchical relationship within the home, society, and the church. Women are allowed to pray and prophesy in the church since it is recognized that these acts of worship are distinct from authoritative speaking, teaching, or ruling. Similarly, women are allowed to assume the office of deaconess and some limited forms of teaching.[7]

The traditional view holds to a strict interpretation of the problem passages. Passages which refer to equality (Gal. 3:26-28) refer only to matters of salvation and positional standing, not in the marriage relationship or in ministry opportunities. To those who hold this view it is obvious what Paul intends when he states that "a woman [should] keep silent in the churches" (1 Cor. 14:34-35) and "not have authority over a man" (1 Tim. 2:11-12). However, the problem with such a strict interpretation of such passages is that they are not consistent with other Pauline teachings regarding what a woman can do in the church—such as pray and prophesy (1 Cor. 11:2-16), teach (Titus 3:14-15), and lead (Rom. 16:2). According to the traditionalist a woman may be allowed to teach children and other women, but definitely not a mixed audience of adults. Based on this view "theological seminaries are advised not to encourage women to enroll in programs which ordinarily lead to pastoral appointments. Those who successfully complete the program are unlikely to find openings as pastors. (For women) there are other more appropriate programs of study."[8]

The Egalitarian view. This view is based upon the belief that any office a man can hold a woman can as well and that anything less is oppression in the name of Christ.[9] This view acknowledges a significant cultural influence in biblical hermeneutics. By passing the problem passages through the lens of culture and historical setting, a different interpretation is developed from the traditional paradigm.

Galatians 3:28 is a banner verse for the egalitarian position: there is no difference between male or female once we are in Christ. Since God does not recognize a distinctive it is wrong for man to view one.

Regarding 1 Corinthians 14, the word "silent" (*sigao*) literally means no talking or utter silence. Given the cultural setting of the day, one must keep in mind that women had not been the beneficiaries of religious education. Having come into the church as new Christians, the women naturally had many questions regarding the teaching of the Word of God. The early church had no feature like our Sunday Schools, where the teacher, whether male or female, might invite questions or debate, so women naturally asked questions during the worship service to gain a clarification on the passage being taught. It is believed that this constant questioning on the part of the women present created a distraction to the teacher and the men in attendance. In order to avoid such confusion and to facilitate more effective communication, Paul simply asks women to ask theological questions at home where they would not interrupt the flow of the worship service. Such a view is consistent with 1 Corinthians 11:2-16 where Paul draws up regulations for women speaking in the worship assembly. Given this interpretation, chapters 11 and 14 of 1 Corinthians do appear to contradict each other.

According to the egalitarian paradigm, the teaching of 1 Timothy 2:11-12 is understood in a similar context of church confusion. The Greek word for silence (*haysukia*) is different from the one found in 1 Corinthians 14. Here it means quietness, calm, and tranquility as opposed to utter silence. It refers to a quiet, nonaggressive demeanor. The word for authority (*authenteo*) is used only here in the New Testament. Its noun form means to have authority, to domineer, or to master. According to the egalitarian, as long as the woman is not creating a confusion with her instruction or not demonstrating an auto-cratic or dictatorial leadership style, she is not forbidden to exercise leader-ship in the church. The essence of this passage refers more to the style of ministry than to the office of ministry. It was never the intent of this passage to preclude women from pastoral roles of service. Whether serving as a deacon, teacher, or senior pastor, this passage was given only to guide women in the formation of positive character qualities to be used in that office.

Summary

The church continues to wrestle with the leadership role available to women in ministry. The Old and New Testaments provide us with examples of women who used their leadership abilities in the home, community, military, and in service of Jehovah. General principles can be drawn on the basis of such examples of leadership, and these can serve as guideposts for the church today.

The ultimate source of direction, however, comes from the passages of Scripture which deal directly with the subject. However, there is no clear consensus regarding the interpretation and application of these passages. For this reason there are opposing views regarding the role of women in ministry for the church today. In addition to the two paradigms presented in this chapter, there are a number of additional views that may be explored by consulting the resources provided at the end of this chapter. Each student must carefully consider the evidence for each paradigm and make a decision. Ultimately, each mature believer must come to his or her own conviction regarding this difficult issue facing the Christian church.

Notes

1. Roberta Hestenes, "Women in Leadership: Finding Ways to Serve the Church," *Christianity Today*, 3 Oct. 1976, 6.

2. Hestenes, "Women in Leadership." 10.

3. Leslie Maxwell, *Women in Ministry.* (Wheaton, Ill.: Victor Books, 1987), 23.

4. Herbert Lockyer, *The Women of the Bible.* (Grand Rapids: Zondervan Publishing House, 1967), 93.

5. William Greathouse, *Beacon Bible Commentary*, vol. 8, (Kansas City, Mo.: Beacon Hill Press, 1968), 277-78.

6. Maxwell, *Women,* 67.

7. Robert Johnston, "The Role of Women in the Church and Home: An Evangelical Testcase in Hermeneutics," W. Ward Gasque and William LaSor, eds., in *Scripture, Tradition and Interpretation.* (Grand Rapids: William B. Eerdmans Publishing Company, 1978), 18.

8. Robert Culver, "Let Your Women Keep Silence." Bonnidell Clouse and Robert Clouse, eds., in *Women in Ministry.* (Downers Grove, Ill.: InterVarsity Press, 1989), 47.

9. Patricia Gundry, "Why We're Here," Alvera Mickelsen, ed., in *Women, Authority and the Bible.* (Downers Grove, Ill.: InterVarsity Press, 1986), 14.

For Further Reading

Clouse, B. and Clouse, R. *Women in Ministry.* Downers Grove, Ill.: InterVarsity Press, 1989.

Garlow, J. *Partners in Ministry*. Kansas City: Beacon Hill Press, 1981.

Howe, M. *Women and Church Leadership*. Grand Rapids: Zondervan Publishing House, 1982.

Hurley, J. *Man and Woman in Biblical Perspective*. Downers Grove, Ill.: InterVarsity Press, 1981.

Knight, G. *The Role Relationship of Men and Women*. Chicago: Moody Press, 1985.

Kobobel, J. *But Can She Type?* Downers Grove, Ill.: InterVarsity Press, 1986.

Maxwell, L. *Women in Ministry*. Wheaton, Ill.: Victor Books, 1987.

Mickelsen, A. *Women, Authority and the Bible*. Downers Grove, Ill.: InterVarsity Press, 1986.

Spencer, A. *Beyond the Curse: Women Called to Ministry*. Nashville: Thomas Nelson Inc., 1985.

Nineteen
Legal and Ethical Issues in Christian Education Ministry

With the exception of what constitutes a nonprofit corporation for income tax purposes, the federal government has, for the most part, steered clear of creating laws governing the practice of religion by local churches or parachurch organizations. Thus the laws governing how a church or religious organization practices its ministry to people are largely left to individual states. These laws differ greatly from state to state.

Most of what follows in the legal issues section of this chapter arises because we live in an increasingly litigious society. Unfortunately, churches, and those who work for them in either professional or voluntary ministry positions, are not immune from law suits which may arise from alleged negligence in some aspect of ministry.

This chapter is not intended to be an exhaustive discussion of all the legal ramifications involved in the practice of ministry. Such an investigation would not be possible due to the number of court cases currently being considered and the diversity of laws from state to state. The legal issues to be discussed here are those issues most likely to be faced by workers in the various Christian Education functions of a church's ministry.

Liability Insurance
Whether or not the state requires it, it's a very wise church which chooses to protect itself with a comprehensive liability insurance policy. Basic liability coverage will protect the church in the event that someone is injured or suffers some other form of damage on church property. A variety of additional coverages can be added to the basic coverage in the form of what the insurance industry calls "riders."

Perhaps one of the most important riders on a liability policy related to

Christian Education ministry is protection against injury or damages suffered by a person while participating in any kind of church-sponsored activity. Many churches provide a wide variety of activities, trips, and experiences for children, youth, and adults; and these churches need a comprehensive liability policy which will protect it and its workers in as many as possible of these situations.

Full Liability Coverage Versus Coinsurance
While the rules can vary somewhat from company to company, a full liability policy will generally pay a claim to an individual for any injury or damage suffered which is not specifically excluded from coverage in the policy. This type of policy will pay the claim regardless of whether the injured individual has other insurance which is equally liable or not.

For example, the youth pastor of First Church recently took a group of high school students roller skating at a local skating rink. Earlier this year, First Church purchased a full coverage liability insurance policy which guarantees coverage of all persons involved in church-sponsored activities, regardless of whether these activities were held at the church or elsewhere. One of the boys in the group fell at the skating rink and broke his arm, requiring immediate emergency medical care, as well as follow up physical therapy for several months following the injury. Because First Church has a full coverage liability insurance policy, the insurance provider will reimburse the injured boy's family for the cost of medical treatment due to the injury, even though both the skating rink and the boy's family also have insurance policies which would have paid for all or part of the costs of treatment.

The cost of full coverage liability insurance has become prohibitive for many churches, especially smaller ones. These churches have discovered that there is a way to protect themselves while at the same time greatly reducing the amount of their budgets which must be set aside for insurance coverage. This is called liability coinsurance. In many states, the annual premium cost for liability coinsurance is less than half that required for full coverage liability insurance. There are several varieties of coinsurance, but the basic idea is that the policy will pay for any injury or damage which is not covered by some other full coverage liability or health insurance policy.

For example, the youth pastor of Second Church took his youth group skating at the roller rink. Second church is new and small, but a growing church which needs to make sure it is getting maximum benefit from all money spent. So Second Church invested in a liability coinsurance policy. At the skating rink that night a student from Second Church fell and was injured and needed immediate emergency, as well as long-term medical treatment. When contacted about the medical claim, Second Church's insurance provider said, "We will gladly pay any claim arising from this injury which isn't also covered by some other type of insurance." In this case, the injured student's family has a family health insurance policy which will pay for 80 percent of the cost of the medical care needed to recover from the injuries suffered. Therefore, the church's coinsurance policy will pay for the 20 percent of the cost which the family's health insurance does not cover.

Exclusionary Riders

Christian Education workers need to carefully study their church's liability insurance policy. If necessary, a church leader who understands insurance policy language should explain any parts of the policy one doesn't understand. Many liability policies include what are referred to in the insurance industry as exclusionary riders. Each of these riders excludes from coverage certain activities or actions which are deemed higher than normal risk. It may be a surprise to discover that a local church's liability policy excludes from coverage some of the activities which have been conducted with children, youth, or adults. Typical exclusions include skiing, rock climbing, white-water rafting, hang gliding, and other recreational activities which are considered to be higher risk activities.

A policy may also have a rider which excludes coverage for any individual whose physical condition puts him or her at higher than normal risk while participating in certain activities. When ministering to individuals who have any kind of physical disability or chronic medical problem, one should check the church insurance policy carefully to make sure adequate liability coverage exists for taking them on an activity.

A third exclusionary rider which may be part of a policy concerns insurance coverage for drivers on officially sponsored church outings. Many Christian Education workers in churches which own buses know the minimum age of drivers covered by their insurance policy. Few Christian Education workers know whether the church liability policy contains a rider stating a minimum age for drivers providing transportation for a church-sponsored outing. It is not uncommon for a church liability policy to contain a rider which states that coverage is extended only for drivers who are 21 years of age or older. Some riders even exclude adult drivers with less than an exemplary driving record.

A final caution: churches covered by a liability coinsurance policy need to inform church families, members, and participants, telling them this is the type of insurance the church has. Not only is this the ethical thing to do, it may protect your church and its insurance provider from a damaging law suit.

For example; the youth pastor of Second Church has not notified parents of the students in his youth group that the church carries liability coinsurance. The student who was injured on the skating outing comes from a non-church family. This student's parents were under the impression that the cost due to any injury suffered by their child while on the church outing would be covered by the church or its insurance provider. They are quite upset upon discovering that they have to file a claim with their own health insurance provider first and then file an additional claim with the church's coinsurance provider for the medical cost not paid by their own insurance. This has resulted in undue inconvenience to this family and a significant delay in their being reimbursed for the medical costs. The result is that they now don't want their child to come to any further youth group activities at Second Church.

None of this would likely have been a problem if the youth pastor had notified the parents of all the young people that the church was covered by a coinsurance policy. This notification could be a statement on a medical release information form.

Medical Release Forms

Every time a Christian Education worker conducts a ministry activity with children or young people under the age of 18, he or she is taking a significant risk. At any time in any place one of those young people could become injured or ill and need medical attention. In most, if not all states, obtaining professional medical care for a minor without the signed consent of his or her parents or legal guardians is extremely difficult and in some cases impossible. In some states, these forms must be signed and the signature notarized by a notary public to be legally binding. A sample medical release form which would be acceptable in the state of California is attached at the end of this chapter. Regulations vary from state to state, so C.E. workers should consult with a hospital or doctor's office in their community to learn what forms are used when parents bring children in for treatment in their state. Under normal circumstances, if you model your form after the ones used by medical professionals in your community you will be safe.

Since the parents or legal guardians will be signing this form, it is appropriate to put other necessary information on it so that their signature indicates that they have read and understand the information on the form. For example, this is a good way to notify parents of the kind of liability insurance a church has and which kinds of activities are excluded from coverage.

Not only should one have a medical release form signed by the parents or legal guardian for each activity which a church sponsors for youth, but medical release forms should be on file in the church office giving permission for medical treatment if needed during routine church activities such as AWANA, VBS, or Sunday School. Many churches have a number of children or youth attending whose parents do not come. Any one of those children or youth could become injured or ill during Sunday School, worship service, or another activity and be in need of emergency medical care. If the parents cannot be reached immediately, it will likely be difficult to get medical treatment quickly. However, with signed consent forms on file (usually updating them annually is sufficient), workers don't have to worry if they cannot get in touch with the injured or ill child's parents right away.

International Travel

In most cases an insurance company does *not* cover travel outside the United States and Canada. This means that a church or parachurch organization opens itself up to potential lawsuits if the students should become injured during an international missions trip. Flight insurance, which can be obtained from a local travel agent or the airport, usually covers items such as baggage loss, terrorism, or cancellation of flights, but doesn't cover the individual against liability claims while on the journey. For this reason many churches have sharply curtailed international missions trips until individuals reach adult age.

A tragic illustration of what can happen recently occurred in California where a youth pastor took his high school group to Mexico for a missions service project. While there one of the students was killed in an accident. The church didn't have international liability coverage, and the resulting loss suit could have serious and long-term consequences for the church itself.

International missions trips are becoming more popular for students underage and a church which sponsors such activities should consult with an attorney to draw up a specific liability waiver form for international trips. The cost is approximately two hours of professional consultation. Such a waiver will inform parents that the students who participate on such trips do so at their own risk.

Confidentiality and Privileged Communication

Another legal and ethical issue which often arises for the Christian Education worker concerns matters of confidentiality communicated either in a counseling session, or perhaps by a colleague in ministry. The question which arises is, "When am I allowed to keep a confidence and when could I be required by law to reveal what I've been told?"

Protection Under the Law

Generally speaking, there are two types of protection of the privilege of confidentiality: 1) protection from voluntary disclosure by the receiver of the information is afforded to the individual being counseled, and 2) protection for the receiver of the information from being compelled to disclose it by state law, a court of law, or a church court.[1] In other words, the parishioner in a counseling situation is protected against the counselor divulging what he or she told the counselor in a counseling situation. Secondly, the ministry worker, in most circumstances, cannot be forced to reveal something that was stated to him or her in confidence.

Communication is deemed confidential when one of the three following criteria is met:

1) confidentiality is a requirement or a tradition of the church,
2) confidentiality is an ethical or legal duty imposed by a license, or
3) confidentiality has been promised by formal or informal agreement between the person giving information and the person receiving it.[2]

An example of the first criterion would be the Roman Catholic Sacrament of Confession. An example of the third criterion is a counseling situation where a C.E. worker has agreed to keep a confidence and the parishioner involved has understood that the information given is to be kept secret. Currently no state issues any kind of a license for lay or professional ministry workers which would have anything to do with confidentiality.

How Does It Apply to Me?

In what context is the Christian Education professional likely to hear information which may need to be kept in confidence? There are at least six situations in which this kind of information may come up:

1) confession of some kind of sin,
2) spiritual counseling,
3) emotional counseling,
4) comment in a small accountability or support group,
5) as a prayer request in a prayer meeting, and
6) casual personal conversation.[3]

The next question which arises for the Christian Education person is, "How do I know if something I heard is something I could be required to voluntarily disclose?" In most states the first consideration leading to an answer is whether or not the worker is an ordained clergy, licensed clergy, or non-ordained church staff. In most situations ordained clergy enjoy rather sweeping and broad protections against being compelled to disclose confidential communications. Licensed clergy, on the other hand, enjoy protections related strictly to the limits of their license. Finally, in most states, there are few protections against compelled disclosure on the part of volunteer workers.[4] It's crucial for C.E. workers to consult with knowledgeable persons in their congregations to learn of the disclosure requirements in their state.

There are two situations in the state of California (and many other states) where a Christian Education worker is required to report information to local authorities. The first of these is when the worker believes the person with whom he or she is dealing represents a potential harm to a third party, and the potential victim is identifiable. In this case, the worker is required by law to 1) warn the potential victim, and 2) involve the necessary authorities to protect the potential victim.[5]

The second case where disclosure is required by California law is in the case of suspected child abuse. California law defines child abuse as: physical injury inflicted by other than accidental means; sexual abuse; unjustifiable punishment or willful cruelty; or neglect, including abuse in an out-of-home care facility.[6] In this case, the C.E. worker should consult immediately with his or her pastor and church board. If there is enough evidence to raise a reasonable suspicion of child abuse, a report must be filed in writing with the local police department within thirty-six hours of the incident.[7]

The C.E. Worker and Church Discipline

The New Testament has much to say about discipline within the local church. Matthew 18 provides a procedure for redress of a grievance between two members of the body. In 1 Corinthians 5 and 2 Corinthians 2 the Apostle Paul addresses some of the disciplinary needs of the church in Corinth and tells them to discipline themselves or he will have to discipline them on his next visit there. In 1 Timothy 5 Paul gives instructions to a young pastor regarding the discipline of the members of his church. The fact is that God expects the church to be a disciplined body.

Secular government has historically realized that it's best to defer to church courts or councils when it comes to disciplinary issues within the body of Christ. However, in recent years there have been several cases where individual parishioners have sued churches and pastors after being made subject to church discipline. How can a church and its workers protect itself from such a court action?

There is no way for a church or its workers to guarantee that it can't be sued for a disciplinary action against an individual member. However, there are some steps which the church and its workers can take to reduce the risk of losing a law suit following a disciplinary action.[8]

1) *Teach regularly and often about the disciplinary role of the church.* Christian Education workers should clearly outline for their students (at the adult level) the disciplinary steps the church will take related to various infractions of the church covenant.

2) *Explain to potential new members the requirements of their commitment and specifics of discipline if they breach it.* Church workers should make sure potential members clearly understand the requirements for membership and the penalties related to violation of those requirements.

3) *Ask new members to sign the vows of their commitment at the time of their membership.* Christian Education workers should seek the affirmation of new members regarding the rights of the church to apply discipline.

4) *When discipline is necessary, carefully follow clearly defined procedures.* C.E. workers should never carry out discipline on their own. Rather, they should seek the support and involvement of the pastoral staff and the official church board. All involved should follow the defined procedures carefully.

5) *Don't allow unsubstantiated charges to be publicly proclaimed by the church.* Church education workers must be extra careful not to be the conduit of unsubstantiated charges. It is both legally dangerous and ethically wrong to spread these charges to other people.

6) *Base disciplinary decisions on biblical grounds and frame them that way.* Christian Education workers should work with the pastoral staff and official church board making sure that Scripture supports the disciplinary actions being proposed and should further be prepared to articulate that biblical position wherever necessary.

7) *Publish the disciplinary action relating only that information which needs to be published and substantiate the whole action with Scriptural support.* Church workers should support the disciplinary action taken by the congregation and refuse to participate in gossip or idle conversation about the one disciplined or the action itself.

Specific Issues Which Arise

This final section contains some practical suggestions which, if followed, will help Christian Education workers to avoid the kind of serious trouble which can come from the most innocent of circumstances.

1) *Do not provide any kind of lodging for a person under age 18 without the signed consent of his or her parents or legal guardian.*

For example: Gary comes home after the curfew hour imposed by his parents and immediately gets into a violent argument with his father. After several minutes of arguing, his father kicks Gary out of the house. Gary needs somewhere to stay so he calls his youth pastor and asks to stay the night until he is able to patch things up with his dad.

Many youth pastors have, without hesitation, agreed to allow students like Gary to spend one or more nights at their own home until reconciliation with the parents can take place. Generally speaking, this should not be done. The person who allows underage students to live or "crash" at his or her home is

288 Foundations of Ministry

inviting charges of kidnapping, alienation of affection, or other criminal or civil charges. Such charges could be brought against both the worker and/or the church by angry parents.

The proper response would be to take the time that night to be an intermediary between Gary and his parents in an attempt to get them to let him return home. Along with this is a promise from the C.E. worker that he or she will meet with the family at their earliest convenience to help resolve the larger conflict which precipitated the outburst. In the event that there is no possibility of Gary returning home that evening, the proper local authorities must be contacted and he should be turned over to their care for the night.

2) *Don't allow minors or unreliable adults to drive other minor students anywhere on an officially sponsored church activity.* Qualifications for official drivers were covered earlier in this chapter. The other question arising from this suggestion is, "What qualifies as an officially sponsored church activity?" This varies from state to state, but generally speaking the following criteria apply. An officially sponsored church activity is one for which the participants are urged to meet at a common location (church, private home, shopping mall, etc.) for the purpose of traveling together to an event and returning together.

Legally, in most states, the church is liable for anything that happens to a participant in this type of activity from the time he or she arrives at the prearranged meeting place until the student returns to the established location for pickup to return home. In a very few states the church's liability is extended from the time the participant leaves home until the time he or she returns home. It is always wise to check local state laws to determine which is the case for a particular local church

For example: Barry recently turned 16 and his parents bought him a new car for his birthday. The church youth group is going on an all-day water skiing outing at a lake about two hours away. All the high school students have been told to meet at the church parking lot, and various parents and other adults have been recruited to provide transportation for the students. But Barry arrives in his new car and informs the youth pastor that he has permission to drive to the lake and back and that he plans to take two of his friends with him. Barry wants to know where he should meet the group at the lake.

The wise worker confronted with this scenario will refuse to let Barry drive his car to the lake. And if he cannot prevent an adamant Barry from doing that, will refuse to allow the friends to ride along because the church's insurance policy will not cover a young driver.

So, the next question is, "How does a worker prevent the above scenario from happening?" The following two steps will keep something like the scenario above from becoming an issue.

• Step 1) Make sure all the students know that persons under the age specified by the church insurance policy (usually 21 years) cannot drive on officially church-sponsored activities.

• Step 2) Suggest to parents who permit their teens to drive to activities that they make arrangements to meet the group at the location of the activity (in the case above, the lake). Thus, the student driving his or her own car should go there directly from home and return directly to home when the activity is over. If Barry had driven straight from his home to the lake, he and those who ride with him are not officially considered to be part of the group covered by church insurance and are traveling at the risk of Barry and his parents and their insurance provider.

However, once Barry arrives at the church (or other designated meeting place), he is assumed by his parents and the law to be part of the officially church-sponsored group and the church could be legally liable for anything that happens to Barry and his passengers on the trip.

3) *When counseling, don't make promises that you can't keep.* As stated earlier, in most states the counselor may be required by law to divulge information gleaned in a private session. A worker can't know in advance of a session whether he or she is going to receive such information. Many youth workers and other Christian Education veterans have been confronted by a counselee who began his or her comments with something like, "I need to tell you something, but before I do, I need you to promise me you won't tell anyone else what I'm about to say."

The advice here is don't make that promise. If the person divulges information that one feels legally or ethically obligated to relate to others, then the counselor has been placed in a very awkward position. When confronted with such a situation, a better response might be, "I can't promise you that I won't tell anyone else, but I can promise that I won't tell anyone who doesn't absolutely have to know what you're about to tell me." This gives the counselor freedom to determine who must be told and in what context to do so.

Summary

We live in a time in which people are anxious to cash in on the booty resulting from civil lawsuits. In many cases the church and its employees have not been at fault and are the innocent victims of harmful litigation. However, in some cases people have been seriously hurt and even killed because of the negligence of well-meaning ministers. There is much that should be done to protect the lives and safety of those for whom the church is responsible. Vehicles and equipment must be properly maintained, volunteer staff must be adequately trained, employees should receive guidance about church policies and procedures, and church boards must be educated about eliminating needless risks.

There is virtually nothing a church can do to keep a determined litigant from suing for civil damages. However, there are many suggestions contained in this chapter that will enable a church to have some confidence that the plaintiff who files a lawsuit against it cannot win the suit in court. Due to the ever changing nature of this subject the wise church board periodically consults with an attorney who specializes in First Amendment or personal injury law for updates and advice. It is up to the church to prove beyond a shadow of a doubt that it has done all that it could reasonably do to protect and serve those who participate in its ministries.

Notes

1. Dennis Kasper, "The Clergy and Legal Liability." Seminar at Fuller Theological Seminary, 29 September 1986.

2. Richard R. Hammar, *Pastor, Church and Law* (Springfield, Mo.: Gospel Publishing House, 1983), 47.

3. Ibid., 49.

4. Kasper, "Legal Liability."

5. H. Newton Maloney, and Thomas L. Needham, *Clergy Malpractice* (Philadelphia: Westminster Press, 1986).

6. Kasper, "Legal Liability."

7. Ibid.

8. Dennis Kaspar, "Legal Issues Raised by Church Counseling and Discipline." *Theology News and Notes — Fuller Theological Seminary*, October 1986, 7.

A Sample Permission Slip

CENTRAL BAPTIST CHURCH
MEDICAL PERMISSION SLIP

Name _____ Phone _____

Address _____

_____

The person named above has an unusual medical need as stated below:

_____

_____

_____

I/we the undersigned do hereby give permission to Central Baptist Church and its representatives to obtain any necessary medical treatment for the person named above during the conduct of any program, ministry or activity sponsored by Central Baptist Church.

_____ I want the person named above to ride only with adult drivers approved for coverage on the church's liability insurance policy.

_____ I will allow the person named above to ride with adult or teenage drivers not officially approved for coverage on the church's liability insurance policy and I/we have our own insurance coverage for this person in the event of injury.

_____
(signature of legal parent or guardian)   Date

NOTE TO PARENTS: Central Baptist carries only liability coinsurance. This means that should your child become injured or ill on a church spon-sored activity, your own family medical insurance will be billed first. If you have no insurance or if your insurance doesn't cover all necessary medical costs, our policy will make up the difference.

PART FOUR.
Specialized Educational Ministries

Twenty
The Ministry of Christian Camping

Camping has emerged over the last 200 years as a natural part of America and its culture. Images of the family station wagon, stuffed full of outdoor gear and family members of all ages and heading for the "great outdoors," is a typical scene of summer. No less typical is the picture of an 8-year-old child, full of anticipation as well as apprehension, leaving on the bus for his first summer camp adventure. A wide variety of organizations have recognized the potentials of the camp setting to provide healthful recreation, serve as an educational environment, and socialize the individual through experiences of group living. Most of these groups affirm the possibilities of the natural environment for "holistic" personal growth. Many of these organizational camps profess a "spiritual" purpose for the growth of campers. Christian camps do share many purposes with secular groups yet must be unique in the spiritual dimension. Their central purpose must be to "use as fully as possible the camp experience as an opportunity for discipling individuals toward maturity in Christ."[1] The methods and means of camping may be changing in many ways, yet this foundational purpose and the biblical truths that support it makes Christian camping distinctive in its field.

The outdoor environment is a powerful setting for spiritual birth and formation. Camps are places for life-changing decisions and growth. It has been estimated that one fourth of all believers began their personal relationship with Christ at a Christian camp.[2] Many missionaries point to a commitment they made while at camp as their call to missions. The church or parachurch organization that understands the uniqueness and benefits of such an environment can greatly enhance both its outreach and discipleship ministry. As an active participant in such a ministry, your understanding of camping can be a vital ingredient in the overall success of a church's Christian Education ministry.

Christian Education Potentials of Camping

One would be hard pressed to find another setting with as much potential to enhance spiritual growth as the Christian camp. Ted Ward, noted Christian educator, in an address to camping professionals, has stated, "A camp setting is the greatest environment for learning today."[3] What are some of the unique potentials of this setting which make it so rich for life-change and development? A broad view of Christ's reconciling work sees Him restoring a person's relationships in four key dimensions: with God, with the self, with other people, and with the created order. The ministry professional or layperson should be aware of the special contribution camping can make in each area.

Relating to God

The primary need of every human being is to begin and nurture a right relationship with the Creator. Exposure to the outdoors gives opportunity to gain knowledge about God and His work. Camping provides the opportunity for the creation to speak eloquently of the power and majesty of God. Lessons from the created world are often used biblically as illustrations of God's providence and works on behalf of His children. Not only can the natural setting facilitate learning *about* God, it can also promote the individual's personal experience *with* God. Many biblical figures, including Abraham, Jacob, Moses, David, Elijah, and Paul, encountered God in the wilderness and were transformed by the experience. Jesus sought moments of solitude with the Father when He went up to the mountain to pray. The wilderness epitomizes the place where a person can draw apart from distractions to wholly focus on God and listen to His voice. Bob Kraning, camping professional, expressed it well in saying, "God continues to use camps and conference centers as a key decision place in the lives of people . . . because of the isolation . . . because of the getting away and getting alone with God."[4] Overall, the camp program must provide times of biblical instruction which draw attention to the character and working of God, as well as provide opportunities for receptive individuals to discover Christ and be transformed through a personal walk with Him.

Relating to One's Self

When people are rightly related to God, they gain for the first time the possibility of knowing who they are and can then experience their full potential as human beings. The Christian camp is an ideal place to facilitate self-understanding and acceptance, as well as to enhance holistic personal development. People were created to develop in a whole array of areas. Jesus Himself was said to have developed mentally, physically, socially, and spiritually (Luke 2:52); balanced growth and lifestyle appear to be in God's design for all believers. The camp is a unique environment in which to introduce counterculture changes and help Christians live life as it was meant to be lived. Two examples, from many that could be cited, follow.

The press of urbanization, rampant "workaholism," and the accelerated pace of life make it imperative that believers understand the need for divinely ordained rest, reflection, and "re-creation."[5] God instituted the Sabbath rest in part to model this for humankind. Christ Himself, at some of the busiest times of His ministry, took time away in a remote setting to be alone with His disciples and the Father. In place of mindless amusements provided by modern electronic entertainment media, the camp offers times for quiet reflection as well as opportunities to develop recreational interests and skills in sports or other hobbies that can provide leisure for a lifetime.

A second example relates to the need of believers to be challenged, tested, and disciplined in their faith. God has commanded that "man's character should be a growth, not a gift."[6] Unless opportunities are provided for the individual to take risks and to be stretched, personal growth is retarded. The wilderness exemplifies a place of testing in Scripture; Abraham, Moses, Elijah and Jesus, among others, all endured important times of testing in remote environments. According to one educator, young people need to be challenged to something greater than themselves, such as sacrificial service to others, in order to grow.[7] The camp setting provides abundant opportunities to provide the missing challenge. For example, a call to growth through stress is the primary mission of many wilderness camps. Other types of camps focus on a challenging call to Christian commitment and training in discipleship skills and habits. In addition, the Christian camp can provide campers the opportunity to try on new roles, experiment with gifts, serve others and develop ministry and leadership skills. In short, it can be an exciting "laboratory for Christian living," full of realistic situations and spiritual potentials waiting to be tested.[8]

Relating to Others

Another human need, increasingly important with the disintegration of families and other social relationships, is that of a supportive and caring community. The outdoor environment can be used by God as a place for His people to learn about as well as actually experience Christian community.[9] One of the primary lessons God taught the Israelites through their wilderness experience was their unity as His congregation, set apart for His special use. Likewise, much of Christ's work in forging His diverse band of followers into the unified leadership of the early church occurred as they lived and traveled together through the countryside of Palestine. He taught that they were a new kind of family; through the difficulties of that life they learned dependence upon Him and love for one another. People of all ages can find a true sense of community among believers at camp and extend this through the communal life of the church. Relationships with counselors, teachers, and other campers can serve as a stabilizing force in the life of the camper. The "around the clock" living situation allows large amounts of time to be spent observing and interacting with maturing and caring leaders as well as peers. The communal life of the group as it worships, fellowships, and learns together is a powerful dynamic for life change as well as for the formation or enhancement of interpersonal relationships. Cabin meetings, meals, and recreation all can serve to provide experiences in interdependence and teamwork.

Relating to Nature
The final relationship which needs restoration is between the human race and the natural world. Scripture reveals that since man disobeyed in the Garden of Eden and neglected his stewardship, the creation has suffered. The contemporary crisis relating to human destruction of the environment is ample evidence of this. While a final solution lies only in the power of the Creator, Christians today need to gain a biblical understanding of their role as stewards in caring for limited natural resources. On this basis they can participate in what Schaeffer terms a "substantial healing" of the creation.[10] Camps have the potential to lead the Christian community in this arena. Nature study naturally integrated with the biblical teaching on creation can deeply affect the perspectives of many young people. Camper involvement in service projects to restore or prevent environmental damage is yet another potential activity fairly unique to a camp setting which could aid this process.

Christian Camping as Educational Ministry
To have maximum impact, the camping ministry must be seen as an integral part of the overall educational ministry of the church. A broad understanding of ministry affirms the unity of the church and camp. Though methods may differ between the two, the purpose of engendering spiritual growth in people is the same. Camping programs must be based on solid spiritual and educational goals and objectives which, in turn, must be built on an analysis of the needs of the campers and the biblical imperatives directed at these needs. Most Christian ministries will find that many of their educational goals and objectives can be achieved with greater success if they use the resources of a camping ministry.

Considering the camp as an extension of the complete educational ministry of the local church has two distinct advantages. First, the camp experience is planned well in advance and within the context of a larger program that has overall goals and direction. The camp educational program can actually begin many months previous to the outing, starting with the active involvement of campers themselves in prayer, team building, planning, promotion, and preparatory biblical learning. After camp, the results of the experience can be conserved and extended through continued relationship building, follow-up on life decisions, discipleship training, and guided reflection. Jogging the student's memory with videotape, slides, writing, or songs can aid in the extension of the ministry experience.

The second advantage of viewing camping as a part of the total ministry of the local church is that the group can utilize the particular strengths of the camp setting to meet objectives that can best be accomplished there. For example, team sports can be played in the city, but developing skills in nature study or wilderness sports might only be possible at camp. Speaker-led Bible teaching times may be effective in either environment, yet individual study in Scripture followed by spirited interaction with cabinmates seldom happens in the city. When choosing the type of camp and its programming, church leaders who are planning on going to camp should consider the unique contributions of camping and select the camp program that best meets their ministry needs.

Options in Christian Camping

Christian camping, like many other ministry areas, is undergoing much change. Bob Cagle's book entitled *Youth Ministry Camping*, identifies a recent trend toward "boundaryless camping." Church youth leaders have felt increasing freedom to go beyond the bounds of what has traditionally been done before. Options for camping ministry may be limited only by the vision and creativity of ministry leadership.[11]

Philosophy of Christian Camping

Camps have been categorized by a number of different criteria. The first and probably the most important division of camps relates to their philosophy, or underlying emphasis. This approach affects almost all other elements of the camp including programming, staff selection, training, facility development, and utilization. The two major philosophical approaches are the *centralized* and the *decentralized*, with a third, the *eclectic*, being a blending of the other two. A detailed contrast between the characteristics of the two major philosophies is found in figure 20.1 on page 300. The centralized approach corresponds to what traditionally has been called the "Bible conference."[13] The Bible conference, a permanent site camp which experienced its beginning development in the 1920s and 1930s in turn grew out of the "old-time camp meeting" held in the 1800s by many evangelical churches.[14]

Comparing General Characteristics: Camping Approaches

Centralized	Decentralized
Large group/all-camp meetings and activities	Small group meetings and activities
Program focuses on a few trained professionals	Program focuses on counselor
Bible taught by platform speaker	Bible taught by cabin counselor
Campers receive Bible content by listening	Campers study Bible content on their own
Mass evangelism	Personal, one-to-one evangelism
Life-decision/commitment-making orientation	Discipleship/spiritual growth orientation
Counselor is in a support role to staff and tends to be primarily a disciplinarian	Counselor teaches and conducts activities
Counselors tend to receive little training	Counselors usually receive extensive training
Dormitory type arrangements	Individual cabin/group arrangements including eating by cabin in dining hall
Central planning of all elements, including programming, by administration	Cooperative, democratic planning of some elements including programming by counselors and campers
Large scale program elements	Small scale program elements
Highly-structured programs and scheduling	Flexibly-structured programs and scheduling allowing some spontaneity
Fast-paced programming	Leisurely-paced programming
Campers are either spectators of exciting entertainment or participants in all-camp events	Campers are involved as active participants
Recreation focuses on team sports and individual sports and activities under program specialists	Recreation focuses on crafts, nature study, and outdoor skills
Competition to promote camp spirit is promoted	Individual competes only with self in personal achievement and performance
Site usage tends toward large buildings and playing fields grouped close together	Site usage tends toward smaller buildings and activity areas that are well separated and which fit into the natural lay of the land

Note: While these elements tend to be present in camps that follow one approach or the other exclusively, this chart is for comparison purposes only and will not hold true in every case.

Figure 20.1

In many ways, the conference approach simply transferred the standard church service to a camp setting. The focus of the centralized approach, as the name implies, would be on large group, standardized activities involving all campers or major segments of the camp population at one time. Programs would tend to focus on accomplished speakers, musical performances, or other forms of mass communications to the large group. Other elements in the program, such as the cabin group or recreational activities, usually are not seen as central to the spiritual purpose of the camp. These camps are often geared toward evangelistic presentations or calls for deeper life-changing commitments to Christ. Often the recreational programs of these camps will be geared toward highly competitive team sports.

The decentralized approach, on the other hand, corresponds to what traditionally has been called the "church camp."[15] Organizational camping, which embodied this approach, did not begin until 1885 with the first YMCA camp, which, at the time, had a strong evangelical emphasis.[16] The camp which follows the decentralized approach emphasizes the small group as the central unit for fulfilling its spiritual purpose. The cabin counselor becomes the focus of ministry; the capabilities of this staff person are crucial to the success of the program. Most of the program, including Bible study and recreation, is accomplished through the activity and dynamic of the small group. Discipleship and accountability along with the building of relationships are emphasized in this approach. Recreation often emphasizes nature study or skills which are appropriate to the natural environment, and camps often make the attempt to integrate such activities with the biblical teaching.

The eclectic approach attempts to take some of the best elements from each of the two distinct approaches and bring them together in one camp setting.[17] For example, the morning Bible study may be led by the cabin counselor while the evening may be reserved for an all-camp rally with a speaker and special music. An increasingly popular compromise, most Christian camps are tending more toward this middle position due to the obvious advantages and disadvantages in each of the two extremes. As Todd and Todd note, the majority of evangelical camps probably fall somewhere between the approaches of the centralized *conference* and the decentralized *camp*, "endeavoring to inject as much 'real camping' as possible in their program while retaining the aspects of conference programming considered essential."[18]

Types of Christian Camps

The major division of camps according to type is *resident* and *nonresident*. As Mattson defines it, a resident camp consists of a permanent campsite where campers spend the majority of their time. The nonresident camp, on the other hand, does not include a permanent site where campers spend consecutive nights.[19] The week-long summer youth camp still predominates as the traditional resident camp. These are often geared toward particular age groupings or specialized avenues of ministry (e.g., sports, music, families, or handicapped). With the tendency toward shorter vacations, the weekend camp or retreat is enjoying great popularity among many church groups. Resident camp facilities have a broad range in the services that they provide. The full-service Christian camp often provides everything for the individual camper or group including cabins, food service, trained staff including counselors, and a program consisting of spiritual teaching and recreational opportunities. A few resident facilities expect the church to provide some of these elements, such as recreation directors and counselors. Resident camp facilities most commonly are either independent in their sponsorship and governed by a board of directors or sponsored by a denomination or other parent organization.

Much of the variety in types of camps in the last thirty years has occurred in nonresident camping. Such camps provide the church or camping group with great flexibility in the type of camp that can be run since it is not usually anchored exclusively to one developed site. On the other hand, nonresident camps will require more extensive planning in advance, since, for example, all supplies must be transported with the group. Included here are *day camps*, often designed for younger children and held at a wide variety of locations from 9 A.M. until 4 P.M. *Travel camping* involves extended trips by means of motorized travel (e.g., car, bus, or recreational vehicle). Visits are made to a number of locations with overnight stops en route. The *family caravan trip* has found popularity with many church groups, combining some of the enjoyments of the family sight-seeing vacation with the benefits of Christian community. One of the most exciting developments in youth ministry in recent years is the *youth missions trip*. While some would consider this a different type of ministry program, many service-oriented trips could fit within the classification of travel camps. *Trip camping* involves a variety of means of non-motorized outdoor travel for extended periods, including by foot, ski, bike, raft, canoe, or pack animal. Within this category, wilderness camps have gained prominence over the past two decades; Mattson divides these into two kinds.[20] The first, the wilderness *trail* camp, requires little previous experience or preparation on the part of the camper and tends to focus on basic outdoor living skills. It usually fits the standard time frame of the resident Christian camp of about one week. The second, the wilderness *stress* camp, emphasizes personal and group growth which comes with endurance and overcoming of hardship. Such programs may be extensive, often three weeks in duration, and include training in advanced outdoor skills as well as a variety of tests of stamina and character. Numerous Christian camping groups specializing in wilderness stress experiences are in existence. Many of these draw on some elements of the "Outward Bound" philosophy of education integrated with spiritual elements unique to the Christian faith. Most of these groups operate independently. A few function under the sponsorship of large resident camp or other parachurch organization.

Utilizing an Existing Camp or Programming Your Own

One final option in camping is of vital interest to most camp leaders in the church and other ministries at one time or another. This regards choosing whether to use the services of an established camping program or running the program "in-house" without the aid of such resources. For some, this may not be a choice at all. Traditional church ties or camp ownership by the organization or denomination may lock a group into a particular experience; lack of proximity to or availability of a suitable established camp may preclude the option as well. Given that the leader or leadership team has an option, there are a number of factors which must be considered.

The advantages of using an existing camp are many: the availability of trained professional staff, provision of a wide variety of services and resources, and a consistent degree of quality would top the list. Because these are provided, leaders are often freed to spend time ministering to their campers rather than being concerned with details. The presence of trained camp professionals becomes especially important in such areas as wilderness camping, when health and safety issues become more critical than they are in camps nearer to civilization. These trained counselors and staff usually are experienced in how to best utilize the camp situation for maximum spiritual impact on the campers.

It has been estimated that there are over 2,000 Christian camps operating in North America.[21] If an existing camp program would be best for a church group, then it is essential to follow the process for selecting the proper camp. First, get recommendations on camps of the type that will fulfill ministry goals. Ask other pastors or youth workers about their experiences with various camps. Membership in the national accrediting organization for camps, American Camping Association or Christian Camping International, is a positive recommendation since each has recognized standards for excellence in camp operation. Both publish guides which contain helpful information on member camps.[22] Next, contact the camp director or ministry relations person. Ask for any published materials or brochures available describing the camp. This should be done well in advance of the date of the camp, anywhere from nine months to a year, since quality camps are often in high demand during the prime summer season. Arrangements should be made to visit the camp, preferably at a time when one can observe the camp during its operation.

Spending time with the camp representative is vital since he or she can help a leader know if the camp will be a good match for the group. Ask questions about anything—observations, concerns, or potential problems. Find out about the camp's history, provisions for the safety and health of the campers, and food and lodging arrangements, as well as programming and ministry options. Find out exactly what services the camp is providing and what they expect from a group. For example, often the camping group is required to supply one counselor for each given number of campers. Be clear on rules and other camp expectations which will affect conduct of the camp and preparation for it. Inquire about size restrictions for groups and whether or not the facility will be shared. In the case of some decentralized and wilderness camps, large undivided groups may not be permitted and may defeat the unique purpose of the camp. Find out the exact cost to the church and specifically what will and will not be covered in that price. Cost alone should not be the major factor in a decision since many other ingredients go into making a successful camp. Also, one should be clear on contractual arrangements, such as amount of deposit required and minimum number of campers to decide if a group can adhere to these standards. C.E. leaders should look for camp personnel with a genuine desire to serve their group and meet their needs, not one interested only in booking the camp. The Christian camp must see itself as a supportive extension of the church or ministry group, not an autonomous ministry of its own. In this way it can serve as a parachurch organization in the finest sense of the term, called alongside to help in a specialized area that would be difficult for the group to accomplish on its own.

After finalizing arrangements and booking the camp, periodic contact should continue with the camp representative to coordinate on any planning details. This person can be a valuable resource for ideas and materials on promoting the camp to a group and aiding them in camp preparation, as well as coordinating during the actual camp experience. After the camp, follow-up contact and evaluation should be conducted with the camp for feedback on the services provided and the degree of effectiveness in reaching the planned objectives. A relationship for years to come between the camp and the group may emerge from a positive camping experience.

Running Your Own Camp Program

The group which elects to run a camp using its own resources may do so for a number of reasons. The most immediate may be the cost of the program. By renting the facility alone, without the program personnel of the camp, substantial savings should be enjoyed. A church group will also have the added advantage of program flexibility that many established camps lack. The group can tailor the camp and the program specifically to meet its own ministry objectives. One final benefit that may be overlooked is the advantage in having the campers themselves involved in the complete planning and execution of the camp. They may achieve a sense of camp "ownership," and a spirit of teamwork with one another, not possible when a complete package is provided for them.

If a church or organization decides to run its own camp to meet its objectives, a whole new set of considerations and responsibilities become important.

The biggest single consideration for a group in deciding to run its camp is the presence of trained, capable staff or volunteers. In fact, lack of skilled small-group counselors is a major deterrent to using the decentralized camp approach. In seeking help, look for spiritually mature and clear-thinking people to serve as solid Christian models for the campers. The proven Christian character of the individual is primary. While camp skills can usually be taught fairly quickly to motivated staff, development of solid character takes a lifetime. Wright and Anthony list a number of additional qualifications for the camp counselor, including knowledge of the Scriptures, positive attitude, love, reliability, flexibility, physical health, and a servant attitude.[23]

Pre-camp training sessions will need to be conducted in a number of areas. These will vary according to the type of camp, but should probably include training in Bible study methods, health and safety rules and procedures, small group leadership, and sports or recreation skills. An important focus must be the age-level needs and abilities of the group to be counseled, so that all teaching and programming can be geared to that developmental level. Staff should be trained for individual counseling in such typical situations as leading a camper to Christ or helping a young person who is homesick. Simulations, role play, and case studies can be particularly helpful in these sessions. A training program can provide the additional benefit of team building among the staff, a vital element for a successful camp.

Another key consideration relates to legal and liability issues. This is a particular area of concern for camps since exposure to physical danger in the outdoor environment is often greater than the risks found in the normal ministry situation. The camp director assumes an important responsibility for the physical well-being of the campers. Areas of concern include medical care, camper physicals, parent permission forms, appropriate insurance, special certification and training of staff, and provision for safe maintenance of vehicles and utilized facilities. Counseling staff should be trained in how to deal with sensitive issues and when to make referrals. In addition, a trend toward more stringent government regulation means camp leaders must be aware of any regulations which will affect a camp's operation. Acquisition of permits and observation of guidelines for use of public lands for wilderness camps are one case in point. Camps involving remote travel place an additional burden of risk on the camp leadership. The leader of such a Christian camp experience is judged by the standards — "current peer practices" — of outdoor professional guides and could be judged legally liable in case of a lawsuit over a camper accident or injury.[24] Unless the camp leader is well qualified and experienced, a professional guide or wilderness camping leader is highly recommended for the margin of safety provided.

A consideration crucial to the success of any camp is the leadership team. In most cases professional staff, laypersons, and campers themselves should all be included on this planning team. Among the many activities of this group will be surveying the campers in regard to their needs and interests, selecting a camp director, choosing a site and major program elements, deciding on a theme, determining a budget, and insuring that all camp responsibilities are delegated and covered adequately. The planning team should begin meeting well in advance of the event, since popular facilities and speakers often must be contacted many months before the event. After the camp, its job is not completed until a thorough post-camp evaluation has been completed.

Finally, a few general programming considerations should be noted. The actual camp planning process, as has been mentioned before, must begin with the goals for the educational ministry based on biblical imperatives and the needs of the campers. Specific objectives should be chosen for a particular camp experience based on these general goals. The philosophy of the camp (centralized vs. decentralized) and the type of camp should be selected based on the probability that the objectives could be achieved best in that setting. Often a camp program will be oriented around a central theme which takes these objectives into consideration. In general, biblical teaching in camp tends to be topical. Each daily Bible study can be planned to develop a particular aspect of the theme. While leader-centered teaching has been traditional, serious thought should be given to inductive Bible study and other methods that allow the camper to be an active and expressive participant in the teaching-learning process. Balance and variety are key concepts to keep in mind in program planning. For example, a structured time for individual reflection and prayer can be balanced by providing group time with sharing and "debriefing." The combination of these two learning environments can be more valuable to the spiritual formation process than either one separately. Also, the more variety in the methods used, the greater the likelihood that all campers will be affected to some degree since campers vary in individual interests and learning styles. In a totally integrated program, almost every activity, if selected and planned carefully, can support the theme and contribute to one or more of the objectives. While many events can be scheduled, others occur unexpectedly. Staff should be aware of the educational potential of the "teachable moments" which transpire in the unplanned program.

Summary

The ministry of the Christian camp has had a long and rich heritage of impacting the world with the message of salvation and spiritual enrichment. Perhaps no other parachurch agency has had such an impact on the church. Its support for the mission of the church and its ability to blend creative programming with an environment conducive to learning has enabled it to make a strong contribution to ministry. Christian Education and Christian camping share many ministry goals and objectives in common. It's for this reason that the church's educational ministry has much to gain from a partnership with a local Christian camp.

Notes

1. Werner Graendorf, *An Introduction to Christian Camping* (Duluth, Minn.: Camping Guideposts, 1984), 25.

2. Norman Wright and Michael J. Anthony, *Help, I'm a Camp Counselor*, rev. ed. (Ventura, Calif.: Regal Books, 1986), 12.

3. Lloyd Mattson, *Build Your Church Through Camping* (Cotton, Minn.: Camping Guideposts, 1984), 10.

4. Robert Kraning, videotaped presentation, Camp Leadership class, Talbot School of Theology, 25 April 1990.

5. For further discussion of this important topic see Tim Hansel's *When I Relax, I Feel Guilty* (Elgin, Ill.: David C. Cook, 1979).

6. Lois LeBar, *Education That Is Christian* (Wheaton, Ill.: Victor Books, 1989), 113.

7. Anthony Campolo, *Growing Up in America* (Grand Rapids: Zondervan Publishing House, 1989), 28-29.

8. James Michael Lee, *The Content of Religious Instruction.* (Birmingham, Ala.: Religious Education Press, 1985), 618-19.

9. For further discussion on how one type of camping can build community see Daryl L. Smith, "Trailcamping—A Microcosm of Community," *Christian Education Journal*, vol. 10, no. 1 (Autumn 1989): 51-62.

10. Francis Schaeffer, *Pollution and the Death of Man: The Christian View of Ecology* (Wheaton, Ill.: Tyndale House Publishers, 1970), 69.

11. Bob Cagle, *Youth Ministry Camping* (Loveland, Colo.: Group Books, 1989), 20-21.

12. Mattson, *Build Your Church*, 49-61.

13. Floyd Todd and Pauline Todd, *Camping for Christian Youth*, rev. ed. (Grand Rapids: Baker Book House, 1969), 30.

14. Ibid., 8-12.

15. Ibid., 30.

16. Ibid., 5.

17. Mattson, *Build Your Church*, 57.

18. Todd and Todd, *Camping*, 32.

19. Mattson, *Build Your Church*, 50.

20. Ibid., 59.

21. Wright and Anthony, *Camp Counselor*, 11.

22. Ibid., 21-30.

23. Ibid.

24. Tim Sanford, "Caution . . ." *Group*, June-August 1987, 17.

For Further Reading:

Ball, A. and Ball, B. *Basic Camp Management*. Martinsville, Ind.: ACA, 1987.

Christian Education Today (Summer 1991). (Issue devoted to Christian camping.)

Madsen, E. *Youth Ministry and Wilderness Camping*. Valley Forge, Pa.: Judson Press, 1982.

Reichter, A. *The Group Retreat Book*. Loveland, Colo.: Group Books, 1983.

Roadcup, D. ed. *Methods for Youth Ministry*. Cincinnati: Standard Publishing Co., 1986.

For Further Information

Organizations:

Christian Camping International
P.O. Box 646, Wheaton, IL 60189
(708) 462-0300

Publications:
Journal of Christian Camping and
Official Guide to Christian Camps and Conference Centers

American Camping Association, Inc.
Bradford Woods, Martinsville, IN 46151-7902
ACA Bookstore 1 (800) 428 - CAMP (for orders)

Publications:
Camping Magazine
Parents' Guide to Accredited Camps
Camp and Program Leader Catalog

Twenty-One
Parachurch Ministries

The last forty years have witnessed a phenomenal multiplication of evangelical Christian organizations which have come to be known as "parachurch ministries."[1] White, in his thorough work on the subject, defines parachurch as, "Any spiritual ministry whose organization is not under the control or authority of a local congregation."[2] These ministries, which conservative estimates put at more than 10,000 in the United States alone, have both produced innovative and effective outreach and stirred up controversy in regard to the local church.[3] Some see the providential hand of God using them to fulfill a unique and prophetic role, while others dispute the legitimacy of their very existence. The parachurch has served to effect spiritual growth and to allow fruitful expression of ministry for many believers, including this writer. Others, particularly those in church pastorates, have been frustrated by these independent ministries, which they see as usurping the ministry of the local church.

This chapter will discuss some key issues concerning the church/parachurch relationship, examine characteristics of parachurch agencies, categorize the various types of ministries, and provide insights for those interested in parachurch vocations. Recommendations will also be provided which should help the local church and parachurch ministries to work in harmony. These suggestions will be followed by a discussion on what the church might learn for its future ministry from the parachurch pioneering efforts.

Tensions between Church and Parachurch Ministries
What are the key issues in the conflict between local church and parachurch organizations? White states that the four major arenas of controversy are the 1) legitimacy of parachurch ministries, 2) the related issue of conflicts in

spiritual authority for those in these ministries, 3) the competition for scarce spiritual leaders, and 4) the contention of both for the same financial resources.[4] The first two issues will be developed here, since the resolution of these directly affect the latter two. Practical suggestions will be made later in the chapter concerning the leadership and financial issues.

The question of the legitimacy of the parachurch ministry and its relationship to the biblical authority of the local church must begin with a scriptural understanding of the church. As mentioned in chapter 1, the Greek term *ecclesia* in the New Testament primarily refers to the church in two distinct senses. In some uses the term refers to the universal church, emphasizing the spiritual unity of all believers in Christ, whether assembled or not. The second and predominant usage refers to a local assembly of those who profess Christ, that is, to a specific local church body. It should be noted that nowhere is the term used to refer to a building or anything resembling a denomination. Neither does the New Testament know anything about members of the universal church who do not fellowship together visibly in a local assembly.[5] While certainly such believers do exist in isolation, in biblical terms, this is an abnormal situation. From the perspective of some, the local fellowship appears to be the only body given specific authority; this authority was given for such purposes as administering discipline and choosing of leadership.[6] Therefore, it seems to be the contention of the New Testament authors that every believer, regardless of the type of ministry in which he or she is engaged, should be under the authority of a local church.

But what of the parachurch ministries themselves? Is there biblical precedent for them and what authority do they have? This section will not draw any definite conclusion on these difficult questions but will primarily seek to show the spectrum of views on this issue. White enumerates a wide variety of theological positions.[7] In one view the parachurch is not a legitimate ministry structure at all in light of New Testament teaching. Those holding this view would contend that there is no specific provision for an authoritative ministering body outside the control and authority of the local church. Another more conciliatory position states that these structures have been raised up on a temporary basis to fulfill service which should be done by the local church. In this vein, Lindsell notes that, overall, such ministries "have been a positive development, showing that when channels are blocked in existing churches, God moves outside then and does new things." He warns, however, that the danger inherent in some parachurch ministries is their tendency to replace the church in the minds of many.[8]

Those favoring full acceptance of the legitimacy of parachurch ministries vary in the type of ministry they view as warranted. One view contends that only those organizations whose objective is solely church planting have a right to exist. Others would extend this validity to all those structures which are mobile mission outreaches for the spread of the Gospel. Ralph Winter, whose "two structure" approach will be detailed later, finds biblical justification for these agencies in the "missions band" of the Apostle Paul as found in the Book of Acts. He views these groups as operating somewhat under their own authority and not that of any one local church, but as raised up by God to do an essential and ongoing work for the spread of the Gospel. He points to the work of William Carey and others as beginning the modern era of Protestant parachurch agencies.[9] Additional support for this position may be gained by noting Christ's provision of gifted leaders for the church in Ephesians 4:11. Only the evangelist, by the very nature of his work, would have a ministry primarily outside the local church body. While such ministry might well be under the authority of a particular local assembly, those such as Phillip the Evangelist seem to operate somewhat independently. The other gifts seem to be meant primarily for function within the local body. It would be harder, it might be argued, to biblically justify parachurch organizations whose basic ministries overlap the primary work of the local church, such as teaching and training disciples. On this basis, such agencies would do well to make every effort to serve and help to build local churches.[10]

Snyder champions a different approach regarding the validity of parachurch structures. He maintains that since the biblical church consists solely of God's people in community, any institution or organization that is not an integral part of that community is actually a parachurch. This would include even some agencies, such as the Sunday School, that operate within the local church organization. The way is therefore opened freely to utilize many different cultural forms and structures to fulfill the church function of ministry. For him, therefore, "the crucial consideration for structure becomes not biblical legitimacy but functional relevancy."[11]

Though apparently not quite as radical in the way he characterizes the parachurch, White supports the "dual legitimacy" position that would affirm a variety of ministries along side the local church. Part of his justification for this position is his agreement with Snyder concerning the great freedom of form and structure which appear in the New Testament to allow the whole church to accomplish its purpose and functions. Another support he appeals to is that such parachurch organizations provide important avenues for individual "believer-priests" to express their ministry in the body of Christ. Any conflicts in authority between the two organizations which lead to a sense of divided loyalties must be resolved based on the primary goal of building the whole body of Christ. The individual parachurch worker on the authority of the priesthood of all believers must make a responsible choice in this regard.[12] Contrary to the position stated earlier, White does not find scriptural support for the contention that all ministry, whether individual or group, must be under local church authority.[13]

Even those who are broad in their acceptance of parachurch agencies argue that not every organization has a valid ministry. The individual contribution of the particular organization to the work of the whole body must be evaluated.[14] One of the major problems, at least in the U.S., may well be the proliferation of a vast number of small, autonomous, nonprofit organizations. Some of these have been founded by leaders with strong individualistic spirits and are not accountable to any local church nor to any other responsible group of believers. Many appear to be inefficient in operation and yet draw resources away from more effective ministries.[15]

Besides the theological issues involved, practical considerations can be advanced in support of certain types of ministries outside the local church. For example, in certain situations, every church having a separate outreach ministry could lead to a duplication of effort and inefficient stewardship of resources. A single parachurch program would likely be able to work more effectively on a college campus than a number of uncoordinated church college groups. A second case where the parachurch might have an advantage is in programs which have a very specialized and focused task. This type of ministry is often so narrow in its scope and so intensive in its use of resources and skilled people that it would be impractical for any one church to support it. Ideally, such groups could come under the direction of one particular church yet be allowed to serve many other churches or needs. An example of this might be a camping program or a home for unwed mothers. This type of arrangement requires a wide breadth of vision on the part of the local church in order to participate in a shared ministry with other bodies. Practically, this does not often happen. These are only two of the ways that these agencies can serve the Christian community in a manner in which the church may not be capable. While one must be careful about attempting to validate ministry simply on a pragmatic basis, most would agree that parachurch agencies have contributed significantly to the work of the kingdom by meeting unfulfilled needs.[16]

Characteristics of the Local Church and the Parachurch

Probably the best way to get a general understanding of the parachurch is to view its characteristics in relief against those of the local church. This contrasting perspective will help to illustrate how each can complement the other in the broad goal of building the kingdom, as well as highlight the inherent weak tendencies of each structure. Winter characterizes the local church as having a vertical structure, which he designates with the sociological term *modality*, because in its essence it is a fellowship which makes no distinctions on the basis of age or sex. The parachurch, on the other hand, has a horizontal structure, termed a *sodality*, which is limited to a particular subgroup based on age, sex, or marital status and which requires an adult second decision beyond that of the modality.[17] By contrasting these two (see figure 21.1 on page 315)[18] it becomes easy to see why some of the classic tensions between these two structures have arisen. This chart is also instructive as to why conflicts arise between the local church as a whole and special interest groups within the church structure. Winter notes, "It may well be true that because these two types of organizations are so different, they will always have to make a special effort to understand each other."[19] These are general characterizations only; many exceptions to these characteristics would be found in the case of specific organizations.

Classifying Parachurch Educational Ministries

Categorizing parachurch ministries at the end of the twentieth century is no easy task. With the increasing trend toward specialization to meet needs of specific interest groups, they present an ever broadening variety of programs, many of which are either wholly or partly educational in nature. While some would limit the category "parachurch" to nonprofit Christian groups, this would leave out many organizations (e.g., some Christian publishers) which provide support and material to aid the church's ministry.[20] In addition, some mission organizations are sponsored exclusively by one church denomination (e.g., Southern Baptist Convention) whereas others are interdenominational and are supported by numerous churches and private funding sources (e.g., Wycliffe). In one approach the spectrum of these agencies is shown relative to their degree of dependence or interdependence from the ministry of the local church, as demonstrated in figure 21.2 on page 316.[21]

This section will classify parachurch ministries into seven general categories based on type of service performed, provide a brief characterization of each type, and give a few notable examples. In some cases, brief comments about vocational opportunities will be given. Some organizations are difficult to classify because their programs bridge a number of categories.

Missions

The years since World War II have witnessed a virtual explosion of overseas mission agencies and their personnel. While denominations are still important sending agencies, the vast majority of these have developed outside any denominational structure and are therefore clearly independent and parachurch in nature. This is not solely an American phenomenon since many non-Western nations have become senders of missionaries.[22] Such agencies range from the large and well-established, such as Africa Inland Missions

Local Church Structure	Parachurch Structure
1. Consists of whole families and ranges of age ("cradle to grave")	1. Consists of motivated individuals
2. Generally "people" oriented	2. Primarily "task" oriented
3. Relatively low level of commitment needed and minimal requirements of members	3. High level of commitment and stringent requirements for workers in addition to that needed from the local church member
4. Decisions generally made by a consensus of leaders or whole church	4. Decisions tend to be made by directive from "prophetic" leadership
5. Participation and inclusion both voluntary and involuntary (children)	5. Participation strictly voluntary
6. Internal diversity of purpose and goals to meet a variety of needs	6. Limited and specific purpose and goals to meet specific needs
7. Broad objectivity and perspective of ministry necessary to protect overall ministry from harm and domination by special interests	7. Narrow perspective tending toward seeing only its own ministry goals and therefore having a tendency to "oversell" its cause to supporters
8. Tends to be immobile and inflexible regarding changing ministry demands	8. Tends to be mobile and flexible to meet changing ministry demands quickly and effectively
9. Tends toward bureaucracy separating financial donors from end results	9. Donors can generally see specifically what contributions are accomplishing
10. Finds it difficult to gain broad support among diverse elements for enterprises beyond its internal needs	10. Offers an outlet for those in the church with diverse and differing visions of ministry
11. Has potential to help or harm the parachurch to the extent that it acknowledges its legitimacy in contributing toward Christ's universal church and by the amount of personal and financial support	11. Has potential to help or harm the local church depending on the degree of submission practiced toward the local church by parachurch workers and their willingness to use spiritual gifts for the building up of the body

Figure 21.1

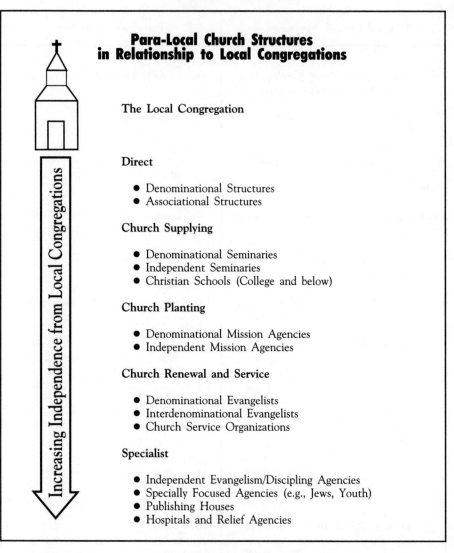

**Para-Local Church Structures
in Relationship to Local Congregations**

The Local Congregation

Direct

- Denominational Structures
- Associational Structures

Church Supplying

- Denominational Seminaries
- Independent Seminaries
- Christian Schools (College and below)

Church Planting

- Denominational Mission Agencies
- Independent Mission Agencies

Church Renewal and Service

- Denominational Evangelists
- Interdenominational Evangelists
- Church Service Organizations

Specialist

- Independent Evangelism/Discipling Agencies
- Specially Focused Agencies (e.g., Jews, Youth)
- Publishing Houses
- Hospitals and Relief Agencies

Increasing Independence from Local Congregations

Figure 21.2

and Overseas Missionary Fellowship, to the smallest faith mission. Their particular mission may be primarily one of relief, such as World Vision, translation work, such as the American Bible Society and Wycliffe, evangelism and discipleship training, or church planting. A vast array of opportunities and needs for vocational workers exist within these organizations. Many believe that the greatest need is for missionaries who can teach indigenous leadership and give them a sound biblical and theological base. Bible training is vital as preparation for such mission as well as cross-cultural studies. Important recent developments in mission training are the growth of institutions such as the U.S. Center for World Missions and the School of Intercultural Studies at Biola University.

Mission agencies on the home front have multiplied as well, notable among these are a great number of agencies working in the inner cities. Organizations such as World Impact and Church Resource Ministries provide a variety of services in these communities. Rescue and relief agencies for such groups as the homeless operate in most urban areas as well. Among a variety of other specialized "home missions" works are prison and jail outreaches such as those conducted by agencies like Prison Fellowship.

Evangelism and Discipleship

Parachurch organizations which focus on the sharing of the Gospel and edification for those of college age and above are considered here. Ministries such as Campus Crusade for Christ and Inter-Varsity Christian Fellowship have had a major impact on the American college campus as well as on the international scene through various ministries. The Navigators, which began its work with military personnel and now works with a variety of adults in this country and abroad, are well known for their structured emphasis on discipling.[23] Requirements for joining the staff of these organizations range according to the particular ministry, with a college degree generally preferred along with some ministry experience and additional training.[24]

Evangelistic ministries with domestic as well as world-wide impact are among the more visible parachurch ministries. Most notable among these over the last half century has been the Billy Graham Evangelistic Association. Dr. Graham and his team have been exemplary in their efforts to win people to Christ, to cooperate and contribute to leadership training in local churches, and to be financially accountable to the Christian community which supports them.

A number of parachurch ministries focusing on Bible knowledge and study for adults have developed nationally. A number of these programs, such as Bible Study Fellowship and Precept Ministries, involve intensive and demanding studies, primarily for women. A novel approach to acquiring an overview of Scripture in a short period of time is used by another group, Walk Thru the Bible Ministries. These organizations often use church facilities for their programs.

Childhood and Adolescent Ministries

These programs running through high school age can be divided into two subcategories, those working primarily through the church's sponsorship and those working chiefly independent of the local body. Organizations such as Awana, Canadian Sunday School Mission, Christian Service Brigade, and Pioneer Girls provide a program and support materials to be utilized by local lay and church staff leaders. Independent works include local club and student communities of national organizations such as Child Evangelism Fellowship, Youth for Christ, and Young Life, led by paid staff or volunteer lay workers. Full-time staff with many of these independent organizations are expected to have a bachelor's degree and usually have had experience working with the ministry on a volunteer basis. Some of these organizations also have significant mission and camping programs.[25]

Camping and Recreation

Since most camping experiences are short in duration, camping must by its very nature be a parachurch ministry, used to enhance the effectiveness of the church or other Christian organizations utilizing it. Camps range greatly in the variety of experiences offered and the degree to which they are flexible to meet the particular needs of the using organization. While many large camps operate as independent agencies (e.g., Word of Life, Kana Kuk Kana Komo), others find sponsorship through denominations (e.g., Glorietta, Ridgecrest), local churches, or national youth organizations (Camp Malibu). Though positions for full-time camp staff are somewhat limited, great opportunities exist for cabin counseling and other part time ministry. (See also chapter 20, *The Ministry of Christian Camping*.)

Schools and Educational Institutions

In recent years Christian day schools at the elementary and secondary levels have multiplied across the nation, offering many families an alternative to publicly sponsored education. Some have begun with denominational support, others through the support of a single local body, while a number have sprung up independent of specific church support. To qualify for teaching positions in most day schools, an undergraduate degree with a teaching credential is usually required and Bible training is preferred. (See also chapter 25, *Public Education, Christian Schools, and Home Schooling*.)

A number of Bible colleges and Christian liberal arts institutions, which seek to integrate evangelical faith and higher learning, offer both undergraduate and advance degrees in a wide range of disciplines. These, as well as a number of conservative theological schools and seminaries serving to train leaders for vocational ministry, are either independent or sponsored by various denominations. Faculty positions in higher education necessitate advanced degree work, with most seminaries preferring those with doctoral degrees as well as field experience.

Media and Technology

With the vast growth in information and technology, parachurch ministries specializing in these areas have experienced incredible growth as well. The printed word is vital to virtually all ministries and especially to educational efforts. Denominational and independent Christian publishers produce texts and reference works as well as popular books. The church profits from their curriculum and other educational support materials as do many mission enterprises. The electronic media ministries such as radio (e.g., Insight for Living, The Haven of Rest) and television (e.g., 700 Club, T.B.N. Broadcast) have claimed high percentages of exposure in audiences across the country.[26] Most are strongly evangelical in theology. Many local churches as well as parachurch organizations have extended their ministries and gained exposure for other programs in this way. While some debate the effectiveness of these media ministries specifically for evangelism, their primary benefit may well be for the edification and education of believers through daily Bible study programs and messages.[27] Clearly, not all applaud the "electronic church," some seeing in it a competitor for local church funding and a contributor toward a passive, vicariously lived spiritual life.[28]

While the cost of producing quality films for the Christian market is becoming prohibitive in some cases, many film companies are moving more toward the cost-effective use of videotaped productions, particularly for use in teaching and training. The ministry of Christian music (e.g., Maranatha Music, Word, Sparrow Records), in all its varieties, is a growing parachurch field as well. Somewhat specialized or technical skills in the areas of communication, journalism, music, and media technology would be required by those desiring to work in such organizations.

Organizations specializing in adaptation for ministry of the new information systems available are also a fairly recent development (e.g., Church Member Services). In seeking to manage their ministries and communicate with constituents, churches and extra-church agencies are becoming increasingly dependent on computers and other recent innovations.

Special Interest

Probably the greatest increase in independent Christian organizations has come as the result of attempts to focus on a particular area of need or concern in the Christian community. Some of these, such as James Dobson's Focus on the Family, have a broad appeal to many and have made substantial impact. Other groups, such as MOPS (Mothers of Pre-Schoolers), seek to serve a smaller segment of the Christian community with a common interest. Many small agencies have a narrower focus still, working with believers within a particular secular vocation, for example. Those ministries concerned with the needs of the handicapped and counseling or recovery centers for those with addictive behaviors would also be considered as part of the parachurch spectrum. Also included in this category would be concerned Christians who have organized to actively support a biblical approach to many of the moral issues in society, such as abortion, pornography, abuse, and poverty. A great diversity of opportunity, vocational and volunteer, is available in this diverse field and the requirements for entry range widely.

Vocations in Parachurch Ministries

The intrinsic rewards of vocational involvement in ministry can be very attractive for those seeking to express their love for the Lord in Christian service. As has been noted, the parachurch field offers an amazing variety of opportunities.

Before launching into any such work, the aspiring parachurch worker should ask a number of self-examination questions as well as inquire about the particular organization of interest. In addition to general questions relating to personal suitability for any vocational ministry, some issues are particularly pertinent to individuals seeking to work outside the church, as the following questions illustrate:

- Can my gifts and abilities best be expressed within the local church ministry, or do they require expression outside this context?
- Am I sufficiently aware of all avenues and possibilities for ministry in order to determine the one to which I am best suited?
- What spiritual gifts and talents do I have and can I best express them through this particular ministry?
- What are the demands for service in this organization, and what will be expected of me?

Because of the critical nature of finances, many parachurch organizations require that staff members raise all or at least a substantial percentage of their own support. The potential worker must honestly assess whether this is a step of faith that can be taken and survey the potential support base available as well.

A number of other questions would focus more on the parachurch agency itself.

- Is the chosen ministry biblically sound in its doctrinal statement and do the staff live out in morals and lifestyle what they claim in this document?
- Does leadership consist of believers of proven Christian character with an evident desire to minister the Gospel?
- Are they actively involved in their own local churches? Are all staff encouraged and supported in their personal spiritual growth and church involvement?

- Is provision made for initial and on-going staff training as well as encouragement toward further education such as seminary?
- Does the ministry have a clear statement of purpose, specific goals, and can progress toward this actually be seen in the field operation?
- What is the history of this organization in regard to effective ministry and wise stewardship of gifted people and resources?
- Does the ministry provide for a short-term volunteer or internship program whereby one can evaluate some of these issues as well as the realities of day-to-day ministry?

Experience may be necessary to gain an objective view of the difference between the popular perception of a ministry and the actualities of daily life, such as may be the case in fields like Christian camping.

Many other questions that are appropriate for particular types of parachurch ministries, such as mission boards or Christian day schools, are beyond the scope of this chapter. Excellent resources are available which examine these and list specific information regarding some of the larger parachurch organizations.[29]

Recommendations for Parachurch Organizations

Some in the Christian community see vast improvements in the relationship between the local church and parachurch agencies. Perhaps some of the tension has been lessened in recent years because, as one writer puts it, "groups are seriously trying to work with the institutional church and not just pay lip service to it."[30] Cooperative ministry is the most appropriate option in light of the needs of the immediate culture and the world.

McKinney draws on White's work and adds a number of his own helpful suggestions which could aid both the church and the parachurch to work harmoniously together.[31] A few of these will be listed and elaborated upon.

1) *The first action that the parachurch can take is to clearly define its mission.* The ministry staff must have a clear vision of its purpose and be able to clearly communicate this to those in the church in order both to focus effort and to avoid misunderstanding. Many of the larger parachurch ministries are currently going through what might be termed an "identity crisis." Some may well have attempted to engage in too many different kinds of programs and, as a result, have lost a single dynamic focus, one of the characteristic advantages of the parachurch structure. As with most innovative organizations, these were founded by strong leaders with a clear vision who have since passed on the mantle to the second and even third generation of leadership.[32] It's up to new leaders to rethink and clarify direction for these ministries in light of changing needs and challenges.

2) The parachurch needs to define its relationship to local churches. This relationship will vary depending on whether the ministry is directed primarily outside the church or is directly contributing toward the program of the local body. McKinney calls for a recognition of the legitimate role of such ministries as part of Christ's ministering body and plan for this age. Such recognition should not be seen as a blanket license for the legitimacy of every organization apart from the ministry of the local church. Some of the smaller ministries might find more stability and effective ministry and escape charges of an independent spirit if they were to come under some type of local church governing structure. The issue of authority is a difficult one, as was seen earlier, but the parachurch should clearly be supportive of the local church and as sensitive as possible regarding possible conflicts in this area.

3) Every parachurch organization should insist that staff members be involved in local churches. Some staff members have failed to avoid the dangerous assumption that the parachurch *is* their church, thus missing the personal edification, pastoral ministry, and opportunity for service which comes from the wide spectrum of believers in the local body.

4) Parachurches should channel the fruit of their ministries into local churches. By having a positive attitude toward the local church and encouraging attendance and involvement, organizational staff contribute to the spiritual growth of their disciples toward biblical obedience and help to counter any charge by the church of personal "kingdom building." Criticism of the local church will only contribute to the breakdown of the harmony so vitally needed.

5) The parachurch must give priority to maintaining regular communication with local churches. People tend to fear things they do not understand, and this includes any group whose doctrines, purpose, or methods are unknown to them. Communication is a critical factor in bringing about trust in any relationship. When a trusting relationship is built between church pastoral staff and parachurch staff, tensions are reduced and opportunities for effective service are extended. Such trust and communication also entails parachurch sensitivity to fund-raising and staff recruitment in the local church environment, following the guidelines established by the church in these regards.

Recommendations for Churches

The church can also take a number of actions, states McKinney, to cooperate with the parachurch.

1) It needs to recognize the parachurch ministry as a legitimate extension of the local church. Such designation recognizes that the body of Christ and its mission should be supported and encouraged wherever it is manifested in genuine service. A spirit of unity among members of the local church is essential regardless of the diverse ministries they are engaged in, either inside or outside the individual church. The local church must have a broad vision for advancing the Gospel in cooperation with a number of ministries.

2) *Secondly, a cooperative spirit should be developed.* Such a spirit will have the long-term effect of building up all the ministries involved and contribute toward avoiding a competitive spirit. Some church leaders fear that trained leadership may be siphoned away by non-church agencies, yet it must be acknowledged that a primary purpose of the church is to equip the saints for just such service. For those desiring vocational ministry involvement, the parachurch often offers opportunities for leadership that may not otherwise be available to those without seminary training. A sometimes overlooked benefit has accrued to the church in the person of those coming out of parachurch backgrounds to train at seminaries for church leadership positions.[33]

3) *The local church should be encouraged to utilize parachurch organizations in their areas of specialization.* As noted, one of the strengths of these organizations is a narrow focus in a specialized area. The church should take advantage of these highly motivated individuals by allowing them to serve and train others in their areas of expertise. Where opportunities permit, a part-time church staff arrangement for parachurch workers might even be possible.

4) *Local churches must encourage greater financial support to parachurch ministries.* This may well help to make the parachurch more accountable to the local church, one of the major points of tension on the part of the church. Individuals and organizations tend to be more accountable to those who control the purse strings. It may well be appropriate to consider funding such organizations through the church's missions budget as many churches do. If a smaller amount of a parachurch organization's funding comes from individual church members and more comes from the local church as a giving body, some of the tensions over the giving of members being split between church and parachurch would be lessened. Responsible stewardship dictates that the local church must show discernment about which parachurch groups it supports financially. Such a need to report and be accountable to others may well be the way that ineffective ministries are restrained.[34]

To clarify a local church's relationship to parachurch organizations, it may be wise for that church to set forth a policy statement concerning this issue. One pastor whose church had a large constituency of parachurch staff viewed as essential a formal declaration expressing a philosophy of church/parachurch relations for their particular situation.[35] This document first set forth the theological basis for the church/parachurch relationship, affirming the primacy of the church and the legitimacy of ministry of the parachurch, followed by the enumeration of the church policies. These are presented as a model (figure 21.3) of what might be done in other church settings. It presents a practical balance in regard to a number of the issues that have been discussed.

Church/Parachurch Policies

A. People

1. It is the responsibility of every believer to be engaged in active worship, training, and service in a local church.

2. It is the right of individual believers to respond to God's call for service according to their own conscience. Service in parachurch structures is as honorable as in local church structures.

3. It is the responsibility of the members of our local church to accept all believers as individuals regardless of their association with parachurch structures.

B. Programs

1. Parachurch programs may be used if they take the pastor and his leadership role seriously.

2. Parachurch programs may be used if they fit into the total plan of our local church.

3. Parachurch programs may be used if the resources needed will not damage or lessen the total effective program of our church.

4. Parachurch programs may be used if they foster a way of life witness in the body.

5. Parachurch programs will receive less consideration the farther the local church is from the center of the program.

6. In all conflicts between parachurch structures and our local church over policies, procedures, programs, methodologies, goals, and doctrinal beliefs, our local church will take priority.

C. Finances

1. Parachurch structures may receive financial support from our local church only as our church maintains 50 percent of its mission giving to (denominational) missions.

2. Parachurch structures may receive financial support as they qualify under our regular missions policies.

3. Individual staff of parachurch organizations may receive support through our regular mission policies.

4. Individual staff of parachurch organizations may not solicit funds from the constituency of our local church without direction of the board of elders.

Figure 21.3

What the Church Can Learn from the Parachurch

Parachurch organizations have proved successful in pioneering many new areas of ministry both inside and outside the Christian community, often due to their very nature, as detailed earlier. It might be profitable for ministries within the local church to observe some of these features and seek to appropriately adapt them to the church in order to respond to future needs. This pattern has already taken place in the case of parachurch youth organizations which have served as examples, at least in part, to help the growth and maturity of youth ministry within the church.[36] In considering insight from the experience of these groups, the church staff should be cautioned that no parachurch program or method can simply be imported into a particular church setting intact without consideration for the local situation.[37]

Researcher George Barna predicts that to be effective into the next century the church will need to take new directions in ministry. A number of these are worthy of note as directions already characterizing many parachurch ministries:

• Church ministries must not downplay the Christian call for discipleship but must instead emphasize belief that is lived out in the whole of life. It must clearly teach the basics of biblical faith in a relevant way.[38]

• Many churches have already adapted discipleship training methods pioneered by parachurch organizations.[39]

• Church programs must challenge and equip the whole body by offering opportunities for service for lay workers and train them in the use of spiritual gifts and abilities.[40]

• The local church cannot expect to have authority simply because of its institutional history as the moral backbone of America, but must use the authority given by Christ to be a vital educational and serving organism which earns respect by the works that it does.[41]

• Church ministries must be increasingly sensitive to address specialized needs and experiences of specific groupings of people and to communicate the whole Gospel message to them in relevant ways.[42]

• Growth will tend to take place in those ministries that are smaller and thus able to respond more flexibly to needs, that are more willing to take risks, and which tend to communicate a greater sense of purpose and urgency.[43]

Many local congregations have been exemplary in their attention to the areas listed above and many parachurch groups do not fit the general pattern described. Each should be aware of the dangers of insensitivity to changing needs and of becoming mired in an institutionalism that renders the organization less effective for building the kingdom.

Summary

The local church can learn a great deal from the pioneering spirit demonstrated in many parachurch organizations. Historically, parachurch organizations have been on the cutting edge of ministry. They are more susceptible to change and do not have the same degree of bureaucracy associated with many church denominational structures. However, in many cases the parachurch has not held itself accountable to the local church which is the biblically established avenue of ministry. As such, many have been guilty of draining essential resources from the church in the name of contemporary ministry.

The needs of this lost world cry out for attention. Obviously, there is a shortage of resources to meet each of these global needs, and it is in a partnership relationship between church and parachurch ministries that we will be able to address these needs. As each recognizes its unique contribution and works together, the kingdom of God will be more firmly established across this planet.

Notes

1. The prefix "para" is a Greek preposition meaning "by, with, or along side of." The parachurch is therefore considered to be an organization which is "along side of" the church.

2. White uses the term "para-local church" because of the often ambiguous use of the term "church." This usage shows the agency in question as separate from the authority of the local church. See Jerry White, *The Church and the Parachurch: An Uneasy Marriage* (Portland: Multnomah Press, 1983), 19.

3. J. Alan Youngren, "Parachurch Proliferation: The Frontier Spirit Caught in Traffic," *Christianity Today*, 6 November 1981, 38.

4. White, *An Uneasy Marriage*, 31-32.

5. Robert L. Saucy, *The Church in God's Program* (Chicago: Moody Press, 1972), 16-18.

6. Saucy, *God's Program*, 115.

7. White, *An Uneasy Marriage*, 65-66.

8. Harold Lindsell, "The Decline of a Church and Its Culture," *Christianity Today*, 17 July 1981, 79.

9. Ralph D. Winter, "The Two Structures of God's Redemptive Mission," in A.F. Glasser, ed., *Crucial Dimensions in World Evangelization* (Pasadena, Calif.: William Carey Library, 1976), 327.

10. Robert L. Saucy, personal communication with author, May, 1991.

11. Howard A. Snyder, *The Problem of Wineskins: Church Structure in a Technological Age* (Downers Grove, Ill.: InterVarsity Press, 1975), 160-61.

12. White, *An Uneasy Marriage*, 85.

13. Ibid., 104

14. Ibid., 84.

15. Youngren, "Parachurch Proliferation," 38.

16. White, *An Uneasy Marriage*, 105.

17. Winter, *The Two Structures*, 332.

18. This chart compiles characteristics drawn from several writings, including Winter, *The Two Structures*, 328; Ralph D. Winter, and R. P. Beaver, *The Warp and the Woof* (Pasadena, Calif.: William Carey Library, 1970), 60; and Ralph D. Winter, *The Twenty-five Unbelievable Years: 1945-1969* (Pasadena, Calif.: William Carey Library, 1970), 111.

19. Winter, *The Twenty-Five Years*, 111.

20. Youngren, "Parachurch Proliferation," 38.

21. White, *An Uneasy Marriage*, 65.

22. Winter and Beaver, *Warp and the Woof*, 31-32.

23. R.G. Hutcheson, Jr., "Where Have All the Young Folks Gone?" *Christianity Today*, 6 November 1981, 33.

24. Warren S. Benson, "Parachurch Vocations in Christian Education" in Werner C. Graendorf, ed., *Introduction to Biblical Christian Education* (Chicago: Moody Press, 1981), 352-53.

25. Ibid., 350-51.

26. Ben Armstrong, *The Electric Church* (Nashville: Thomas Nelson Publishing, Inc., 1979), 7.

27. Ibid., 160.

28. Howard A. Snyder, "Why the Local Church is Becoming More and Less," *Christianity Today*, 17 July 1981, 66.

29. Benson, *"Parachurch Vocations,"* This chapter contains a valuable discussion of parachurch vocations, requirements for vocational entry, and a wealth of related bibliographic data.

30. Ron Wilson, "Parachurch: Becoming Part of the Body," *Christianity Today*, 19 September 1980, 20.

31. Larry J. McKinney, "The Church-Parachurch Conflict: A Proposed Solution," *Christian Education Journal*, vol. 10, no. 3 (1990), 73-79; and White, *An Uneasy Marriage*, 117-59.

32. Wilson, "Parachurch," 18.

33. D.A. Hubbard, "Parachurch Fallout: Seminary Students," *Christianity Today*, 6 November 1981, 36.

34. Youngren, "Parachurch Proliferation," 41.

35. Gary L. McIntosh, "The Parachurch Dilemma: A Policy Statement," Unpublished manuscript, Fuller Theological Seminary, 1980, 15-17.

36. Brian Bird, "Have High School and College Ministries Outlived Their Purpose?" *Christianity Today*, 7 March 1986, 44.

37. McIntosh, "Parachurch Dilemma," 14.

38. George Barna, *The Frog in the Kettle* (Ventura, Calif.: Regal Books, 1990), 123-25.

39. Snyder, "Why the Local Church," 67.

40. Barna, *The Frog*, 148-50.

41. Ibid., 179-80.

42. Ibid., 147.

43. Ibid., 143-44.

For Further Reading

Armstrong, B. *The Electric Church*. Nashville: Thomas Nelson Publishing, Inc., 1979.

Benson, W.S. "Parachurch Vocations in Christian Education." In *Introduction to Biblical Christian Education*, ed. by W.C. Graendorf. Chicago: Moody Press, 1981.

Bird, B. "Have High School and College Ministries Outlived Their Purpose?" *Christianity Today* (7 March 1986): 44-45.

Board, S. "The Great Evangelical Power Shift." *Eternity* (June 1979): 55.

Hutcheson, R.G., Jr. "Where Have All the Young Folks Gone?" *Christianity Today* (6 November 1981): 32-35.

McKinney, L.J. "The Church-Parachurch Conflict: A Proposed Solution." *Christian Education Journal*, no. 3 (Spring 1990): 73-79.

Snyder, H.A. *The Problem of Wineskins: Church Structure in a Technological Age*. Downers Grove, Ill.: InterVarsity Press, 1975.

White, J. *The Church and the Parachurch: An Uneasy Marriage*. Portland, Ore.: Multnomah Press, 1983.

Wilson, R. "Parachurch: Becoming Part of the Body." *Christianity Today* (19 September 1990): 18-20.

Winter, R.D. "The Two Structures of God's Redemptive Mission." In *Crucial Dimensions in World Evangelization*, Edited by Arthur F. Glasser. Pasadena, Calif.: William Carey Library, 1976.

Winter, R.D. and Beaver, R.P. *The Warp and the Woof*. Pasadena, Calif.: William Carey Library, 1970.

Youngren, J. A. "Parachurch Proliferation: The Frontier Spirit Caught in Traffic." *Christianity Today* (6 November 1981): 38-41.

Twenty-Two
Counseling Ministry in the Church

Each new generation in our society continues to feel the impact of declining social and moral values. These secular values slowly but steadily erode the foundation of the American family. The effects of alcohol, drugs, violence, and the lowering of sexual standards, which once didn't produce their effects until high school, are now impacting our elementary schools. The result is a new generation of people who are living with fractured and imbalanced lives. When these individuals become Christians they are declared new creations in Christ (2 Cor. 5:17). However, many of them come into the church still bearing the scars of their previous lifestyles. The church can continue to help set these people free from the physical and emotional bonds which entangle them by providing biblically based counseling. Counseling of this nature is designed to help them see who they are in Christ and to provide them with the scriptural foundation which they need for consistent Christian living.

For the believer to experience a more vibrant life in Christ, the family and the church need to join forces. When there is a deficit in a member of a family, there is also one in the church body. Church leaders need to learn how to recognize, accept, understand, and provide assistance to hurting members of our communities. That help may be in the form of prevention, enrichment, remedial care, and/ or equipping. Too often the church has looked outside of itself to help those struggling emotionally. This has resulted in a separation between faith development and emotional development. In reality, both are closely related to the proper understanding and integration of scriptural truths.

Philosophical Foundations of Counseling

Scripture as Foundation. Counseling needs to be seen as a legitimate ministry in the church. Legitimate because the Bible, from the creation of Eve for

Adam, calls us into relationship. God declared that it was not good for man to dwell apart from interpersonal relationships with others. We need relationships because although we were perfectly formed, the consequences of living in a fallen world have resulted in broken lives. It is in relationship that we find completeness and it is in the context of relationship that healing takes place. Because there are deficits in each of us, the work of the church is far greater than any one or several leaders can fill.

Through the resource of God's special revelation, His written Word, we are able to form a grid of biblical truth. This truth tells us a great deal about the nature and condition of human beings, the character of God, and the solution to sin. It is through this grid that we view the findings and discoveries of science and medical research. The contributions of sociology, psychology, and personality theory serve as a supplemental resource for the Christian counselor and used with wisdom can form a complementary relationship. "The study of normal psychology helps us see what it means to be a whole human person. Jesus Christ told His followers to be 'perfect, therefore as your heavenly Father is perfect' (Matt. 5:48). Jesus knew that no mere human creature could attain the sinless moral perfection of God. He was not setting an impossible standard before us, as some have interpreted the passage. Rather, He used the word *perfection* in the sense of completeness. We are to be like our heavenly Father in every way, fully, completely. In other words, we are to be whole persons."[1]

Speaking of the need for completeness in the body of Christ, Paul wrote, "Then we will no longer be infants, tossed back and forth by the waves, and blown here and there by every wind of teaching and by the cunning and craftiness of men in their deceitful scheming. Instead, speaking the truth in love, we will in all things grow up into Him who is the Head, that is, Christ. From Him the whole body, joined and held together by every supporting ligament, grows and builds itself up in love, as each part does its work" (Eph. 4:14-16).

Biblical Perspectives of Counseling

Counseling was taking place in the church long before it was a formalized program. If one uses the broader definition of counseling as one who comes along side and brings comfort, corrects, or provides guidance, then the Bible has many instances of counseling.

1) Moses was one of the first counselors listed in Scripture. Much of his day while on his wilderness trek was spent listening and judging the complaints of the people. His wise judgment and counsel provided the people with guidance with which to live their daily lives (Ex. 18:15-16).

2) Jethro, Moses' father-in-law organized the people into groups so others

could assist him in counseling (Ex. 18:21-22). If the problem was too complex for one counselor to understand, the individual was referred to a higher judge, until if needed, Moses would hear the problem.

3) Job's friends came to him to provide counsel, encouragement, and support during his time of personal crisis (Job 2:11, 13).

4) The young shepherd David was brought to King Saul to console him with music. To Saul, who at the time was experiencing great emotional distress, David's music was a form of therapeutic support. It allowed him to experience periods of emotional and mental healing (1 Sam. 16:23). Shepherds duties were counseling related. They involved strengthening the weak, helping the crippled, healing the sick, and finding the lost.

5) Prophets such as Elijah and Elisha provided counsel in the form of preaching and expounding God's Word to the people (1 Kings 17–19). Their advice, though not often followed by the people, provided clear indication of God's prescription for peace. These men of God were sought out for their wise counsel and advice by kings and military leaders from the nations around Israel.

6) The ministry of Jesus often involved counseling others. He provided His listeners with guidance on how to enter the kingdom of God (Matt. 19:23-30), how to receive healing (John 3:1-16; Matt. 12:10-14), and ways to restore fractured relationships (Matt. 5:23-26). The prophecy of Isaiah stated that "Counselor" would be one of His names (Isa. 9:6). He talked about listening, an important counseling skill, over 200 times. He modeled acceptance, warmth, and gentleness with the woman at the well (John 4) and the adulterous woman (John 8). Jesus demonstrated counseling skills through His listening (Luke 24:17-24), His ability to confront (Luke 24:25; Matt. 8:26), His understanding of people (Matt. 19:16-22), and in His ability to relate the words of Scripture to human need (Luke 6:47-49).

7) The Apostle Paul demonstrated empathy and care to the Ephesian elders (Eph. 1:1, 16-18). As he went from house-to-house teaching the Word of God no doubt he became involved in many counseling experiences. Paul's letters to the church demonstrate his close relationships with people (Col. 4; Rom. 16). Many of his writings were motivated by his desire to solve an important problem facing the church body or an individual within the church (see Phile., 1 Cor.).

The early church appointed laymen to determine community needs and to administer appropriate assistance (Acts 6:1-7). Meeting the physical, emotional, and spiritual needs of people has been a consistent theme throughout the history of the church. Although methods and techniques for coming to the assistance of people in need may vary from generation to generation, the church has always been a place where people came during times of physical,

emotional, or spiritual distress. Christ commanded the church to model unconditional love and acceptance to anyone in need.

The Distinctives of Christian Counseling

Christians are encouraged to build up one another to maturity in Christ. This
includes a responsibility to help individual members so the body of Christ will
be strengthened.

Minirth, Meier, and Wichern list six reasons why Christian counseling is
unique:

1) Christian counseling accepts the Bible as the final standard of authority. Christians are not left to be "tossed back and forth" but can look
to a final authority for human behavior. The Bible not only gives insights into the design of human behavior, but also puts it into proper
perspective. It tells us who we are, where we came from, our nature, and
our ultimate purpose.

2) Christian counseling is unique because it depends not only on the
human will to be responsible, but also on the enabling, indwelling power
of the Holy Spirit to conquer human problems.

3) Christian counseling is unique because although by nature human
beings are selfish and tend to ignore or hate God (Rom. 1:16ff), Christians through faith (Rom. 8:12ff) receive the Spirit who gives them
victory in overpowering their sin nature.

4) Christian counseling is unique because it effectively deals with the
counselee's past. Because Christians find themselves forgiven for past
life events, they can be guilt-free (1 John 1:9) and look forward to the
future (Phil. 3:13-14). Even if some past events require insight and
specific prayer to remove resentment and bitterness, believers have a
secure position in Christ as being "washed clean."

5) Christian counseling is unique because it is based on God's love. God
loves us (1 John 4:10) and as His love flows through us we love others
and care for them (Rom. 12:9-21). A Christian counselor feels a spiritual relationship to other Christians and helps them to grow in Christ as
they solve their problems.

6) Christian counseling is unique because it deals with the whole
person. The Christian counselor is aware that the physical, psychological, and spiritual aspects of human beings are intricately related.[2]

First Peter 2:5, 9 teaches, all believers are part of a universal priesthood
which calls us to minister to one another to achieve the goal of maturity. In
order for this unity of the body to be achieved, each member needs to

exercise his or her unique gifts—ones that were given and planned during formation before birth (Ps. 139).

Counseling in the church is helping people understand and accept their strengths and deficits so that they can minister out of their strengths and be ministered to by the body to fill their deficits. Most deficits needing to be filled by the body fall into the areas of love, trust, self-esteem, power, and identity. God, through His Son, perfectly fills each of these areas of deficit, but we experience this filling by receiving from the parts of the body of Christ with whom we are in relationship. The problem comes when one's deficits begin inhibiting one's faith development. When this occurs one believer is called to come along side the other to provide guidance and support.

The Integration of Theology and Psychology

The relationship between theology and psychology has long been debated. Since the first century, mental illness has been a struggle for theologians. The struggle has been how to separate the psychological from the spiritual when the two are so intricately woven together within a person. Some people see these elements as unrelated, some as being completely integrated, and still others see them as being antagonistic.

Theology is man's rational description of God and His relationship with man. The method used by theology is to take Scripture as truth and relate it to human experience. Psychology, on the other hand, is the scientific study of human behavior, thinking, and feeling. The method used by psychology is to study behavior in a way that can be statistically analyzed. Psychology is a science because it is based on scientific data gathered through the five senses. Theology, however, is not a science since it is based on revelation. Integration is not just combining these two areas of study. Rather, it is living what we know to be truth. Carter and Narramore speak of this integration when they state: "We all find security in our traditional ways of viewing things and tend to be threatened by new or different ideas and perceptions. The pastor who has years of training and experience in viewing maladjustment as sin may be threatened by the psychologist's view that this is really a psychological distur-bance. The psychologist has no less difficulty with the pastor's view that what the psychologist calls pathology is really sin. It is no easy task to move beyond our initial anxiety, defensiveness, and even resentment at representatives of other disciplines and begin to develop a truly integrative way of looking at things."[3]

The challenge is to live congruently with what we know to be true in Scripture; that is, for our behavior and feelings to be consistent with the truth we know. If any one of the three are not congruent, we need to work at discovering why. For example, the Bible says that joy is a characteristic of the

Christian life (John 15:11), but when a person cannot find joy in the life of faith she needs to find why her emotions are incongruent with what she knows to be true.

The Counseling Process

The process of counseling is the process of redemption (Col. 1:13-23) or the process of buying back, making reconciliation possible. There are three stages to this process: relationship, realization, and responsibility. Each of these stages is important to the process of redemption. Any one stage alone is incomplete, but followed in order, redemptive work begins to take place. With each stage reviewed there are corresponding skills that the reader is encouraged to develop over time.

Stage 1: Relationship

The building of a solid trusting relationship is foundational and essential to create a healing context in which realization and responsibility can take place. A counseling relationship is more than a friendship. Trust, respect, and love develop creating an atmosphere of hope for healing.

The bridge of relationship is built by establishing rapport with the client by entering his or her frame of reference. One "gets in anothers' shoes" by being a good receiver of what the counselee says. This involves five skills:

1) *Attending.* A counselor represents God in hearing people who are aching to be heard. Attending involves giving attention to counselees, focusing on them, being present with them, and carefully observing things such as eye contact, body posture, gestures, facial expressions, dress, tone of voice, as well as noting what they are and aren't saying, the intensity of their words, and the kinds of words they use. Attending is important because it helps people establish rapport, it reduces anxiety, increases self-confidence, helps them to explore values, and increases motivation to pull together their resources to establish new goals.

2) *Concreteness.* When people reach out, they usually do so in a vague way. This skill gets them to be specific by asking questions and making tentative statements. Ask them to make their experiences more concrete by finding out who, what, where, when, and how. We want them to be specific in three areas: their behavior, feelings, and thoughts. Our goal is to integrate and have these three critical parts of any experience be congruent.

3) *Compassion.* This critical skill is the ability to reflect back to a person both the feelings and the content of what he or she said to create a deeper level of understanding. Compassion mirrors incarnation—God walking in human form like us. This skill gives a person the sense of being completely heard and consequently builds interpersonal connection. The safety created by this

skill creates the atmosphere of vulnerability, change, and growth.

4) Genuineness. This is the skill of being honest about oneself and not wearing masks of hypocrisy. Genuineness comes through when we deal with things that are going on inside ourselves, when we are really being real and owning the fact that we are still growing. Genuineness reduces the pedestal effect and makes confession safe.

5) Respect. This is to prize or value an individual because God made him or her. Valuing people for their uniqueness gives them significance and security.

These skills of building relationship model God's unconditional love for the counselee and should continue through each stage of the counseling process.

Stage 2: Realization

In this stage, the counselor helps a person to gain insight into themselves. Counselees begin to discover the incongruencies between thoughts and feelings, feelings and behavior, or thoughts and behavior. During this stage, the foundation of trust built in the relationship frees them to feel safe enough to lay aside some of the resistance they feel and explore experiences, thoughts, or feelings they have previously kept hidden. This can be a difficult and painful time in counseling, but also a time of building hope because they finally understand why they act, feel, or think the way they do and that someone else is walking with them in understanding too. The skills of this stage are many and take a lot of practice.

1) Identifying themes and implications. This is discovering themes in a counselee's life such as power, trust, self-image, role playing, performing, crises, perfection, conforming, guilt, dependency, and rescue.

2) Process reflection. This is looking at the process of each experience and finding alternative responses, connecting puzzle pieces, and examining alternative ways of handling an issue.

3) Discovering incongruencies. Finding incongruencies between thoughts, feelings, and behaviors.

4) Recognizing defenses. Discovering how the counselee protects against pain: denial, anger, rationalization, projection.

5) Use of analogies. Use of word pictures to help the counselee gain insight and understanding.

6) Confrontation. Learning to combine truth and grace in confronting a counselee.

7) Immediacy. Focusing on the here and now relationship between the counselor and counselee.

8) Transparency. Learning how and when to let the counselee see the counselor's experience, behavior, thoughts, or feelings.

These skills all need to be understood, learned, and practiced. Pertinent books and resources for learning these skills are listed at the end of the chapter.

Stage 3: Responsibility
This is the last stage of counseling, here a person actually begins to become responsible for the insight gained in the realization stage. The skills involved in this stage are:

1) Forming a statement of intent. Beginning to respond in behavior to realization.

2) Building a workable goal. Helping a counselee create a goal that is ownable, reachable, and measurable.

3) Working on the goal. Determining the time frame, what resources are needed, who is involved, and who is in control.

4) Building an action plan. Discovering the facilitating and restraining forces, benefits to the counselee, others, and God, and the possible sabotages to the plan.

5) Rewards. Finding people who will reward the counselee and rewards that motivate the counselee to continue carrying out the plan.

In the process of counseling, these three stages don't always follow in order. Rather, the counselee may be in different stages with different issues in life. For example, a person may have enough trust in the counseling relationship and realization to begin taking responsibility in her marriage, but be still building trust in the area of childhood experiences that are affecting her life today. It is a counselor's responsibility to empower a counselee to move forward to the next stage, but only when the counselee is ready.

The Qualifications of the Christian Counselor
There are many questions as to who is qualified to do what in regards to helping others. Can pastors help people who are struggling emotionally? Can therapists help people who are struggling spiritually? And the person struggling asks, "Who do I go to for help?" Those in the counseling profession have a variety of labels—psychiatrist, psychotherapist, psychologist, counselor—which also adds to the confusion. To the unskilled layperson these labels can create confusion and a degree of apprehension about seeking help.

People in our churches are struggling more with basic issues of life than ever before. Why? Because the basics aren't basic anymore. "We are too quick to resent and feel what we suffer from others, but fail to consider how much others suffer from us. Whoever considers his own defects will find no reason to judge others harshly."[4] According to Dr. Larry Crabb:

In the name of submission, wives have endured every imaginable form of abuse. They worry that God requires them to sit still while their husbands beat them; they push themselves to cooperate sexually even when exhausted to avoid God's displeasure and their husband's scorn. Men, on the other hand, have crumbled under the weight of wrong perceptions of husbanding, knowing that they simply are not as strong or as wise as they think they should be. Sometimes defeated men have turned to pornography, adultery, depression, and workaholism to find relief from the intolerable burden to be more than they are. Adultery clearly is wrong and so is the demand for relief that fuels it. But the pressure to meet false standards can be so immense that whatever provides relief seems justified.[5]

Being addicted has become a common way to cope with life because it brings a temporary relief whether in the form of food, sex, work, or drugs. People no longer determine right from wrong, rather they determine what will make life better right now.

One expert states that 21 percent of people seeking help go to psychologists, 29 percent go to psychiatrists, and 42 percent go to their pastor.[6] Although 42 percent of people turn to their pastors, pastors say they are not trained to handle the complex problems coming to them and are burning out from their counseling load. Discouraged, they aren't able to do the tasks they were trained to do. Oftentimes, the pastoral needs to take care of people and to gain approval or acceptance feed the desire to help more people than they are able and consequently they burn out.

Pastors need to sort out what they are called to do: preach, facilitate equipping the body, counsel, administrate, or develop a helping ministry. As a church grows, very soon one person cannot do it all so a pastor's job description should narrow down and become more specialized. Oftentimes a pastor cannot let go of what he is doing because his emotional needs of acceptance, approval, and love are being met through the very things of which he needs to let go.

Many churches today need a staff person, either part-time or full-time, who is trained in counseling. This person should not be responsible for all the counseling but should be the facilitator for meeting the counseling needs of the church. This could include training, supervising, supporting, and encouraging those people with the gift of helping.

All Christians are ministers and can help with the process of growth and healing of another person. The number one qualification for ministering to another is being human and therefore needing relationship with another. The needy longing of our souls brings us to God, the only one who can really fill that need. The rest of our years are spent working through the process of making our lives congruent, inwardly in our thoughts and feelings and outwardly in our behavior to be more consistent with our position in Christ. Other Christians in the body who have strengths in areas of others' weaknesses can help make the body whole. This ministry of sharing is one which gives hope and promise.

Other qualities of a wise Christian is one who:
- is in pursuit of God,
- knows God's Word in a living way,
- knows the importance of prayer,
- values fellowship with godly people,
- shares the truth of the Word of God.[7]

These characteristics should be found in all Christians, but particularly in those who desire to counsel others. Some Christians build competencies and skills which further increase their ability to help others. These skills need to be integrated into their already God-given ministry which is to be a part of the priesthood of all believers.

The church today needs all believers fulfilling their part in the functioning of the body. Each believer having strengths, skills, gifts, competencies, and weaknesses that are a unique part of the whole. Each one needs to be aware of what they can give and where they need to be receiving. No one in the body is ever beyond the place of needing others. No matter how skilled, trained, or competent, we all need relationships within the body of believers.

The job of pastors and leaders in the church is twofold. First, they need to model through openness and vulnerability our own weaknesses and how we receive help through relationships in the body. We need to model that spiritual and emotional health are intricately woven together. What hinders or helps our relationships with others often tends to hinder or help our relationship with God the same way. For example, if we are depressed it not only hinders our relationship with others, but also our relationship with God. Secondly, leaders need to facilitate the working out of the priesthood of all believers. This task will become overwhelming if leaders are not carrying out number one as stated above, in fact it will become impossible. Visible vulnerability and receiving from the body by leaders will facilitate others to begin to do the same.

Skilled Helpers

For members of the body who are gifted in helping others and desire to be further trained there are a number of other characteristics beyond the ones stated above that are vital to be skilled in helping others.

1) *Vulnerability.* Being aware of one's own strengths, weaknesses, and unresolved issues and taking responsibility for them when appropriate.

2) *Attitude of acceptance.* Evaluating and judging keeps people at a distance, whereas an attitude of acceptance helps another person to look at themselves (Gal. 6:1).

3) *Ability to listen.* Listening with understanding can be developed if one has the desire to hear another (James 1:19).

4) *Compassionate Heart.* True compassion can be developed if one is open and able to feel feelings with another person (Rom. 12:15; Gal. 6:2). When our own feelings are not being allowed expression because of our own pain, it's difficult and sometimes impossible to feel the pain of another.

5) *Dependent on God.* Being able to submit to a higher authority keeps believers humble and also aware that only God, through the work of the Holy Spirit, can change the heart of another.

6) *Desire to develop a knowledge of proper technique.* Helpers need to know the proper timing for asking questions, being direct, showing compassion, or revealing vulnerability. Counseling is hard work and one needs preparation to be skilled at helping others.

7) *Knowledge of Scripture and its appropriate use.* Using Scripture when another can't receive it because of pain in his life, may hinder rather than help a person grow in spiritual maturity.

8) *Trustworthy and confidential.* Trustworthiness as a counselor is a prerequisite for a person needing to trust another (Prov. 11:13; 21:23).

9) *Recognize and know one's limitations.* No one person has the ability to meet every need another could bring. Counselors need to acknowledge their strengths and weaknesses. They need to know their limitations and be able to refer to others when necessary. Every counselor should have a referral list of people who have strengths or skills that he or she does not have.

10) *Willing to be accountable.* No Christian counselor should be helping others without a place of accountability. Why? Because counselors are human rather than perfect. Counselors who don't have a place to be accountable are in danger of hurting someone who comes to them for help.

Christian counseling within the body of Christ is an awesome responsibility. Prayerful consideration should be given to one's giftedness, dedication, and preparation before entering the role of counselor.

It's the church's responsibility to thoroughly screen those who desire to become counselors. Screening should take place before entering a training program and throughout preparation. Screening prior to entry should include a battery of psychological evaluations. Some tests that could be used are:

- The Minnesota Multiphasic Personality Inventory (MMPI)
- Taylor-Johnson Temperament Analysis (TJTA)
- Myers-Briggs Temperament Indicator (MBTI)
- Family History Analysis (FHA)

Also included should be interviews with a psychologist, pastor, and counseling facilitator. When these are completed and evaluated satisfactorily, a time commitment for training should be received.

Training and Supervision
Training should be seen as valuable and necessary, with only excused absences allowed. Evaluation of skills should take place throughout the training process so each trainee knows where more practice is needed.

Supervision begins when a new helper is assigned the first counselee. This is probably the single most important part of the training process and should continue as long as a person is counseling. This is their place of accountability. Each counselor should be prepared to present their client load for evaluation of progress and direction for coming sessions. Counselors in training should begin with one counselee and not progress to more until the supervisor evaluates readiness to add others.

Supervision should take place one hour per week in small groups of four or five with individual time available if needed. The supervisor should be a trained pastoral counselor with a network of licensed Christian counselors for referral and consultation. Supervisors should be available for emergencies throughout the week or to provide resources of trained counselors who are available. *Supervisors should assess a counselor's ability to:*

1) empathize or feel with the counselee,
2) think through the issues of the counselee,
3) discern alternative responses to the issues, and
4) motivate the counselee to build a goal-directed action plan.

Supervisors should also
1) discern whether the counselor's own personal issues are entangling with the counselee's issues;
2) support, encourage, and pray with the counselors.

All people needing help should be screened through tests and interview assessment by a trained counselor, so each person is placed with a counselor who has the appropriate strengths, skills, and training to help. Persons with severe and chronic histories of mental illness including borderline, character, or narcissistic personality disorders should not be given to a lay counselor in training. Persons with suicidal ideations or currently using psychotropic medications should also be referred to licensed therapists. Again, a supervisor should know a counselor's limitations and continually assess a counselor's strengths and growth in their ability to help.

Summary

Christians today need to belong to churches which are living out Christ's command to be a body active in creating wholeness. Leaders in church and parachurch ministries can help facilitate this inner spiritual and emotional healing by modeling it before the congregation.

Our churches need to be places of prevention of pain, healing of hurts, enrichment of strengths, and equipping and training of new skills. Each person in the body, including the leadership, need relationships to *heal in* and relationships to *give to* if we truly believe in the priesthood of all believers. If the church was truly utilizing its strengths in the body and connecting through weaknesses, it wouldn't have to look outside its walls frequently for healing.

Notes

1. Frank B. Minirth, Paul D. Meier, and Frank B. Wichern, *Introduction to Psychology and Counseling* (Grand Rapids: Baker Book House, 1982), 26.

2. Ibid., 65.

3. Bruce Narramore and John Carter, *Integration of Psychology and Theology* (Grand Rapids: Zondervan Publishing House, 1979), 118.

4. Larry Crabb, *Men and Women* (Colorado Springs, Colo.: NavPress, 1991), 39.

5. Ibid., 32-33.

6. Frank Tillapaugh, *The Church Unleashed* (Ventura, Calif.: Regal Books, 1982), 144.

7. Minirth, Meier, and Wichern, *Introduction*, 295.

For Further Reading

Anderson, R.S. *Christians Who Counsel*. Grand Rapids: Zondervan Publishing House, 1990.

Drakeford, J.W. *Counseling for Church Leaders*. Nashville: Broadman Press, 1961.

Egan, G. *The Skilled Helper.* Belmont, Calif.: Brooks/Cole Publishing Co., 1982.

Hyder, O.Q. *The Christian's Handbook of Psychiatry.* Old Tappan, N.J: Fleming H. Revell Co., 1973.

Innovations in Learning. *Equipping Christians for Helping Ministries.* LaPalma, Calif.: Innovations In Learning, 1986.

Minirth, F.B., Meier, P.D., Wichern, F.B., and Ratcliff, D.E. *Introduction to Psychology and Counseling.* 2nd ed. Grand Rapids: Baker Book House, 1991.

Miller, P.M. *Peer Counseling in the Church.* Kitchener, Ont.: Herald Press, 1973.

Okun, B. F. *Effective Helping.* Monterey, Calif.: Brooks/Cole Publishing Co., 1982.

Tan, S. *Lay Counseling.* Grand Rapids: Zondervan Publishing House, 1991.

Tillapaugh, F.R. *The Church Unleashed.* Ventura, Calif.: Regal Books, 1982.

Tweedie, D.F. *The Church and the Couch.* Grand Rapids: Baker Book House, 1963.

Wright, H.N. *Training Christians to Counsel.* Denver: Christian Marriage Enrichment, 1977.

Twenty-Three
Mission Education in the Local Church

She was only thirteen when the rosy cheeked, blonde girl went forward in church to dedicate herself to a life of service for Christ, to go anywhere and do anything He would choose for her. At fifteen she had a Samuel-like dream in which God called her name three times and, as Samuel did, she responded on the third call to hear the Lord say that her service was to be in Latin America. As a North Dakota high school senior she began an investigation of missionary opportunities in Latin America and gained an unmistakable sense of direction to Brazil.

Meanwhile, 400 miles away in a nearby state, a sixteen-year-old youth experienced the same heart surrender to Christ's service. On reading a missionary biography he committed himself to become a missionary. At twenty it was unquestionably revealed where God wanted him to serve: Brazil.

In mysterious ways this young man and woman attended the same college, became casual friends and, only upon learning later of their independent missionary calls to the same place, let love blossom. Marriage and missionary service followed. Both made career commitments to serve Christ in cross-cultural ministry as a result of mission instruction in their lives. Both believed this ministry was God's choice for them, accepting as fact the historical challenge of Count Nicholas von Zinzendorf, the Czech Moravian missionary leader, who said, "Why stoop so low to be a king if God has called you to be a missionary?" The young man and the young lady are this author and his wife.

The impact of strong mission emphasis in our personal lives illustrates the power it holds for the local church. This chapter will review the privileges of mission service, the principles of a mission curriculum, and the context of mission education for the local church. Further, it will give suggestions for partnership with and participation in mission through a quality local church mission education ministry.

The Privileges of Mission Education

Faithful mission educators will receive praise from Christ at heaven's awards ceremony. It is with such a spirit of respect, held high as an honor before the members of our local churches, that teachers should accept the challenge to instruct others for mission.

But the teacher should beware: to teach about missions is convicting; it will lead to soul-searchings and cravings within the heart to be completely surrendered to God's passion for the world. It is risky to teach about missions because one will have to practice it—the true stewardship of the teacher's life. Stewardship is, after all, simply shorthand for "God will one day hold you accountable for all the money, talent, and brains He has given to you."[1] Absolute surrender to be and do anything and go anywhere for Christ is the "bottom-line" for Christians, out of such surrender flows the worldwide work of the church.

God chose the church to be His change agent to spread the Gospel throughout the world. The local church, therefore, is the hearth out from which the servants of the Word are to be nurtured, encouraged, and sent. God begins by challenging and calling us to serve Him based upon the information received. Mission instruction informs listeners with the facets and issues the Holy Spirit will use to fulfill His plan for individuals. He will give them a Christian world perspective, call some in specific directions, and make correctives in spiritual vision so they will participate in evangelism and church planting, both local and afar.

Who Are Mission Educators?

Comprehensive mission education should begin in the mind-set of the Christian home, then permeate the local church through the educational and pulpit ministries. The church should celebrate the victories of converts won and churches planted as missionary representatives return home to speak of them. It should encourage every-member participation in the proclamation of the Gospel through the testimony of godly living, well-suited words of appropriate witness, surrender of one's goods to the work of Christ, and life lived from the viewpoint of eternity rather than the materialistic present.

Mission education involves all who possess the channels to motivate and mobilize the church for ventures in mission. Classroom teachers of all levels, reaching the entire age span, should possess an integration of Great Commission truth as a normal part of the teaching curriculum.

It is the teacher's role, in essence, to instruct the next generation of the church with a God-oriented world view and an understanding of Scripture that will make them aware of Christ's reason for coming into the world and what that coming implies: the Great Commission. Preparation for mission ought to begin in one's childhood and youth. It should continue over into young adulthood where mobilization for practical missionary causes may become a normal part of a church's program, moving on into middle and later adulthood when different dimensions of mission ministry and intercessory and financial participation are emphasized.

The Principles of Mission Curriculum

1) *Mission curriculum must be spiritual.* The first and greatest lesson in educating people for mission is to teach the prominence of prayer. Missions is God's work; it is carried out primarily on one's knees. To the degree that men and women are privileged to carry the Gospel out they must enjoy open channels of dependence on and interchange with their Heavenly Father. They must learn the art of intercession to unleash the forces of heaven. The teacher ought to grow in intimacy with God through a full life of prayer, teaching from the overflow of grace.

To teach the art of intercession successfully on behalf of pastors, missionaries, ethnic groups around the world, unsaved friends and relatives, and local and world outreach ministries is perhaps the greatest triumph a teacher could ever attain. This accomplishment comes from one's own concept of God. No one questions the importance of intercession who has learned the awesome power of its effect. If it is part of the curriculum, where a teacher instructs by example, by practice with the students, and then by giving opportunity to join in prolonged times of effectual prayer and celebration for God's world cause, it can become part of the students' lives. A student who learns the art of prayer learns what mission is from the throne itself.

2) *Mission curriculum must be missiological.* In a desire to help students capture current thinking of mission, one needs to be clear about terms and concepts used. Terms help understand emphases given to aspects of the missionary task. Here is a brief glossary of contemporary missiological terms:

• *Evangelism.* Coming from the Greek word *evangelion*, or good news, it means to bring the glad tidings of the Gospel of Christ to those who have never heard it.

• *Witness.* One who shares a first hand account of what he or she has seen or experienced as conversion from sin to Jesus Christ. The term is used to refer to a private sharing, whereas *testimony* usually refers to a public avowal of beliefs. They are often used interchangeably.

• *Cross-cultural evangelism.* We live in a multicultural world. People are not all alike. Each ethnic group possesses a hidden pattern of thinking and acting which may only be detected by behavior that seems strange to an outsider. Evangelism with peoples different from ourselves is cross-cultural evangelism. (See chapter 7.)

● *Mission.* From the Latin *missio*, which means sending one out to fulfill an assignment. It is used also to refer to an organization for mission service. A person who carries out a mission is called a missionary. Missions is a word used for organizations involved in mission work as well as programs or courses taught for the missionary task. It is no longer as common a term as a generation ago, in preference to the singular form, mission, which has replaced it in much of the literature.

● *Missiology.* This term refers to the specialized study of the mission process. From theology, history, theories of social science, and research, it is a recognized broad-based discipline for teaching and investigation.

● *Missionary Candidate.* These are persons who have expressed a desire to serve with a mission agency by making application for service. On approval they change from candidates, or recruits, to *missionary appointees.*

● *Career and Short-term Missionary.* These refer to the length of service intended by either the person or the task. Career refers to individuals whose intentions are to serve in mission all of their professional lives. Short-term, accordingly, means those who take mission ministry as a short duration, from a few months to a full term of service. Sometimes "short-termers" decide to change to career work once they have been involved in the work on the field and have made the appropriate cultural adjustments.

● *Home and Foreign Missions.* Home mission refers to an organization that works within a subgroup of the host country, as in Appalachia, skid-row, Native American reservations, or Jewish evangelism. Foreign, refers only to overseas missions, so a more precise term would include ministries across national borders, that is, international missions. It is important to note, however, that as the world changes and becomes technologically closer and more international, these terms have become less important. Many mission agencies embrace both ministry with home and international ministries.

● *Self-supporting missionary.* Tentmaking is a concept as old as the Apostle Paul who sometimes supported his ministry by making tents. This idea has become important today with the growth of professions, especially in those situations where normal mission work is forbidden or restricted by government or ethnic policies. In countries open to the Gospel, some individuals integrate their professional employment with an association with local missionaries since self-supporting witnesses have the opportunity to reach a population for Christ that missionaries would not be likely to touch. There are often the restrictions of time and situations, but this is a valid ministry, particularly if converts are brought into the national evangelical church.

Christian Peace Corps volunteers, businesspersons, government officials, and educators have sometimes chosen to be overseas tentmakers and serve the Lord by friendship and personal evangelism and through Bible studies and discipleship ministries.

3) *Mission curriculum must be rooted in biblical theology.* Teachers should recognize that world evangelism is the theme of the entire Bible. In the Old Testament we find the witness of God committed to a chosen people, Israel. From their ethnocentricity and unwillingness to obey the Lord, we learn how cultural arrogance and selfishness held them back from sharing the Word of the Lord with the other nations of world. They were to be a kingdom of priests on behalf of the world before God (Ex. 19:6). Their refusal to evangelize makes the testimony of those who did all the more remarkable. Daniel's witness of his faith in the Lord in Babylon led Nebuchadnezzar to confess the greatness of the Lord. The three Hebrew children's faithfulness doubtlessly affected a generation. Jonah's begrudging message is legendary for its effect upon Ninevah. God often called on others outside of Israel to come to Him because He loves every person He has made. It's interesting that today it is largely the non-Jewish world that has responded to the invitation of the God the Jews refused to follow completely.

The New Testament is to some degree a missionary tract written to persuade the world to believe on Christ. It records the process of evangelism and church planting of the early Church. It calls for the total commitment of all believers. We read of the ministry of Philip the evangelist, the Apostle Peter's outreach, of Barnabas and Silas, and Paul of Tarsus. We learn of the work of the Apostle Thomas only from secular history. He apparently went to Southern India in A.D. 52, where he preached for twenty years, planting what is now known as the Mar Thoma Church before his martyrdom near Madras.[2]

Theological doctrines impact directly what we teach about mission and should include adequate views of God, man, sin, and the church. These and others are significant biblical teachings which will motivate believers for mission. Following are some theological doctrines crucial to the mission curriculum of the local church.

● *The doctrine of humanity.* Missions needs to understand humankind for what it is. We were made in God's image (Gen. 1:26) and possess a spirit, like God, which came from God Himself (God-breathed life), one that never dies. Created from one bloodline, everyone is important to Him (Acts 17:26). Christ died for the sins of every person on earth, everyone from the past, present, and the future.

● *The doctrine of original sin.* All have been alienated from God by their fallen, sinful nature inherited from Adam and Eve. No one is perfect or without sin, for we all break His law (Rom. 3:9-18). Thus, all feel a spiritual vacuum and try to find some deity to appease, reaching beyond to fill that spiritual void. Many have created gods, both religious and secular, to satisfy their longing, but each is only a false and degrading expression of the one true God. All need to know that "there is but one only, the living and true God."

• *The doctrine of God's nature.* Believers who grasp an accurate perception of God's nature begin amazing transformations. It is because they have gained an understanding of the magnitude of the God they claimed to worship, but whose character was never understood.[3] They will begin to trust in the Lord's power to answer prayer, for a small God-concept produces small requests in prayer, but a great God-concept results in big requests and great answers. What creates such differences? Unleashing the power of God by accepting Him for Who He is. The Trinity becomes a meaningful truth to the serious student of God. God the Father becomes a loving "Daddy" *(Abba)* with whom an intimate relationship can thrive. Jesus Christ, the Son, becomes one's dearest friend, brother, and example. The Holy Spirit becomes a comforting companion who comes alongside to empower us.

• *The doctrine related to Satan.* It is also important to acknowledge our great foe and God's implacable enemy, the devil. His skill at hiding his true character in subtle and beautiful things makes him hard to discern. But Satan is angry about God's masterstroke on the cross where he thought he was defeating God, only to discover that it marked his own impending doom. He will try to discourage the world from believing on Christ. The apostle sums up this struggle, "If our Gospel is 'veiled,' the veil must be in the minds of those who are spiritually dying. The god of this world has blinded the minds of those who do not believe, and prevents the light of the glorious Gospel of Christ, the image of God, from shining on them" (2 Cor. 4:4).

• *The doctrine of salvation.* Since humans are irreparably sinful, they cannot enter heaven unless they're given citizenship. No non-citizens are permitted to enter heaven, unlike earthly countries. Instead they are citizens of another city, hell (Ps. 1:6). Hell is real; a horrible place of eternal suffering for sin. Heaven is also real, with the promise of being in God's presence eternally for His redeemed children.

The only way to become a citizen of heaven is by conversion to Christ. Because of His great love for humanity God took the initiative in *sending* His Son. Jesus came on a mission to earth to arrange the way for us to be forgiven and become citizens of heaven. Thus Jesus was, in essence, the model career missionary, giving Himself for the people. Even in the Garden of Eden it was God who sought man, not man seeking God, taking the initiative when our first parents didn't want to face Him after they disobeyed His commands. The heart of the Gospel is that out of His love God sent Christ to die as our personal sin substitute that we may trust in Him and be saved from eternal hell (John 3:16). Those who trust Him are redeemed, ransomed from hell, and forgiven of all sins of the past, present, and future. They are justified, making them suited to enter heaven with no stain on their record, that is, Christ's perfect account is transferred to them. Because of this transfer believers are accepted by the Father as His children. They are born a second time, this one by God's Spirit into God's family and thus given the same citizenship as the Lord Himself, that of heaven. There is a new start to life. "For if a man is in Christ he becomes a new person altogether — the past is finished and gone, everything has become fresh and new" (2 Cor. 5:17).

● *The doctrine of the church.* The universal church is composed of believers from all eras, generations, languages, races, and places — all who have put the weight of their confidence on God's forgiving grace. The local church is a living expression of the great universal body of Christ. One might, in another way, describe Christ's body as composed of the "church triumphant," those who have passed through the gates of heaven already having completed their journey on earth, and the "church militant," those who today face the battlefield and boldly spread the Good News in obedience to the Lord.

● *The doctrine of reconciliation.* Mission means at its base, being an agent of reconciliation between two parties: humankind which wants to go its own way apart from God's Law, and God, who is offended by sin and unrighteousness. As agents of reconciliation, believers become special envoys, ambassadors speaking God's official message to the world on His behalf. As His personal representatives we say, "Make your peace with God" (2 Cor. 5:20).

4) Mission curriculum must be practical. This matter will be discussed in greater detail in the next section. Those who possess a good biblical understanding of mission must be ready to expand in the directions of their talents and spiritual gifts, as the situation and the calling of God may be on individual lives. Those who teach mission in the local church must be willing to model their commitment to supporting the cause of mission in their local community and in other areas around the world.

Local Church Partnership in Mission Education

We know that education for mission is successful when it produces results. Good theology produces good sociology. A strong biblical foundation along with appropriate facts and meaningful discussions will result in fruitful expression of the Great Commission at all levels of life. The following suggestions will help a church to develop a partnership between local church members and mission service.

1) Mission partnership should involve the individual. Partnership in mission begins with a person's own response to God's claims on one's life and the opportunity to become a co-laborer with God in His work. There are endless ways by which one may work with the Lord for mission, some of which are addressed here.

2) Teach a partnership of commitment. Each Christian will have to give an account to the Lord someday about his or her degree of surrender to Christ as Lord and response to Christ's commission to evangelize the world. "For everyone of us will have to stand without pretense before Christ our Judge, and we shall each receive our due for what we did when we lived in our bodies, whether it was good or bad" (2 Cor. 5:10). Each person owes his or her life to Christ; each is asked to surrender completely to the will of God and be available to serve in the great missionary design of the Lord. Nothing less than accepting spiritual slavery, total servitude to the Lord Jesus will do. Although all should be surrendered and open to do anything, anytime, and anywhere for Christ, most will be given responsibilities at home.

Pastors are a special class of individuals charged by God to live as models for their flocks of what it means to surrender. Some avoid surrendering to the idea of personal participation in mission for fear that God might require them to become a part of it, to leave their churches and homelands for what is perceived by them as less glamorous service. Some pastors will only allow missionaries to speak in their pulpits when they are out of town. Too few seminarians give the idea of mission work a serious consideration. Yet it is the pastor who faces God squarely on this issue who experiences the dynamic spiritual power and the greatest effectiveness. On such kind God can pour His fire.

3) Teach a partnership of intercessory prayer. Each day one can preach the Gospel in Brazil, Japan and other areas of the world. It can be done from a living room chair. One may travel to those places by means of intercessory prayer.

The Christian who understands the true impact of talking with the Father will find no trouble scheduling times with Him for triumphant prayer. Individuals use many memory aids to help them pray for others. Some use prayer reminders of pictures or cards, missionary letters, mission project notices, news items, and the names of persons they feel burdened for, laying them out before the Lord in loving intercessory prayer. It is also common to create a personalized prayer list, divide the list up into five or more days to provide regularity in praying for others. The intercessor already shares in God's victories and blessings now, and in the end, will receive part of the eternal reward.

4) Teach a partnership of mission correspondence. Every adult Christian should adopt a personal missionary for special attention, focused prayer, correspondence, birthdays, anniversaries, Christmas, and special "care" packages. Children and youth should also be encouraged to correspond with missionaries. A deep bond develops between them, and it makes for a rich encounter for both the adopted missionary and the one adopting him or her when the missionary returns on leave.

5) *Teach a partnership of financial substitution.* As in intercession, so also through financial participation in mission outreach the giver preaches the Gospel and plants churches all around the world. While all believers aren't able to go and do the hands-on ministry of the field, by investing a meaningful part of their income to enable others they serve there by financial substitution. God's bookkeeping system counts those who must remain in the homeland to share in the rewards of the spiritual victories (see 1 Sam. 30:24). It's interesting to observe that those who begin a lifestyle of intercession typically become avid contributors to missionary concerns out of the great sense of privilege it brings.

6) *Teach a partnership of experience.* Individuals who are able to make visits overseas to observe mission fields have their perspectives greatly changed by the experience. Nothing will impact people so dramatically as a personal view of the work. Transportation costs are usually modest for a single adult or couple to travel anywhere on earth. Work trips, another way to experience the mission field, have the stated objective of accomplishing a task on behalf of the ministry. Such trips normally last from a few days to a few weeks. Builders, teachers, medical professionals, mechanics, semi-skilled or unskilled folks can offer their time on such excursions to serve where they are needed. The results can be electrifying to themselves and their home churches.

Recently it has become more common for individuals to invest a year or two in short-term missions. Not sensing God's direction to enter career service, these servants of God want to contribute a part of their lives to mission work. This option ought to become an emphasis in congregations for both young and old, single or married, college age, or retired. Churches should encourage each Christian to consider this idea. Many "short-termers" return to the field as career workers because they caught a vision for the work. Others become the missionary zealots and leaders of mission-minded churches.

There are many ways to learn about mission beyond the normal educational program of the local church. Recognizing that good teaching and preaching about mission can have a startling effect, the most powerful result of that groundwork is when an individual gets *personally involved* in some partnership — indicating that the Lord is at work in His child to help bring the Gospel to the world.

Mission Partnership Should Involve the Family

Mission opportunities suitable for an individual may also apply to families. But families are able to do things collectively that single persons find difficult.

Nothing else can duplicate the shaping power that the Christian home has on the next generation. The following suggestions will be helpful to the family that seeks to become more involved in missions.

1) *Teaching family partnership in missionary thinking.* A veteran missionary once was asked where he received his training for his years of fruitful missionary service. "Most of my actual missionary training," he replied, "was received at home." Although he had college and seminary training, he traced his deep interest in missions to a home centered around missionary interests, where missionary plaques and pictures were hung on the wall, missionary letters read regularly at family devotions and visiting missionaries were dinner guests.[4]

Families uniting for the benefit of the work of God find that one of the primary results is on the family group itself. It draws the family closer through a common objective. Every member has the potential to become fully mission-centered, focused on Christ. Children are taught the Lord's values instead of the world's. For example, teaching children how to make a missionary bank, to save their money for missions, is a great Sunday School project. Children can learn early the blessing of financial investment in heaven.

2) *Teaching family partnership of missionary adoption.* A family may "adopt" an entire missionary family, collectively joining forces to focus their prayers and activities to minister to that family in the Lord's name. Both focused prayer and letterwriting ministries would bring amazing encouragement to those missionaries. If a home that has children adopts a missionary family having young ones of similar ages, the bonding can lead to lifelong friendships and produce in the children a greater vision and willingness to serve God.

3) *Teaching family partnership of missionary hosting.* A wonderful way to introduce children to the world of missions is by having missionaries as dinner guests. Whether for a meal or as a houseguest, there is no substitute for private interaction with a missionary or a missionary family to plant God's wonder and challenge in young lives. Adults, youth, and children all benefit from this exposure. It is a two-way street of blessing, for in reaching out to missionaries we help the Lord's workers feel restored, loved, and refreshed, and host families are themselves encouraged. The actual guest is Christ Himself (Matt. 10:41-42).

Mission Partnership Should Involve the Congregation

A church will never have a successful mission program until it involves all of the congregation, but this is no small task. The following suggestions will help the local church teach mission to its congregation.

1) *Teaching congregational partnership in prayer.* At its essence, the church is to be a movement of prayer. Worship and intercession is its heart. When that dies the fervor goes. Fire has a tendency to go out; therefore believers must

continue to provide fuel by lives of prayer. Congregations who meet for concerted prayer—who really know how to pray—are God's favorite dwelling places. Leaders need to model this attitude about prayer, for it's in such an atmosphere that God might choose to pour out a reviving movement, doing amazing things in the church and community because of genuine prayer.

2) Teaching congregational partnership in training. The church was the seminary of the New Testament. In many ways it should still be. Certain matters are relayed best in the natural setting of the local church and cannot be taught on academic turf.

Training begins in the pulpit. Pastors should have hearts which weave the truths of worldwide evangelism into the normal pulpit ministry. Missionary speakers should be heard regularly in the pulpit. Other options include reading prayer letters or interviewing missionaries during the worship service. These have a strategic effect upon the way a congregation responds to mission. The pulpit emphasis will be a key block in the mission program of a local church.

The training should continue in the classroom. The education program, at all levels, should tastefully apply the implications for world evangelism, whenever such an application is appropriate. Sunday School classes could take study units to examine other ethnic groups and their religions and needs. Missionary guests could visit classes (and also youth groups). Classes may adopt missionaries themselves. Videos can be shown on any occasion. Discipleship classes for small groups of zealous learners could teach persons how to develop a God-oriented worldview and concern. Evangelism should be studied, witnessing skills examined, practiced, and incorporated into the lifestyles of members. One who learns how to evangelize makes a great potential missionary. Field exposure of some kind is an ultimate laboratory experience. Nothing so impacts a church as when the pastors and leaders participate in mission visits and work trips. A pastor could take his or her "sabbatical" overseas on the mission field.

3) Teaching congregational partnership in social concerns. "We don't feed hungry people because of the Great Commission; we preach the Gospel because of the Great Commission. The only excuse we need to feed hungry people is that we are Christian."[5] Mercy is one of God's attributes. Compassion is the overflow of a heart in one with Christ.

We must not pass by Lazarus at our gate as the rich man did in the Gospel story. "The blind man with two amputated legs seated on a storefront step selling pencils; the homeless family of four sleeping in their automobile under a bridge; the unshaven transient seeking work in exchange for a hot meal; the bag lady rummaging through a garbage bin. Each one is not just poor, but destitute. These are the Lazaruses of the 1990s."[6]

Opportunities for helping the poor, sick, handicapped, broken, or imprisoned are all expressions of Christ at work in His Church. To be biblical a
local congregation must carry Christ's burden for the unfortunate. They are
special to Him (Matt. 11:5). He will hold us accountable for them and reward
us for our compassion (Prov. 14:31; 21:13; 22:22-23; 28:27).

4) *Teaching congregational partnership in investment.* No churches receive
more blessing than those that supply funds to provide for the ministry of
missionaries at work in the harvest. It's important for Christian educators to
teach how easy it is to give.

A church of only 100 givers can provide fully for one or more missionaries
with minimal effort. In the example below let us say that a given congregation
has agreed that each person should give up one 60¢ soda per day and contribute that amount to world missions. Here is what would happen using such a
small amount:

100 members @ 60¢ per day	
1 day	$ 60.
1 week	$ 420.
1 month	$ 1,800.
1 year	$ 21,900.

Figure 23.1

It's no secret that very few churches of 100 members contribute even this
small amount annually to missions, and yet this congregation hasn't begun to
tithe or take a major mission offering, just a minor inconvenience of pocket
change. Imagine their surprise when, in a moment of realization of what they
could accomplish, they decide to double their designation to the equivalent of
two sodas per day. All the above figures could be doubled. Missionaries can
easily be supported by most churches.

When we use the same sixty cents daily example with churches of more
than 100 members the sums are numbing. (See page 356.) And that which
was given was pocket change, only sixty cents per day. The potential for
missionary investment is enormous. Remember, what is shown is not formal
mission giving but simple replacement of one or two daily cups of beverage.
This ministry of giving, of financial substitution is not because God wants
money, but our hearts. If He owns our hearts He holds the string to our
purses and leads us to invest in eternity.

5) *Teaching congregational partnership in celebration.* Christians have reason
to celebrate: our Lord is winning. His servants ought to share in the joy of the
victories. We celebrate and educate in mission. One way to do so is by
missionary festivals or conferences. Nothing generates more interest, educa-

Church members:	300	400	500	1,000
1 day	$ 180.	$ 240.	$ 300.	$ 600.
1 week	1,260.	1,680.	2,100.	4,200.
1 month	5,400.	7,200.	9,000.	18,000.
1 year	$65,700.	$87,600.	$109,500.	$219,000.

Figure 23.2

tion, and enthusiasm than the celebration of what God has done on the mission field. At such festivals missionaries can rehearse all that God has done in opening the door of faith so others can know Christ. At these times people commit their lives to serve Christ, come to grips with missionary calls, decide to commit financial investments for heaven's work, and strengthen the spirit of missionaries through the fellowship of God's people at home.[7] International dinners of foods of the world, make good mid-year celebrations on mission themes, particularly focusing on those areas where missionaries are supported. Videos, films, and slides can make frequent contributions to the knowledge of the mission field and work.

6) *Teaching congregational partnership in recruitment.* The local church is the maternity ward for missionary recruits. Out of it come those who respond and follow Him to other lands in fulfillment of the Great Commission. The church becomes the training school where hearts and minds are nurtured and prepared to serve. Each church should set the objective of becoming a plenteous supplier of the next generation of pastors and missionaries.

Congregations should cooperate with mission sending agencies, whether denominational, interchurch, or parachurch, in order to send their missionaries to the field. The task is beyond a single congregation and only the family of Christ in union will bring world evangelization about. The objective is that everyone will find some avenue by which to participate in taking the Gospel to the world.

Local Church Participation in Mission Practice

The end result of a good mission education program in the local church will be participation in mission. Some avenues by which the local church can directly participate in the worldwide harvest include:

1) *Teach evangelism as a lifestyle.* All Christians have the obligation to participate in evangelism. Not all have the gifts of an evangelist, but all are expected to take some part in the common objective of bringing others to Christ. No missionary should be sent to the overseas task without having known some experience in leading others to the Savior. Churches should teach, demonstrate, and expect evangelism. New believers should be immediately encouraged to share their witness with others, thus beginning a lifelong pattern of personal evangelism.

2) Encourage reaching vocational communities. Wherever believers are called vocationally, their godly lifestyles and sanctified words should allow them to reach out to their colleagues. The church must supply the necessary tools and resources to encourage its congregants to integrate their faith with their workplace. Many vocations offer unique opportunities for evangelism and witness.

One example of this is the opportunity open to Christians to influence the field of secular education. Conservative Christians in the past have tended to shy away from the philosophical struggles and social conflicts within academe, choosing rather to stay within the safe fences of Christian institutions. Today, believing scholars are again responding to the challenge of leaving religious institutions of higher learning to become God's change agents in the class-rooms of secular educational institutions. Many students, faculty, and administrators are facing for the first time godly examples within a nonbelieving setting. Faithful Christian academics will discover a good harvest of seekers who watch their lifestyles and their caring hearts. This is yet another field for mission.

3) Encourage international student evangelism. Great opportunities exist in North America for reaching international students with the Gospel. Whereas the missionary task usually reaches only the lower levels of the highly strati-fied, class-oriented societies of the Third World, where the middle and upper classes that form the power structure are often untouched, God, in His kindness and wisdom, has sent thousands of representatives of the upper and middle social groups from nearly every country in the world to the doorsteps of the West. There, attending classes at their nearest college or university, churches will find the very students who will become tomorrow's intelligen-tsia — government officials, generals and admirals, educational and business leaders, physicians, and engineers among the foreign visitors. In making a concentrated effort — as individuals, families, and congregations — by helping, hosting, and "adopting" both single internationals and entire families, local churches may bring them to a knowledge of Christ while they are open to the hospitality of our shores in a way in which it would be nearly impossible in their national setting. In fact, many international Christian leaders have found Christ while students in the West.

4) Encourage self-supporting witnesses overseas. No country is totally closed to the Gospel, if workers enter as professionals. Some do not allow vocational missionaries, but will permit government and military personnel, businesspeople, teachers, and other specialists to come and help them. One might even enroll as a student in a national university, studying only a course or two per term for an almost unlimited time, with the real motive of witnessing through friendship evangelism and discipleship, helping to plant Christ's church.

In this fashion one becomes similar to the Apostle Paul who both was and was not a tentmaker. True, he made tents as needed, but his true vocation was evangelism and church planting. Except for Gospel broadcasts, tentmaking is the main avenue available to us in most Moslem countries. It was by much the same channel that Arabic traders brought Islam to Africa and the Orient in past centuries. How effective the self-employed businessman was for Islam! Should the bearers of the truth of the Gospel do any less? And even if one goes to a country which allows missionary work, the self-employed worker can communicate with a social group that the missionary will not be able to reach. In this case the professional can collaborate with missionaries and local churches. Fresh evangelistic strategies are needed for not all are directed to careers in ministry overseas but choose to work overseas by God's design anyway, helping to bring nationals into the kingdom.

5) *Reach expatriates overseas.* One overseas group that Christian workers probably neglect more than any other may be the international community, the English-speaking officials, teachers, businessmen, their spouses and families. They are far from the circle of the church. Having left a "Christian" homeland, there is often no one to reach out to them and meet their spiritual needs. Most do not seek or find persons who can help them amidst life's clouds and sorrows. The vast majority of Americans and other English speaking expatriates overseas are untouched.

For many seasoned or retired pastors, and others looking for a meaningful challenge, there is the opportunity to plant churches in the overseas international setting. This avenue of reaching compatriots has the advantages of homeside holidays and seasons which can bring the community together for friendship, evangelistic Bible studies, small group discipleship, and collective worship. Frequently there are calls for pastors for already established English language churches. There is usually an adequate salary and the responsibilities are not dissimilar from pastoring stateside. The overseas English language church is a most unique and important ministry neglected by mission strategists of the West.

Summary

Teaching mission in the context of a church Christian Education program is an important responsibility. This instruction must go beyond simple classroom presentations of world need. It must also strike at the heart of our students. Students must get a glimpse of how God sees the world and at the destiny of those who enter into eternity without a knowledge of the Savior. A comprehensive mission education program should involve the listener at many levels. Mission education within the local church must be well-designed, clearly communicated, and supported by the personal experiences of the teacher.

As we seek to educate students we must remember that world evangelism is one of the essential activities of the church's mission. We must undertake such a task with a heartfelt desire to reach the lost and to send the message of hope, love, and redemption to those in and around our church communities as well as the world.

Notes

1. Donald R. Brown, Editorial, *Action*, March-April, 1990, 1.

2. J. Herbert Kane, *Understanding Christian Missions* (Grand Rapids: Baker Book House, 1986), 197.

3. Ibid., 86-137 for an interesting survey of biblical and theological issues.

4. For example, "How to Emphasize Missions in the Home," pamphlet, World Vision, n.d.

5. Richard Buck, "The Harvest," *Baptist Mid-Missions* (Spring 1991): 1.

6. Frederick G. Boden, Jr., "Poor, Yet Rich in Christ," *Portals of Prayer*, vol. 54, no. 331, 5 June 1991, 187.

7. See "How to Plan a Missionary Conference," pamphlet, World Vision, n.d.

For Further Reading

Green, M. *Evangelism in the Early Church*. Grand Rapids: Wm. B. Eerdmans Pub. Co., 1970.

Hesselgrave, D.J. *Planting Churches Cross-Culturally: A Guide for Home and Foreign Missions*. Grand Rapids: Baker Book House, 1980.

Kane, J.H. *Understanding Christian Missions*. Grand Rapids: Baker Book House, 1986.

Missions Education Handbook. Wheaton, Ill.: Association of Church Missions Committees, 1985.

Peterson, J. *Evangelism as a Lifestyle: Reaching into Your World with the Gospel*. Colorado Springs: NavPress, 1980.

Twenty-Four
Special Education Ministries

Our contemporary society is driven by the need for status, prestige, material possessions, and other outward signs of achievement. The media demonstrates this compulsion by establishing the criteria for the person who has attained social rank: one who is attractive, has a pleasant personality, wears the right fashions, and drives the best car. The media dictates our values and sets the patterns for what society considers important. How unfortunate it is that we are guilty of weighing the merits of individuals based solely upon extrinsic qualities. For in so doing, we have isolated ourselves from one of America's untapped and undiscovered beauties—the intellectually impaired. This chapter is designed to provide the reader with a brief overview of the classification and characteristics of mental impairment and what the church can do to minister to both individuals who are impaired and also their families.

Orientation to Intellectual Impairment

Every year approximately 130,000 children are born intellectually impaired in the United States. In Canada, approximately 17,000 babies are born in this condition. It is generally agreed that approximately 3 percent of the North American population could be classified as intellectually impaired. That means approximately 7 million mentally retarded people live in the United States.[1] It should be noted, however, that great caution should be used in the consideration of these figures for several reasons. First, in many cases the basis by which mental retardation is classified depends upon a standardized IQ test which has different variances and limits from one state to another. Since there are more people in a given classification as the IQ number increases, one researcher who uses the IQ limit of 70 will have a far different approximation than the researcher who uses 75 as his limit. Second, it is important to note that people are not static. If environment truly does play a part in a person's performance ability then these approximations will vary as people progress and regress through various predetermined limits. Finally, recent medical advances are also able to help some individuals rise above former standings.[2]

Terms such as "retarded," "handicapped," "disabled," "exceptional," and "impaired" are used are descriptors for these people in the literature. In most educational settings these individuals are labeled "special education" students. In some cases this designation also includes those who are physically impaired as well as those who are mentally impaired.

Historical Development of Special Education

In reviewing the history of society's reaction to retardates, one learns that early civilization kept them away from "normal" society. During the days of the Greeks and the Romans, children who were born mentally retarded were often destroyed. They were seen as an unnecessary burden on the family, and parents were legally allowed to abandon their retarded babies in the fields or have them put to death. History tells us that there were virtually no social provisions for these special children. Occasionally a family kept their retarded child, but once the parents died the retarded adult's future was bleak. They would be ridiculed or held up for open shame as the town idiots. They lived as homeless adults with a meaningless existence or were imprisoned for the remainder of their lives.[3]

It was not until the nineteenth century that any major work was attempted to better the condition of the intellectually impaired through the means of education. The first residential school for the retarded can be traced back to 1837 which was established by Edward Sequin as part of the famous Bicetre Hospital. Along with this school, he added greatly to the early understanding of the retardate with his classic 1846 work, *The Moral Treatment, Hygiene, and Education of Idiots and Other Backward Children*. Sequin was been recognized as the leading international figure in the research of mental retardation.

In these early years of American history most intellectually impaired children were taught in an institutional setting. Students remained in these residential schools for most of the year, only returning to their parents homes for brief periods such as summer vacation and seasonal holidays. In many cases, parents of mentally impaired children felt ill prepared to provide for their children's needs and were compelled to place them in these institutional settings. There they would receive specialized care in areas such as diet, physical therapy, education, personal safety, and socialization with other children in like condition. Laws dating back to 1873 can be found which began to look for the provision of educational benefits for the retardate. From this point until the early 1900s progress was slow in the development of educational institutions committed solely for the advancement and care of the mentally impaired.[4]

The impetus which the "mental retardation movement" received in the early years of the twentieth century was hampered by the pressures of the Depression followed by World War II. "Immediately after the war, interest spread rapidly. There was a resurgence of effort and purpose. The phenomenal growth and development of interest in mental retardation after World War II can probably be attributed to four events: 1) a thorough revulsion toward the Nazi mass slaughter of retarded persons; 2) a reawakening of interest on the part of biological and social scientists; 3) renewed public awareness of how little had been done for these 'forgotten people;' and 4) an adamant, unashamed, and well-organized parent movement."[5]

After the 1950s parents became the recipients of more educational opportunities and were more likely to keep their retarded children at home. They formed community support groups where they could share ideas, provide knowledgeable advice, and give emotional support to other parents. Colleges began to offer courses in areas related to the psychology, sociology, and educational development of those who were intellectually impaired. Today, residential schools still provide a service to families with intellectually impaired children, particularly for those who are severely impaired.

There have been three major movements in the historical development of care for the intellectually impaired person. The first, ranging from 1850-1900, saw the birth and early growth of institutional care; the second stage, being 1900-1950, saw the development of measurable standards, tests, and personality profiles; and lastly, the stage which we are presently in, 1950 to present. This current stage shows the greatest hope for the intellectually impaired by demonstrating an emphasis upon his or her productivity and usefulness to society.[6]

Classification of the Intellectually Impaired

Like the historical development of care for the retardate, early attempts to classify and compartmentalize retardates seem to indicate confusion over what differentiates a retardate from a slow learner. Much of this confusion was abated by the development of the intelligence test. Of the many means of classifying retardates, the most accurate seems to be the standard IQ test developed by Binet-Simon. This scale, which was developed in 1905, helped move toward a more accurate and universal standard of intelligence measurement. Three standard forms of classification (figure 24.1) have prevailed over the years of study.[7]

Classification:	Educable (EMR)	Trainable (TMR)	Profound (PMR)
IQ Score:	70 – 50	50 – 20	Below 20
Percentage of Impaired Population:	84%	13%	3%
Brief Description:	Able to learn but progress is slow.	Able to learn self-help skills, some socialization, and simple household chores.	Gross retardation. Minimal capacity for learning.
Academic Achievement:	Able to read, write, and do a variety of math computations.	Able to learn to recognize their own name. May be able to print their name and address.	May respond to minimum or limited training in self-help.
Social Achievement:	Can learn to live independently in a community.	Can learn to behave properly. The TMR can not live independently in the community.	Very limited social skills of any kind.
Occupational Potential:	Able to work in jobs requiring limited cognitive skills.	Able to work in a sheltered form of vocational workshop.	Requires complete care and custodial supervision.

Figure 24.1

Not all national organizations agree on the classifications which are listed in figure 24.1. For example, the American Association of Mental Deficiency has five categories: borderline, mild, moderate, severe, and profound. The American Psychiatric Association classifies mentally impaired into three categories: mild (IQ range of 85-75), moderate (IQ range of 75-50), and severe (IQ range of 50-0). The National Association of Retarded Children's classification includes: marginally dependent (IQ range of 75-50), semi-dependent (IQ range of 50-30), and the dependent (IQ range below 30).

As with any field related to the study of psychology, there is a danger in stereotyping an individual within a given classification. Care must be taken that performance on an intelligence test is not the only criteria used in the classification of a potential retardate. Other factors would include hereditary occurrences, environmental conditions, etiological symptoms, behavioral abnormalities, and cultural norms. All of these factors must be included in order to achieve an accurate appraisal of a persons "normality."

Characteristics of the Intellectually Impaired

Educable Intellectually Impaired (EMR)
Physical. These children would be the least likely to be recognized as mentally deficient by the average person. They will seem almost normal except for slightly less coordinated motor skills. These individuals are more likely to have hearing, speech, and visual deficiencies than the average child.

Cognitive. The EMR learns slowly. They do not have the ability to think in abstract concepts. "The more concrete the task, the better they will function. Retarded children (EMR) are limited in such capacities as comprehension, generalization, association, symbolization, judgment, comparison, and fluidity of thought."[8]

Social. In the past few decades these children have been "mainstreamed" through the public educational system. This has allowed them to make friends with other peers and to have somewhat normal social lives. Obviously, some care should be taken in supervising their social relationships since their sense of judgment is not as finely developed as the average child of their age.

Emotional. Many EMR individuals understand that they are different from their friends and peers. This difference can create some anxiety or emotional discomfort if expectations for performance are not realistically balanced. In some cases this anxiety can lead to discouragement and depression.

Spiritual. The EMR is able to grasp simple spiritual truths. These students should be told that God loves them and is concerned about them as individuals. They should be encouraged to develop a self-image based on how God views them and not on the society's norms. Stories should be simple, without complex symbolism, and should relate to real life experiences.

Trainable Intellectually Impaired (TMR)
Physical. The TMR may look physically different than the average child their age. They tend to have growth abnormalities in height and weight, for example, their torsos are shorter and wider and they may have larger than average heads. They may appear to be in a dazed condition with odd body and facial mannerisms. It is also not uncommon for TMR children to have cerebral palsy.

Cognitive. The TMR is able to show signs of mental growth although they will be quite slow in emerging. A summary of their abilities includes: "poor reasoning, ineffective use of language, inability to think abstractly, low concentration level, lack of motivation; have trouble carrying a task to completion; lack imagination and creativity; rate of academic development is around one-half to three-fourths that of the average person; is slower in conceptual and perceptual abilities."[9]

Social. Individuals are not capable of consistent social behavior. Their degree of socialization may allow them to be able to recognize who they are and who is consistently nearby.

Emotional. They are able to perform independent functions provided they receive constant supervision. Some students may appear to be quietly withdrawn from those around them, while others are loud and quite outgoing in nature. Like all people, their personalities generate individual differences making concise descriptions difficult to generalize.

Spiritual. Individuals may be able to understand that God is like a father who loves them. They should be able to understand right and wrong. They will enjoy brief stories about nature and animals.

Profound Intellectually Impaired (PMR)

Physical. These individuals will require constant supervision. In many cases they will have to wear protective apparel. The most severe cases will be institutionalized and confined to a bed or wheelchair. These will be unable to care for their own personal needs such as dressing, eating, bathing, or hygiene.

Cognitive. The PMR person is severely limited in cognitive functioning and academic development. There is little capacity for learning although some limited progress can be achieved over a long period of time.

Social. They are usually quite limited due to their inability to speak in intelligible words. Their decreased mobility lessens the chance for interaction with peers although they may establish their own form of social interaction with peers in an institutional setting. Socialization is very difficult due to slurred speech, drooling, and incoherent audible patterns.

Emotional. The PMR is able to express emotions such as excitement, happiness, joy, fear, anxiety, or crying. Thus, emotional characteristics are evident but not consistent or dependable.

Spiritual. Development in this dimension is very limited in nature. Students enjoy it when people around them sing songs, hold their hands, and stimulate their senses of sound, touch, and smell.

The Church's Role in the Lives of the Intellectually Impaired

Due to medical and research advances in the study of the intellectually impaired, we have been able to see them make significant progress in their physical, mental, social, and emotional development. Yet there is a long way to go in realizing the vision of all that can be accomplished to aid the intellectually impaired person in becoming a whole person. The spiritual dimension of their lives is equally important, yet often overlooked when speaking of retardates. The EMR and TMR individual is able to accept a limited degree of spiritual training and produce what could be associated with "fruit." Of course, it is only the church that can become the vehicle for such growth and development. No state or federal institution is capable of meeting so important a need. The church does have a part to play in the development of an intellectually impaired person. We have a responsibility which must be met.

The church today has been slow in recognizing the need to develop special education programs for the intellectually impaired. For those few churches that have undertaken the task, they have seen ministry take place in three areas: 1) the *intellectually impaired individual* grows personally and spiritually as a result of the increased attention put on him by the Sunday School teacher; 2) the *family of the intellectually impaired person* is oftentimes reached for Christ as they see genuine Christlike concern for their family member; and 3) the *church* grows through the experience. Not only numerically as new families join the church, but also qualitatively as church members realize the meaning of Jesus' words, "To the extent that you did it to one of these brothers of Mine, even the least of them, you did it to Me" (Matt. 25:40). The staff of a special education program learn valuable lessons of incarnational theology.

God gave many instructions for us to heed when it came time to help the needs of those who were less fortunate than ourselves. The Books of Psalms and Proverbs speak to us of His concern for the fatherless, the widow, and the destitute of society. Concern for the needy is a common theme found throughout God's Word.

Ministry to the Intellectually Impaired.
Jesus exemplified the need for involvement as He displayed His love for children. The average mentally retarded person's mental capacity may never rise much above a sixth grade level, however, 84 percent of the retarded population is in the educable category. Many of those EMRs have reached an age of accountability.[10] The church, therefore, has a responsibility to provide the Gospel message to them in a manner which is appropriate to their level of understanding. A survey of applicable biblical commands and instructions follows:

We are commanded to love.	"A new commandment I give to you, that you love one another, even as I have loved you, that you also love one another" (John 13:34).

We are commanded to teach.

"Go therefore and make disciples of all the nations, baptizing them in the name of the Father, and the Son and the Holy Spirit, teaching them to observe all that I have commanded you" (Matt. 28:19-20).

Abundant life for the retardate.

"I came that they might have life, and might have it abundantly" (John 10:10).

Social adjustment for the retardate.

"Train up a child in the way he should go, even when he is old he will not depart from it" (Prov. 22:6).

God has chosen the foolish to confound the wise.

"God has chosen the foolish things of the world to shame the wise, and God has chosen the weak things of the world to shame the things which are strong" (1 Cor. 1:27).

God does not show partiality.

"And opening his mouth, Peter said, 'I most certainly understand now that God is not one to show partiality' " (Acts 10:34).

The Holy Spirit is able to discern spiritual truth in a person.

"For to us God revealed them through the Spirit; for the Spirit searches all things, even the depths of God. For who among men knows the thoughts of a man except the spirit of the man, which is in him? Even so, the thoughts of God no ones knows except the Spirit of God" (1 Cor. 2:10-11).

Jesus' love for children (and those of childlike mental capacity).

"Permit the children to come to Me, and stop hindering them, for the kingdom of God belongs to such as these. Truly I say to you, whoever does not receive the kingdom of God like a small child shall not enter it at all" (Luke 18:16-17).

God wants those who cannot provide for their own needs to be invited to come into the kingdom of
God.

"When you give a luncheon or a dinner,
do not invite your friends, or your
brothers, or your relatives, or rich
neighbors, lest they also invite you in
return, and repayment come to you. But
when you give a reception, invite the
poor, the crippled, the lame, the blind,
and you will be blessed, since they do
not have the means to repay you; for
you will be repaid at the resurrection of
the righteous" (Luke 14:12-14).

Ministry to the Family

Along with the ever increasing population of mentally retarded persons, there is
a ministry potential to be found in their families as well. "Over 4 million
American families are affected by mental retardation! That is a startling estimate
that is far from radical. It is through these families that most Sunday Schools will
be able to reach mentally retarded families."[11] The stress associated with a family
member who is intellectually impaired can be overwhelming. Parents may blame
themselves for the cause; brothers and sisters feel trauma because they don't
know how to respond or react to the retarded family member. It's not uncommon for families of retarded persons to be living in great emotional turmoil.
"Professionals in the field of mental retardation have found that the religious
teachings and spiritual strength of the parents have a significant effect on the
way they and other family members respond to a child who is mentally
retarded."[12]

The church can play a vital role in ministry to the family of an intellectually impaired person in at least seven constructive ways. First, it can aid the
other family members in their understanding of what causes intellectual impairment. Family members should be reassured about the differences between myths
and facts concerning intellectual impairment. Second, the church can help the
husband and wife to open communication lines which perhaps have been
strained through years of turmoil. This can be achieved through weekend marriage and family enrichment seminars for parents in the church with intellectually impaired family members. Third, for families with young children who are
impaired, the church can assist parents in learning correct methods of discipline
for the child. Fourth, for the impaired adults, guided workshop projects could be
established that would allow the EMR and TMR to fulfill useful chores around
the church. This will allow free time for other family members who must watch
and care for them. Fifth, the church is capable of assisting the educational and
spiritual needs of family members by providing special education Sunday School

classes. This frees other family members to be able to worship and participate on Sunday morning without having to provide constant supervision. Sixth, the church can visit family members to seek to win them to Christ or establish a contact for future church membership. Seventh, the local church can help children of intellectually impaired adults by encouraging and reaffirming their support during times of difficulty as children make important decisions that affect the well-being of their parents. As the local body of Christ, we must not neglect our ministry to the families of intellectually impaired persons.

The family that is supported and reinforced by the church will have a happier life together and will also play an important role in the development of the impaired adult. When visiting the family of an intellectually impaired person, consider the following list of important suggestions:

1) Call ahead and set an appointment. Consider their needs and schedules (school, therapy, care of person, etc.).

2) Plan your visit—set a time limit and know what you want to talk about.

3) Be neat in appearance. Dress according to the neighborhood.

4) Make a mental note of obvious family needs (e.g., baby-sitting, finances, material things, home repairs).

5) Uncover family interests, if any (e.g., hobbies, travel, church, friends).

6) Don't ask awkward questions. Listen carefully to their dialogue and notice "body language."

7) Take note of family attitudes about the person and his/her handicap.

8) Write up their comments and your impressions *after* the visit—not during it.[13]

These should help to make visits a more pleasant and enjoyable experience for all involved. Families need loving support and the church must not fall short of its commission to reach out to those in need.

Benefits for the Church

Another major focus of ministry that the local church can perform for mentally retarded adults is to help integrate them into the social and worshiping community of the church. This may be met with opposition as uneducated, perhaps well-meaning, church members would prefer not to be reminded of disabled or handicapped persons. This can be a stretching and growing experience for church members as they recognize and respond to God's command to be compassionate to the less fortunate of our society. We can learn a great deal from their simplistic lifestyle and needs.

Integrating the intellectually impaired into the church can be a threatening experience for them so great care should be taken to insure success. This integration process should only be attempted for the mildly impaired. Those who are TMR should be provided with facilities and staff better equipped and trained to handle their unique needs. The following list of prerequisites will help ensure a successful integrative experience:[14]

1) Ensure that the retardate is bathed and dressed properly. This will help him feel more comfortable and will help other adults feel more relaxed with him.

2) Be glad to have the retardate. Let her know that you care and love her. This can be expressed by your sincere and thoughtful comments to her.

3) Enlist enough workers so as to meet the special demands of the retardate. This should be done so as not to deprive any of the others in the room of needed items.

4) Build a spirit of understanding with others. Often they will ignore a retarded person's actions. If her actions are disturbing, however, she may need to be placed in a special group.

5) Try and enlist the retarded person's involvement during group activities. Limit the size of his group to just a few members and encourage him to take a part in the learning activity as long as it is not frustrating to him. Avoid activities like reading or writing as they may make him frustrated in his inability to "keep up" or perform like everyone else.

6) Seek to engage the retarded person in conversation. Help him talk about his daily experiences, family, or friends. Allow him to express himself without trying to "finish his sentence for him" while he is talking. This is important to them since most retarded persons have difficulty speaking and this allows them the sense of belonging.

7) As long as she is an accepted member of her chronological age group, promote the person into further grades with other members.

Steps to Implementing a Special Education Program in the Local Church

The following steps should be helpful to the local church that seeks to implement a special education ministry in the Christian Education program.

1) *Pastoral support.* Seek and develop pastoral support for the special education ministry. The pastor of the church must be wholeheartedly in favor of this ministry. Each member of the pastoral staff who will be responsible for this ministry must be committed to it.

2) *Establish a special education committee.* This committee can provide the church with the leadership base that it will need to adequately develop such a labor intensive program. Members should be involved in assessing the needs for such a program in the local community, developing the goals and objectives for the program, recruiting the necessary workers, and developing a training program that will adequately prepare the volunteers for service.

3) *Explore alternative means.* There are a number of creative alternatives for ministering to the intellectually impaired in different communities. Some churches may object to having the impaired in their fellowship for a variety of reasons. For these churches, it may be more appropriate to send the special education teachers to the impaired students. Another option may be a midweek program when most of the congregation is not present. For resistant churches, a phase-in period may be needed to properly educate and prepare the congregation.

4) *Provide transportation.* Typically, the intellectually impaired will need transportation to the church. If it's not possible for the church to supply transportation, a car pool arrangement may be developed with the parents of the intellectually impaired children. Alternatives for the church may include public transportation, a church bus ministry, church members providing rides, a church shuttle van service, community van programs for the elderly and mobility impaired, or family members who can drive.

5) *Teacher training and equipping.* Churches need to provide specialized training to help workers understand the unique elements of special education curriculum and teaching methods.

6) *Implement the program.* Once the ground work has been completed, a church should implement the program on a small scale first. This will allow a church to be sure that it is fully prepared for all elements of a special education ministry. As confidence develops the church may feel more comfortable advertising its program and increasing the amount of individuals they can handle.

7) *Evaluate the program.* Periodic and annual evaluations of the special education ministry should be conducted to make sure that it's accomplishing all that it was designed to do. If changes are warranted, it's easier to make them in process rather than waiting for a crisis to develop needed change.

Teacher Training for Special Education Ministries

The next major step is the development of a teacher training program. This program must be taught by someone experienced in working with intellectually impaired persons. Teaching in such a department is not for everyone. Potential teachers should be challenged to examine their reasons for desiring such a ministry. Working with intellectually impaired persons can be hard, tiring, and draining work. Some important qualities to look for in a special education teacher are:

- Persons who enjoy association with persons who are intellectually impaired.
- Sensitive to the needs of mentally retarded persons, particularly to their spiritual needs.
- Knowledgeable of the world in which retarded persons live and move; familiar with their interests, their everyday experiences, their hopes, and their fears.
- Willing to learn through study and experience, and from members, parents, and other teachers.
- Familiar with materials and methods that will meet the needs of impaired persons; and committed to studying, preparing, and using the resources in effective teaching.
- Enablers—doing with—not for their pupils.
- Persons who can minister in the homes of members sharing in family joys and accomplishments as well as in problems, disappointments, and sorrows.[15]

Once workers are located, they should complete an introductory training course on the special needs of the intellectually impaired. Some sort of an ongoing program of teacher training needs to be made available for answering questions and special problems which may arise during the course of the year. Such an orientation course should include study in some of the basic areas listed in figure 24.2 on page 374.

The training program is essential for the well-being of teachers who are perhaps unsure of their ability to work with intellectually impaired persons. In the weeks of training, visit other Sunday Schools with special education programs, state schools, and homes of members who have intellectually impaired family members. There is no substitute for experience, but a good orientation and training program will certainly go a long way in preparing the worker for the time when he or she will be teaching in the classroom.

The classroom structure may vary from the existing situation in many churches because of some unique needs intellectually impaired persons have.

The following are examples of supplies that a special education class should have: books, art supplies, large print Bibles, large pictures with uncluttered backgrounds, audiovisual equipment, TV with VCR, games, puzzles, and chalkboard.[16]

Teaching in a Special Education Program

When working with the intellectually impaired student in the classroom, the following suggestions should prove helpful for the teacher or volunteer worker:

1) Success Provide experiences at which they can be successful. If they experience success, they will be more willing to try new activities.

2) Individualization Activities and lessons should be individualized to the abilities of each participant.

3) Simplicity Instructions should be simple and concise. Complex commands will be confusing to the impaired.

4) Brevity Activities should be geared to a shortened attention span. If proper activities and materials are utilized, a longer duration of attention will result.

5) Examples Concrete examples should be employed whenever possible. Abstract discussions should be avoided.

6) Repetition In order for the impaired to learn, repetition must be used. For maximum retention of a concept, overlearning should take place.

7) Reinforcement Reinforcement should take place immediately after the correct response has been given. With the impaired, verbal praise is generally the best reinforcement.

8) Consistency To be effective with the impaired, consistency is essential. When a proper behavior is exhibited the individual should be praised. When an improper behavior is demonstrated, the individual should be corrected.

9) Input When instructing the impaired, a multisensory approach

Teacher Training Seminar Outline
for Special Education Ministries

Unit One—Orientation to Mental Retardation

    A. Definition and causes
    B. Classifications
    C. Historical setting and influences
    D. Characteristics of retardates

Unit Two—Classroom Management

    A. Discipline
    B. Motivation
    C. Behavior modification techniques

Unit Three—Teaching Techniques

    A. Curriculum adaptation
    B. Available resources
    C. Special music, art and drama
    D. Crafts
    E. Storytelling
    F. Reading and writing

Unit Four—Family Ministry

    A. Parents
    B. Children
    C. Relatives
    D. Peers

Unit Five—Discerning Spiritual Growth

    A. Salvation: When, how, where
    B. Rededication
    C. Manifesting fruit of the Spirit

Unit Six—Special Cases

    A. Multiple handicap persons
    B. Seizures
    C. Medications
    D. Down's Syndrome
    E. Cerebral Palsy
    F. Respiratory Disorders
    G. First Aid

Figure 24.2

should be utilized. The sense of vision, hearing, and touch should be employed whenever possible.

10) Firmness   Be firm (and loving) when working with the impaired. Often the retarded need to be encouraged to participate in activities.

11) Expectations   The same behavior should be expected from the impaired that would be proper for a nonhandicapped young person. We are *not* helping them if we tolerate improper behavior.

12) Touch   The sense of touch is important to the impaired. Most retardates desire physical contact; therefore, a hug or a pat can communicate "love" much more effectively than words.

13) Involvement   Involve higher functioning retardates as helpers. They will enjoy the responsibility.

14) Encouragement Impaired persons should be encouraged to do things for themselves as much as possible.

15) Prayer   When praying with an intellectually impaired participant, use short, simple phrases. Have them repeat each phrase.

A very important issue for the special education teacher is classroom and activity discipline. Little has been written on this subject as it relates to the intellectually impaired but the following suggestions may be of help:

1) Discipline the impaired adult according to his or her mental age. In many cases that means approximately the age of 5. If you view them in this way they will respond better to you at that level.

2) Every impaired student is different. Care must be taken to ensure that the discipline is tailored to fit each student, since no two intellectually impaired persons are alike.

3) Be aware of their abrupt mood swings and try not to respond to them on their level. Discipline must be consistent, firm, yet loving.

4) Sometimes they can be reasoned with by using statements like, "You know what will happen if you do that, don't you?"

5) Knowing their personal likes and dislikes will help in modifying their behavior. For example, many impaired adult women are overweight and prefer diet drinks. Positive and negative reinforcement of this privilege may help one achieve the desired behavior.[17]

Classroom management is essential for creating a healthy and successful learning environment. There is no substitution for order and discipline in a class of special education students. Once control is lost it will be difficult to regain. Teachers should strive to learn the early warning signs of deviant behavior.

Summary

Christian educators must have a holistic look at intellectually impaired individuals. Workers must see them for who they are and strive to assist them in becoming all they can be. They have the ability, in some cases, of being receptive to spiritual things. Some can realize what it means to come to a saving knowledge of Jesus Christ, and some can demonstrate the fruits of a new life in Christ. We must be careful not to stereotype them together, but realize their uniqueness and potential. They should be seen in the context of their environment, family, behavior, spiritual awareness, as well as intellectual capacity.

Workers in the special education classes should strive to demonstrate a Christlike concern for them—not out of an attitude of superiority, but out of an attitude of humility and servanthood. Ministry to the intellectually impaired is carried out through role modeling Christ's example.

The church must rise to the occasion of providing an environment for intellectually impaired persons that will provide for their emotional, physical, mental, and spiritual development. It's only in this way that we will be able to present Christ to *all* humankind.

Notes

1. Robert Clark, Joanne Brubaker, and Roy Zuck, eds., *Childhood Education in the Church* (Chicago: Moody Press, 1986), 183-84.

2. Darrick Cunnar, *Challenges in Mental Retardation* (New York: Columbia University Press, 1964), 5.

3. James Stein, "The Potential of Physical Activity for the Mentally Retarded Child," *Journal of Health, Physical Education, and Recreation*, vol. 37, no. 25 (April 1966): 25-27.

4. Jerome Rothstein, *Mental Retardation: Readings and Resources* (New York: Holt, Rinehart, & Winston, Inc., 1971), 25.

5. Ibid., 28.

6. Ibid., 33.

7. Gene Newman and Pat Hamman, *Teacher Training: A Training Manual for Special Ministry Teachers* (Hermosa Beach, Calif.: ACAMPAR Programs, Inc., n.d.), 7.

8. M. Hutt and R. Gibby, *The Mentally Retarded Child* (Boston: Allyn and Bacon, Inc., 1958), 106.

9. Clark, Brubaker, and Zuck, *Childhood Education*, 188.

10. Newman and Hamman, *Teacher Training*, 10.

11. Doris Monroe, *Reaching and Teaching Mentally Retarded Adults* (Nashville: Convention Press, 1980), 37.

12. Ibid., 38.

13. Newman and Hamman, *Teacher Training*, 78.

14. *Your Church and the Mentally Retarded.* (Nashville: Sunday School Board of the Southern Baptist Convention, 1976), 7.

15. Monroe, *Reaching and Teaching*, 54-55.

16. Ibid., 118-19.

17. Jackie Evans, Children's Ministry Director, Ryanwood Baptist Church, Fort Worth, Texas, interview with author, 3 March 1982.

For Further Reading

Burton, T. *The Trainable Mentally Retarded.* Columbus: Merrill Publishing, Co., 1975.

Cheine, J. *The Learning Disabled in Your Church School.* St. Louis: Concordia, 1983.

Clark, D., and Lesser, G. *Emotional Disturbance and School Learning: A Book of Readings.* Chicago: Science Research Assoc., 1975.

Frankel, M., Happ, W., and Smith, M. *Functional Teaching of the Mentally Retarded.* Springfield, Ill.: Charles C. Thomas Pub., 1975.

Hadley, G. *How to Teach the Mentally Retarded.* Wheaton, Ill.: Victor Books, 1978).

Huff, O. "Not Smart Enough for Church," *Christianity Today* (August 1981): 45-47.

Hutt, M. and Gibby, R. *The Mentally Retarded Child.* Boston: Allyn and Bacon, Inc., 1975.

Payne, J., Polloway, E., and Smith, E. *Strategies for Teaching the Mentally Retarded.* Columbus: Merrill Publishing Co., 1981.

Perske, R. *Hope for the Families: New Directions for Parents of Persons with Retardation or Other Disabilities.* Nashville: Abingdon Press, 1981.

Pierson, J., and Korth, B. *Reaching Out to Special People: A Resource for Ministry with Persons Who Have Disabilities.* Cincinnati: Standard Publishing, 1989.

Stubblefield, H. *The Church's Ministry in Mental Retardation.* Nashville: Broadman Press, 1965.

Wood, A. *Unto the Least of These: Special Education in the Church.* Schaumburg, Ill.: Regular Baptist, 1984.

Twenty-Five
Public Education, Christian Schools, and Home Schooling

The educational systems of America have long been the subject of debate in education, psychology, sociology, business, public policy formation, and in society as a whole. The seeds of a pluralistic educational emphasis began to take root early in the formative years of institutionalized education in America. The relationship of Christian and secular educational systems must be understood within the context of its historical antecedents.[1] History teaches that there has been a great deal of confusion and misunderstanding over the role of education and religion in the past 200 years.

This chapter will provide the reader with an overview of the three major approaches to education that are prevalent within society today. We will begin with a brief look at their historical development and an overview of their philosophical presuppositions. In addition, arguments for and against each system will be provided, and lastly, criteria will be established to serve as the basis for determining quality control of each system.

Historical Development in Public Education
The roots of the American and Canadian public school system trace back to the influence of the British Empire. The King of England dictated much of the policy by which schools were to operate. Parliament supported these dictates and generally went along with the king's edicts. With the establishment of the new colonies in America came a change in educational philosophy. Although the schools in the new world began with a close relationship to the teachings of the church, school and government officials soon came to the realization that true "freedom" meant the ability to determine one's own set of standards and beliefs throughout all of society.

Those who laid the foundations of American colonial government also set the parameters for future educational policy. As they declared their political independence, they also had to consider the consequences of guiding principles that would demand a reexamination of the practices and priorities of public education. Two such principles to be considered were the right of people to govern themselves and the right to worship according to the dictates of one's own conscience. These came to be known as the twin accords of civil and religious freedom.[2] Thus, from the earliest stages of American history there has been a strong defense for the separation of church and state. However, the Constitution of the United States in its original form makes neither provision for, nor mention of, general education. The result has been a long-standing debate concerning the influence of one over the other.

The nation's schools were not always established and maintained by the state. "In early colonial times the church assumed responsibility for education. Sectarian rivalry, however, tended to make education a theological battlefield rather than a church-sponsored program of instruction."[3] Laws soon began to emerge which sought to prevent the merging of religious indoctrination with educational instruction. Soon after these laws began to receive support from the courts, America became the recipient of a dualistic educational system: a secular system which taught the free exchange of educational ideas and a second religious system sponsored and controlled by ecclesiastical authority.

"A pluralistic religious society, with each sectarian group zealous to protect its young from heresy, reluctantly came to the conclusion that religion was too important and too divisive to be entrusted to a common or public school system. Coming to a similar result through a far different rationale were those who saw religious instruction in a public school system as a threat to religious liberty."[4] Thus, for nearly two centuries America has operated with two distinct school systems: a public school sponsored by federal and state tax dollars, and private schools sponsored by religious or private funding. The people, acting on their highly valued "freedom of choice" could choose which system they preferred for the education of their children.

Up until the beginning of the twentieth century this plurality remained unchallenged. However, in 1920 the citizens of Oregon were put to the test when a law was passed which required all children of the state to attend public schools. The Catholic church challenged the law all the way to the Supreme Court (Pierce vs. the Society of Sisters of the Holy Names of Jesus and Mary). They won their argument that freedom of choice guaranteed by the constitution should also apply to the education of one's children.

A 1962 Supreme Court ruling further illustrates the state's resolve to maintain the separation of religion and education. The high court ruled in Engel vs. Vitale that the Regents' prayer, a short invocation for use in New York classrooms, was unconstitutional. One year later, in the midst of public outcry over the Regents' prayer issue, the court also ruled that Bible reading (Abington School District vs. Schempp) and reciting the Lord's Prayer (Murray vs. Curlett) were also unconstitutional. It was due to cases such as these that many Catholic and Protestant educators began to cry for the removal of their members' children from the public school systems across America. The result was a major surge in the number of children enrolled in church-related institutions across the nation.

Philosophical Perspectives

No two schools are alike across this land. How a school is run and what philosophical tenets it supports are determined by at least five different variables: 1) state and federal regulations, programs, and grants, 2) school district policies, dictated by officials and/or board members, 3) school administrators, 4) classroom teachers and aides, and 5) amount of parental and other community involvement.[5] Each of these variables plays a large part in the character and makeup of the school.

Factors such as curriculum choice, discipline techniques, level of class competition, methods of socialization, respect for authority, values formation, and a host of other issues are all determined by a combination of politicians, administrators, teachers, and parents.

Though each school has a different philosophical base for operation, each holds to a common goal of preparing a child for life in our society. "Besides buildings, cash flow, a powerful establishment of professionals, and a legal structure that maintains and regulates it all at taxpayer expense, public education is also a process whereby the American youngster is molded into an American adult."[6] Regardless of chosen vocation, the student will live in a society in which they will be expected to act in accordance with prescribed standards of conduct. Teaching students to value these standards is a major philosophical mandate from government regulators.

The Condition of the American Educational System

Mention of the public school system typically draws diverse opinions about how it is doing and what it could be doing better. Few people remain neutral about it. Most offer criticism about its lack of vision, coordination, and promise. As one author opines, "After more than 100 years of universal public education, we can say that it nowhere resembles the utopian vision that drove its proponents to create it. It has not produced the morally improved human beings that our founding fathers had envisioned . . . the Catholics were aware enough to see what it would all lead to and bolted from the public school rather than accept the destruction of their faith . . . The whole experiment has been a colossal failure."[7]

Though such comments are strong and perhaps somewhat overreactive, it stands to reason that improvement in a system so large can always be singled out by someone. For America's public schools, it can be said that the last decade has been the worst of times and the best of times. Never before have public schools been subjected to savage criticism for failing to meet nationally prescribed standards of performance—yet never before have governments been so aggressively dedicated to identifying the schools' problems and allocating the needed resources for resolving them.[8]

The 1983 call to reform, *The Nation at Risk,* was a warning from the National Commission on Excellence in Education that our public schools were rapidly deteriorating and were "awash in a rising tide of mediocrity." The report went on to say, "if an unfriendly foreign power had attempted to impose on America the mediocre educational performance that exists today, we might well have viewed it as an act of war."[9]

Indicators such as the rise in public school violence, lowering of test scores, increase in drug use on campus, sexual abuse, and student apathy are evident to even a novice investigator. Currently, about 25 percent of all U.S. high school students—some 750,000 each year—simply drop out.[10] For example, the 1984 National Assessment of Education Progress showed that slightly more than 60 percent of 17-year-old students lack the ability to find, understand, summarize, and explain relatively complicated information, including information about topics they study in school.[11] Often they do not have the basic reading and comprehension skills needed to secure or hold down a job in American industry. The need for educational reform is apparent!

In every corridor of American life the cry for educational reform has been sounded. Indications are that the cries are being heard and that reforms are having their effect. Early test results in the 1990s are showing some improvement. The demands of parents and local school boards for increased accountability and discipline are beginning to pay dividends. SAT scores among college-bound high schoolers are showing some signs of progress on a national basis. Funding from federal, state, and local governments are beginning to reflect more priority being placed on education in America. It will take time but the volume of federal and state reports that were generated in the 1980s all held a resounding similar theme—reform is needed, and it is needed now.

Historical Development of the Christian School Movement

As a result of our society's disillusionment, a rapidly growing number of parents are pulling their children out of the public school system and finding or creating alternative ways of educating them. This has resulted in the increase in private schools, Basic schools, parochial schools, correspondence schools, and Christian schools.[13] The fastest growing segment of American elementary and secondary education across this country is that of private, conservative, Protestant schools.[14]

Why have these schools grown? To a large degree these schools arose to pursue a different educational agenda. Since an increasing number of parents believe the public schools have been negligent in their ability to perform in terms of academics, moral and value development, and religious instruction, they have abandoned them for what they believe is a better alternative.

Christian schools have existed in the United States since the early settlers. In a very real sense, the first American schools were established and operated by the church. Until the end of the Civil War American Protestants viewed the public school as their own creation. These early schools reflected the religious beliefs and values of American society as a whole. Bible reading was part of their curriculum and daily prayers were consistently practiced. It was not until the states began to eliminate these components of the public school system that the church created its own distinct schools.[15]

Between 1945 and 1985 the number of Christian schools expanded from the occasional exception to at least 3,100 schools with over 552,000 students. Today, the number of Christian schools across America has continued a steady rise in popularity. The dramatic increase in Christian schools which has become evident in the United States over the past few years must really be traced back to the mid 1940s.[16] At that point Christians were taught to be the "salt of the earth" and were expected to remain "in the world" to exercise their spiritual effect. To send one's children to a Christian school was to abandon one's mission to the world by isolating them from the people who needed the message the most. In essence, these parents were accused of placing their children in a "greenhouse," far removed from the effects of the real world. However, with the Supreme Court decisions in the early 1960s (previously cited), the American Christian public decided the fight to defend the traditional public school education was already lost.

Philosophical Perspectives
The Christian school philosophy is significantly different from public education. Christian schools have moral absolutes. Their educational philosophy is based upon a God-centered view of the world and humanity as taught in the Bible. The Scriptures provide us with guidance regarding important educational presuppositions such as curriculum development, discipline techniques, socialization methods, teaching morals and ethical standards of conduct, and a host of other related issues.

Every Christian school needs to have a written statement of its Christian educational philosophy, detailing the biblical imperatives of its existence and the integration of biblical truth with its curriculum. Every portion of its philosophy should be supported by the Word of God, which serves as the foundation for everything that is taught in the Christian school.[17]

The following statements of educational philosophy, purpose, and objectives are typical of Christian schools:[18]

1) God is the Creator and Sustainer of all things and the Source of all truth.

2) Because of sin, man tends to omit God and thus fails to relate himself and his knowledge to God, the Source of all wisdom.

3) Regeneration is by faith in Jesus Christ. True meanings and values can be ascertained only in light of His person, purpose, and work.

4) The home, the church, and the school should complement each other, promoting the student's spiritual, academic, social, and physical growth.

5) God has given differing abilities to each student. It is the teacher's responsibility to challenge each child according to his ability and to seek to teach him at his academic level.

6) The Christian is not to be conformed to the world, but must accept his responsibility and his role in our democratic society.

7) The student's home, church, and school experience should be a preparation for a life of fellowship with God and service to man.

Out of these somewhat general philosophical statements flow the corporate objectives of each institution. These corporate objectives may vary from school to school depending on the age level served, the denominational affiliation of the school, parental emphasis, and other factors. A list of typical Christian school corporate objectives follows:[19]

1) To teach that the Bible is the inspired and only infallible authoritative Word of God, thus developing attitudes of love and respect toward it (2 Tim. 3:15-17; 2 Peter 1:20-21).

2) To provide opportunities for students to confess Christ as Savior and Lord (Rom. 10:9-10).

3) To teach students to know and obey the will of God as revealed in the Scriptures, thus equipping them to carry out God's will daily (Rom. 12:1-2; 2 Tim. 2:14; Deut. 26:16-17).

4) To impart an understanding of each Christian's place in the body of Christ and its worldwide mission, providing opportunities for student involvement in this task (Eph. 4:12; 1 Cor. 12:1-31; Matt. 28:19-20).

5) To teach biblical character qualities and provide opportunities for students to demonstrate these qualities (1 Sam. 16:7; Gal. 5:22-23).

6) To help students develop self-images as unique individuals created in the image of God, so that they may attain their fullest potential (Ps. 139:13-16).

7) To teach students how to become contributing members of society by realizing the need to serve others (Gal. 5:13; Rom. 12:10).

8) To teach students biblical skills for personal and social relationships (Ps. 119:9; Eph. 4:12).

9) To teach students biblical attitudes toward material things and the responsibility for using them for God's glory (1 Tim. 6:17-19; Matt. 6:19-20; 1 Cor. 10:31).

10) To teach students creative and critical thinking based upon the proper use of biblical criteria for evaluation (2 Tim. 3:14-17).

A school's educational philosophy and its corresponding corporate objectives should encompass all elements of its influence over the student: instruction, extracurricular, athletic events, and social functions. Consistency between each of these functions and the teachings of the Word of God will help ensure a properly integrated Christian experience for students.

The Christian School: Arguments for and against
There are differing views regarding the merits of Christian schools today. A brief overview of each side's arguments will be beneficial for the individual who may be considering their use.

Arguments in Favor of Christian Schools
Those who support the use of Christian schools in America generally have the same issues in mind when they discuss them. A summary of these supportive issues follows:[20]

1) The teachers are born-again Christians and have a high level of desire to be in their job. In essence, it isn't just a job to them but a calling which they seek to fulfill.

2) Parents have a higher level of involvement in the welfare of their child's educational development. Since the parents are having to pay tuition for their child's schooling, they will desire more involvement in the experience.

3) Exceptionally good relationships exist between the school and the home since each views the other with mutual respect. They view each other as essential members of the same team striving for the same goals and objectives.

4) Christian schools provide a healthier teacher:student ratio for classroom instruction. Last minute demographic changes, budgetary

variances, and political maneuvering are less likely to adversely affect this important instructional element.

5) In general, students do not have learning or behavioral problems. This is not to say that such problems do not exist, but in the Christian school context they don't seem to exist in the same proportions as in the general population.

6) The faculty in Christian schools have a deeper sense of loyalty and commitment to the system under which the school operates. This cohesion translates into higher morale and positive teacher attitudes.

7) Relationships between faculty and administration are better than in a public school context. The adversarial role that administrators must sometimes assume in the public school is not as evident in a Christian school.

8) Opportunities are provided for each student to learn from the Word of God about important life issues. The Word of God serves as the foundational absolute for believers and serves as a standard for objective decision making.

9) The student's academic work is integrated with the Bible. Students in science, mathematics, athletics, and social studies have much to learn from the integration of faith and living.

Arguments against the Use of Christian Schools
It would seem that Christian schools are the answer to all of society's ills. However, in reality, the Christian school is not without its detractors. Their arguments deserve careful thought and reflection and should be seen as a basis for continual efforts to improve Christian Education:

1) Facilities are often inadequate or inferior. Without the resources of federal, state, or county funds, many Christian schools are forced to operate on meager resources. Used equipment is donated from a variety of sources and is often times inadequate or unsafe.

2) Program offerings are usually restricted compared to public schools. Resources which require a sizable amount of capital expenditures such as musical instruments, athletics, and science labs may be far below public school standards.

3) Students are sheltered from "real life" experiences. Many parents feel their children need to be exposed to the real issues facing children and adolescents in society (competition, peer influence, drugs, sexuality, alcohol, etc.) and failure to do that while parents are around to interpret these issues may be detrimental to the children's development.

4) Christian teachers and students are needed in the public educational system to provide a Christian witness to the lost. Removing all

believers from so great an audience is not responsible evangelism to the local community.

5) Christian schools are notorious for housing students who cannot do well in other schools. These students are socially fixated, isolated, or withdrawn. In some cases they are delinquents who were removed from public schools and now turn to Christian schools as a last resort.

6) The teachers of Christian schools are not as highly trained as public school teachers. Some schools, those who are not members of national credentialing associations, such as the Association of Christian Schools International, may have lower standards than public schools. Some Christian schools do not require their teachers to have state teaching credentials, so there is no guarantee of teacher quality.

7) The finances are too meager to provide quality instruction. This argument states that higher funding ensures better quality administrators and teachers. In essence, the more funding that is available to a school the better the educational personnel they can provide for their students.

8) Principals of Christian schools are not highly trained. In some cases the principal's duties are assumed by a local pastor. Such personnel are not trained in educational psychology, philosophy, or curriculum design. This lack of professional education training lessens their credibility among the school's personnel.

9) Faculty and administrative turnover is excessive. This is due to a number of factors such as low pay, ever changing school district standards, political maneuvering, and a low level of commitment to the profession.

10) The money spent on schools should go to foreign missions where it can be of more use. Many foreign countries have no public school system for their children and financing two systems in North America is seen by some as overindulgence and poor stewardship.

11) The tuition costs are too high. Many parents who would like to send their children to a Christian school, and who could genuinely benefit from it (e.g. single parents, disadvantaged children, underprivileged children, etc.), cannot afford the privilege. Due to the high cost of tuition, many Christian schools have become a privilege the wealthy alone can afford.

Such sweeping generalizations for arguments both for and against must be taken in context with each school. Since each Christian school is independent, apart from those which belong to a Christian school district, care should be taken before carelessly labeling their merits or limitations.

Criteria for Quality Control

Parents and church leaders should consider carefully the qualifications of a Christian school. Of course, the quality of such institutions varies greatly. The title Christian school does not guarantee a quality educational experience for children. There are a number of crucial factors that need to be carefully examined in looking for a good school:

1) *Educational philosophy.* The board of education, administrators, and teachers should all have a sound understanding of the distinctives of a Christian-based philosophy of education. Each member should be able to articulate in word and deed such a philosophy in seeing that a school's objectives are carried out thoroughly.

2) *School board.* Does the school board have qualified individuals serving on it? Do the members have degrees in education and have teaching experience? Are they godly men and women who genuinely desire what's best for the students? Is there parent involvement with the board and is this involvement encouraged?

3) *Administrators.* Do the school administrators have the necessary spiritual, academic, biblical, and administrative qualifications for their positions? Are they trained in their field and do they show signs of continuing their professional development through participation at national or regional training seminars and workshops? Are they consistent spiritual leaders in their own homes, churches, and communities?

4) *Teachers.* A number of questions need to be asked concerning teachers. Are each of the teachers born-again Christians? Are they screened for previous criminal violations? Do they have state teaching credentials? What percentage of the teachers have a state credential? Do the teachers speak highly of their administrative personnel? Are they involved in regular and systematic in-service training opportunities? Do they express a desire for parents to play an active role in the educational process? Are parents invited to attend classes and to serve as volunteers in the classroom?

5) *Resources.* Take a tour of the school's facilities and examine their quality. Do they shows signs of wear and abuse or are they well maintained. Visit the gymnasium, library, infirmary, science labs, music classroom, cafeteria, teacher's lounge, playground, and student restrooms. Each of these resources will tell you a great deal about their values and priorities.

6) *Chapel service.* Each Christian school should have some regular chapel service for their students. Who provides the oversight for the chapel and what are their qualifications? Do the students receive the opportunity to hear guest speakers and how often?

7) *Adequate financial resources.* Do the administrators and teachers get a fair and reasonable salary for their service? Because they are Christians serving the Lord is no excuse for poor and beleaguered faculty. They need to be able to work without the undue pressure of worrying about receiving a fair wage and receiving it on time.

8) *Turnover rate among administrators and faculty.* A high level of turnover may indicate a problem under the surface. Be sure that administrators and faculty are happy in their positions and are content in what the Lord has provided for them.

9) *Curriculum.* Examine the curriculum and see that it coincides with the church's or family's beliefs and values. Are the textbooks of sufficient quality and academic rigor? Ask about student academic performance compared to state standards.

10) *Spiritual tone.* This is a difficult element to measure, but during an observational visit one should be able to sense something of the school's atmosphere. Are the staff conscious of their calling to serve Christ in this school? Do each of the personnel take their responsibility seriously?

Christian schools are fast becoming an alternative for the Christian parent. The rapid growth of Christian schools across the United States and Canada is among one of the more significant developments within the body of Christ today. While not all are enthusiastic about them they are certainly meeting the need for many. Careful prayer and thought should go into the decision to place a child in such a school. Where appropriate, the student should have the opportunity to express his or her feelings about attending a Christian school. Together with the home and the church, the Christian school can be a valuable resource for strengthening a Christian's commitment for serving Christ.

Home Schooling
Many parents, faced with the thought of sending their children to secular public schools, have chosen to educate their children themselves. Citing the increased secularization of public schools, the highly competitive nature of early childhood socialization, textbooks based on secular humanistic philosophies, and a morally corrupt environment, many parents have given up on the public school system altogether. Many of these parents cannot afford the high tuition rates of private schools and have chosen the only other alternative. One which they feel is far better for their children—home schooling.

This home schooling approach to childhood education is not new. It began in the pages of Hebrew Scripture. Jewish parents were given the responsibility to raise and nurture their children and to instruct them in the Word of God at an early age (Deut. 4:9; 6:7). Home schooling was a fulfillment of the biblical command to "train up a child in the way he should go" (Prov. 22:6). Hebrew parents were to teach their children the Law and to pass it down from generation to generation (Ps. 78:5-8). Children are entrusted to parents by God (Ps. 127:3). They belong to God and He has given them to the care of parents until they return to Him. As sovereign ruler of the universe God has chosen each family according to the specific needs of each child He gives. No child is an accidental gift from God! It is therefore the primary duty of parents to educate and train their children in such a way that they will come to know God and respect His Word as a final authority for their lives.

When the New England settlers first arrived in Colonial America they taught their children in their homes. "These families were highly educated, had a strong work ethic, total commitment to God, and the conviction to disciple their own children. Education was essential, especially reading, so they could read the Bible for themselves."[22] This home schooling approach to early childhood education continued until a small town was formed and tax revenues could be collected which would in turn support the upkeep of a small community schoolhouse.

Children were taught a trade through the context of a parent. For example, girls were taught how to bake, sew, and perform household duties by the mother. Young boys were taught skills such as farming, woodworking, blacksmithing by their fathers, or through an apprenticeship from local adults. Both the Pilgrims and the early settlers in the frontier regions of America required their children to attend schools (when they were available) by the age of 6.

Arguments for Home Schooling

The apex of the argument for home schooling is the recognition that development of a healthy self-image in a child is a direct result of positive and healthy interpersonal relationships with adults. A home schooling environment would obviously provide such a climate and atmosphere.[23]

A second argument in favor of home schooling is that it fosters a better relationship between child and parent. The amount of personal interaction that a parent and child have together during the home schooling process will strengthen and support the parent-child relationship for years to come. Even if the child is placed into a school system after the age of nine or ten, the years of bonding and interaction during the first few years of home schooling will pay rich dividends throughout the years to come.

A major argument for home schooling is that it does not replicate the highly competitive nature found in most schools today. Most public schools, and even the curriculum of some Christian schools, place too much pressure on children to learn to read. The research presented by David Elkind in his book *The Hurried Child* indicates that children who are taught to read later in life will eventually stabilize with those children who were taught to read earlier.[24]

Another argument says that home schooling aids the child in the development of healthy emotional development. Peers, even at an early age, can greatly affect the emotional fabric of a young child. Their comments can bruise and crush a young child's spirit for years to come. The security of a home environment helps protect against such damage.

Proper values and ethical standards can be taught to the child in this environment as well. The humanistic tenets of values clarification taught in many schools today can have far reaching implications for a formative young mind. Parents who home school their children want them to develop biblical standards of conduct with proper reinforcement, before being heavily influenced by a fallen society.

The ability to teach sound methods of discipline that are consistent with biblical principles is also a reason for home schooling. The motivation level of many students is strongly related to their self-discipline. A poor level of discipline will affect their rate of learning, social conduct, socialization at later development, and eventually impact their work ethic.

A child that has special learning problems will also greatly benefit from home schooling. "The tutorial potential which a parent has in dealing with his child one-on-one gives him a great advantage in meeting the child's special needs, especially in nurturing his self-concept with a healthy biblical perspective."[25]

The last argument for home schooling relates to families who, due to geographical location, find that they are unable to send their children to either a public or Christian school. This is particularly true for missionaries on a foreign field who don't view sending their children away to a boarding school as a biblically responsible alternative to parenting or education.

Arguments against Home Schooling

The first argument to be sounded against home schooling comes from teachers themselves. They claim that most parents are not qualified to be teachers and further, such qualifications should come from formal education alone. Even parents who hold college degrees are not experienced in educational elements such as curriculum design, methods of instruction, or testing and measurements. Most parents do not possess a sufficient understanding of mathematics, science, English, history, music, or other subjects to be able to teach their own children.

Limitation of resources is another argument against home schooling. A proper education requires certain resources which are best supplied by a school. Material needs such as books, films and graphic aids, art supplies, and science materials cannot be supplied by the average parent. A lack of such educational resources will greatly undermine the quality of education that the parent is providing.

The legality of such an approach to education is also an important consideration. Many states require parents to bring their children to school by the age of 6. To refuse to do so would be a violation of the state law. According to Romans 13, local governments are established by God and believers are to obey the law and send their children to public or private school. Each state has different laws and regulations about home schooling. Some states allow a parent to home school provided they register with the local school district and can prove reasonable academic progress is being made by the child. Each state's authorities should be consulted to learn its law's requirements.

Although there are many more arguments against home schooling these represent the primary issues. One alternative which many parents are using to avoid these arguments is to set up what is called "an umbrella arrangement" with a Christian school. This arrangement allows the parents to home school their child yet still receive consultation, guidance, curriculum, and advice from qualified people who care. Such an arrangement satisfies the requirements of many states since the Christian school provides each family with 1) a permanent file in the school records, 2) a prescribed curriculum for each age/grade of the child, 3) a timetable for progressing through the curriculum, 4) a transcript which the child may use if he/she transfers to another community, 5) a means for testing the child with standardized state and local tests to ensure proper progress and documentation of successful achievement, and 6) a liaison with credentialed school personnel who can come to the assistance of a parent or child who may need special help. Such an arrangement is strongly encouraged for parents who elect the home schooling alternative for their children.

Criteria for Quality Control

Raymond Moore, in his book *Homespun Schools*, advocates a small list of qualifications for parents who desire to home school their children. He writes, "The requirements are not complex. Parents need only be loving, responsive, and reasonably consistent, and salt these qualities with a little imagination, common sense, and willingness to follow a few simple suggestions."[26] Some home educators would claim such a list is a bit too brief but it does point out their conclusion that a good home teacher is more a matter of character qualities than skills, knowledge, and degrees.

For further information on any of the issues raised in this section on home schooling consult the reading list at the end of this chapter. In addition, it may be very helpful for parents to join a home schooling network set up in many local communities. These networks share resources, learning experiences, transportation to field trips, and are a valuable help, especially for new home schooling parents. A list of these home school associations according to state is provided in the back of *Successful Home Schooling.*

Home schooling may not be for every parent. It requires a great deal of forethought and prayer. Schooling children also requires a time commitment on the part of both parents and additional financial expenses for curriculum, an umbrella association, and learning resources. But for those who are truly committed to the process it has become a popular and growing alternative to the public or Christian school.

Notes

1. Glen Heck and Robert Meyers, "Education in Secular and Christian Perspective," in *Introduction to Biblical Christian Education,* ed. Werner Graendorf (Chicago: Moody Press, 1981), 304.

2. Ibid., 305.

3. Peter Person, *An Introduction to Christian Education* (Grand Rapids: Baker Book House, 1979), 193.

4. Heck and Meyers, "Education," 311.

5. Ethel Herr, *Schools: How Parents Can Make a Difference* (Chicago: Moody Press, 1981), 53.

6. Samuel Blumfield, *Is Public Education Necessary?* (Old Greenwich, Conn.: The Devin-Adair Co., 1981), 6.

7. Ibid., 248.

8. John Chubb and Terry Moe, "America's Public Schools: The Need for Choice," *Current* 328 (Dec. 1990): 4.

9. National Commission on Excellence in Education. *A Nation at Risk: The Imperative for Educational Reform* (Washington, D.C.: U.S. Government Printing Office, 1983), 5.

10. Nancy Perry, "How to Help America's School," *Fortune*, 4 Dec. 1989, 137.

11. Michael Cohen, "Restructuring the System," *Society*, vol. 26, no. 4, May/June 1989: 40.

12. Nancy Henderson, "Sizing Up Your Local School," *Changing Times*, Nov. 1989, 102-04.

13. Herr, *How Parents*, 52.

14. Virginia Mardin and William Turner, "More Than Segregation Academies: The Growing Protestant Fundamentalist Schools," *Phi Delta Kappa*, vol. 61 (Feb. 1980): 391-94.

15. Frederick Wilson, "The Dramatic Growth of Christian Schools: 1945-1985," *Journal of Christian Education*, vol. 9, no. 1 (Autumn 1989): 11.

16. Ibid.

17. Claude Schindler, "Planning and Achieving Curricular Excellence," *Journal of Christian Education*, vol. 9, no. 1 (Autumn 1988): 38-39.

18. Roy Lowrie and David Roth, "The Role of the Christian School," in *Childhood Education in the Church*, ed. Robert Clark, Joanne Brubaker, and Roy Zuck (Chicago: Moody Press, 1986), 606-07.

19. Schindler, "Planning and Achieving, 39-40.

20. Lowrie and Roth, "Role of School," 608.

21. Ibid.

22. J. Richard Fugate, *Will Early Education Ruin Your Child?* (Tempe, Ariz.: Aletheia Division of Alpha Omega Publications, 1990), 56.

23. Raymond Moore and Dorothy Moore, *Home Grown Kids.* (Waco, Texas: Word Inc., 1982), 32-33.

24. David Elkind, *The Hurried Child.* (Reading, Mass.: Addison-Wesley, 1981), 33.

25. Michael Beidel, "The Role of Home Schooling in Childhood Education," in *Childhood Education in the Church*, ed. Robert Clark, Joanne

Brubaker, and Roy Zuck (Chicago: Moody Press, 1986), 598.

26. Raymond Moore and Dorothy Moore, *Homespun Schools* (Waco, Texas: Word, Inc., 1987), 12.

For Further Reading

Public Schools

Brainbridge, W. and Sundre, S. "Parents as Consumers of Public Education." *The Education Digest,* vol. 56, no. 4 (1990): 41-42.

Gallup, A. "The 21st Annual Gallup Poll of the Public's Attitudes toward the Public Schools." *Phi Delta Kappa,* vol. 71, no. 1 (September 1989): 41-53.

Gow, K. *Yes, Virginia, There Is Right and Wrong.* Wheaton, Ill.: Tyndale House Pub., 1985.

Kozol, J. "A Report Card on School after 20 Years." *The Education Digest,* vol. 54, no. 4 (1989): 7-9.

Van Alshire, G. *The Christian and the Public School.* Nashville: Partheon Press, 1982.

Christian Schools

Baker, A. *The Successful Christian School.* Pensacola, Fla.: Beka Books, 1979.

Billings, R. *A Guide to the Christian School.* Hammond, Ind.: Hyles-Anderson, 1971.

Kienel, P. *The Christian School: Why Is It Right for Your Child?* Wheaton, Ill.: Victor Books, 1974.

_____. *Reasons for Sending Your Child to a Christian School.* La Habra, Calif.: P.K. Books, 1974.

_____. *The Philosophy of Christian Schools.* Whittier, Calif.: Western Association of Christian Schools, 1978.

Home Schools

Fugate, J. *What the Bible Says about . . . Child Training.* Tempe, Ariz.: Aletheia Division of Alpha Omega Pub., 1990.

_____. *Successful Home Schooling.* Tempe, Ariz.: Aletheia Division of Alpha Omega Pub., 1990.

_____. *Will Early Education Ruin Your Child?* Tempe, Ariz.: Aletheia Division of Alpha Omega Pub., 1990.

Moore, R. and Moore, D. *Better Late Than Early.* Berrien Springs, Mich.: The Hewitt Foundation, 1975.

_____. *School Can Wait.* Berrien Springs, Mich.: The Hewitt Foundation, 1979.

_____. *Home Grown Kids.* Waco, Texas: Word Inc., 1981.

_____. *Homespun Schools.* Waco, Texas: Word Inc., 1987.

Selected Christian School Organizations

American Association of Christian Schools. 1017 N. School St., Normal, IL 61761

Association of Christian School, International. P.O. Box 4097, Whittier, CA 90607

National Christian School Education Association. 464 Main Rd., Newtown Square, PA 19073.

National Union of Christian Schools. P.O. Box 8709, 3350 East Paris Ave., Grand Rapids, MI 49508.

Western Association of Christian Schools. P.O. Box 4097, Whittier, CA 90607.

Author Biographies

Michael J. Anthony
Michael has an Ed.D. degree in Educational Administration from Southwestern Baptist Theological Seminary and also a Ph.D. degree in education with an emphasis in lifespan development from the Claremont Graduate School. He is the Chairman of the Christian Education Department at Biola University's Talbot School of Theology. He has served on staff with five churches and several parachurch organizations. He has authored several books, numerous articles, and has conducted Christian Education ministries in over fifteen countries. Michael also serves part-time as Minister to Young Families at Mariner's Church in Newport Beach. He and his wife, Michelle, have one child and live in Irvine.

Michael A. Bechtle
Michael has an Ed.D. degree in Administration of Higher Education from Arizona State University. He has worked in a variety of church ministry positions and has served as Registrar and Chairman of the Christian Education Department at Arizona College of the Bible. In addition to authoring a book, Mike has written over 200 pieces of curriculum for David C. Cook Publishing Company. He has done consulting in time management, project management, and organizational effectiveness with over 100 Fortune 500 corporations. He and his wife, Diane, have two children and live in Brea.

Reuben H. Brooks
Reuben brought a tremendous heart for world evangelism and missions to the Christian Education Department. He has a Ph.D. from the University of Colorado. He has served in a variety of mission positions including a mission-

ary to Brazil; Executive Secretary of the Brazil Gospel Fellowship Mission; Chairman of the Department for Missions at Oak Hills Bible College; Missions Director for InterVarsity Christian Fellowship; and Professor of World Missions at Trinity Evangelical Divinity School. He has also served as the Academic Dean at Sterling College. In addition to teaching doctoral courses in the Christian Education Department, Dr. Brooks also served as Chaplain and Dean of Student Ministries at Biola. He is currently head of the Department of History, Geography, and Political Science at Tennessee State University (Nashville).

Shelly M. Cunningham
Shelly is a Christian educator whose ministry experience includes work with youth, singles, women, and directing the Christian Education program in a local church. She is a candidate for the Ed.D. degree at Talbot School of Theology. Her areas of specialization include age-level ministries, educational theory, and the practice of teaching. Shelly continues to be involved in the local church through teaching children's ministries, speaking at retreats, and directing teacher training workshops. Shelly and her husband, Ed, live in Fullerton.

Dennis H. Dirks
In addition to teaching in the Christian Education Department, Dennis also serves at Talbot School of Theology as the Dean of Administration. Dennis earned his Ph.D. degree in Education from the Claremont Graduate School. He has contributed articles for numerous journal publications and has written chapters for several Christian Education books. Dennis has served on the board of directors for the North American Professors of Christian Education and is a widely sought conference speaker. He teaches an inter-generational Sunday School class at his home church, First Evangelical Free of Fullerton.

Kenneth R. Garland
Ken received his Ed.D. degree from Talbot School of Theology. He lives in Southern California with his wife, Karen, and four children. Ken has spent twenty years in local church youth ministry in California and Oregon and has served as president of the Greater Los Angeles Sunday School Convention. Program Director for Talbot's Master of Arts in Youth Ministry program, Ken also serves as an interim pastor to local churches throughout Los Angeles.

Rex E. Johnson
Rex has been teaching Christian Education at Talbot for over fifteen years and currently directs the M.A. in Marriage and Family Ministries program

within the C.E. department. He has written several books and speaks on marriage and family issues in churches nationwide. Rex lives his message at home with his wife, Eve, and their four children. He also develops video-assisted and computer-assisted leadership training curricula through Innovations in Learning, a company he founded in 1979.

Richard J. Leyda

Richard has earned an M.Div. degree from Talbot School of Theology and is also a candidate for the Ed.D. degree. With a varied background of participation and coaching in intercollegiate athletics and outdoor sports, Richard is vitally concerned for the integration of biblical truth with the whole-life experience of the student. He has directed both parachurch and school-based wilderness camping programs and was a guidance counselor and teacher of religion at a Christian secondary school. Richard has also served as a deacon in his home church at First Presbyterian Church of Hollywood. He and his wife, Ellen, have two children and live in La Canada.

Daniel C. Stevens

Daniel received his Th.M. degree from Dallas Theological Seminary and his Ph.D. in education from Ohio State University. He began teaching Christian Education in 1975 and specializes in biblical and philosophical components of C.E. and higher education curriculum development. Dan has served in a variety of roles in Christian higher education including registrar, director of development, department chairman, and executive dean of two seminary extension campuses. Dan and his wife, Sue, have four sons. Dan currently serves part-time as Pastor of Small Group Ministries at Grace Church of Los Alamitos.

Judy K. Ten Elshof

Judy has an M.A. degree in Marriage and Family Ministries from Talbot School of Theology and is currently working on her Psy.D. degree at Rosemead School of Psychology. In addition to teaching full-time at Talbot, Judy is Vice President of Personnel and Management for Ministry Associates, a non-profit Christian organization for counseling and teaching families. She maintains a private counseling practice and is also a popular seminar and conference speaker. She lives with her husband, Gene, in La Palma, having parented two children.